# Defeating Hitler

# Defeating Hitler

## Whitehall's Secret Report on Why Hitler Lost the War

*Paul Winter*

continuum

**Continuum International Publishing Group**

The Tower Building          80 Maiden Lane
11 York Road                Suite 704
London SE1 7NX              New York, NY 10038

**www.continuumbooks.com**

The original report *Some Weaknesses in German Strategy and Organisation 1933–1945: Report by the Joint Intelligence Sub-Committee, 20th October, 1946* – The National Archives, ref: CAB 146/497

**British Library Cataloguing-in-Publication Data**
A catalogue record for this book is available from the British Library.

ISBN: HB: 978-1-4411-9635-4

**Library of Congress Cataloging-in-Publication Data**
A catalog record for this book is available from the Library of Congress.

Typeset by Newgen Imaging Systems Pvt Ltd, Chennai, India
Printed and bound in India

Defeating Hitler *is dedicated to my Grandfather, Lionel Watson,*
*who, as a young gunner in the 10*[th] *Medium Regiment,*
*Royal Artillery, experienced at close-quarters the full-might*
*of Hitler's war machine on the battlefields of Normandy,*
*the Low Countries and Nazi Germany.*

# Contents

# *Chronology of Events: 1933–45*

**1933**

| | |
|---|---|
| 30 January | Adolf Hitler appointed Chancellor of Germany |
| 22 March | First concentration camp for political opponents is set up at Dachau |
| 27 April | Hitler appoints Rudolf Hess his official deputy for all matters concerning the NSDAP |
| 14 October | Hitler announces on German radio his intention to leave the League of Nations |

**1934**

| | |
|---|---|
| 2 June | Hitler orders the C-in-C of the German Navy, Admiral Erich Raeder, to keep the construction of U-Boats a secret |
| 6 June | Hitler orders the expansion of the *Reichswehr* from 100,000 to 300,000 men |
| 30 June | 'Night of the Long Knives' leading SA figures such as Ernst Rohm and opponents of the Nazi regime are murdered by Himmler's SS in a bloody purge |
| 25 July | Austrian Nazis attempt a *coup d'état* in Austria during which Chancellor Dollfuss is murdered |
| 2 August | President Paul von Hindenburg dies |
| 2 August | Soldiers of the *Reichswehr* ordered to swear an oath of personal allegiance to Hitler |
| 4 August | Hitler appoints himself Supreme Commander of the *Reichswehr* |
| 13 December | Hermann Goering appointed Hitler's deputy and successor in the event of the Führer's death |

**1935**

| | |
|---|---|
| 9 March | The existence of the *Luftwaffe* is revealed |
| 16 March | German military conscription is reintroduced in flagrant breach of the Treaty of Versailles |
| 18 June | Anglo-German Naval Agreement signed limiting German Naval construction to 35% of total British tonnage for the Royal Navy |

**1936**

| | |
|---|---|
| 7 March | German forces re-occupy the demilitarized Rhineland |
| June | British Joint Intelligence Committee (JIC) set up |
| 17 June | Heinrich Himmler promoted to head of the entire German police force |
| 11 August | Hitler appoints Joachim von Ribbentrop German Ambassador to Britain |
| 18 October | Hitler signs the directive for the Four-Year Plan of which Goering is placed in charge |
| 25 November | Germany and Japan sign the Anti-Comintern Pact |
| 25 December | Dr Theo Morell appointed Hitler's personal physician |

**1937**

| | |
|---|---|
| 25–29 September | Mussolini's first state visit to Germany |
| 5 November | Hitler holds a secret military conference attended by leading Nazis and military commanders at which he sets out his long-term politico-military aims. The Führer's military adjutant, Colonel Hossbach, compiles a memorandum on the meeting detailing the extent of Hitler's ambitions |

**1938**

| | |
|---|---|
| 4 February | Hitler appoints himself Reich War Minister and abolishes the Reich War Ministry replacing it with the *Oberkommando der Wehrmacht* (the Armed Forces High Command) with General Wilhelm Keitel as its head |
| 12 March | Hitler invades Austria during Operation 'Otto' thereby securing the *Anschluss* (Annexation) of his native country |
| 18 August | General Ludwig Beck, Chief of the Army General Staff, resigns over Hitler's plan (Case Green) to invade Czechoslovakia. The Führer appoints General Franz Halder as Beck's replacement |
| 15 September | British Prime Minister Neville Chamberlain flies to Munich in order to dissuade Hitler from going to war over Czechoslovakia |
| 22 September | Chamberlain flies again to Germany and meets the Nazi leader in Bad Godesberg in order to broker a deal over the Sudetenland |
| 29 September | Munich Agreement signed by Nazi Germany, Great Britain, France and Italy |
| 1 October | German Army occupies the Sudetenland |

**1939**

| | |
|---|---|
| 16 March | Hitler invades Czechoslovakia and marches into Prague |
| 23 August | Nazi-Soviet Non-Aggression Pact signed by Ribbentrop and Molotov |
| 1 September | Hitler invades Poland |
| 3 September | Great Britain declares war on Nazi Germany |

| 9 November | Two officers from the British Secret Intelligence Service (SIS), Major Stevens and Captain Best are kidnapped by the German *Sicherheitsdienst* (SD) at the town of Venlo on the Dutch-German border. Best and Stevens were deceived into thinking they were dealing with anti-Hitler elements within the *Wehrmacht* |

**1940**

| 9 April | German forces invade Norway and Denmark |
| 10 May | Winston Churchill becomes Prime Minister and Minister of Defence. Hitler launches his Blitzkrieg in the West against Holland, Belgium, France and Luxembourg |
| 10 June | Italy declares war on Britain |
| 23 June | France capitulates |
| 10 July | Official start of the Battle of Britain |
| 16 July | The Special Operations Executive (SOE) is created to 'set Europe ablaze' |
| 12 August | As a prelude to an invasion of Britain Hermann Goering's *Luftwaffe* launch 'Adler Tag' (Eagle Day) intended to destroy the RAF |
| 13 September | Italians invade Egypt |
| 31 October | Official end of the Battle of Britain |
| 26 November | Future Operations Enemy Section (FOES) set up to draft strategic assessments for the JIC and Chiefs of Staff |

**1941**

| 12 February | Rommel and the *Afrika Korps* arrive in Tripoli |
| 7 March | British troops arrive in Greece |
| 22 March | Creation of the Axis Planning Section (APS), successor to the FOES |
| 6 April | Germans invade Yugoslavia and Greece |
| 29 April | British forces evacuate Greece |
| 10 May | Deputy Führer, Rudolf Hess, parachutes into Scotland ostensibly on a peace mission |
| 15 May | Formation of the Joint Intelligence Staff (JIS) successor to the APS |
| 20 May | German airborne troops attack Crete |
| 22 June | The launch of Operation *Barbarossa* the German invasion of the Soviet Union |
| 14 August | Atlantic Charter signed by Roosevelt and Churchill |
| 7 December | Japanese surprise attack on US Pacific Fleet at Pearl Harbor. American declaration of war against Japan |
| 8 December | German Army Group Centre offensive halted before Moscow |
| 11 December | Hitler declares war on the United States |
| 19 December | Hitler appoints himself Commander-in-Chief of the Army |

**1942**

| | |
|---|---|
| 15 February | The surrender of the British and Commonwealth garrison at Singapore |
| 28 March | British Commandos raid the dry-dock at St Nazaire in France (Operation *Chariot*) in order to prevent its use by the Tirpitz and other German raiders |
| 21 June | Fall of Tobruk |
| 30 June | Rommel checked at El Alamein |
| 19 August | British and Canadian forces raid Dieppe during Operation *Jubilee*. German Army Group B besieges the symbolic city of Stalingrad |
| 25 September | Hitler dismisses General Franz Halder as Chief of the Army General Staff OKH |
| 23 October | General Erwin Rommel's *Afrika Korps* is attacked by General Montgomery's 8th Army at the Battle of El Alamein in North Africa |
| 8 November | Anglo-American forces land in North-West Africa during Operation *Torch* |

**1943**

| | |
|---|---|
| 14 January | President Roosevelt and Winston Churchill call for the 'unconditional surrender' of Germany and her Axis allies at the Casablanca conference |
| 30 January | Admiral Doenitz replaces Admiral Erich Raeder as Commander-in- Chief of the German Navy |
| 31 January | Field Marshal von Paulus's German Sixth Army surrenders to the Red Army at Stalingrad |
| 19 February | German forces attack the Americans at the Kasserine Pass |
| 11 May | Third Washington meeting between Roosevelt and Churchill codenamed 'Trident' |
| 13 May | German surrender in Tunisia |
| 16/17 May | Lancaster bombers from the RAF's 617 Squadron attack the strategically important Mohne, Eder and Sorpe Dams in the Ruhr |
| 23 May | Doenitz withdraws U-Boats from the Battle of the Atlantic |
| 4 July | Hitler launches Operation *Citadel* on the Eastern Front in order to eradicate the Kursk salient. The battle of Kursk becomes the greatest tank battle in history |
| 10 July | Allies land in Sicily during Operation *Husky* |
| 25 July | Mussolini deposed and arrested |
| 17 August | Quebec Conference, codenamed 'Quadrant', attended by the British, American and Canadian governments |
| 9 September | Allies land at Salerno during Operation *Avalanche* |
| 1 October | Allies enter Naples |
| 22 November | Cairo Conference ('Sextant') attended by Roosevelt, Churchill and Chiang Kai-Shek |
| 28 November | Churchill, Roosevelt and Stalin meet at Tehren ('Eureka') to discuss Allied strategy |

**1944**

| | |
|---|---|
| 22 January | Allies land at Anzio during Operation *Shingle* |
| 18 March | Germans occupy Hungary |
| 11 May | Operation *Diadem* Allied offensive in Italy |
| 4 June | General Mark Clark's 5th US Army enters Rome |
| 6 June | The Allies launch Operation *Overlord*, the greatest seaborne invasion in history along the Normandy coast |
| 13 June | First V-1 pilotless rocket lands in London |
| 20 July | Colonel Count Claus von Stauffenberg attempts to assassinate Hitler by means of a bomb planted at the *Führerhauptquartier* (FHQ), the *Wolfsschanze* (Wolf's Lair) in Rastenburg, East Prussia |
| 25 July | Operation *Cobra* commences heralding Allied breakout of Normandy |
| 13–20 August | Battle of Falaise Pocket in Normandy |
| 15 August | Operation *Dragoon* is launched by the Allies in southern France |
| 25 August | Paris is liberated by the US 4th Infantry Division and General Leclerc's Free French 2nd Armoured Division |
| 3 September | Brussels liberated by the British Second Army |
| 4 September | The strategically important port of Antwerp is captured by British Second Army |
| 8 September | V-2 rockets are fired on London for the first time |
| 17 September | The ill-fated Operation *Market Garden* commences in Holland |
| 26 September | British 1st Airborne Division is ordered to withdraw from Arnhem |
| 1–8 November | The Dutch island of Walcheren cleared by British and Canadian forces during Operation *Infatuate* |
| 16 December | Hitler launches Operation *Herbstnebel* ('Autumn Mist') in the Ardennes signalling the last major German offensive in the West |

**1945**

| | |
|---|---|
| 1 January | Operation *Bodenplatte* – the *Luftwaffe* mounts its last major air offensive in the West against Allied airfields |
| 4 February | Yalta Conference ('Argonaut') attended by Roosevelt, Churchill and Stalin |
| 23 March | Allies cross the Rhine during Operation *Plunder* |
| 12 April | Death of President Roosevelt |
| 29 April | German surrender in Italy |
| 30 April | Hitler commits suicide in the Führer bunker, Berlin |
| 8 May | VE Day |
| 17 July | Potsdam Conference convenes in Berlin |
| 6 August | First Atomic Bomb dropped on the Japanese city of Hiroshima |
| 9 August | Second Atomic bomb dropped on the Japanese city of Nagasaki |
| 15 August | VJ Day |

# *Dramatis Personae*

## Werner von Blomberg (1878–1946)

*Generalfeldmarschall* von Blomberg. Appointed Minister of Defence in 1933 and Minister of War and Commander-in-Chief of the Armed Forces in 1935. In April 1936 he became Hitler's first Field Marshal. Forced to resign in 1938 due to a personal scandal involving his second wife, von Blomberg played no major role in the Second World War but was captured by the Allies in 1945. He subsequently gave evidence against leading Nazis at the Nuremberg War Crime Trials. He died in March 1946 while in Allied custody.

## Martin Bormann (1900–45)

Appointed Reich Leader of the Nazi Party in 1933. Private Secretary to Rudolf Hess from 1933 to 1941. Promoted to Head of the Party Chancellery following the mysterious flight to Scotland by Hess in May 1941. Appointed *Reichsminister* in charge of the Party Secretariat and Staff 1942. Chosen by Hitler to be his Private Secretary in April 1943. Selected as commander of the *Volkssturm* (People's Army) October 1944. One of the last to escape the Führer bunker in May 1945, Bormann's whereabouts and ultimate fate remained a mystery obliging the International Criminal Court at Nuremberg to condemn him to death *in absentia* in October 1946. It was not until 1972, however, that his remains were discovered by workmen in Berlin.

# Walther von Brauchitsch (1881–1948)

*Generalfeldmarschall* von Brauchitsch. Commander-in-Chief Army (*Oberbefehlshaber des Heers*) from 4 February 1938 until 19 December 1941 when he was forced to resign by Hitler following the failure of Army Group Centre to capture Moscow. Charged with war crimes after the war, Brauchitsch died in British captivity on 18 October 1948 before he could be tried.

# Wilhelm Canaris (1887–1945)

Admiral Canaris, Chief of the *Abwehr* from 1935 to 1944. Naval officer, anti-Nazi conspirator and sub-source of intelligence for the British Secret Service. Arrested in July 1944, Canaris was eventually hanged at Flossenburg concentration camp on 9 April 1945 for his indirect involvement with the July Bomb Plot conspiracy against Hitler.

# Karl Doenitz (1891–1980)

Grand Admiral Doenitz. Commander of U-Boats, 1 January 1936 to 1 May 1945. Commander-in-Chief *Kriegsmarine*, 30 January 1943 to 1 May 1945. Commander-in-Chief Operations (North) 17 April 1945 to 23 May 1945. Appointed Hitler's successor and became *Reichspräsident* and Commander-in-Chief of Armed Forces, 1 May 1945 to 23 May 1945. Sentenced at Nuremberg to ten years' imprisonment in 1947. Released from prison in October 1956.

# Joseph Goebbels (1897–1945)

Journalist and Doctor of Philosophy in Literature. One of Hitler's closest associates and a leading anti-Semite. Became a member of the Nazi Party in 1924. Made Gauleiter of Berlin in October 1926. Reich Minister of Propaganda from 1933 to 1945, and from July 1944 onwards General Plenipotentiary for Total War. Committed suicide with his wife and family in Berlin on 1 May 1945.

# Hermann Goering (1893–1946)

First World War fighter ace. Reichsminister for Air. Commander-in-Chief of the *Luftwaffe* from 1933 to 1945. Appointed Plenipotentiary for the implementation of the Four Year Plan for Re-armament in 1936. *Reichsmarschall* and deputy/successor to Hitler. Captured by the Americans in May 1945, Goering was sentenced to death at the Nuremberg War Crime Trials in October 1946 but committed suicide before the sentence was carried out.

# Heinz Guderian (1888–1954)

*Generaloberst* Guderian. Pioneer of armoured warfare and leading proponent of the Panzer and *Blitzkrieg*. Commander of XIX Panzer Corps during the Polish and French campaigns of September 1939 to June 1940. Commander 2nd Panzer Army from 5 October 1941 to 25 December 1941. Dismissed by Hitler in December 1941 for criticizing German strategy. Rehabilitated in February 1943 and appointed Inspector-General of Armoured Troops. Chief of Army General Staff from 21 July 1944 to 28 March 1945. Dismissed again by Hitler for insubordination. Captured by US troops in May 1945 but not charged with war crimes. Released from custody as a prisoner of war in June 1948.

# Franz Halder (1884–1972)

*Generaloberst* Halder. Chief of the Army General Staff from 1 November 1938 until 24 September 1942 when he was dismissed by Hitler and replaced by *Generaloberst* Kurt Zeitzler. Implicated in the July Bomb Plot of 1944, Halder was arrested by the *Gestapo* and placed in Flossenburg and Dachau concentration camps. He was later transferred to Tyrol where he was liberated by US forces on 5 May 1945. He spent the next two years as a prisoner of war and gave evidence against leading Nazis at the Nuremberg War Crimes Trials. He later became an advisor to the US Army Historical Division and to the new West German Army.

# Rudolf Hess (1894–1987)

Deputy Führer of the Nazi Party. First World War fighter pilot. Joined the
Nazi Party in 1921 as one of its earliest members. Imprisoned with Hitler in
Landsberg Prison following the failed 'Beer Hall Putsch' of November 1923,
Hess became the Nazi leader's private secretary transcribing and editing *Mein
Kampf*. Appointed deputy Führer on Hitler's accession to power in 1933 thereby
becoming one of the most powerful figures in the Third Reich. Disillusioned
with Germany's war with Britain, Hess flew to Scotland on 10 May 1941 in
order to broker a peace deal. Disowned by Hitler, he spent the rest of the war in
British captivity and was tried at Nuremberg in 1946 for war crimes. Sentenced
to life imprisonment, Hess spent the next 41 years in Spandau Prison in Berlin
where he committed suicide on 17 August 1987.

# Reinhard Heydrich (1904–42)

*SS-Obergruppenführer und General der Polizei* Heydrich. Nicknamed 'the
Hangman' and 'the Butcher of Prague'. Chief of the Reich Main Security Office
(RSHA) from September 1939 to 4 June 1942. President of Interpol from 24
August 1940 to 4 June 1942. Chairman of the Wannsee Conference on the
'Final Solution' to the 'Jewish problem' 20 January 1942. Deputy Protector
of Bohemia and Moravia from 29 September 1941 to 4 June 1942. Mortally
wounded in Prague by Special Operations Executive (SOE) trained Czech
patriots on 27 May 1942. Died of wounds on 4 June 1942 in the Czech capital.

# Heinrich Himmler (1900–45)

*Reichsführer-SS* from 1929 to 1945. Became head of the Gestapo in 1936 and
Minister of the Interior from 1943 to 1945. One of the most powerful figures
in the Third Reich and much feared by his Nazi colleagues, Himmler was one
of Hitler's most trusted lieutenants. As such, he was instrumental in executing
the Führer's orders for the 'Final Solution' to the 'Jewish problem'. Appointed
Commander of the Replacement (Home) Army in July 1944. Commanded both
the Army Group Upper Rhine in December 1944 and Army Group Vistula in
January 1945. Discovered to have been negotiating a separate peace with the

Allies, Himmler was stripped of all his Party and state offices by Hitler, who ordered his arrest. On the run from both the Nazis and the Allies, Himmler was finally captured by the British on 22 May 1945, but committed suicide the next day while in their custody.

## Adolf Hitler (1889–1945)

Austrian-born artist, writer, German politician, First World War veteran and leader of the Nazi Party from 1921 to 1945. Chancellor of Germany from January 1933 to April 1945, and head of State (Führer) from August 1934 to April 1945. Supreme Commander of Germany's Armed Forces from February 1938 to April 1945. Committed suicide in Berlin on 30 April 1945.

## Alfred Jodl (1890–1946)

*Generaloberst* Jodl. Chief of Operations Staff of the High Command of the Armed Forces (OKW) from 1939 to 1945. One of Hitler's closest military advisers, Jodl drafted many of the 74 Führer Directives issued during the war. Condemned to death at Nuremberg and hanged on 16 October 1946.

## Ernst Kaltenbrunner (1903–46)

*Obergruppenführer und General der Polizei und Waffen SS* Dr Kaltenbrunner. Appointed Chief of the Security Police and SD (RSHA) on 30 January 1943. One of Himmler's trusted subordinates. Captured by the Americans in May 1945 and sentenced to death at Nuremberg for war crimes. Executed on 16 October 1946.

## Wilhelm Keitel (1882–1946)

*Generalfeldmarschall* Keitel. Chief of the High Command of Armed Forces (*Oberkommando der Wehrmacht*) from 1939 to 1945. Nicknamed 'lackey' due to his servility towards Hitler, Keitel was the dictator's most senior military adviser. Condemned to death at Nuremberg and hanged on 16 October 1946.

# Albert Kesselring (1885–1960)

*Generalfeldmarschall* Kesselring. Commander-in-Chief Armed Forces South (Mediterranean), 2 December 1941 to 10 March 1945. Commander-in-Chief Armed Forces West from 11 March to 25 March 1945. Commander-in-Chief Armed Forces South from 25 March to 6 May 1945. Condemned to death for war crimes by a British Military court in Venice in February 1947. Death sentence commuted to life imprisonment in October 1947. Pardoned and released from prison in October 1952 due to ill-health.

# Erich von Manstein (1887–1973)

*Generalfeldmarschall* von Manstein. Hitler's finest military strategist. Commander Army Group II from 18 September 1941 to 21 November 1942. Commander Army Group Don from 28 November 1942 to 14 February 1943. Commander Army Group South from 14 February 1943 to 30 March 1944. Dismissed by Hitler on 30 March 1944 due to divergences of opinion on German strategy. Replaced as C-in-C Army Group South by *Generalfeldmarschall* Walther Model. Although retired von Manstein was arrested by British troops in August 1945 and subsequently tried for war crimes before a British Military Tribunal in Hamburg in August 1949. Sentenced to 18 years in prison, later commuted to 12, von Manstein was eventually released in May 1953 on medical grounds.

# Erhard Milch (1892–1972)

*Generalfeldmarschall* Milch. Appointed State Secretary of the Reich Aviation Ministry in 1933. Oversaw the development of the *Luftwaffe* during the inter-war period. Commanded *Luftflotte* 5 during the Norwegian campaign and was promoted in 1941 to the post of Air Inspector General following Ernst Udet's suicide. In 1947, Milch was tried at Nuremberg for war crimes and received a sentence of life imprisonment later commuted to 15 years. Released in June 1954.

# Benito Mussolini (1883–1945)

Leader of the National Fascist Party in Italy. Made Prime Minister of Italy 1922. Known as *Il Duce* from 1925 onwards. Declared war on Britain and France on 10 June 1940. Deposed on 24 July 1943 by the Fascist Grand Council. Arrested and detained at Gran Sasso he was eventually rescued by *SS-Obersturmbannführer* Otto Skorzeny on 12 September 1943. Head of State of the Italian Social Republic from 23 September 1943 to 25 April 1945. Mussolini and his mistress, Clara Petacchi, were eventually captured by Communist Partisans near Lake Como on 27 April 1945. They were duly executed and their bodies hung upside down outside a petrol station in Milan.

# Erich Raeder (1876–1960)

Admiral Raeder. Commander-in-Chief *Kriegsmarine* from 1935 until 1943 when he was replaced by Grand Admiral Karl Doenitz. Sentenced to life imprisonment at Nuremberg in 1946. Released in 1955.

# Joachim von Ribbentrop (1893–1946)

Soldier, journalist and champagne salesman. Friend of one-time German Chancellor, Franz von Papen. First met Hitler in 1928 and joined the Nazi Party in May 1932. Became foreign policy advisor to Hitler and later Reich Minister Ambassador-Plenipotentiary at Large (1935–36). Negotiated the Anglo-German Naval Agreement of 1935. German Ambassador to the Court of St James's from October 1936 to February 1938. Created Reich Minister for Foreign Affairs on 4 February 1938 holding the post until 30 April 1945. Signatory to the Nazi-Soviet Pact of August 1939. Captured in June 1945 and tried for war crimes at Nuremberg in October 1946. Found guilty and hanged on 16 October 1946.

# Erwin Rommel (1891–1944)

*Generalfeldmarschall* Rommel. Commander of 7th Panzer Division during the French Campaign of May–June 1940, Rommel came to prominence commanding the *Deutsche Afrika Korps* during the North African campaign of

1941 to 1943. Nicknamed the 'Desert Fox', Rommel was given command of Army Group E in Greece in April 1943 and in November 1943 was sent to France to take up the post of commander of Army Group B with instructions to prevent the Allies from landing successfully on the west coast of Europe. Implicated in the July Bomb Plot of 1944 Rommel was forced to commit suicide in October 1944.

## Gerd von Rundstedt (1875–1953)

*Generalfeldmarschall* von Rundstedt. Commander of Army Group South during the Polish campaign of September 1939. Commander of Army Group South during Operation *Barbarossa*, the invasion of the Soviet Union June 1941. Suffering a heart attack in November 1941, von Rundstedt was replaced by *Generalfeldmarschall* Walther Reichenau. Recalled from retirement in March 1942, von Rundstedt was appointed Commander-in-Chief West. Replaced by *Generalfeldmarschall* Günther von Kluge on 2 July 1944, who in turn was succeeded by *Generalfeldmarschall* Walther Model on 16 August 1944, von Rundstedt was reappointed Commander-in-Chief West on 1 September 1944. Finally relieved of his command in March 1945 after urging Hitler to make peace with the Allies. Captured by US forces in May 1945, he was charged with war crimes by the British. However, he was later released in July 1948 due to ill-health.

## Walter Schellenberg (1910–52)

*SS-Brigadeführer* Schellenberg. Pre-war counter-intelligence officer in the SD. Personal aide to Heinrich Himmler and deputy leader under Reinhard Heydrich of the RSHA from 1939 to 1942. Architect of the 'Venlo Incident' in November 1939 when two SIS officers were abducted at the Dutch-German border town by Schellenberg's men. Appointed head of foreign intelligence in 1944 following the abolition of the *Abwehr* and its absorption into the RSHA. Captured by the British in Denmark in 1945 he subsequently gave evidence against leading Nazis at the Nuremberg Trials. Convicted of war crimes in 1949 at the 'Ministries Trial', Schellenberg was sentenced to six years' imprisonment. Released in 1951 on health grounds he died in 1952 of liver cancer.

# Hans von Seeckt (1866–1936)

*Generaloberst* von Seeckt. Member of the Prussian General Staff from 1897. Chief of Staff of the Army from 1919 to 1920. Chief organizer and architect of the *Reichswehr*, the 100,000 strong army allowed Germany by the Versailles Treaty of 1919. Commander-in-Chief of the *Reichswehr* from 1920 to 1926. Member of the Reichstag from 1930 to 1932 subsequently aligning himself with the Nazis. Military adviser to Chiang Kai-Shek in China from 1934 to 1935.

# Albert Speer (1905–81)

Professor of Architecture. Appointed Inspector General of the Reich in 1937. Became Reich minister for Armaments and War Production following the death of Fritz Todt in February 1942. Member of Doenitz's short-lived 'Flensburg Government', May 1945. Condemned at Nuremberg for war crimes in 1946 and sentenced to 20 years' imprisonment. Released in October 1966.

# Dr Fritz Todt (1891–1942)

Civil Engineer. Inspector General German Roadways, July 1933. Founder of 'Organisation Todt' (public works system) 1938. Creator of the Siegfried Line 1938 to 1940. *Reichsminister* for Armaments and Munitions from March 1940 until his death in an air accident on 8 February 1942.

# Ernst Udet (1896–1941)

*Generaloberst* Udet. First World War fighter ace. A member of the Nazi Party from 1933 Udet became a leading advocate of the *Luftwaffe* in the inter-war period becoming in 1936 head of the Reich Air Ministry's development branch. Promoted again in 1939 to the position of the *Luftwaffe's* Director-General of Equipment Udet committed suicide in November 1941 due largely to an increasingly fractious relationship with Hermann Goering.

## Walter Warlimont (1894–1976)

*General der Artillerie* Warlimont. Deputy Chief of Operations Staff (*Wehrmachtführungsstab*, WFSt, Armed Forces Operations Staff) from November 1938 to September 1944. Sentenced to life imprisonment at Nuremberg in 1948. Released in 1954.

## Kurt Zeitzler (1895–1963)

*Generaloberst* Zeitzler. Chief of Staff XXII Korps of XIV Army from 1939 to 1940. Chief of Staff *Panzergruppe* A from 1940 to 1941. Chief of Staff 1st Panzer Army 1941 to 1942. Chief of Staff to Commander-in-Chief West 1942. Chief of Staff Army Group D 1942. Succeeded Franz Halder as Chief of the Army General Staff. Served in this role from 24 September 1942 to 20 July 1944 when he resigned through ill-health. Remained on the 'Reserve List' for the rest of the war. Dismissed from the Army by Hitler in January 1945. Made a British PoW in 1947.

# *Foreword*

I have been looking forward to this moment since I first caught a whiff of this fascinating document in Noel Annan's *Changing Enemies* in 1995. I can remember encouraging Paul Winter to go and find it at The National Archives when he set out on what has proved to be his own highly fruitful search for the documentary trail of secret Whitehall's wartime efforts to fathom the mind of Hitler.

Dr Winter is especially well placed to guide his readers through this remarkable Joint Intelligence Committee document. It will fascinate anyone with an appetite for intelligence history or possessing a curiosity about the course of the Second World War.

Lord Hennessy of Nympsfield, FBA,
Attlee Professor of Contemporary British History,
Queen Mary, University of London.

# Introduction

## I. Historical context

Referred to erroneously in several historical accounts as 'Why the Germans Lost',[1] *Some Weaknesses in German Strategy and Organisation, 1933–1945* has never before been published or quoted in its entirety.[2] Held under Section 3 (4) of the Public Records Act for almost half a century, *Some Weaknesses* was finally declassified in October 1991 and released the same year into the protective custody of the old Public Record Office (PRO), Kew under catalogue heading CAB 146/497. Just one of many intelligence-related documents to be liberated by the 'Waldegrave Initiative' of 1992, which facilitated the declassification of hitherto highly sensitive government files, *Some Weaknesses* runs to 200 pages and addresses the underlying reasons why Adolf Hitler and the German high command lost the Second World War. These ranged from the peculiar idiosyncrasies of Hitler's personality, and their negative impact on German strategy, to the failures and weaknesses of the German Intelligence Services (GIS). Yet before consulting the document itself, certain pertinent questions need to be posed such as when and why it was written? Who penned it and for whom?

Begun in March 1945, in response to the growing weight of captured documentation and prisoner-of-war interrogations facilitated by the collapse of the Third Reich, a 'preliminary draft' of the report was completed in October 1945 by members of the Joint Intelligence Staff (JIS). Formed in May 1941 to act as a central assessment staff to the Joint Intelligence Committee (JIC), or as one former chairman has referred to it, the 'high table' of British intelligence, the *raison d'être* of the JIS was to co-ordinate, assess and disseminate strategic intelligence for the JIC in considered inter-service appreciations. This was essential work inasmuch as the JIC, created in June 1936 to act as single voice on security and intelligence matters,[3] and whose membership from May 1940 onwards comprised the heads of the main constituent departments of Britain's intelligence community, reported directly to the British Chiefs of Staff (CoS) and in turn the Prime Minister on all matters regarding the secret world.[4]

Yet notably, if rough drafts of the report, which are held within file CAB 146/498 and entitled 'MI14 Draft for JIC', are consulted, it becomes apparent that virtually all the intellectual preparation for JIC (46) 33 (Final), as *Some Weaknesses* was to be referred to bureaucratically, was conducted by officers from MI14, the War Office's German Section.[5] Established on 15 May 1940,[6] and tasked with handling all intelligence pertaining to the German war machine, MI14 would eventually consist of eleven sub-sections ranging from MI14(a) to MI14(k), which handled everything from the German Army's order of battle to the *dramatis personae* of the *Wehrmacht*'s high command. Yet its real purpose, according to Noel Annan, who served in both MI14 and the JIS during the war, was not only to 'advise the Chief of the Imperial General Staff [as to] what Hitler would do next',[7] but to act as a form of 'lightning conductor, giving the Director of Military Intelligence and the CIGS some protection from Churchill's erratic interpretations' of secret intelligence.[8]

Aside from exposing the inexplicable decision on the part of the JIC to conceal the involvement of MI14 in the project, and instead to credit the JIS with the authorship of *Some Weaknesses*, the contents of 'MI14 Draft for JIC' also serve to shed some light upon those figures intimately involved in its drafting. This is fortunate in that the few existing accounts which do allude to the report, namely Donald McLachlan's *Room 39* and Sir Percy Cradock's *Know Your Enemy*, fail to enlighten readers as to the identities or positions of those engaged in its compilation. Yet by means of scribbled notes and memoranda preserved within the covers of CAB 146/498, we now know that a Major O'Donovan of MI14 and a M. J. Creswell, Foreign Office representative to the JIC and signatory to the final report, were the true architects of the project, instrumental in managing the commission and ensuring its successful completion.

Eventually submitted by the JIC to the Chiefs of Staff on 20 October 1946 as a 'leaving present to its masters', *Some Weaknesses*, which was 'orientated from the German point of view', sought to act as a 'check', so its preface avowed, on the accuracy and validity of JIC papers submitted to the heads of Britain's armed forces throughout the war. Subordinate to this, but nevertheless just as important, was the need to educate British officialdom as to the 'principal causes of German collapse, inherent in Germany's political and military organisation, in German personalities and in Germany's war machine and methods of production'. Amounting to what would now be termed a 'mission statement', the JIS declared in the report's foreword:

> We consider it desirable to set down certain aspects of the War whilst there are still sources available who were closely connected with the events described. We believe that when it is finally possible to make a balanced historical survey, some of the acutely critical moments which are vividly remembered now are likely to become confused with the passage of time, and that there will be a tendency to take for granted Allied superiority and to underestimate the great and evident strength of the German war machine.[9]

Yet 50 years later a leading historian, Professor Richard Overy, published a book, which, retrospectively, confirmed their original fears. Entitled *Why the Allies Won*,[10] this tome not only exhibited a 'tendency to take Allied superiority for granted' but also 'underestimated' the German war machine and in particular its supreme commander, Adolf Hitler. As well as being diametrically opposed to the less-attractive proposition 'Why the Germans Lost', held by some wartime intelligence figures as being closer to the truth,[11] *Why the Allies Won* also eschewed addressing the vitally important issue of intelligence and its impact on the course of the war.

Ignoring the verdict reached by the official historian of wartime British intelligence, Sir Harry Hinsley, namely that the war had been shortened by at least one or two years due to the miracles of ULTRA, the product of Bletchley Park's decryption of German high-grade codes,[12] Overy stated in his preface that, 'It is fashionable to see the use of intelligence as a critical difference between the two sides, but I am not sufficiently persuaded of this to give the subject a chapter of its own'.[13] For the eminent 'warrior-scholar', Professor Sir Michael Howard, author of the official history of British wartime deception, 'to write the history of the war without mentioning it [intelligence] was like writing *Hamlet* without the Ghost'.[14] That

Overy was so dismissive of 'intelligence' and its influence on Allied operations and strategy is not only startling, but highly questionable in the light of over three decades' worth of research on the subject. Such indifference is even more puzzling when one considers the critical role played by intelligence, as evidenced in *Some Weaknesses*, in the rise, decline and fall of the Allies' opposite numbers in Berlin.

## II. Contents

In terms of structure and content, this official *aide mémoire* is organized into three main sections each containing distinct sub-sections. The first addresses Hitler's 'grand design' for the domination of Europe and the world by Nazi Germany; the major events which interfered with his plans, such as the declaration of war by Great Britain in September 1939; the inability of the *Luftwaffe* to win air superiority over England during the summer of 1940 thereby forcing the cancellation of Operation *Sealion*, the proposed invasion of Britain; the failure of Operation *Barbarossa*, the German offensive against the Soviet Union in June 1941; and the entry into the war of the United States in December 1941. Section I also chronicles the slow but inexorable defeat of the Nazi war machine from 1942 onwards after it lost the strategic initiative to the Allies. Section II, meanwhile, focuses on the inherent weaknesses of Germany's war effort, which were recorded as Hitler's idiosyncratic style of command, the absence of a joint command structure within the *Wehrmacht*, the flawed nature of the German Intelligence Services, and the organization of German war production, which up to 1943 was simply not geared to waging 'Total War'.

The last section, which consists of 19 appendices, 'describes', in the words of the report's authors, 'the chronological sequence of events from 1939 onwards in the different theatres of war, on land, on sea and in the air, and in the fields of war production and military supply'.[15] This approach, so the report claimed, was 'in order to illustrate the manner in which the various German weaknesses played their part in Germany's defeat'.[16] Nevertheless, for those whose pulses do not race at the thought of Nazi economics and industrial output, two of the most fascinating and engaging chapters to be found in *Some Weaknesses* are those devoted to the mental peculiarities of the Führer and the activities of his principal espionage agencies, namely the *Abwehr*, the German Military Intelligence section of the *Oberkommando der Wehrmacht* (OKW),[17] and the *Sicherheitsdienst* (SD), the intelligence service of Heinrich Himmler's *Schutzstaffel* or SS.

## Der Führer

The quest to fathom the Führer, however, was not the sole preserve of Whitehall's central intelligence machine. At almost the same time as MI14 and the JIC were embarking upon their own intellectual journey, the future Regius Professor of Modern History at Oxford, Hugh Trevor-Roper, who had served within the ranks of the wartime Secret Intelligence Service (SIS), was compiling his own unique insight into the Nazi dictator's character and mental universe. Commissioned in September 1945 by the MI5 officer Brigadier Dick White[18] to investigate the exact circumstances surrounding the fate of Adolf Hitler and his Nazi 'court', Trevor-Roper's tireless enquiries and final counter-intelligence report, which he submitted to his superiors at the Supreme Headquarters Allied Expeditionary Force (SHAEF) in November 1945, would come to represent the basis for a best-selling book, *The Last Days of Hitler*.[19]

Remarkably, 60 years on, and in its ninth edition, *The Last Days of Hitler*, first published in March 1947, was, in the opinion of Noel Annan, 'an account that still stands despite the mountains of material that later became available'.[20] Later feted by the media as *the* 'Hitler expert', and regarded in the immediate post-war period by the Foreign Office's Information Research Department (IRD), dealing with psychological warfare, as the 'principal student of German mentality under war conditions',[21] Trevor-Roper had, by means of his treatise, initiated a literary process, which to date has produced countless books and articles on Hitler and the Third Reich.

In keeping with the overall conclusions reached by Trevor-Roper in 1945, it is generally agreed by historians that Adolf Hitler was responsible not only for starting the Second World War in 1939 but perpetuating it well into 1945. His importance and centrality to the story of the war are now beyond doubt. In the opinion of one distinguished academic, the 'Second World War' was, first and foremost, 'Hitler's personal war in many senses. He intended it, he prepared for it, he chose the moment for launching it; and for three years, in the main, he planned its course'.[22] Such a contention is also championed by the multi-volume German official history, *Germany and the Second World War*, which has not only reasoned that, 'The European war that broke out on 1 September 1939 would not have done so but for Hitler',[23] but has also contended that once the war became a truly global conflict in 1941 involving, as it did, ideologically driven totalitarian states, Hitler became in effect 'the totally dominant figure of this ideologized warfare'.[24]

Yet astonishingly, Britain's wartime central intelligence machine failed consistently to acknowledge the Führer's supremacy in politico-military affairs. Only in *Some Weaknesses* did the JIS and JIC finally recognize this, albeit far too late to affect the accuracy of their wartime reporting to Churchill and the Chiefs of Staff. Further issues on which the apex of British intelligence failed to report during the war, but deemed important enough to include in its farewell paper, are Hitler's personality and cognitive processes, as well as his mental and physical health.

During the period March 1945 to October 1946, the JIS had come to discern several 'defects' in Hitler's character which, they claimed, had had a ruinous effect upon Germany's ability to execute a successful war. His so-called intuition, 'obstinacy', failure to 'appreciate the opinions and reactions of Foreign Countries', 'opportunism', 'over-centralization and obsession with detail' were all cited.[25] Yet thanks to 60 years' worth of academic study devoted to this topic, several other idiosyncrasies and personality traits can be added to this list, namely the exhibition of a volatile mix of ethnocentric biases, ideological and racist prejudices, secretiveness, fanaticism, megalomania, paranoia and obsession. What is more, we now know that these facets of Hitler's mental make-up were accentuated by serious physical health problems precipitated in part by an over-reliance upon drugs and an injurious lifestyle.[26]

Crucially, the JIS were in no doubt that the 'main defects of Hitler's character' had indeed had an 'important influence on the way in which Germany waged the war'[27] and that the 'cumulative effect of these defects . . . eventually made a very great contribution to the breakdown of the whole German war machine'.[28] That the JIS should have devoted a whole chapter in *Some Weaknesses* to Hitler's personality and its impact upon German strategy, however, is somewhat surprising in light of recent research among the surviving records of the wartime JIC. This has revealed that the committee and its assessment staff failed largely to place Hitler in his proper context and to ascertain exactly where he stood in relation to the conception, planning and direction of German strategy and operations. To compound matters, the JIC and JIS assumed, quite falsely, that the OKH and OKW were in reality devising strategy while acting at the same time as a brake on Hitler's more questionable actions.[29]

Tellingly, as much was admitted to in 1946 by the report's authors. Having acknowledged, *ex post facto*, that no other figure in Germany had exerted the same degree of 'major influence on German strategy or foreign policy' as had the Führer – a fact attributed to his having 'remained the dictator and undisputed ruler of National Socialist Germany right up to a few days before his death' – they conceded that, 'This was much more so than was often assumed by Allied assessments made during the war'.[30] What is more, the JIS was also at pains to point out that contrary to what the JIC had conjectured at the time, 'Even the most powerful of his subordinates acted only by Hitler's grace', and that, 'Many of the policies attributed to Himmler, Goebbels or Ribbentrop [actually] originated from Hitler himself'.[31]

As for the mind-set and psychology of the Nazi leader, the paucity of wartime intelligence on these matters is evidenced in the post-war findings of the JIS, who, when pressed to pass judgement confessed: 'We lack the evidence on which to attempt an analysis of Hitler's mental processes; it is, indeed, open to doubt whether a satisfactory judgment on this difficult topic will ever be reached' they concluded.[32] Difficult or not, Britain's secret state never stood a chance in second-guessing the Führer's thought-processes due to the simple fact that throughout the war they eschewed the psychological profiling of foreign leaders.

This was, however, in stark contrast to US intelligence, and in particular the Office of Strategic Services (OSS), the American equivalent of Britain's SIS, who during the spring of 1943 embarked up two audacious and comprehensive psychological studies of Adolf Hitler: 'Analysis of the

Personality of Adolph Hitler With Predictions of His Future Behaviour and Suggestions for Dealing with Him Now and After Germany's Surrender' by Dr Henry A. Murray;[33] and Dr Walter C. Langer's, 'A Psychological Analysis of Adolph Hitler: His Life and Legend'.[34] Unlike JIC assessments, these evaluations attempted to identify, *inter alia*, a direct correlation between Hitler's personality and his actions in the hope of predicting his future intentions *vis-à-vis* the Allies. Overall, these two reports were, in the opinion of one author, 'remarkably accurate in some respects',[35] giving US intelligence at least some clue as to what made their adversary 'tick'.

## Hitler's mental and physical health

Since his suicide in April 1945, the state of Hitler's physical and mental health has been a subject of prolonged debate by historians. Numerous books have been devoted to this subject, but perhaps the most successful has been Fritz Redlich's 'pathography' of the Nazi leader, *Hitler: Diagnosis of a Destructive Prophet*,[36] which posed the key question: could 'physical illness or mental disorder . . . contribute to an understanding of [the Nazi leader's] behaviour'?[37]

Unlike his British counter-part, Winston Churchill, Hitler did not possess a figure equivalent to that of Lord Moran, who, as Churchill's personal doctor, helped nurse the ageing leader through his finest hour.[38] Instead, the Nazi leader placed himself at the mercy of a quack and charlatan, namely Dr Theodor Morell, who from 1936 onwards was Hitler's personal physician.[39] Churchill's drinking habits have on occasions been seized upon by some historians to explain some of the wartime Premier's more erratic behaviour and strategic ideas. Yet, as the great man once quipped, 'I have taken more out of alcohol than alcohol has taken out of me'.[40] The same, however, could not be said of Adolf Hitler and his dependency on narcotic stimulants.

The dictator's reliance upon Morell and the drugs he administered was a direct result of his own mental and physical disorders, which grew in severity as Germany's war unfolded. In August 1941 electrocardiograms indicated that Hitler had become afflicted by 'rapidly progressive coronary sclerosis',[41] which in conjunction with gastrointestinal problems, insomnia, depression and a general malaise, heralded the beginning of deteriorating health for the Führer.

However, the most serious signs of ill-health began to display themselves in 1942 when Hitler started to exhibit 'an uncontrollable trembling of the left arm, jerking in his left leg, and a shuffling gait . . .',[42] unmistakable indications of Parkinson's disease.

To offset the debilitating effects of these maladies, Morell subjected the Nazi leader to a regime of pills and injections. One historian has calculated that Morell administered 90 varieties of pills and injections during the war, with Hitler taking up to 28 different types of tablets each day.[43] Significantly, this medication took the form of amphetamines, opiates, bromides, barbiturates and cocaine, a chemical cocktail made more potent by the introduction of 'large doses of Dexedrine . . . caffeine . . . and huge quantities of Dr Koester's Anti-Gas Pills, which contained small doses of the poison Strychnine and atropine'.[44] Yet, despite the mind-blowing strength of such drugs, there is a general consensus that, with the exception of amphetamines, Hitler never succumbed to the addictive qualities of these pills.

It was, however, the abuse of amphetamines which appears to have had the most deleterious effect upon Hitler's physical and cognitive processes. This substance abuse, as noted by one commentator, took place between 1939 and 1943, a period in which the dictator took some of his most important strategic decisions, and resulted in the Führer being at times 'temporarily impaired'.[45] This was perhaps unsurprising when one acknowledges the severe side-effects of prolonged amphetamine abuse, specifically: 'increased anger and anxiety', hallucinations, paranoid delusions, 'schizophrenia-like psychotic episodes with dangerously violent behaviour', elevated blood pressure, chest pains and convulsions.[46] Despite inexplicably discontinuing its use during the last two years of war, 'Could some of Hitler's major tactical or strategic errors, such as impulsive military decisions, or enormous, multi-casual decisions such as declaration of war, be ascribed to amphetamine abuse?'[47] Redlich demurs maintaining rather equivocally that the 'Existing evidence does not permit this conclusion beyond any reasonable doubt'.[48]

In terms of Hitler's mental health there has been much debate as to whether or not he was a psychotic, a schizophrenic or just plain 'mad'. For Dr David Owen, author of *In Sickness and in Power*, 'The popular assumption of . . . Hitler's madness rests in part on the enormity of his crimes but also, perhaps, on his style, or at least on his rhetorical style . . .'[49] Yet, as Owen himself has stated, 'There is no convincing evidence that makes it possible for Hitler to be categorized as mentally ill . . .'[50] This diagnosis is also supported by the exhaustive researches of Fritz Redlich, who has concluded that although the Führer did not suffer from 'any of the major psychotic disorders' such as schizophrenia or psychoses, he may well have been encumbered by an 'anti-social personality disorder and borderline personality disorder'.[51] Clearly, Hitler's crimes and strategic misjudgements cannot be attributed to insanity or mental illness. However, could errors in judgement and decision-making on the part of the Führer be ascribed to physical ill-health and to the malign effects of drug abuse?

The consensus among most historians is a categorical 'no'. John Lukacs, author of *The Hitler of History*, has avowed: 'there is absolutely no convincing evidence to the effect that his physical ailments affected or obscured his thinking and his judgment to the point of irrationality';[52] while the distinguished writer, Sebastian Haffner, asserted: 'Accounts presenting Hitler during the final years of the war as a mere shadow of himself, a pitiable human wreck, are all hopelessly overdrawn. Hitler's disastrous failures from 1941 to 1945 . . . cannot be explained by physical or mental decline'.[53] Moreover, Ian Kershaw is adamant that, 'Morell and his medicines were neither a major nor even a minor part of the explanation of Germany's plight . . .'[54] during the latter stages of the war. Not even the degenerative nature of Parkinson's disease has been afforded a role in explaining away Hitler's highly-questionable politico-military choices. For one leading medical practitioner, 'his capacity for problem-solving and information processing was not impaired'[55] by the disease, nor did it, in Owen's opinion, '. . . much affect his key decision-making', which was already 'fixed by his own overambitious strategic objectives'.[56]

What is indisputable, however, was the 'extremely rapid bodily and mental decline' Hitler suffered between 1942 and 1945.[57] This was attested to by two of the Führer's closest subordinates, his SS Adjutant, Otto Günsche, and Heniz Linge, his personal valet. Under severe torture and interrogation by their Soviet captors, the two admitted that as the war progressed the dictator had suffered more and more dizzy spells and illnesses,[58] adding that by 1944 Hitler simply 'could not live without the stimulants and tranquillisers' Morell prescribed.[59] It would appear that during their lengthy interrogations, Günsche and Linge supplied their NKVD inquisitors with plentiful evidence of 'Hitler's mental absence, even disorientation, and of his complete indifference to his surroundings'.[60]

This overall impression of physical and psychological decrepitude is supported by *Oberst* Bernd Freytag von Loringhoven, *aide-de-camp* to Hitler's last two chiefs of staff, who, 60 years after the war, recollected that by 1944 and 'At fifty-five years old, he [Hitler] truly looked an old man, stooping, hunched, head drooping, skin greyish, face deathly pale, eyes lacklustre . . .'[61] As it was, Hitler's health and Germany's military fortunes mirrored one another, deteriorating steadily throughout the winter of 1944–45 and eventually expiring that following spring.

Yet, despite the claims of historians and commentators such as Kershaw, Lukacs and Redlich, namely that Hitler's physiological and psychological condition would not have seriously impaired his judgement, or ability to take rational decisions (conclusions which may well derive from a reluctance to hand the Führer's supporters an apologia for his heinous crimes and actions), it is very doubtful whether any human being could function properly in a state of such mental and physical decay. Furthermore, the mixture and quantity of drugs taken by Hitler, particularly from 1941 onwards, also pose further valid questions as to his fitness for command and his capacity to conceive, plan and direct strategy.

Aside from the abundance of material made available to Whitehall by the collapse of the Third Reich, the state of the Führer's physical and mental health, as already noted, went largely unreported by the highest forum of Britain's intelligence community. The extant records of the JIC show that neither the committee nor its assessment staff took this subject seriously, despite the existence of credible evidence in other department's files, subsequently omitting this potentially significant subject from their appreciations. In doing so, they failed to draw the attention of the Chiefs of Staff to a potential correlation between Hitler's deteriorating mental and physical health and the course of German strategy, which became ever more erratic and illogical as the war progressed. Only in *Some Weaknesses* did the JIC finally acknowledge the relevance of this issue, notifying its readership that although the Führer had, 'offset his mental and physical exhaustion by means of artificial stimulants', by war's end these short-term solutions had merely 'increased his incapacity to take decisions, which he put off from day to day even when every hour was vital'.[62]

## Failures and weaknesses of the German Intelligence Services

Despite the protestations of some historians to the contrary, any explanation as to why Hitler and his generals ultimately lost the war is simply incomplete without reference to the role of intelligence in both the Allied and Nazi camps. At least in respect of Hitler's intelligence machine, the JIC's farewell paper does not disappoint, devoting one chapter (Chapter III of Section II 'The Weakness of German Intelligence') and an appendix (Appendix V the 'German Secret Intelligence Service (G.S.I.S.)') to Nazi Germany's covert agencies. Prominent among these, as the report makes clear, were the *Abwehr* and *Sicherheitsdienst* both of which were instrumental in helping to undermine the Third Reich, albeit for diametrically opposing reasons.

Established in 1921 as the 'only form of intelligence department permitted to Germany by the Versailles Treaty'[63] and headed from 1935 onwards by the *éminence grise* of German Intelligence, Admiral Wilhelm Canaris, the *Abwehr* was, in essence, the secret service of the OKW. Tasked primarily with the acquisition of military intelligence, the *Abwehr* in fact consisted of three main sections, I, II and III, dealing with foreign intelligence gathering, sabotage and covert operations and security and counter-espionage respectively.[64] Each of these 'specialist' sections were represented within a 'network of stations inside and outside the Reich': those inside the 'Reich and German-occupied territories' were designated *Abwehrstellen* (Ast); while those in neutral states, such as Sweden, Turkey and Spain, were referred to as *Kriegsorganisationen* (KOs).[65] Despite the existence of Section VI of the SD, which also specialized in foreign intelligence, Canaris's organization managed to achieve primacy in this particular arena of espionage. This was due in no small part to the abilities of Canaris and the fact that the *Abwehr* was held in such high esteem by Hitler who, for many years, was in awe of its cloak-and-dagger activities.

Yet the collective wisdom of the JIC, as distilled within the pages of *Some Weaknesses*, maintained that the standing and success of Canaris's organization had peaked during the years 1939–41. This was due largely to the successes of the German Army in the field, which ironically owed little to intelligence, and the effectiveness of *Abwehr* counter-espionage operations against foreign agents in Western Europe, which most certainly did. The JIC argued, moreover, that this 'golden period' for the *Abwehr* had given way during the years 1942–44 to one of almost 'uniform failure' inasmuch as the German secret service signally failed to acquire crucial intelligence on Allied strategic and operational intentions prior to the amphibious landings in North Africa, Sicily, Italy and Normandy.

The fate of the *Abwehr* was finally sealed, however, in February 1944 when Canaris was relieved of his command ostensibly for not countering Allied intelligence operations in Spain. The situation was compounded still further by the defection to the Allies of the *Abwehr* official Erich Vermehren and his wife that very month. Led by *Oberst* Georg Hansen from March onwards, Canaris's beloved service would eventually become entirely subsumed within the *Reichssicherheitshauptamt* (RSHA) for its role in the Bomb Plot of 20 July 1944 when disaffected *Wehrmacht* officers attempted to assassinate Hitler and trigger a *coup d'état* against the Nazi regime.[66]

It is on the question of its failures and weaknesses as a covert intelligence gathering and analytical service that the report excels. Drawing heavily, one detects, upon the Top Secret report compiled on the *Abwehr* and SD by Hugh Trevor-Roper in 1945,[67] *Some Weaknesses* enumerates the inherent flaws of Hitler's intelligence machinery and the suspect methodology employed by his spies. These ranged from their inability to 'speak truth unto power' inasmuch as their intelligence had to be skewered to fit with the particular preconceptions and *Weltanschauung* ('world view') of Hitler and his henchmen; through 'the absence of any inter-service staff,' such as the JIC and JIS, for the 'co-ordination and appreciation of intelligence';[68] to the marked disinclination of the various German Intelligence Services to co-operate and co-ordinate with one another, which was symptomatic of the 'divide and rule' policy so actively encouraged by the Führer. To round matters off, the report's authors also alluded to the fact that the *Abwehr*, in particular, was 'idle and corrupt' and rife with 'financial corruption and political disaffection'.[69] There is no doubt, therefore, that these

serious defects in Nazi intelligence contributed significantly to the defeat of
Hitler and his Third Reich.

Nevertheless, the wartime record of the *Abwehr*, SD, *Gestapo* and RSHA
as a whole was not all bad. Fashionable as it has become to dismiss and ridicule Hitler's spies, *Some Weaknesses* makes clear that these organizations did
in fact achieve notable wartime successes against the Allies. Perhaps their most
significant success was in penetrating the various agent networks set-up and
run by the Special Operations Executive (SOE) and SIS in the Low Countries.
In particular, *der Englandspiel*, or the 'England Game', whereby British agents
dropped into Holland during the period 1942–44 were captured and 'played
back' to their handlers in London, came to exemplify the ruthless efficiency
of the German Intelligence Services and the skill with which they operated
against their British adversaries.[70]

The kidnapping of two SIS officers, Major Richard Stevens and Captain
Sigismund Payne Best, by the SD at the Dutch-German frontier town of Venlo
on 9 November 1939, was an even earlier success for Nazi intelligence. Lured
to this unremarkable town by supposed representatives of the German military opposition to Hitler, Stevens and Best unfortunately fell into a carefully
laid trap set by the leading SD officer, *SS Brigadeführer* Walther Schellenberg.
Spirited across the German border by their SS abductors, the two intelligence
officers would reveal much under interrogation about SIS, its staff and organization thereby fatally weakening its operations in the Low Countries.[71]

Further successes acknowledged by *Some Weaknesses* focus on the ability
of the RSHA not only to penetrate Allied and neutral embassies, but to undertake 'spectacular sabotage and terrorist activities' against its enemies, many
being organized by the legendary *SS Obersturmbannführer* Otto Skorzeny; the
accumulation of vital information by the *Gestapo* on Soviet military potential
during the period 1939 to 1941 through the detailed questioning of German
workers and technicians returning from the Soviet Union; the formidable success of the *Gestapo* in counter-intelligence and the repression of conspiracy and
unrest in Germany and occupied Europe; and finally its deep penetration of
French resistance networks in the run-up to the D-Day landings of June 1944,
which resulted in its detecting the imminence of the Allied offensive before
its rivals in the *Abwehr* and SD. Missing from *Some Weaknesses*, however, are

some of the other major successes achieved by the *Abwehr*, specifically the early penetration of MI5,[72] the acquisition of the blueprints for the top-secret US 'Norden' bombsight and the setting up of extensive agent networks in the Soviet Union and the United States.[73] In light of these achievements, it is clear that Canaris's agents were not all 'idle and corrupt' incompetents.

# III. Omissions in the report

Significantly, what is not mentioned in the report is just as fascinating and important as what is. To those conscious of the crucial role intelligence played helping Britain and her Allies win the war, the conspicuous absence of any reference in *Some Weaknesses* to signals intelligence (SIGINT), and in particular ULTRA is arresting. The same applies to strategic deception, which reached new heights of ingenuity and success due to the work of the Double-Cross or XX Committee, which from January 1941 until the end of the war ran an exotic cast of double agents, mostly *Abwehr* spies sent to Britain, captured and eventually 'turned' by the Security Service, MI5. Also omitted is the role of human intelligence (HUMINT), the work of spies and in particular the activities of deep penetration agents situated in the very heart of Hitler's high command.[74] The subversive activities of key figures within the ranks of the Third Reich, who actively conspired against it, are also airbrushed from history by the report's draftsmen.

## *Spies and 'Traitors'*

Startlingly, recent archival research has revealed that British intelligence possessed at least three 'moles' within the OKW and RSHA. From early 1940 until September 1942 SIS ran a high-level asset inside the supreme command of the *Wehrmacht*. Codenamed 'Warlock' this agent fed his handlers valuable information on the strategic and operational intentions of the German military machine. By early 1941, however, it had become apparent to certain sections of Whitehall's intelligence community, namely MI14 and the JIS, that 'Warlock' had been caught and 'turned' by Himmler's security services. This dawning realization stemmed from the fact that the material supplied by 'Warlock' did not tally with the intelligence they were acquiring via ULTRA and other secret sources. A pattern of discrepancies or contradictions in such information would have alerted British intelligence officers to such a scenario. Yet why SIS continued to believe in their much-prized agent far into 1942, when sister organizations were preaching extreme caution, remains a mystery.[75]

A further cast of top-level agents discovered in the files of British intelligence appear to have infiltrated the very highest echelons of the German high command and its intelligence apparatus. Despite not having a codename we now know through a declassified CX report that SIS possessed an asset with very close connections to the RSHA and Walther Schellenberg himself.[76] Confirmed by material located in the records of the American Office for Strategic Services (OSS),[77] it would appear that as late as February 1945 this particular spy was relaying back to London critical information on the activities, personalities and rivalries of Hitler's security agencies. Frustratingly, the identity of this agent remains a mystery, but deep suspicion falls upon Kurt Jahnke, an officer in Amt VI, the foreign intelligence branch of the RSHA, who was a trusted confidant of Schellenberg's.[78]

Perhaps one of the greatest sources of wartime HUMINT, however, was agent 'Knopf'. Run by the Polish Secret Service (II Bureau of the Polish general staff), from at least early 1941 until late 1943, 'Knopf' was a German national, possibly a staff officer, whose sub-sources in the OKW and OKH provided him with top-grade strategic and operational intelligence on the *Wehrmacht* during some of the most critical stages of the war. Passed on to SIS by the Poles, who cultivated a very close wartime relationship with their British counterparts, the material collected by 'Knopf' and his sources ranged from the actual date of Hitler's offensive against the Soviet Union, Operation *Barbarossa*, to the existence of the Führer's headquarters in East Prussia, the *Wolfsschanze* (Wolf's Lair). Further intelligence on German intentions in North Africa, the Mediterranean and on the Eastern Front was also forwarded to Whitehall by this remarkable network. So highly was 'Knopf's' product regarded that it was disseminated to and read by General Sir Alan Brooke, Chief of the Imperial General Staff (CIGS) and Winston Churchill himself.[79]

Two of the most noteworthy 'traitors' to Hitler, who actively sought to undermine the Third Reich from within, were Admiral Wilhelm Canaris and his deputy, Colonel Hans Oster. Known as the 'little admiral', Canaris was an ardent anti-Nazi who had, since the late 1930s, conspired with other disaffected German officers to topple the Nazi dictator and his regime. Much ink has been spilled over the years by historians in their quest to ascertain the exact nature of Canaris's 'treason'. To varying degrees, all have muddied the waters. Yet we now know that despite distancing himself from the July Bomb Plot conspirators, who formed the nucleus of the German Opposition to Hitler, the chief of the *Abwehr* did pass on valuable intelligence to SIS.

This is confirmed in the Service's recent official history which relates that Canaris, known as 'Theodor' to the British, drip-fed politico-military secrets to a Polish intelligence agent, Halina Szymańska, codenamed 'Z.5/I', who worked ostensibly as a secretary in the Polish legation in Berne, Switzerland. This secret back-channel was via an *Abwehr* subordinate, Hans-Bernd Gisevius, who from August 1940 until December 1942 supplied Szymańska, and in turn, Whitehall's secret servants, with a variety of classified material. So close was the relationship between Canaris and Szymańska (the two had first met in Poland in September 1939) that on one occasion in October 1941, Hitler's spymaster even had dinner with her in Berne in order to reveal the extent of German difficulties on the Eastern Front.[80] Ironically, Canaris was later hanged by the Nazis not, it must be noted, for leaking secrets to the enemy, but for his association with leading anti-Nazis.

No less important, however, were the activities of Hans Oster. Outspoken, reckless and overtly anti-Nazi, Oster was almost the mirror-opposite of his more calculating boss. Appalled by the excesses of the Nazis and convinced that Germany would lose the war Hitler had initiated, Oster sought to undermine the Third Reich by leaking to the Allies the military plans of the German high Command. The high-water mark of his espionage activities occurred in the autumn and spring of 1939–40 just as the *Wehrmacht* was poised to invade in the West. Determined to fatally compromise the planned German offensive, the deputy head of the *Abwehr* re-activated an old friendship with the Dutch Military Attaché in Berlin, Major Gijsbertus Jacobus Sas, in order to betray Hitler's aggressive intentions. Details of 'Case Yellow', the blueprint for the invasion of France and the Low Countries, were personally communicated to Sas by Oster, who encouraged his friend to disseminate them to his counter-parts in Belgian and British intelligence. Frustratingly, like earlier failed attempts to alert the Danes and Norwegians of impending attack, Oster's warnings were ignored, dismissed or acted upon half-heartedly by the Dutch, Belgians and British with tragic consequences.[81]

Let down by the Allies, Oster committed himself thereafter to the over-throw of the Nazi regime by means of a *coup d'état*. A one-man dynamo, Oster would work tirelessly during the next three years to galvanize a cabal of disaffected *Wehrmacht* officers who shared his ultimate goal: the elimina-tion of Hitler. Yet his personal crusade was jeopardized in April 1943 when he was dismissed from his post as *Abwehr* deputy for helping Jews evade their Nazi persecutors. This, coupled with the dismissal of Canaris in February 1944, ensured that the *Abwehr* was no longer the epicentre of the German Opposition. Yet on 20 July 1944 their co-conspirators very nearly succeeded in killing the Führer and triggering a military coup in Berlin. Tragically, Hitler survived and the subsequent man-hunt by Himmler's security serv-ices ensured that many of those implicated, including Oster, were arrested by the *Gestapo* and duly executed or imprisoned. For his 'crimes' against the Reich, Oster was hanged, along with his old boss Canaris, on 9 April 1945 at Flossenburg concentration camp.

Unsurprisingly, none of the incredible facts cited above are recorded or even hinted at within the covers of *Some Weaknesses*. The reason for such omis-sions is, however, rather prosaic. Quite simply, the remit of *Some Weaknesses*, as set down by the relevant commissioning authorities, never allowed for the report's scribes to disclose the critical role SIGINT, HUMINT and the Double-Cross system played in defeating Hitler's war machine. Such matters were far too sensitive and secret to divulge to a wider, uninitiated audience. The wartime policy of 'need to know' remained, un-astonishingly, paramount throughout. Consequently, the report received a very low security classifi-cation from Whitehall's secret servants, namely 'confidential' as opposed to 'Secret' or 'Top Secret'. Frozen by official secrecy for the next 30 years, it was not until 1974, when Group Captain Frederick Winterbotham published his book, *The Ultra Secret*, that the work of Bletchley Park was revealed to the general public.[82] Moreover, it has taken even longer for Britain's foreign intelligence gathering service, SIS, to avow officially its wartime agent networks and clandestine operations.[83]

## Nazi atomic and chemical weapons programmes

What is also absent from this account is any reference to the German's atomic weapon programme, informally known as the *Uranverein* or the 'Uranium Club' which commenced work shortly before the outbreak of war. One of the project's leading scientists, the German physicist Werner Heisenberg, was instrumental in harnessing the research and development facilities of the Third Reich in order to investigate the feasibility of building an atomic bomb. Yet Heisenberg's work, and indeed that of the entire programme, was gravely undermined by Hitler's racial laws and the politicization of academia, which forced some of the world's greatest physicists, many of whom were Jewish, to leave Nazi Germany and Fascist Italy and head to the safety of the United States. By means of this 'brain drain' the Nazis fatally crippled their own programme and endowed their current and future enemies with the requisite mental horsepower required to win the race for nuclear supremacy. The failure of the Third Reich to attain the atom bomb, therefore, must surely rank among one of the most important reasons why Hitler did not win the Second World War, or at the very least reach a politico-military stalemate *vis-à-vis* the Allied powers.

*Some Weaknesses* is also silent about those atomic programmes run by Britain, Canada and their American ally, codenamed TUBE ALLOYS and the MANHATTAN Project respectively. Yet this is curious in light of the first successful test of the atom bomb at the Alamogordo test range, New Mexico on 16 July 1945, and is doubly so when considering the obvious publicity surrounding the dropping of the uranium (codenamed 'Little Boy') and plutonium ('Fat Man') atomic bombs on Hiroshima and Nagasaki on 6 August and 9 August 1945. This deafening silence also conceals the fact that the atomic bomb had originally been intended for use against Nazi Germany. In light of post-war disclosures, it is safe to conclude that had Grand Admiral Karl Doenitz's 'Flensburg government' refused to capitulate in May 1945, thereby prolonging hostilities, the cities of Berlin and Nuremberg would most likely have been reduced to radioactive ash by the Allies' new super weapon.[84]

Never likely to be a war-winning strategy *per se*, the deployment of chemical weapons by Hitler's scientists, the *bête noire* of British planners, may, nevertheless, have changed not only the course of the war but its character. Although historians are fully conscious that the Nazi dictator never initiated gas warfare, even *in extremis*, the reasons for such restraint have nonetheless baffled them. While some commentators have ventured that this was due largely to the Führer's own experience of being temporarily blinded by mustard gas during the First World War,[85] others have stated, quite erroneously, that even before the outbreak of war in September 1939 Hitler had banned their offensive use.[86] A number have even conceded, moreover, that the rationale behind the Nazi despot's decision not to use gas 'can only be a matter of conjecture'.[87]

However, as Gerhard L. Weinberg's magisterial treatment of the Second World War, *A World At Arms*,[88] makes clear, far from prohibiting the development of chemical weapons, Hitler had actually initiated a programme for producing nerve agents such as Tabun, Sarin and Soman.[89] Terrifyingly, wartime British intelligence, according to its official history, 'failed "to secure any definite lead on the German work on their Tabun type gases" either before or during the Second World War', and critically 'did not receive intelligence of German work on nerve gases until the first stocks of Tabun weapons had been captured in 1945'.[90]

Such mystification also afflicted, unsurprisingly, the JIS and JIC whose collective wartime thinking was vexed periodically by this potential threat. Although *Some Weaknesses* is, with one exception, mute on the issue of gas warfare and its attendant 'intelligence failures' on the part of the British,[91] it is now clear that instead of diminishing as the war progressed, Whitehall's anxiety over whether Hitler might commit some 'mad dog act' by introducing gas warfare onto the battlefield actually grew. British officialdom was not alone in this, however. Both the Americans and Soviets 'remained', in the words of F. H. Hinsley's official history, 'uncertain about the enemy's policy with regard to chemical warfare' throughout the war.[92]

Nevertheless, we now know that Nazi policy regarding the development and eventual use of chemical weapons was predicated on the certain belief that the Third Reich held a 'monopoly' on nerve agents. Yet on 15 May 1943 a seismic shift in strategic policy occurred in Berlin when Hitler received news that, contrary to received wisdom, Germany did not, in reality, have sole ownership of nerve agents.[93] Mistakenly led to believe by faulty intelligence that his enemies had successfully manufactured and stockpiled similar toxins, Germany's leader had no choice but to refrain from employing chemical weapons against the Allies for fear of massive reprisals against the German population, who lacked, *inter alia*, a ready supply of gas masks.[94] In fact, unbeknownst to the Germans, Britain, America and the Soviet Union possessed no such comparable hardware in their respective arsenals.

## Post-war intelligence reviews

Nuclear and chemical warfare aside, anyone scouring the pages of the report for introspection or self-examination on the part of Britain's central intelligence apparatus will also be greatly disappointed. Apart from brief allusions to the failure of Whitehall in 1940 to place the economy onto a 'total war' footing,[95] and the fact that Allied intelligence grossly underestimated the power and influence of the Führer apropos the conception, planning and execution of German politico-military policy,[96] there are virtually no 'lessons learned' incorporated into the 200 pages of historical analysis produced by the JIC. This may, however, be explained in part by the fact that an internal review of Britain's secret state had already been penned by the wartime Chairman of the JIC, Victor Cavendish-Bentinck, who on 10 January 1945 submitted to the Chiefs of Staff a report entitled *The Intelligence Machine*, which, unlike *Some Weaknesses*, was classified 'Top Secret'.[97]

Distinctly different in scope and content from the historical treatment supplied by the JIS, Cavendish-Bentinck's review was, in the opinion of Michael Herman, an expert on the uses and abuses of intelligence, the 'first serious British attempt – possibly the first attempt anywhere – to set out a plan for . . . a complete, interlocking, peacetime system' of intelligence reporting.[98] Yet, in keeping with *Some Weaknesses*, the notion that *The Intelligence Machine* should set out to evaluate the accuracy of wartime reporting on the part of the JIS and JIC appears to have been far from paramount in the minds of those with a vested interest in its findings. As Herman has opined, while the appraisal 'was a vision of a post-war system written from the centre of wartime action', it was, however, 'stronger on vision than on reflection . . .'.[99] To the mind of the modern scholar this shortage of self-scrutiny and censure appears to have been the *leitmotif* of British official reporting at this time.

Nonetheless, on 6 November 1947, just a year after the dissemination of *Some Weaknesses*, a further review of Britain's intelligence services was circulated within the inner-loop of Whitehall. Eponymously entitled the 'Evill Report' after its author, Air Chief Marshal Sir Douglas Evill, but officially designated *Review of Intelligence Organization 1947*, the report's rationale was to review the post-war arrangements already put in place by Cavendish-Bentinck.[100] Running to 45 pages and addressing, *inter alia*, the individual components, mechanics and future requirements of Whitehall's intelligence community, Evill's report, which was also classified 'Top Secret', appears to have been somewhat superfluous inasmuch as his findings merely vindicated those already reached by Cavendish-Bentinck two years before. As is plain, *Some Weaknesses* was but one of a multiplicity of reports commissioned by Whitehall in the immediate post-war period whose respective aims were not only to bridge gaps in existing knowledge, but to inform the future development of British intelligence through the study of its past and that of its former enemies.

## IV. Inaccuracies in the report

Although errors of fact or interpretation are surprisingly scarce within *Some Weaknesses*, one of its more notable inaccuracies appears right at the beginning of the report on page three. Addressing the matter of Hitler's political polemic, *Mein Kampf*, the JIC asserted that the book had been 'written between 1923 and 1930'. Although technically correct, Hitler in fact published the first volume on 19 July 1925 with the second made available to the public on 11 December 1926. Such imprecision, however, was in fact symptomatic of a deeper intellectual malaise which had affected wartime British intelligence, namely its inexplicable disinclination to read, dissect and analyse *Mein Kampf* in the pursuit of possible insights into the mind and intentions of the Führer. As historians are now aware, this was a notable blunder and one that revealed the cognitive limitations of Britain's intelligence services at this time.

While *Mein Kampf* cannot be regarded as an exact blueprint of Hitler's future intentions,[101] it nevertheless provided its readership with an 'uncompromising statement of Hitler's political principles, his "world view", his sense of his own "mission", his "vision" of society, and his long-term aims'.[102] What is more, according to the official historians of Germany's role in the Second World War, 'anyone who wanted to know what Hitler said and planned could easily find out. At the very least, his ambitious plans of warlike expansion were not unknown, and, as they contained "elements of purposeful planning and designs for the future", it was not possible simply to dismiss them as absurd'.[103] In light of this, *Mein Kampf* can therefore be treated as a very important, if not indispensable, source of 'open' intelligence on Hitler and his mind-set.

The disinclination on the part of British intelligence, particularly during the early years of the war, to scrutinize *Mein Kampf* goes some way in supporting the contention that Whitehall's secret state simply did not regard Hitler as a serious political thinker or international player. Such a notion was championed by Major-General Sir Kenneth Strong, one-time head of MI14 and G-2 (head of intelligence) to General Eisenhower at SHAEF, who later recalled that in Whitehall 'the fulminations of *Mein Kampf* were generally regarded by officialdom as having little or no practical value, even as a guide to German thinking, let alone German intentions'.[104] Strong was not alone in this view, however. Hugh Trevor-Roper was to lament in his 1968 book, *The Philby Affair*, that, 'I doubt if there was one man among the professionals of SIS, at that time, who had read *Mein Kampf* . . .'[105]

Such contentions are supported still further by the fact that during an extensive trawl of the wartime records of the JIC not a single reference to *Mein Kampf* was unearthed in the multitude of assessments commissioned by the committee. That said, what appears to be the sole exception manifests itself in a rough draft of a two-page JIC paper entitled, 'Germany's Next Move' and dated 30 June 1940, in which Professor Noel Hall, the Ministry of Economic

Warfare's representative on the committee, refers to 'Hitler's emotional preoccupation with "Lebensraum"' or 'living space', an oblique allusion to one of the
central tenets of the Führer's ideological manifesto.[106]

Yet in *Some Weaknesses* the JIC informed the Chiefs of Staff that the Führer,
'in his direction of German policy between 1935 and 1945, carried into execution the main design foreshadowed in *Mein Kampf*...',[107] adding that, 'Our study
is much assisted by having, in *Mein Kampf*, the blueprint against which the finished product can be placed for purposes of comparison'. The report's authors
concluded, moreover, that, 'Rarely in history can there have been a case where
the principal player in the game of war opened by so clearly showing his hand'.[108]
If this had been so, why then did British intelligence and its politico-military
'customers' ignore such a crucial source of 'open' intelligence throughout the
war?[109] The inescapable impression left by this passage is that on the issue of
Hitler's political autobiography and its utility, Whitehall's secret servants were
not only disingenuous in their reporting, but indubitably wise with hindsight.

# V. Conclusion

In April 1963, the distinguished American journalist, Philip L. Graham, coined
the now immortal phrase the 'first rough draft of history' while describing the
art of journalism and its concomitant duty to explain, on a daily basis, world
events to a universal readership.[110] Aptly, the parallels with intelligence reporting could not be more piquant. Allowing for the fact that it was intended for a
restricted circle of Whitehall officials, *Some Weaknesses* can indeed be viewed
as the 'first rough draft' of an historical discourse on the Second World War
that continues to this day. Well-researched, succinctly written and persuasively
argued the report appears to have quenched the intellectual curiosity displayed
by the JIC and Chiefs of Staff as to the underlying reasons why Hitler and his
high command lost the war in the manner they did.

Sixty years after its circulation, this *aide mémoire* also serves as a valuable
corrective to a dangerous tendency exhibited by some historians in recent years,
namely to forget the military professionalism and successes of the *Wehrmacht*
and to focus instead on the much vaunted 'superiority' of the Allies. As the

high priest of wartime British intelligence, Victor Cavendish-Bentinck, later asserted, the Germans could easily have 'won the war five times over' had the Führer and his commanders not made so many errors of judgement.[111] If nothing else, the publication of *Some Weaknesses* will serve to dissuade present and future students of history from underestimating the potency of Hitler's war machine and from forgetting how close it came to winning the war.

Yet, as we have seen, the report is far from perfect. Aside from its various omissions and occasional errors, *Some Weaknesses* also fails to deliver on one of its central mission statements, specifically to serve as a 'check' on the accuracy of JIC papers submitted to the wartime Chiefs of Staff.[112] From a purely scholastic point of view this is regrettable inasmuch as to date no overall assessment of the committee's performance in predicting German strategy exists. This evident lack of self-scrutiny on the part of the JIS and JIC may well be construed, in light of recent historical research, as an implicit acknowledgement that Whitehall's central intelligence machine had been less than adept at fathoming the strategic mind-set of Hitler and his military advisers. This particular thesis certainly accords with that proferred by Noel Annan, who later lamented in his thought-provoking book, *Changing Enemies*, that, 'Perhaps our greatest, and yet most comprehensive, failure was to get inside Hitler's mind and think like him'. To 'fathom the workings of Hitler's mind', so Annan admitted, would have 'required intelligence of a very high order'.[113]

This conclusion very much dove-tails that reached by Lieutenant-Commander Ewen Montagu RNVR. A member of the Naval Intelligence Division (NID), with a seat on the XX Committee, Montagu was one of the architects of Operation *Mincemeat*, a spectacular piece of strategic deception launched in April 1943 to convince the OKW into thinking the Allies would land in Sardinia or Greece instead of their true objective, Sicily.[114] While mindful of the many successes achieved by Whitehall's politico-military elite, Montagu's abiding impression of the wartime Chiefs of Staff, however, was that they simply '*couldn't make themselves think as Germans*'.[115] As the Joint Intelligence Committee and its assessment staff did the thinking for the Chiefs of Staff Committee, responsibility for this shortcoming rests heavily with them.

The commissioning of *Some Weaknesses* can therefore be viewed as a direct attempt by the 'high table' of Britain's intelligence services to rectify this deficit in wartime knowledge and to ascertain exactly what had occurred 'on the other side of the hill' between 1939 and 1945.[116] Yet, by a stroke of irony, in highlighting the deficiencies of Nazi Germany they inadvertently brought attention upon their own. That said, for all its shortfalls and omissions , *Some Weaknesses in German Strategy and Organisation, 1933–1945* remains recommended reading for scholar and general reader alike chronicling, as it does, the rise, decline and fall of Hitler's military machine as seen through the prism and focus of British intelligence reporting.

CONFIDENTIAL.                                      Copy No. 344

**J.I.C. (46) 33 (Final).**

*20ᵗʰ October,* 1946.

## CHIEFS OF STAFF COMMITTEE

### JOINT INTELLIGENCE SUB-COMMITTEE

# SOME WEAKNESSES IN GERMAN STRATEGY AND ORGANISATION 1933-1945

## Report by the
## Joint Intelligence Sub-Committee

## NOTE

In approving this report, the Chiefs of Staff emphasised that
Appendices VIII-XIX, containing a chronological statement of
events in the different theatres of war and in the fields of strategy,
war production and military supply, should not be considered as
authoritative histories, nor as a complete or balanced narrative
of those events. It may well be that the official histories, when
compiled, may show that there are errors and omissions in these
Appendices. Consequently, as indicated in paragraphs 2 and 5
of the covering note by the Joint Intelligence Sub-Committee to
the report, they should be considered purely as illustrations of
the manner in which various German weaknesses played their
part in Germany's defeat, orientated from the German point of
view.

*Offices of the Cabinet and Minister of Defence, 20th October* 1946

## CHIEFS OF STAFF COMMITTEE

### Joint Intelligence Sub-Committee

# SOME WEAKNESSES IN GERMAN STRATEGY AND ORGANISATION, 1933-1945

## Report by the Joint Intelligence Sub-Committee

In March 1945 the flow of intelligence which we were obtaining from the interrogation of German prisoners-of-war and from captured German documents had reached such proportions that we thought it useful to begin the preparation of a report on German Strategy, so as to check from German sources the various appreciations which we had submitted to the Chiefs of Staff earlier in the war.

2. With the collapse of German in May 1945 the volume of material available to us was increased by the overrunning of the various German archives, such as those of the Supreme Command of the Armed Forces (OKW) and the Ministry of Foreign Affairs. This enabled us to expand this study to include a mass of technical information which we considered would be of use to future historians, and in particular, would give a broad review of the course of German high policy and strategy leading up to the defeat of Germany by the Allied Powers. The study would also draw attention to certain weaknesses from which our own organisation of defence might in turn benefit, and would present as much factual and technical information as could properly be brought into the compass of a Joint Intelligence Sub-Committee appreciation.

3. A preliminary draft of this report was completed in October 1945 by those Officers who, as members of the Joint Intelligence Staff, had themselves taken part in the preparation of Joint Intelligence Sub-Committee papers during the war. This draft was made the basis of a special interrogation by

General Jodl, Chief of the Operational Staff of the OKW, who confirmed the accuracy of its broad conclusions, and an examination was also made of evidence collected for the Nuremberg trial. Subsequently, we included further information, which came to light some months after the end of the war in Europe and in the Far East.

4. We submit, therefore, in the attached Report a provisional study, in broad outline, of the weaknesses in German strategy and organisation during and immediately prior to the War. Our purpose is to bring to notice some of the principal causes of German collapse, inherent in Germany's political and military organisation, in German personalities and in Germany's war machine and methods of production. These have been brought to light by Intelligence scrutiny of captured documents and in interrogations by the Allied military authorities.

5. The report cannot be more than a purely provisional one. It does not attempt to make a final assessment of the German weaknesses. That must be left to the historians. The events which we describe are too recent and the mass of material, of which only a small portion has been examined, too voluminous for a historical survey to be made at the present time. We are well aware of the defects of the report, which are inevitable in an attempt to describe a complicated chain of events of such recent occurrence, at a time when the assistance of many of those with an intimate knowledge of those events is no longer available. We do, however, attempt to describe the basic German plan to set out the different factors which interfered with its fulfilment, and to identify a number of weaknesses in the German war machine which are thereby revealed.

6. We consider it desirable to set down certain aspects of the War whilst there are still sources available who were closely connected with the events described. We believe that when it is finally possible to make a balanced historical survey, some of the acutely critical moments which are vividly remembered now are likely to become confused with the passage of time, and that there will be a tendency to take for granted Allied superiority and to underestimate the great and evident strength of the German war machine.

7. Our study is orientated from the German point of view, and though we touch from time to time on several phases of Allied strategy, in so far as they served to dislocate the German design and to bring to light the basic German weaknesses, we do not otherwise attempt to study Allied strategy or to examine its developments in the course of the War. In Section I of the Report we describe what we believe to have been the main design

of Hitler's strategy and describe the manner in which it was pursued up to the outbreak of War. We then examine the impact of certain events which, though some of them may have been foreseen and discounted by Hitler, nevertheless affected his strategy from 1939 onwards and interfered with the execution of his design. And finally we describe very briefly from the German point of view the evolution of war strategy after 1942, when Germany had lost the strategical initiative. Since that initiative was then in Allied hands, our description can only be of the briefest, since an attempt to relate the evolution of the war itself in that period would amount to an historical review covering both Allied and German strategy. In Section II we describe certain weaknesses as they became apparent in the course of the war. Finally, in Section III, we describe in a series of chapters the chronological sequence of events from 1939 onwards in the different theatres of war, on land, on sea and in the air, and in the fields of war production and military supply, in order to illustrate the manner in which the various German weaknesses played their part in Germany's defeat.

*Traditional German Policy.*

8. There is one further point which we wish to make at the outset in order to give historical perspective. The National Socialist Revolution in Germany and the rôle played by Hitler in directing German rearmament and strategy, make it inevitable that in examining Germany's war effort we should concentrate largely upon his policy and design. It would, however, be a fundamental mistake to suggest in any way that the policy pursued by Hitler was different from the policy basically desired by the General Staff and by the German people. "A war to wipe out the desecration involved in the creation of the Polish Corridor and to lessen the threat to separated East Prussia was regarded as a sacred duty, though a sad necessity. This was one of chief reasons behind the partially secret rearmament which began about ten years before Hitler came to power and which was accentuated by Nazi rule."*[1] It is true that Hitler forced the pace in German rearmament and in the development of German policy; it is also true that in many ways his personal influence caused deviation from the strategy which the General Staff would themselves have preferred to pursue; but it is nevertheless important to emphasise that the policy pursued by Hitler was a logical development of Germany's nationalist revival, which began immediately after the defeat of Germany in 1918 and whose purpose it was to reverse the verdict of the

---

* Affidavit sworn by von Blomberg, War Minister from 1933 to 1938

last war. The enormous popularity obtained between 1933 and 1937 by the Nazi movement and the almost unanimous support for Hitler from the German people during those years showed to what extent the people were identified psychologically with Hitler's general outlook and policy.

(Signed)    E.G.N. RUSHBROOKE.

G.W.R. TEMPLAR.

R.E. VINTRAS.

(for A.C.A.S. (I)).

M.J. CRESWELL.

*Offices of the Cabinet and*

*Minister of Defence, S.W.1.*

*30ᵗʰ September,* 1946

# SOME WEAKNESSES IN GERMAN STRATEGY AND ORGANISATION, 1933-1945.

## Report by the Joint Intelligence Sub-Committee.

# CONTENTS

# SOME WEAKNESSES IN GERMAN STRATEGY AND ORGANISATION 1933-1945.

# SECTION I

# Chapter I. –
# Hitler's Grand Design

HITLER in his direction of German policy between 1935 and 1945, carried into execution the main design foreshadowed in *Mein Kampf* (written between 1923 and 1930). Our study is much assisted by having, in *Mein Kampf*, the blueprint against which the finished product can be placed for purposes of comparison. Barely in history can there have been a case where the principal player in the game of war opened by so clearly showing his hand.

2. Hitler's design, as expounded in *Mein Kampf*, was to re-establish Germany, both politically and as a military Power, by reversing the provisions of the Treaty of Versailles; to incorporate all Germans within one Reich, including those in the lands previously forming part of the Austro-Hungarian Empire; and to provide more "living space" for the German people. In the west, he desired above all a settlement of accounts with France, so that the shame of Versailles should be redeemed and France should no longer impede German aspirations in other directions. The attainment of these objectives implied the German domination of Europe. Her only possible future challenge for this predominant position appeared to be the U.S.S.R., though it would probably take years for Russia to develop her military potential. In all Hitler's speeches and pronouncements ran the constant theme of hostility to the Soviet Union.

3. In the field of strategy, however, the main theme of *Mein Kampf* and of Hitler's theories expounded in speeches and staff conferences was the disastrous effect on Germany, as proved in 1914-18, of a simultaneous war on two fronts. To this, to the strategical errors of the General Staff and, above all, to the *betrayal* of the German front line soldier by the politicians and civilians, especially the Communists and pacifists, he attributed Germany's failure in 1918.

4. Hitler openly discussed in *Mein Kampf* how to achieve German domination of the world. We believe that this was his underlying purpose, though Germany was so

weak when he first came to power that he had to concentrate first upon reconstruction, defence and the attainment of a predominant position in Europe. He worked on a basis of expediency and probably had no clear idea at that early stage how he was going to achieve his ultimate objective. He may have thought at moments of achieving it through an Anglo-German alliance. Eventually, however, he realised that the British Commonwealth would not accept his terms. We describe in the following paragraphs the rough outline of events as, step by step, Hitler put Germany into a position to dominate Europe and to threaten the world.

# THE PREPARATORY PHASE

5. Before beginning the active phase of his strategy, which opened in February 1938 with the substitution of men like Ribbentrop, Keitel and Brauchitsch, who subscribed to the policy he wanted for the more responsible Neurath, Blomberg and Fritsch, Hitler spent three years mobilising the defence of the Third Reich, on the training of whose aggressive spirit he had already by 1935 spent two years of intensive propaganda and mass-psychology. The foundations of German rearmament had already been laid by von Seeckt and the Reichswehr soon after the Treaty of Versailles. After several years' constant training of the S.A. and later the S.S., after eliminating by the purge on the 30th June 1934, the party radicals who sought to set up the party forces instead of the German army as the focus for national resurgence, Hitler introduced conscription in March 1935 and unveiled the Luftwaffe as a new air weapon (in open defiance of the Treaty of Versailles), in the same month. After a further year of intensive military preparations and training he marched into the Rhineland in March1936 at a time when Britain and France and the League of Nations were preoccupied with the Italo-Abyssinian crisis. He thus put himself in a position to fortify his western frontier and prepared to defy the Western Powers.

6. At the same time Hitler reorganised [the] German economy, developing greater self-sufficiency for war by inaugurating the Four Years' Plan in the autumn of 1936, and obtained that "strong alliance" which he had stated in *Mein Kampf* was to be the basis of Germany's foreign policy, by creating the Rome-Berlin Axis in 1936. As the first military expression of this alliance he at once joined with Mussolini in their common felonious enterprise of intervention in the Spanish Civil War. By his alliance with Italy he sought to remove the chief barrier against German designs in Austria.

7. In each of his preliminary steps Hitler gambled on the success of his plan, and knew that he would not have been able to afford failure. As he said in his speeches, he did not admit the existence of the word "impossible." The strength of his position lay, as he well knew, in the fact that his opponents were too timid and too disunited to call his bluff. He profited throughout by this disunity and defied them one by one. When, in 1938 and 1939, they awoke, though remarkably slowly, to his real intentions, his bluff was bluff no longer, and he was determined to carry out his design, cost what it might.

8. In these first stages in Hitler's policy it is possible to discern two characteristics. Hitler gambled on success, and had no alternative plans in the event of failure. Though constantly aware of his ultimate aim he did not plan more than one step ahead. This was partly due to the fact that he was an opportunist and partly to distrust of his collaborators and military advisers.

## THE ACTIVE PHASE

*Austria, Czechoslovakia, Poland.*

9. It is arguable whether, before 1937, Hitler had formed any very firm opinions as to how his grand design was, in practice, to be executed. On the 10th November of that year, he summoned the Chiefs of his Armed Forces and explained his future policy. He outlined it as follows:-

(a) Germany must have more "living space".
(b) This could best be found in eastern Europe (*i.e.*, Poland, White Russia, the Ukraine).
(c) To obtain it involved war.
(d) Germany must make war at the first favourable opportunity in order to use the advantages of rearmament and of the tide of patriotic fervour aroused and stimulated by the Nazis, and to deal with her possible opponents before they were ready to fight.
(e) He considered that Germany would have to reckon with her two "hateful enemies", England and France, to whom a German colossus in the centre of Europe would be intolerable.

In the same month Lord Halifax visited Berlin and Berchtesgaden and found that, far from there being any possibility of coming to some understanding with Hitler on the basis of an equal share for Germany in colonial trade from territories in Central Africa, all that Hitler would talk about with any interest was "Lebensraum" in Europe and the questions of Austria and Czechoslovakia.

10. We now have evidence that Neurath and Fritsch (representing the traditional German Nationalist view in the Foreign Office and Army respectively) and even the servile Blomberg (influenced no doubt by Fritsch and the Officer Corps) felt serious misgivings about this policy. When, therefore, the time came to put it into execution Hitler threw them out and by a decree of the 4th February, 1938, assumed the Supreme Command of the Armed Forces himself. Within ten days Schuschnigg was summoned to Berchtesgaden, was directly intimidated by gangster methods from the moment he set foot over the frontier at Freilassing, and was bullied into accepting Hitler's men of straw into his Cabinet. A fortnight later Schuschnigg rallied, tried to make a stand by calling a plebiscite and Hitler, seeing his first objective beginning to slip from his grasp, abandoned "legal" means of effecting the "Anschluss", invaded Austria and absorbed it into the Reich.

11. The next step was "to smash Czechoslovakia through military action". Two months later therefore, on the 30th May, 1938, Hitler signed the directive giving his final decision to destroy Czechoslovakia, thereby initiating the military preparations. Beck, the Army Chief of Staff, stated in a lecture two months later that while Germany was crushing Czechoslovakia the French Army would invade and defeat Germany. As a result of this lecture he was dismissed by Hitler. Hitler had proved he was right in believing that France would not attack when he advanced into the Rhineland in March 1936, and he was to prove himself right again over Czechoslovakia in spite of the fears of the General Staff.

12. On the 8th September the High Command put the finishing touches to the operational orders, and all was in readiness. The directive of the 30th May had ordered Keitel to guarantee execution of the operation by the 1st October. The Munich Agreement was signed on the 29th September and the German forces entered Czechoslovakia the following day.

13. The annexation of the Sudeten territories, however, did not achieve Hitler's object; it merely deprived Czechoslovakia of her defences. In March 1939, again abandoning "legal" means, and confirmed by the attitude of the Western Powers at Munich in his belief that they would not oppose his designs, Hitler invaded Bohemia and

Moravia and marched into Prague. By securing the armament production of Austria, Bohemia and Moravia, and by immensely strengthening Germany's strategic position in the south-east, he had reached his first objectives. Goering said at the time that the transfer of Czech armament potential to Germany had considerably strengthened the Axis and would be an advantage in the event of an attack against Poland.

14. During the months after the Munich Agreement, however, Hitler made every attempt to obtain Polish concurrence in Germany's designs on Russia and on the Western Powers. On the 24th October, 1938, Ribbentrop proposed to the Polish Ambassador that Poland should join the Anti-Comintern Pact and should support German colonial claims. Similar proposals were made by Hitler to the Polish Foreign Minister, and by Ribbentrop when he visited Warsaw in January 1939. But Poland refused, re-affirmed the Russo-Polish pact of non-aggression, and on the 31st March 1939, received the Anglo-French guarantee. Hitler, thereupon, decided to attack. On the 23rd May, 1939, Hitler summoned a conference of the Chiefs of his Armed Forces. He now proceeded to announce his decision "to attack Poland at the first suitable opportunity". He explained :-

(a) That Poland would always make common cause with Germany's enemies in the West.

(b) That the existence of Poland was an obstacle in Germany's quest for "Lebensraum".

(c) That Poland was of doubtful value as a barrier against Russia and would not resist pressure from the Soviet Union.

Hitler thus considered an attack on Poland necessary, not only to conquer new space for Germany, but also to eliminate a threat from the East in the case of war with the West and as a means of ensuring the use of Poland in his final struggle with Russia.

15. Although Hitler may have hoped that he could attack Poland without the intervention of the Western Powers, he nevertheless reckoned with that eventuality: his policy was –

(i) By completing the West Wall and taking other defensive measures in the Rhineland and by threatening the ruthless use of his air force, to make intervention appear to the Western Powers likely to be both profitless and costly.

(ii) If the Western Powers declared war, to treat them as the principal enemy,
and to over-run Holland, Belgium and France as soon as possible after the war
had been declared. He would thus secure the "fundamental conditions" for a
successful naval and air war against England.

Nevertheless, Hitler was never in fact prepared for an immediate naval war against
England. He allowed Admiral Raeder to continue his long-term planning on the
assumption that there would be no war against England until 1942 at the earliest,
though on another occasion he gave 1944 as the earliest date. If Hitler could have
avoided war until he had reached the 35 per cent. of British strength allowed him
under the London Treaty of 1935, it would have changed the situation at sea very
much in Germany's favour, but when war with England broke out Germany was
below the maximum allowed her.

# THE DOMINATION OF EUROPE

16. It is clear that Hitler considered the scene of Germany's future expansion covered not merely Central Europe and Poland, but South-East Europe, the Ukraine
and European Russia. He regarded war with the Soviet Union as inevitable and as the
main objective of his policy. Having made temporary use of Russia during the Polish
occupation, much as he had made use of Poland during the Czech operation, it was
probably his intention to repeat the same technique by attacking Russia after having
made the necessary preparatory moves by securing his positions in Finland, Slovakia,
Hungary, Roumania and Bulgaria. Both the design, composition and balance of his
armed forces, and the production programme for their support as originally planned
in the years 1935-1938, confirm that this was his ultimate objective.

17. We consider it probable that Hitler had originally timed his attack on Russia
for a date no later than 1943-45. On the 12th December 1944, in a lecture delivered
to army and corps commanders on the eve of the Ardennes offensive, he said that
the war, inevitable sooner or later, had come at the right time. "It was not possible
that after 5 or 10 years Germany would still possess technical supremacy. A more
favourable moment than the year 1939 would never exist. I therefore personally considered it right to exploit the situation as early as possible and clear such matters as
were necessary should Germany be attacked". Later in the speech he defined "such

matters" as "the final reckoning with Poland in order to put German Reich territory into a defensive position". By December 1944, Hitler was already preparing his own defence and spoke repeatedly of the "preventive" purpose of the war. We examine later in this paper the crucial question of whether Hitler really believed, in 1941, that Russia would attack first.

# WORLD DOMINATION

18. We have referred above to Hitler's underlying purpose of achieving German domination of the world. His plans for this belong, however, to a later phase than those for continental war and called for quite a different balance of armaments. It may be that had Hitler avoided intervention of the western Powers over the Polish issue and then later over the Russian issue, he expected to be able to reduce France to vassaldom without defeating her. In the case of this country it is doubtful whether, in the long run, he ever expected to do more than lull a future enemy into a sense of false security, obtaining our connivance in his attack on Russia (as he had obtained Russian connivance for the Polish, and Polish connivance for the Czechoslovak campaigns) until the time came for his final reckoning with us.

19. We have little information upon which to base an estimate of the nature of the strategy which Hitler would have adopted in a later struggle with Great Britain and America, had he been successful in carrying through his continental war without British intervention. There are, however, one or two pointers to the strategy which he contemplated when he realised, towards the end of 1940, that his efforts to eliminate Great Britain had been in vain. At about this time he ordered some slowing down of the scale of production of munitions for use by his land forces, though the production of aircraft continued unabated and the expansion of U-Boat production, which had been allowed to lag behind the planned figure, was for the first time since the outbreak of war given the highest priority. These and other indications show that, by the end of 1940, Hitler was contemplating a later phase of warfare, using not only a different strategy but different armaments, and an economy directed not so much to land armaments but to the production of all weapons for the destruction of British shipping and supplies. The establishment of German bases in the Atlantic Islands and along the Atlantic Coast of North-West Africa was also contemplated as part of this phase of strategy.

20. There is also little definite evidence of the use to which Hitler expected to put his alliance with Japan in such a later phase. The German policy of friendship with Japan was, we consider, primarily due to Hitler's ultimate objective of war against the Soviet Union. Its first open expression was the signature of the anti-Comintern Pact on 25th November, 1936, the Secret Protocol to which provided for the consultation in the event of an attack by the Soviet Union. It is probable that Ribbentrop, who pursued this policy with such enthusiasm, was at least equally hopeful of using Germany's Japanese ally in the war against England; and the idea of giving Japan a predominant position in South-East Asia after the defeat of the British Empire was probably present in Hitler's mind from the start. (Such a division of the world was indeed provided for in the later Tripartite Pact – signed on the 27th September 1940.) Nevertheless, though Hitler realised the value of Japan to divert British Naval Forces to Far Eastern waters and to tie down man-power in South-East Asia and in India, the evidence in our possession suggests that the primary purpose of his Japanese policy was to involve Japan in hostilities against Russia.

21. Such was the design. We consider in the next Chapter of this report how its execution was affected by different factors which emerged subsequent to the attack on Poland in 1939.

# Chapter II. –

# Events which Interfered with the Execution of the Design.

22. Like other dictators Hitler gained his ends at first, because he knew what he wanted and struck ruthlessly and at his chosen moment. Once battle had been joined, however, the war spread and could no longer be controlled by his own initiative. We discuss in this section the effect on his strategy of events which interfered with his designs. Some of these he may have foreseen, but discounted. Others caught him unawares. The effect of them all was to reveal weaknesses in German planning and organisation, and to face Hitler with that war on two fronts which it had been his purpose to avoid.

## *Declaration of War by Great Britain.*

23. Once again, it is worth-while going back to *Mein Kampf* to trace the evolution of Hitler's attitude to the Western Powers, particularly to England. At that time Hitler regarded a conflict with France as inevitable and necessary to protect Germany's rear when France attempted to intervene, as he felt sure she would, between Germany and her eastern prey. England presented a special problem. Hitler constantly criticised pre-1914 German policy, saying that Germany had in 1914 brought England into the war unnecessarily by thinking, not in continental terms, but of overseas colonies, of exports and of a High Seas Fleet. He probably hoped that so long as our sea communications were in no way threatened either by competition in Naval rearmaments, by designs on overseas bases and Colonies, or by expansion of Germany's export trade,

England would remain a passive onlooker whilst Germany dealt with her continental enemies one by one.

24. In November 1937, in a conference in the Reichskanzlei, Hitler showed a more realistic understanding of the essence of the foreign policy of the Western Powers. "German politics", he pointed out, "must reckon with its two hateful enemies, England and France, to whom a strong German colossus in the centre of Europe would be intolerable". At that time, however, he felt certain that England would not be in a position to oppose German designs in Eastern Europe; for he thought that the British Empire, in view of its internal weaknesses, would not face the prospect of another long-drawn-out European war. He considered, too, that England was traditionally hostile to Russia, and Ribbentrop had impressed upon him the strength and prevalence of anti-Communism in British Government circles. Again France would not attack without British support.

25. In May 1939, he was still less sure of his ground. In a conference on 23$^{rd}$ May, he fully realised that his attack on Poland would involve a grave risk of war with the Western Powers, which would assuredly be a life-and-death struggle. The immediate problem was to hold any attacks from the west until he had achieved the conquest of Poland. Meanwhile, he would have to make plans for a counter-offensive in the west.

26. War with France had long been provided for. To Hitler, though not to the German General Staff, it presented no very formidable task. He had slight regard for the fighting qualities of the French divisions, or for their cumbrous and antiquated equipment. He knew, probably better than his military advisers, the moral lethargy and political disintegration into which France had fallen. He was prepared, therefore, to rely on the West Wall, to which the highest constructional priority had been given since the entry into the Rhineland, backed by a handful of infantry divisions, to hold back the French while Poland was being over-run.

27. Although Hitler frequently stated that he hoped above all else for an understanding with England, yet from the moment he began the active phase of his policy in 1938, it is probable that he considered ultimate conflict with this country inevitable. Ribbentrop, indeed, has stated that war with England was unavoidable when he left the London Embassy at the time of the Austrian crisis. Hitler would probably have made every attempt to avoid it, at any rate until his continental position had become impregnable, and his navy had reached a strength sufficient to challenge British sea power.

28. The documentary evidence is conflicting, but it seems likely that to the last Hitler thought there was a chance that he might yet establish a German hegemony in Europe without British intervention. In this again he was probably influenced by Ribbentrop's contemptuous estimates of the British will to fight. Ribbentrop told Stalin in Moscow on the 24th August, 1939, that "England was weak and wanted to let others fight for her arrogant claim to world domination". He described the letter from Chamberlain, delivered to Hitler the day before, in which the attitude of His Majesty's Government on the Polish question was made perfectly clear, as a "manoeuvre typical of British stupidity". He added that he had himself advised Hitler that "the British should be told that, in the event of a German-Polish conflict, Germany would reply to any hostile British action by bombing London". Though he now denies it, he evidently believed at the time that this intimidation and the shock caused by the diplomatic coalition between Germany and Soviet Russia would be sufficient to keep the United Kingdom out of war. The Dominions, he thought, would not give their support to the "war party" in London.

29. Hitler was determined in any case to proceed with his plan. If England could be kept out at any rate until France had been over-run, she would be deprived of her continental base for offensive operations. She would then fall a victim to German blockade and air attack, and Hitler would have carried to its logical conclusion his policy of dealing with his enemies one by one.

30. The effect of British intervention on German strategy in the Low Countries is suggested by the notes on Hitler's conference of November 1937:-

> "Without England's support (for France), it would not be necessary to take into consideration a march by France through Belgium and Holland, and this would also not have to be reckoned with by us in case of a conflict with France, as in every case it would be as a consequence of the enmity of Great Britain".

In 1937, there seemed no danger of British intervention. After Britain's entry into the war, a German occupation of the Low Countries became urgent, not only to prevent the Allies from advancing to within air and artillery range of the vital industries of the Ruhr but to provide bases for air and naval warfare by which, Hitler was convinced, England could be brought to her knees. By November 1939, however, he was less happy and said in a talk to Supreme Commanders: "I am disturbed about the stronger and stronger appearance of the English. They are a tough enemy above all in defence . . . We have an Achilles' heel, the Ruhr".

31. A second effect of British intervention, not apparently foreseen until the early spring of 1940, was the need for a German occupation of Norway and Denmark. This was urgent for both defensive and offensive reasons. A British occupation of Norway and Denmark, which the Germans believed to be imminent, would threaten Germany with strategic encirclement from the north. It would, moreover, seriously threaten her imports of high-grade Swedish iron ore, one of the main bases of her war production, and would block the entrance to the Baltic. For an offensive war against England, in which the submarine campaign would take a leading part, it would be of the greatest use to have air and naval bases in Norway and Denmark. The sudden and urgent need to forestall the Allies in the Low Countries and the new and unforeseen commitment involved in the invasion of Scandinavia were, therefore, primarily imposed on Germany by the British declaration of war.

## Inability to Attack in the West in Autumn of 1939.

32. Until October 1939, despite all the misgivings of the German General Staff, Hitler's plans had been successful. In that month, he received his first rebuff. If the Allies were to be forestalled in the Low Countries, he declared, the German attack must take place that autumn. First, the Army General Staff were not ready. Then, with bad weather threatening to immobilise the troops and paralyse the Air Force, they were unwilling to risk operations despite Hitler's protests and his fears that Allied operations would begin first. At last on the 10th January, Hitler made up his mind to launch the attack on the 17th. It was called off again on the 13th January ostensibly because of weather, but this cancellation may have been due to the fact that on the 10th January a German Staff Officer had made a forced landing in Belgium carrying secret plans which he was unable to destroy, and which revealed much of German intentions. There were no further orders for attack until Hitler's decision, on the 9th May, to attack the next day. In after years, he cited this enforced delay as a classical instance of obstruction on the part of the General Staff; claiming that had he had his way, he would have been able to attack Russia in 1940.

## Unexpected speed of advance in the West, 1940.

33. The speed and decisive success of the campaign in the West took the General Staff completely by surprise. By the 26th May the Germans were already within

12 miles of Dunkirk. There a strange incident occurred. The Allied evacuation, which was to continue until the 4th June, had just begun when Hitler personally called his armoured divisions to a halt. Despite the vigorous protests of his Army commanders, he remained adamant. The reason for this sudden decision is still obscure. Hitler may, as Rundstedt suggests, have been conserving his armoured forces for the second part of the French campaign, and there may be some truth in the rumour that Keitel had shaken his nerve by his stories of Flanders mud in the last war which made him afraid that losses in tanks would be so heavy as to prejudice future operations. He appears, in any case, to have had exaggerated faith in the capabilities of the Luftwaffe, to whom he entrusted the destruction of the encircled Allied troops. If the German commanders had had their way, the story of Dunkirk might have been very different.

## Failure to eliminate Britain.

34. In July 1940 Hitler was faced with the first major unexpected check to his strategy. He had outrun his immediate plans and was confronted with the problem of eliminating this country, in order to avoid a long-drawn-out struggle with the consequent danger that, if the time came for his final reckoning with Soviet Russia, Germany would be involved in a war on two fronts. Such was the military situation after Dunkirk, that Hitler appears to have believed that Britain would be prepared to make peace. But planning for the invasion of England was immediately begun, and as this threat was developed efforts were made to obtain a compromise peace. Meanwhile diplomatic pressure was applied to Spain in order to induce her to enter the war to allow the passage of German troops to Gibraltar and the establishment of German bases in the Atlantic Islands and on the North-West coast of Africa.

## The Problem of Invasion

35. There had been no long-term planning for the invasion of England. The first mention of it was on the 21st May, 1940, when Admiral Raeder discussed it with Hitler and stated that plans had been elaborated by the Naval Operations Division since November 1939. On the 2nd July, 1940, Hitler ordered intelligence appreciations to be prepared and planning to begin for Operation "Sealion" (the invasion of England). On the 16th July, 1940, Hitler issued a directive which stated: "Since England, in spite of her militarily hopeless situation, shows no signs of coming to terms, I have decided

to prepare a landing operation against England and, if necessary, to carry it out . . . The preparations for the entire operation must be completed by mid-August." The German staffs were therefore given a bare month in which to make all preparations.

36. The preparatory phase of this operation was to be an air offensive whose objectives were the destruction of the R.A.F. in the air and on the ground, and the destruction of ports and communications and of food storage depots in London. The air offensive was to begin on the 5th August, though owing to naval factors it would be impossible for the invasion itself to take place until the 15th September. A decision would be taken later, in the light of the success of such preparations, as to whether the operation could take place at all that year. This would depend on two factors: whether the G.A.F. could neutralise the R.A.F. and so obtain air mastery over the whole invasion area, and whether the G.A.F. could provide protection for the invasion forces and prevent attacks by the British Navy. This protection the German Navy was completely inadequate to provide.

37. The orders issued subsequently showed that Hitler continued to hold up a decision on Operation "Sealion" and was most reluctant to commit himself. On the 16th August, an order was issued to the effect that a decision was still being held up, but that preparations should continue up to the 15th September. On the 27th August, orders were issued to prepare for embarkation at Rotterdam, Antwerp and Le Havre. At the same time, forces in Poland were to be strengthened by 10 divisions plus two armoured divisions, presumably as insurance against a possible Russian threat. On the 3rd September, D-Day was fixed for the 21st September, but it was decided that the order for the execution of the operation would not be given until D minus 10, that the final decision would be taken at the latest on D minus 3, and that all operations were liable to cancellation 24 hours before zero hour. On the 17th September, Hitler decided on the further postponement of the operation, and on the 19th September, orders were given to discontinue the strategic concentration of shipping and to disperse existing concentrations of craft in view of Allied air attacks.

On the 12th October, the operation was called off until the Spring, though deception measures were to continue. This deception was maintained through the Spring and early Summer of 1941, and in July 1941, Hitler again postponed the operation until the Spring of 1942 "by which time the Russian campaign would be completed".

38. It is certain that the General Staff had no taste for the adventure. The advance to the coast had been unexpectedly rapid, and no plans had been prepared for such an

ambitious undertaking. Part of the Luftwaffe had already been redeployed elsewhere. Assault shipping was limited to such barges and river boats as could be brought from Germany or the Netherlands, incapable of standing up to anything but a calm sea, or of disembarking tanks or vehicles without elaborate conversion. The troops had no training in amphibious assaults, the staffs no experience in this unaccustomed technique. In the last resort, everything depended on the ability of the Navy and the Air Force to transport and cover the invading forces.

39. Doenitz has now stated his view that the German Navy was no match for the Royal Navy, which would be presumably thrown in to the last man and the last vessel to counter a landing. It therefore became the responsibility of the G.A.F. both to hold the R.A.F. and to hold the Royal Navy from attacking a landing force. The G.A.F., he said, was incapable of either of these tasks. If it had succeeded in defeating the R.A.F. in the Battle of Britain, it would still have been incapable of keeping the Royal Navy off a seaborne landing force because it had not the necessary weapons; the bombs in use at that time were of far too small a calibre to have been able effectually to prevent heavy ships from coming to grips with the landing force; the German Navy was totally inadequate for these tasks.

40. Goering, however, was confident of the ability of the G.A.F. to carry out the tasks allotted to it. Both Jodl and Keitel accepted his view, and made the final decision for the landings dependent on the ability of the Navy to fulfil certain essential requirements of the Army. According to Doenitz these requirements could have been fulfilled, and the Navy would have had no difficulty in transporting the landing force in the vessels then available. There is, therefore, no doubt that the plan would have been carried out, if air mastery had been obtained, and the Battle of Britain were therefore the decisive issue on whose outcome the whole operation depended.

## The attempt to obtain a compromise peace

41. Ribbentrop has stated during one of his interrogations that shortly after Dunkirk and before the signature of the armistice with France on 22$^{nd}$ June, 1940, Hitler stated that he wished to conclude a peace with England on the basis of leaving the British Empire intact except for the return of the former German colonies. On the 19$^{th}$ July, an offer of this kind was made by Hitler in a Reichstag speech.

42. The flight undertaken by Hess to England, in 1941, was also to some extent a reflection of Hitler's mood at this time. On the 18th September, 1940, Hess paid a visit to a certain Albrecht Haushofer, a personal friend whom he considered an expert on English public opinion and as having many English friends. He said that Hitler was now anxious to explore the possibilities of a peace with this country and wished for a channel of communication. Haushofer pointed out the many difficulties but agreed to act as an intermediary. He therefore wrote a letter dated the 23rd September, 1940, to the Duke of Hamilton, suggesting a meeting at Lisbon, but since nothing came of this proposal, Hess planned his flight to Scotland. After three unsuccessful attempts, the flight finally took place on the 10th May, 1941. Hess subsequently explained that had he undertaken this mission while Germany was suffering reverses it would have been taken as a sign of weakness, and that he therefore waited until after Germany had gained successes in North Africa and Greece.

43. Hess almost certainly felt at the time of his first visit to Haushofer that he was carrying out Hitler's wishes. By May 1941, however, Hitler's view had changed, and his mind was made up. In his speech to the Reichstag on the 4th May, and still more clearly in his speech to Party Leaders immediately before the Reichstag meeting, he made it clear that he had given up all hopes of peace with England and that he had resolved on a long-drawn-out blockade. He spoke in the secret session of the double game being played by Russia, and of his fear of American intervention, to which, now that he had resolved to settle accounts with Russia, he could no longer pretend to be indifferent.

## Alternative Strategy

44. It is possible that Hitler had no real confidence in the successful invasion of England. The whole essence of his long-term plan against England, formulated at his Conference in May 1939, had been to bring her to her knees by intensive sea and air operations, thereby conserving his land forces for the main battle against Russia. He was willing to take advantage of the unexpected extent of the success in France if he could do so easily, but not jeopardise his operations against Russia.

45. In his appreciation dated the 15th August, 1940, of the factors likely to affect the success of "Sealion", General Jodl pointed out that there were other means whereby England could be defeated – prolonged air warfare, the stepping-up of U-Boat warfare, the capture of Egypt, the capture of Gibraltar, and the necessity of

avoiding all other operations (*e.g.*, in Yugoslavia) which could be held over till after the conquest of England. For this alternative strategy, he maintained, a much closer co-operation of the Axis Powers was necessary. Italy and Germany should march "not side by side, but together". Italian air forces should take part in the bombing of England and Italian U-Boats should operate with the Germans from French bases. Egypt should be taken "if necessary with Italian help". In agreement with the Spanish and Italians, Gibraltar should be captured.

## Relations with Spain and the Gibraltar Plan.

46. It was realised that the plan worked out for the assault on Gibraltar would, for its success, require the good offices of the Spanish Government in permitting the passage of troops through Spain. General Franco had early in June taken the initiative in this matter by sending a letter to Hitler congratulating him on his victories and assuring him of Spain's support. A fortnight later, the Spanish Embassy in Berlin presented an official note advancing claims to French Morocco and to other French territory in North and West Africa and stating that, should England continue the fight, Spain would be prepared to enter the war, in which case she would require certain indispensable war material. Germany took little overt interest in this Spanish approach. Hitler's attention was probably confined to completing the defeat of France and to preparing for the invasion of England. At Ribbentrop's instance Franco turned to Mussolini. He received a reply encouraging him to enter the war but offering no support for Spanish territorial claims.

47. In mid-September, Señor Serrano Suner visited Berlin as a special emissary of General Franco. He reiterated Spanish territorial claims, and repeated that Spain wanted to enter the war and was waiting to attack Gibraltar; she would be ready as soon as Germany could deliver the indispensable equipment. Hitler and Ribbentrop showed interest in concerting plans for the capture of Gibraltar, but in return for the cession of Morocco Hitler stipulated that he would need the cession of one of the Canary Islands as a German base, the retention for Germany of bases and enclaves in French Morocco, at Agadir and Mogador, and the cession by Spain of Spanish Guinea and Fernando Po. Spain's entry into the war was to take place simultaneously with the attack on Gibraltar and would follow as soon as possible the completion of the installation of heavy artillery on Spanish territory near Gibraltar. He proposed that a

ten-year pact between Germany, Spain and Italy should come into force on the same day. Franco resisted the cession of Agadir and Mogador and was adamant about the Canaries, Spanish Guinea and Fernando Po. He complained that Germany showed a lack of understanding for Spanish economic needs, and that he would be unable to avoid unrest among the Spanish people while German troops were passing through the country, unless they could be assured of a complete solution of their difficulties resulting from the shortage of imported wheat and petroleum products.

48. On the 23rd October, in an effort to clarify mutual intentions, a meeting took place at Hendaye between Hitler and Franco. By then Hitler was apparently convinced – after an interview with Pétain – of the necessity of keeping Vichy France as a member of the coalition against England, and he no longer maintained his offer of French Morocco. All he would offer Spain was "Gibraltar plus certain territories in North Africa equal to those given to France in compensation elsewhere". In November, when Serrano Suner was summoned to Berchtesgaden, Hitler began to express impatience that Spain should enter the war. The Battle of Britain had been lost, Italy was already involved in Greece and in North Africa. The Mediterranean was beginning to draw his attention. This time Serrano Suner was unresponsive, and emphasised Spain's economic difficulties.

49. Three weeks later Admiral Canaris was sent to Madrid to arrange the details for Spain's entry into the war, which he suggested should take place on the 10th January with the entry of German troops into Spain in preparation for an attack on Gibraltar on the 30th January. To his surprise, Canaris was informed by Franco that it was impossible for Spain to enter the war on the date suggested. The reasons given included fear of losing Atlantic Islands and colonies to the British Navy, inadequacy of defensive measures, lack of food and inability to stand a long war. Franco also argued that he would not move until Suez was in Axis hands, since not until then would he have the assurance that the crisis in the Mediterranean would be over quickly and that Spain would not be involved in long-drawn-out hostilities.

50. On the 6th February, 1941, Hitler sent a letter to Franco appealing in strong and urgent terms that Franco should enter the war without further delay. Franco replied expressing undying loyalty and suggesting that preparations for the attack on Gibraltar be continued with renewed vigour, but stating firmly that, for economic reasons alone, Spain could not then enter the war. Ribbentrop then realised that General Franco had no intention of entering the war, and Hitler desisted from his plan.

## *Italy's Entry into the War.*

51. We have no conclusive evidence to show whether or not Italy's entry into the war in June 1940 was in accordance with a preconceived and concerted Axis Plan. Evidence to the effect that the German Intelligence network in the Middle East area was dependent upon the use of Italian diplomatic and consular facilities, and had nothing to put in their place when Italy declared war, suggests that part at least of German planning was based upon the assumption of a neutral Italy. On the other hand, Hitler is believed to have held up the attack on Poland for two days owing to his uncertainty of Mussolini's intentions; and this suggested that he was counting on Italy's participation.

52. The generally opportunist basis of the Rome-Berlin Axis, already instanced, for example, by Hitler's uncertainty up to the last moment in 1938 whether Mussolini would oppose his invasion of Austria, is consistent with the lack of any concrete understanding on Axis collaboration in future phases of the war; and it is probable that Hitler was the victim of his own mistrust of his allies and collaborators. In consequence of this, not only had no long-term strategic plans for Italian participation in the war been made but also no pre-arranged organisation existed for Italian collaboration.

53. The effect of Italy's entry into the war upon the main lines of German strategy was a double one. On the one hand, as later events proved, it made it impossible to avoid the extension of the war into new theatres, and it is possible to discern a fear of the effect of such extension both in Jodl's argument, in the study of the 15th August, 1940, already referred to, that a longer-term strategy against England involved the necessity of avoiding other operations which could be held over until later; and also in Hitler's anxiety, repeatedly expressed in his later conversations with Molotov (see paragraph 71 below) to avoid any further extension of the war.

54. On the other hand, Italian participation was necessary for that alternative strategy. The Middle East was the one theatre where Germany could seek a decision with British forces on land, and the closing of the Mediterranean to British sea-power was an essential part of the Jodl plan. That plan, however, depended upon close integration of the German and Italian war machines; there was no long-term planning for such integration, and belated efforts to attain it were to prove most difficult and embarrassing for the Germans. As Jodl himself has admitted, "I made only one mistake – and that was as regards the political and military dependability of the Italians.

What Hindenburg said is true, that even Mussolini 'could not make anything out of the Italians but Italians'".

55. It is doubtful whether the full possibilities of the Mediterranean theatre were ever properly grasped by the OKW. Hitler's basic strategy consisted of campaigns on the Western and Eastern fronts so timed to avoid a war, and especially a war of long duration, on the two fronts simultaneously. His attempt to effect that timing ultimately broke down and involved him in a war of precisely that nature; the significance of Italy's entry into the war is to be seen in the extent to which the inadequately coordinated operations in the Mediterranean theatre ultimately resulted in considerable diversion of effort, measured in the last phase by the tying up of valuable divisions in Italy in the winter of 1944-45.

## *Complications in South-East Europe.*

56. While Hitler's attention in the late summer of 1940 was still concentrated on the problem of invading England, complications were beginning to arise in South-East Europe. Russian troops entered Bessarabia and the Bukovina during the summer, and Russian expansion further into the Balkan area appeared probable. During Hitler's return journey from his conversations with Pétain at Montoire, and with Franco at Hendaye, news was suddenly brought to him that Mussolini had, on the 28th October, launched an attack on Greece without previous consultation with his ally.

57. It is clear that, until Mussolini's attack on Greece, the German General Staff and Hitler wished to leave Bulgaria, Greece and Yugoslavia well alone. On the 12th November, 1940, Hitler issued a directive to OKH to prepare for a possible invasion of Greek Thrace from Bulgaria with a force of some ten divisions. An early fancy of Hitler's – to send a mountain division to Albania to reinforce the Italians and thus eventually enable them to attack the Salonika defile from the rear, in conjunction with the attack from Bulgaria – did not survive the administrative objections of Mussolini and the military objections of the German General Staff.

58. By mid-February, 1941, German plans for the occupation of Bulgaria and for pushing on into Greek Thrace were complete (Operation "Marita"), and the number of divisions had risen to seventeen, some of which were, in fact, used in Yugoslavia, including finally five Panzer divisions. Furthermore, the Balkan campaign entailed a major diversion of air strength, amounting to 1,000 operational aircraft, away from the Western Front.

59. The first division crossed the Danube on the 2$^{nd}$ March (the day after Bulgaria joined the Axis) and the last was scheduled to cross on the 31$^{st}$ March. Thus, at a time when concentration against Russia was proceeding actively, the German planned to tie up nearly one quarter of their total Panzer force on the wrong side of the Danube, one of the worst communications bottlenecks in Europe. Halder explains the large number of forces sent into Bulgaria by the need to protect the Turkish and Yugoslav flanks, about which Bulgaria was particularly anxious.

60. Before the invasion of Greece could begin, a new factor emerged in the shape of the Simovic *coup d'État* in Belgrade. It is abundantly clear that up till this time the Germans had intended to respect Yugoslavia's sovereignty during the invasion of Greece, hoping, no doubt, to gain their ends in the former country later, at a more convenient time and in less costly manner. OKH were given eight days in which to improvise an invasion of Yugoslavia, originally without using routes through Hungary, although in the event, this condition was not strictly observed. The plan put into operation provided for, firstly, a thrust by four divisions from Bulgaria (12$^{th}$ Army) towards Skoplje with the aim of relieving the Italian East Flank in Albania; secondly, a thrust by five divisions from Bulgaria (also 12$^{th}$ Army) via Nish towards Belgrade; and thirdly, the deployment of seven divisions through Styria and Hungary to complete the destruction of the Yugoslav army.

61. There can be no doubt that the necessity to intervene in Greece and Yugoslavia was a grave embarrassment to the German High Command. It may also have imposed a delay of a month on the attack on Russia. One of the documents speaks of the 15$^{th}$ May as a provisional planning date for the attack on Russia (as against the actual date, the 22$^{nd}$ June). It is possible, however, that the floods in Poland that summer might have caused an equivalent delay in any case.

62. Italian action had thus resulted in the extension of the war into two new theatres, neither of which formed a part of the essential German strategy – first North Africa, and then the Balkans.

## Hitler's inability to wait before attacking Russia.

63. We have referred above to Hitler's probable intention of settling accounts with Russia at a date not later than 1943-45. Though he seems to have had no clear idea of a long-term plan to enable him to avoid a war on two fronts, it is probable that,

once the Western Powers had intervened at the time of his attack in Poland, he planned to complete his conquest in the West before turning against Russia. This plan would have worked if he had had France alone to deal with, or even after the declaration of war by the U.K., if he had been successful in eliminating this country in 1940. But the failure of his plans for a rapid solution of the problem of the U.K. whether by invasion or by compromise, and the substitution of a longer term strategy – prolonged U-Boat warfare and air attack – meant that he would be compelled either to postpone that attack on Russia until its completion, or to run a considerable risk of the dreaded war on two fronts which it was his purpose to avoid.

64. In the summer of 1940, the problem of whether Hitler could afford any longer to risk devoting his attention to the reduction of the U.K. while the Russian question was left unresolved, entered upon a critical phase. The annexation of the Baltic States by Russia, and the movement of Russian troops into Bessarabia and the Bukovina seemed to be signs of coming Russian moves into the Baltic area and into the Balkans. In particular there seemed grounds for the feat that Russia would deprive Germany of the Roumanian oil fields and thus rob her of an essential source of supply for a prolonged naval and air war against England. It may be that the fear of Russian moves exercised a certain indirect influence on the German scale of air attack at the time of the Battle of Britain. Jodl, in his address to the Gauleiters on the 11th December, 1943, stated that the invasion of England had proved impossible because it could not be carried out without air supremacy and that "no one could take it upon himself to let the G.A.F. bleed to death in view of the struggle which lay before us against Soviet Russia".

65. Already at the time of the Battle of France Hitler had asked Jodl to investigate the possibility of an attack against Russia in the autumn of 1940, and Jodl had replied that the troops could not be switched in time. By August, 1940 Hitler was planning for a Spring Offensive against Russia. He gave orders that he wanted punctual delivery of goods to Russia to continue under the terms of the German-Soviet Pact of 1939, but only until the Spring of 1941. According to an OKW directive of the 6th September, 1940, the German forces in the East were to be increased, but "for security reasons this should not create the impression that Germany is preparing for an Eastern offensive". Raeder, we was kept in ignorance of Hitler's real intentions some time after they were known to the OKW, stated that, "The fear that control of the Air over the Channel could no longer be attained caused the Fuehrer . . . to consider

whether, even prior to victory in the West, an Eastern campaign would not be feasible, with the object of eliminating our last serious opponents on the Continent".

66. The fact that Hitler at so early a date ordered preliminary investigations to be undertaken in preparation for an attack on Russia goes some way to discredit the theory that Hitler finally attacked owing to the fear that if he did not do so Russia would herself attack. We consider that Hitler was influenced in this decision first by his determination, dating from the earliest days of his war preparations, to attack Russia at a suitable moment in order to obtain for Germany living space and raw materials in the East; second by the need of raw materials, especially oil, for the task, which he now realised might be a long one, of subduing the United Kingdom by blockade and air attack; and thirdly by the faulty appreciations of German Intelligence and his own lack of judgment, which made Hitler believe that he had at least as good a prospect of a successful lightning war against Russia in 1941 as he had against the armies of the Western Powers in 1940.

67. Hitler expected to complete the conquest of European Russia by the defeat of the Red Armies in a period of about 2 months, which would enable him to turn back upon England and, assured of the raw materials, oil and food-stuffs needed for sustained attack, to reduce this island at his leisure. After his defeat of Russia, he did not consider that the British Empire would be in any position to strike at Germany, while he himself would have ample to time to build up his forces.

68. Such considerations also afford an explanation of the apparent paradox of the relatively small scale and limited scope of German intervention in the Mediterranean and North Africa in late 1940 and early 1941, when Jodl had already mentioned the capture of Egypt as an objective which formed part of the long-term strategy against England, and when the OKW in resuming the plan for the invasion of England recognised the importance of the Mediterranean as a theatre for Axis naval attack on the British Empire. The former German Naval C.-in-C. Mediterranean has stated that "the Supreme Command believed that the favourite opportunity presented by Britain's isolation and weakness could be put on ice until Russia had been completely defeated on the Continent".

69. The study made by OKH in July, 1941, called "Orient", provided for a main effort against the British position in the Middle East made through Turkey and the Caucasus *after* the successful conclusion of operations against Russia, while North Africa would always remain a minor theatre owing to the "greater difficulties

in reinforcement which would be experienced by the Axis as compared with the Allies." Hitler later confirmed that this was his strategy and, in a conversation with the Japanese Ambassador in Berlin on the 14th December, 1941, he stated that he would attack in S. Russia in the Spring of 1942 to seize the Baku oilfields and pass through Iraq and Persia to threaten India. Meanwhile he would give close attention to N. Africa and the Mediterranean where "they would torpedo every ship they met". The three-pronged attack on the Middle East thus had its place in German strategy, but depended for its existence on a prior victory over Russia. This victory seemed to Hitler, at the end of 1940, more nearly within his grasp than a combined victory, together with Italy, in the Mediterranean theatre.

70. In November 1940, though his decision to attack Russia in the following year had probably already been taken, Hitler availed himself of Molotov's visit to Berlin to try and ascertain Russian intentions. It is probable that he regarded these conversations as a final test to confirm him in his belief that he could not afford to devote a further year to attacks on Great Britain while the campaign against Russia still lay ahead. He may well have feared that, during that year, Russia would advance her influence still further westward, on the Finnish and Roumanian flanks, and might even deprive him of Roumanian oil.

71. On Molotov's arrival in Berlin, he was told by Hitler and Ribbentrop that :-

(a) Germany needed above all a reinsurance with Russia to cover her rear when engaging in the blockade and eventual assault on England.

(b) At the same time, Hitler wished to avoid an extension of the war into new theatres, as he believed that British strategy was unpredictable and might make some sudden attack which, from the orthodox point of view of the German General Staff, would appear unthinkable; he mentioned his apprehension of the establishment of a British base at Salonika and of a possible British thrust northwards to the Roumanian oilfields.

(c) Germany wished to attain these aims by a four-Power agreement between Russia and the Axis Powers defining spheres of interest, carving up the British Empire between them and containing a declaration that Russia was opposed to an extension of the war.

72. Molotov's attitude to these proposals was negative. He showed no interest at the offer of a slice of the British Empire, nor at the suggestion that Russia

might like access to the sea in the Persian Gulf, nor even at the strong hint dropped in the last conversation, that Germany would like to see Russia in possession of India. He appeared to be unmoved by Hitler's undertaking that no more German troops would be sent to Finland and by his statement that Germany had no territorial claims in Finland, Turkey, the Balkans or in Asia. On the subject of Finland, his conversation with Hitler became so heated that Ribbentrop was obliged to intervene. Molotov appeared unaffected by the general "pep-talk" he received to the effect that Britain was already on her knees. In the last conversation he said that, although Russia agreed to the general principles, she needed more time for detailed consideration, and that "what had been begun must first be finished before further questions could be discussed".

73. At one point in the conversation, Molotov asked whether Germany considered that the secret protocol of 1940 was still in force as regards Poland and what Axis intentions were in Poland, Yugoslavia and Greece. He declared also that, as part of the settlement of the Straits question, a Russian guarantee to Bulgaria providing also for Bulgarian access to the Ægean sea was an essential part of Russia's plan. Such remarks may well have been disconcerting to the Germans. Later, Hitler said that during Molotov's visit it had been easy to see how much hatred for Germany was felt in Russia, and that Russian intentions to encroach further into Finland and the Dardanelles were unchanged. He was, no doubt, already anxious about the safety of his flanks in his planned operation. Later, during the campaign, he again and again showed great preoccupation with these flanks: the Molotov conversations show a diplomatic parallel to that strategy.

74. It was clear to Hitler that Russia was not prepared to be intimidated, and he was confirmed in his view that he could not afford to wait. In the next month, December 1940, "Plan Barbarossa" was completed and Hitler issued a main directive that "German armed forces must be prepared to defeat Soviet Russia in a rapid campaign even before the end of the war against England". It was laid down that preparations for the attack were to be camouflaged so that they should appear as part of the preparations for the invasion of England; it was to be the "greatest deception in the history of warfare".

## *Failure of the lightning attack on Russia.*

75. The keynote of Hitler's plan against Russia, issued on the 28th December, 1940, was the destruction of the bulk of the Russian Army, which was in Western Russia, in

bold operations with deep armoured thrusts. Hitler also laid down the broad grouping of forces – two Army Groups North of the Pripet Marshes and one South – which
was eventually followed.

76. According to Halder, OKH's plan of operations only envisaged the achievement
of first objectives, which were fixed at such a distance that, on the one hand, the complete destruction of the Russian forces employed at the beginning of the war could be
ensured, and, on the other hand, the danger of air attack against the Reich eliminated.
OKH maintained that a firm decision on the further course of operations could only be
taken after these first objectives had been reached, and the results of the frontier battles
assessed, but that Moscow would have a decisive rôle, in that it constituted a military,
political and industrial nerve centre whose capture would have incalculable effects.
Hitler, however, had already decided on priority for the reduction of Leningrad – a
decision which was a foretaste of his fatal intuition that the best prospects of success
in the East lay with the two outer Groups of Armies. Hitler's plan for the final objective was the formation of a defensive screen against Asiatic Russia on the general line
Archangel-Volga; the difficulties of maintaining this 2,000-mile front were apparently
of such small importance to him as not to require detailed consideration.

77. When the Russian campaign opened, Hitler had, in Halder's opinion, the preconceived idea that Russia would, despite the advanced season, be forced by the speed
and weight of the German advance to make peace in 1941, thus making further prosecution of the war hopeless for the Western Allies. According to Halder, these views
were not shared, much less encouraged, by the Army General Staff. Hitler, however,
spoiled by the quick success of his early campaigns, refused to take account of road
conditions and terrain. Moreover, the German Intelligence system failed signally in
its estimate of Russia's military reserves and strategic resources.

78. The attack on Russia was launched on the 22$^{nd}$ June, 1941; maps available make
it clear that OKH succeeded in persuading Hitler to adhere, at least in principle, to
their plan of gaining first objectives, which involved along almost the whole front
drives to a depth of nearly 300 miles into Russian territory, and on the front of Army
Group Centre to a depth of 450 miles. By the third week in July, the first phase of the
campaign was over, and the objectives set by OKH substantially reached.

79. In mid-August, 1941, Panzer Group Guderian (the Southernmost Panzer Group
of Army Group Centre) attacked towards Army Group South, and by the first week in
September a vast pocket of Russian forces was being formed in the Kiev area. Hitler

expected this battle to end quickly, and thus make available forces for an attack by Army Group Centre at about the end of September, which would encircle Timoshenko's armies and carry on to Moscow. But despite skilful handling, the battle of Kiev was not complete until the 24th September. In consequence, forces switched back from the Ukraine for Army Group Centre's offensive, which began on the 2nd October, were exhausted. Nevertheless, the attack made good progress, and by the end of October the Germans stood less than 40 miles West of Moscow. (It is even reported that in mid-October, German troops entered the actual suburbs of Moscow.) At the same time, according to Guderian, there came a marked stiffening in Russian resistance.

80. On the 13th November, 1941, Hitler issued orders for an "autumn campaign" designed to take Moscow before the end of 1941. Despite strenuous opposition from experienced Army commanders, who wished to dig in for the winter, the attack was launched, but owing to the extremely cold weather, progress in the initial stages was slow, and the main attack, launched on the 4th December, completely misfired. Retreat became inevitable, but Hitler insisted that no major withdrawal should be made, and that Army Group Centre must fight for every inch of ground until reserves came from the West. Only then could it withdraw to the planned rearward position. This decision led to the retirement of von Brauchitsch, Commander-in-Chief of the Army.

81. Hitler now assumed direct command of the Army on the Eastern front, and his refusal to make strategic withdrawals resulted, when the front was finally stabilised in mid-January, 1942, in a series of uneconomical and dangerous salients.

## Entry of U.S.A. into the War.

82. We have no evidence upon which to assess whether or not, before the declaration of war by the U.K. in 1939, Hitler considered that his plan for world domination would involve Germany, at a later stage, in war with the U.S.A. But during 1940 there are one or two indications of preparation for such a war. In his first conversation with Molotov in Berlin on the 12th November, 1940, Hitler stated that "Germany saw great danger to the rest of the world coming from America in about the period 1970-1980. European countries should organise to prevent the establishment of Anglo-Saxon bases". To counteract the effect of possible American intervention and to support his policy of blockade, Hitler proposed to Serrano Suner and to Franco the capture of Gibraltar and the establishment of German bases in the Canary and Cape

Verde Islands, and along the Atlantic coast of North-West Africa. When the Spanish negotiations broke down, he obtained from de Brinon a formal guarantee of German bases in Morocco and at Dakar in the event of the United States entering the war.

83. In February, 1941, both Germany and Japan wished to avoid being involved in early hostilities with the United States, but Hitler, preparing his attack on Russia, had decided that the time had come to bring Japan into the war against the British Commonwealth. On the 23rd February Ribbentrop urged that Japan should enter the war against England at an early date by making a sudden attack on Singapore; an OKW directive of the 5th March laid down that the entry of Japan into the war was a main aim of German policy. Though evidence on this point is lacking, it seems probable that the purpose of this policy was as much to involve Japan in the war as a belligerent ally of Germany simultaneously with the attack on Russia, as to use Japanese intervention in the long-term war against the British Empire. The OKW directive indeed states that "Operation Barbarossa" would create "specially favourable conditions" for a Japanese operation against Singapore.

84. It is not yet clear, in view of the disingenuity of German policy towards Japan, how far the Germans appreciated that their Japanese policy would ultimately involve them in war with the United States. Ribbentrop, speaking to the Japanese, was certainly at pains to discount this possibility. In his conversation with the Japanese Ambassador on the 23rd February, 1941, he stated that a lightning attack by Japan on Singapore "would keep America out of the war", and that it was in Germany's interest to do so, though America would be unable to go to war militarily, as a landing in Europe or Africa would be impossible, and the United States fleet would not venture beyond Hawaii. The Japanese Government were nevertheless most concerned with the possibility of American intervention, and, according to a report made to Hitler on the 14th March, 1941, by Admiral Raeder, they were only prepared to attack Singapore in the event of actual invasion of England by Germany, calculating no doubt that in that event the war would soon be at an end.

85. Though the German proposals were welcomed by Matsuoka, the Japanese Foreign Minister, he was unable to obtain the agreement of his Government. When he visited Berlin in March-April, 1941, therefore, he frequently stated that he could only express personal views. Japan, he said, would do her utmost to avoid war with the United States. He believed he would be able to stave off this danger for the period of six months which he estimated might be needed to reduce Singapore, but he also pointed to the danger for

Japan of guerrilla warfare against the United States which might last for some five years. He stated that he himself considered that Japan should strike a decisive blow, timed for the right moment, to gain predominance in the South Seas. He added that the Japanese navy had to prepare immediately for conflict with the U.S.A. and he asked for technical assistance from Germany. At the same time he received from Hitler a categorical assurance that Germany would strike without delay in the case of a conflict between American [sic] and Japan "because the strength of the tripartite Powers lies in their joint action; their weakness would be if they allowed themselves to be beaten individually".

86. From the record of the Matsuoka conversations it is clear that Hitler was at that time much concerned with the possibility of American intervention, though he was at pains to conceal his concern from the Japanese. "Germany", he said, "wished to avoid conflict with the U.S.A., though he had already made allowances for such a contingency". He would not now hesitate for a moment to take the responsibility of extending the war, whether to Russia or the U.S.A. "England would have given in long ago but for Roosevelt's encouragement to Churchill. . .Every effort must be made to keep the U.S.A. out of the war and to prevent her help to England becoming effective". At one point in the conversations also Matsuoka asked Ribbentrop what the attitude of Germany would be to the U.S.A. after England's defeat. Ribbentrop refused to commit himself; he replied that this would depend upon the attitude of the U.S. Government. In a previous conversation with the Japanese Ambassador he had said that, in that event, Germany might break off diplomatic relations with the U.S.A., adding that it would teach United States public opinion a lesson and increase isolationist spirit.

87. Matsuoka was not told of the impending German attack on Russia, though Ribbentrop made several remarks which strongly implied it. He spoke of the Russo-German "situation being such that such a conflict, even if it were not probable, would have to be considered possible". He also said that, should Japan fall in with Germany's desire that she should attack Singapore at once, and should she be attacked by Russia in consequence, "Germany would strike immediately against Russia, and the U.S.S.R. would be finished off within a few months". On Matsuoka's return journey to Tokyo, he signed in Moscow the Russo-Japanese Treaty of Neutrality; when in Berlin he had mentioned to Ribbentrop the possibility of engaging in discussions for a non-aggression pact, and Ribbentrop had "advised against it", though he does not appear to have reacted against this proposal so strongly as might have been expected. Far from falling in with Germany's plan by making an attack on Singapore, which would have brought her into

the war against Britain at Germany's side on the eve of the attack against Russia, Japan was able, by this treaty, to secure her own rear in the event of war with the United States. Matsuoka had also succeeded in obtaining an assurance of Hitler's support in such an eventuality, without giving the impression that the attack would take place.

88. After the attack on Russia, repeated efforts were made to bring Japan into the war against the Soviet Union, particularly in Hitler's interview with the Japanese Ambassador on the 15th July, and by Ribbentrop on the 25th August, when he urged that Japan should not attack Singapore and the Dutch East Indies until after she had protected her rear by an attack on Russia the following autumn. On the 10th July, 1941, telegraphing from Hitler's special train, he instructed the German Ambassador in Tokyo to urge Japan's immediate participation in the war against Russia "to join hands with Germany on the Trans-Siberian railway".

89. Japan gave Germany and Italy several days' warning of the opening of hostilities against the U.S.A. The Japanese Ambassador at Rome told Mussolini on the 3rd December that hostilities were likely "in the immediate future" (the attack on Pearl Harbour took place on the 8th December), [sic] and Ciano records in his diary that both Mussolini and Ribbentrop were delighted at the prospect. Ribbentrop had, indeed, on the 28th November told the Japanese Ambassador in Berlin that Japan would never have so good an opportunity again and should "silently attack" the U.S.A. The German Ambassador in Tokyo informed the Japanese Foreign Minister on the 30th November, 1941, that in the event of a breakdown of the negotiations between the U.S. and Japan, Germany would stand by the side of Japan, and he assented to the Japanese interpretation of these words that "Germany would consider her relationship to Japan as that of a community of fate". Similar instructions were telegraphed to the Ambassador on the 5th December by Ribbentrop, who said that "the Axis Powers and Japan find themselves thrust into a struggle fraught with destiny, which they must fight out together to the end".

90. By the time the Pearl Harbour attack took place, Germany probably realised that American intervention in the War was already inevitable. Hitler still hoped for an early conclusion of the war against Russia, and still expected Japanese assistance in that war. On at least three subsequent occasions, July 1942 and March and April 1943, Ribbentrop urged that the time was favourable for a Japanese attack on Russia, and indeed he went on urging this to the end. Yet there can be no doubt that the entry of the United States into the War marked the final breakdown of Hitler's strategy, the basic purpose of which had been to strike down his enemies one by one, and to avoid a war on two fronts.

# Chapter III. –
# Decline and Final Defeat.

## The Turning of the Tide.

91. We have described in the above paragraphs the different events which consecutively hindered the execution of Hitler's design and culminated in a situation in the Autumn of 1942 which was all that he had hitherto sought to avoid. Germany was now confronted with the dreaded war on two fronts against a coalition of Great Powers whose total population and resources far exceeded those of Germany and German-occupied Europe. As we shall endeavour to point out in the next part of the paper, German economy and Hitler's strategy were alike unsuited for dealing with such a situation. The Allies now had the strategical initiative, and after three years of war the only policy which remained to Germany was – as it was described in 1943 by General Jodl – "to live upon the capital sum of space which had been built up for Germany by fighting along the periphery". The tide had turned.

### *The Final Failure.*

92. With the defeat before Stalingrad and at El Alamein and the Allied landing in North Africa, Germany not only failed to achieve the material gains which she had already partly discounted but also lost her stake, and with it the initiative. Great hopes, for example, had been placed in the acquisition of the Caucasus oil, and stocks had been spent in anticipation of replenishment from this source. The losses suffered in man-power and material at this time left a gap which could not immediately be filled and deprived Germany, at any rate for the time being, of the possibility of maintaining the centrally-placed free strategic reserve which was vital to the successful prosecution of a defensive war on two, and probably three, fronts. The situation

called for a major overhaul of strategy; but there is no evidence that it was under-taken. No comprehensive strategical appreciation of Germany's prospects and course of action in the new circumstances has been discovered, and we have the testimony of those Germans who should know to the effect that none was made. In the 2½ years from September 1939, German production of armaments were more than tripled and in the middle of 1944 it was over three times the level of the beginning of 1942. There was no attempt, however, to draw in the periphery of defence so that this increased production could be made effective.

## German Strategy after 1942.

93. The main lines of German strategy, as they slowly evolved, are, however, toler-ably clear. On land, Hitler hoped by grimly contesting every yard of ground and by fierce and continual counter-offensives in the East to hold the fronts on the periphery of Germany's conquests, to keep the war as far away from the Reich as possible, and to provoke a test of endurance in which he hoped that the physical and moral energy of the Allies would flag and dissensions would arise. To sustain the army in this task the Reich combed for reinforcements of man-power and army weapon production took a defensive turn and concentrated more and more on building up the defensive fire-power of the field divisions and in developing the effectiveness of flak artillery. To provide air defence, the Air Force planned a large increase in defensive fighter pro-duction. In the West, any attempt at the invasion of France was to be repelled on the beaches, with fearful losses, by the coastal fortifications, to the construction of which additional priority was given. At sea, the rôle of the navy was to delay the build-up for the invasion and to sap the endurance of the British by intensified U-boat warfare. New U-boats with greatly improved under-water performance and incorporating new anti-detection devices were designed and put into production. Existing U-boats were rapidly equipped with devices enabling them to remain submerged for weeks at a time. These new U-boats offered Germany her last hope of effective blockade, of which she was robbed by Allied bombing.

94. Germany could not hope to regain superiority in men and material on which her strategy had hitherto been based, although she still had great hopes of being able to make up man-power deficiencies by drawing on every available foreign worker. An attempt was made to offset these fundamental weaknesses by producing better tanks

and better guns and in this they continued to outpace the Allies. They also developed novel weapons; new types of midget surface and submerged craft were to assist in guarding the coasts of Europe against invasion and in hampering and taking toll of the build-up of our invasion forces. V.1 flying bombs and V.2 rockets and long-range artillery were to be used for attacks on our cities, assembly ports and internal communications which her diminishing Air Force could no longer undertake.

95. With the total mobilisation of the man-power and material resources of Germany and of the occupied Territories Speer, who became Minister of Armaments and War Production in September 1943, calculated he could produce sufficient to equip and maintain all the field forces which Germany would have available. As stated, he also hoped to ensure German supremacy in the technical sphere. If such a plan had been coolly and clearly drawn up and consistently enforced, it might have had more than an outside chance of succeeding in considerably prolonging the war. But, in practice, weaknesses cropped up at every turn, and in every variety of way confused the aims and confounded the execution of every plan so that, from the start, it became a losing battle.

96. On the Eastern Front Hitler's refusal to give ground in any circumstances prevented the formation of a strategic reserve without which his policy of peripheral defence was inevitably and fatally handicapped. His tenacity was pushed to extreme lengths and had extreme results. Instances are known when he ordered positions to be held for the protection of economic resources which, in the opinion of his economic advisers, were less important than the lives and equipment of the men expended in their defence and than other resources which were thereby left uncovered. The resultant recurring cycle of disasters hoisted the wastage of weapons and munitions to a level with which the best efforts of industry could never compete. Moreover, the policy of peripheral defence positively increased Germany's commitments in that it inevitably involved the provision of material assistance to the weaker Axis allies who were called upon to hold parts of the line or to organise maintenance facilities in the back areas. Only in Italy did the Germans (after the Allied landings in the Summer of 1943) contemplate a strategic withdrawal. But even here, after the "incredible" failure of the Allies to follow up their initial landings in the expected manner, the Germans changed their minds.

97. Although war production showed substantial gains, it failed, through weaknesses in organisation and the imperfect realisation of Speer's attempts at full

mobilisation, to meet the requirements of the Forces. The very large quantities of weapons and equipment which were, nevertheless, produced were often frittered away by Hitler's strategy and the erratic and faulty distribution policy of OKW. When the Allied bombing offensive reached its full stature at midsummer 1944, production wilted rapidly and the successful attacks on oil, for which no adequate defensive preparations had been made, deprived the Armed Forces, and particularly the Air Force, of the means of making full use of even the inadequate equipment which they possessed.

98. The development of the new naval weapons was too late to affect the build-up of the invasion or to disturb its execution. Similarly the development of the terror weapons on which Hitler clearly based exaggerated hopes, was exposed by Allied Intelligence, and their bases were subjected to devastating counter-measures and overrun by the Allied armies before these weapons could be brought to perfection. The tactical possibilities of the jet aircraft were largely nullified by Hitler's disregard of professional advice and his own mistaken decision regarding its employment. It was the shortcomings of German strategy, resulting to a great extent from the shortcomings of German intelligence, which turned the Atlantic wall into a trap in which the losses of men and equipment were heavier than in the retreat from Stalingrad.

## *The Final Phase.*

99. For many Germans, still capable of objective thought, the establishment of Allied armies in the West marked the imminence of inevitable defeat, in view of which further resistance could only prejudice Germany's post-war recovery, and might even prevent her survival as a nation. On the 20th July, 1944, an explosion occurred in one of the huts of Supreme Headquarters at Angerburg, and for some hours many Germans believed that Hitler was dead. The immediate consequence was the biggest purge in the history of the Nazi regime. In all 4,980 persons were executed in connection with the plot, and Field-Marshal Von Witzleben, General Von Hasse and five other high-ranking generals were hanged. The plot, however, was not organised by a handful of high-ranking officers of the German armed forces, but mainly civilians drawn from all the opposition groups in Germany. The result of its failure was that Hitler was more firmly convinced than ever, by his narrow escape, that he was

specially protected by Providence. His followers, as a result of the purge, thought that the last traces of opposition to the regime had been crushed and that their position was, therefore, safe.

100. Thereafter Hitler surrounded himself entirely with sycophants, and took upon himself the entire responsibility for conducting operations. In December 1944, while the Eastern Front was relatively quiet, he staged his last fling in the West, in the shape of the Ardennes offensive, intended to push through to the North, take Antwerp and isolate the British 21$^{st}$ Army Group. Despite the attempts of his commanders in the field to persuade him to accept a less ambitious plan more in keeping with his limited, and rapidly dwindling resources, Hitler allowed the operation to drag on with inadequate forces and supplies, and involving heavy casualties until the Allied pressure and the opening of the new Russian winter offensive in the East compelled retreat. The losses of men and material in this precarious adventure once and for all removed any hopes of a further counter-offensive in the West.

101. In the East, despite the fact that the main Russian effort was being made through Poland and North-Westwards through East Prussia, German dispositions, especially of armour, suggested that, compared with Hungary, all other sectors were of secondary importance. Hitler's reason for squandering most of Germany's best remaining resources of man-power and armour in Hungary when reserves were so urgently needed elsewhere is, and may remain, uncertain. Jodl ascribes it to the urgent necessity of preserving Germany's most important remaining supplies of oil, and it is certain that Speer had left Hitler in no doubt regarding the importance of the Hungarian oilfields while, at the same time, making it perfectly clear that he shared the view of the General Staff that an offensive to stabilise the position in Silesia was of even greater, and indeed quite critical, urgency.

## Defeat.

102. The loss of Silesia and the virtual isolation of the Ruhr by the end of January 1945 convinced Speer – possibly, with Goebbels, the most steadfast and disinterested of Hitler's supporters – that the end was near. Thereafter his own efforts were mainly concerned with attempts to frustrate the destruction of all basic facilities for economic life as enjoined in the stream of scorched earth directives emanating from Hitler who appears to have been determined to make good his long-standing vow that

the German nation should perish with him in the event of defeat. By March it was obvious to the High Command that the rapid Allied advance into Germany from both sides would split the country into two. Jodl states that, late in March or early in April, orders were given for an area in the Alpine Redoubt to be prepared for final defence. At the same time plans were made for continuing resistance separately in the North and eventually in Norway. But these plans could not proceed owing to the disastrous state of communications and the rapid collapse of the Southern sector of the Western front. As Hitler may have known when he decided to make his last stand in Berlin, these preparations were left much too late to be any practical significance.

103. It is remarkable that even at this late stage there remained among the masses in Germany a strong belief in the ability of Hitler to pull them through and turn defeat into victory. Speer, who was at the time travelling Germany from end to end on his self-imposed mission of salvage and was then concerned to disillusion them, has repeatedly commented upon this phenomenon. It is clear that this was no synthetic emotion stimulated by the terror of the Gestapo or even by the propaganda of Goebbels. It provides some measure of the extent to which Hitler had captured the soul and personified the aspirations of the German people, and merits remembrance even though soldiers and civilians alike may now revile his memory and heap all responsibility for their misfortunes upon his head.

# SECTION II.

# GERMAN WEAKNESSES.

# INTRODUCTION.

104. In the first Section of this report we have shown that the factors which first and fundamentally interfered with the basic German strategy were:-

(a) Germany's failure to appreciate the long-term consequences of Great Britain's entering the war when she did, and her failure to eliminate Great Britain before becoming engaged with Russia.

(b) Germany's misapprehension that Russia could be disposed of very quickly, which resulted in the fatal war on two fronts.

105. Among the weaknesses that came to light as a result of these fundamental errors, we consider it of interest to examine the following: -

(a) Characteristics inherent in Hitler's personality as leader of the State and Supreme Commander of the German Armed Forces.

(b) The deficiencies of the working of the machinery of joint command, as shown in practice.

(c) The inadequacies of German Intelligence.

(d) The organisation of German war production.

106. These weaknesses are examined in this Section of the paper. The attached Appendices provide a chronological survey of the several campaigns and show in more detail how these weaknesses affected them.

107. Government under Hitler had the advantages and disadvantages inherent in dictatorships. Decisions could be quickly taken and rapidly executed, but this was usually at the expense of joint consultation and of advice by services and departments. So long as she had the initiative, overwhelming force and no moral restraints, the advantage lay with Germany, as was shown by her rapid rearmament and mobilisation and by her successes in the early use of her armed forces. Had Germany won the war by the end of 1942, future historians might well have attributed her success very largely to Hitler's personality and his centralised direction of the war, and the deficiencies of the German Intelligence system might never have become apparent. As events turned out, however, and Germany lost the initiative, these very factors which had made possible her lightning successes proved to be weaknesses and progressively accelerated the speed of her defeat.

108. We lack the evidence on which to attempt an analysis of Hitler's mental processes; it is, indeed, open to doubt whether a satisfactory judgment on this difficult topic will ever be reached. Most of the information obtainable comes from the interrogation of personalities who are now in a position to be wise after the event. Those among his close collaborators who admired him describe him (in the words of Speer) as "an undoubted genius with an amazing capacity for detail and hard work" – inferring that he was led astray by evil associates who pandered to his weaknesses and concealed the truth from him. Others (like Halder), who had direct experience only of his intolerance, impatience and obstinacy, and who suffered persecution at his hands, regard him as a maniac whose diabolical frenzy has destroyed the German people. We can only hope to record some respects in which the impact of Hitler's personality on public business prejudiced its efficient conduct, and contributed to the defeat of his own plans. It is, however, proper to add that in other respects Hitler's leadership suited the needs of the German nation, and that the force of his personality galvanised it into efforts and sacrifices of which it would, by itself, have been incapable. He was, above all, a consummate master of the art of handling Germans. Although himself slightly exotic – he was an Alpine and not a Nordic type – he was able to play upon their deepest feelings both individually and, with the expert assistance of Goebbels, collectively, in such a way that, though personally unimpressive to most cultivated foreigners, he seemed to Germans to be endowed with a personal magnetism and genius approaching the superhuman.

# Chapter 1. – Hitler.

## Hitler's Personality.

109. Like other dictators, Hitler had perforce as his first objective in any enterprise the preservation of his own supremacy, without which it would have been impossible to carry out his great design for the resurgence of Germany. He was, therefore, in principle, opposed to free consultation and joint counsel. His position made him distrustful of his collaborators, from whom he withheld his plans until he thought the moment had come for detailed planning. He thereby prevented opposition to his policy and kept the power in his own hands. He chose advisers who did not question his directions and, since he would not face unpalatable facts, there were few who would tell him the truth when things went wrong.

110. Hitler's so-called "intuition" had been developed by a high sense of self-preservation and from living by his wits during his rise to power in the early days of the Party. Particularly when Germany had the initiative, his "intuitions" were often right but, as the war progressed and began to go against Germany Hitler had to take over more and more responsibilities, in order to execute command, instead of being able to decentralise to trusted colleagues; he thereby became overburdened with business and detail and "intuition" progressively failed him.

111. The main defects in Hitler's character which had an important influence on the way in which Germany waged the war are discussed below under the following general headings: -

(a) His obstinacy and refusal to listen to, or accept, unpalatable facts or advice which ran contrary to his own preconceived ideas. These ideas were not the outcome of a considered appreciation but of his so-called "intuitive" thought. (Paras. 113-123.)

(Incidentally this attitude of mind would have prevented his impartial assessment of intelligence even if it had been presented to him.)

(b) His persistent failure to understand the opinions and reactions of foreign countries, due in part to his limited education, ignorance of international affairs, and lack of foreign travel. (Para. 124.)

(c) He was an opportunist and, therefore, never formulated a considered long term plan (this lack of a long term plan may, in fact, have been more apparent than real, see Para. 126). He unquestionably failed to adjust such plans as he had, when it should have been clear that their prosecution was no longer profitable. The effect of this opportunism may even have been to Germany's advantage while she had the initiative, but was disastrous when she was being pressed back on all fronts. (Paras. 125-126)

(d) These characteristics made it inevitable that, as the tide of war turned against Germany, Hitler should himself assume more and more responsibilities. Not only did he thus become overburdened and obsessed with the detailed direction of the war but his mental and physical abilities also suffered. (Paras. 127-132)

112. The cumulative effect of these defects in Hitler's character eventually made a very great contribution to the breakdown of the whole German war machine.

## *His obstinacy and inability to accept sound advice.*

113. There is abundant evidence of Hitler's obstinacy and refusal to admit, or even listen to, unpalatable facts, especially when he heard them from men whom he regarded as "professional obstructionists". On the dismissal of those of his responsible subordinates who had become unbearable to him, he frequently reacted by taking all direct responsibility himself or appointing "men of straw". He was in the end overpowered by the burden which he continued incessantly to pile upon his own shoulders, and which culminated in his mental and physical collapse. We have already described how in February, 1938, he dismissed Neurath, Blomberg and Fritsch, and himself took over the Supreme Command of the Armed Forces. Later, in December, 1941, after complaining for some months about him, he dismissed General von Brauchitsch and a number of other generals, such as Guderian, who had occupied leading positions in the winter campaign against Russia, and himself took over the

post of Commander-in-Chief of the Army. Again in the summer of 1942 he dismissed Halder from his position as Chief of Staff of the Army, while in June, 1944, there was another upheaval, resulting in the dismissal of Rundstedt and Geyr von Schweppenburg in the West and von Kleist, von Manstein and Busch in the East. Finally, after the shock of the bomb attempt against him on the 20th July, 1944, there followed a holocaust of generals, including the dismissal of General Zeitzler, Halder's successor as Chief of Staff of the Army.

114. Throughout this time, Hitler became increasingly dependent upon men whom he regarded as subscribing to his own ideas and who, although full of drive, were unorthodox or lacked the essential objectivity of military experience and strategical judgment.

115. The advancement of mediocre men began with Keitel himself, who brought him colleagues of his own mental calibre out of an instinct of self-preservation. Hitler would only keep his advisers if from the start they were such types. Zeitzler and Guderian tried to contradict and had to go. Hitler's "young Field Marshals" such as Rommel, Model, Schoerner, Kesselring, Hube and Dietl always in his presence submitted to the laws of his entourage and only occasionally and tentatively spoke their minds. They took careful account of Hitler's peculiarities. The fact that Hitler stifled the expression of opinion by them meant that they in stifled the expression of opinion by their subordinates. Hitler adopted the same methods with regard to the Navy. He did not like Raeder's views on strategy and he was replaced as Commander-in-Chief of the Navy in January 1943 by Doenitz, who had already gained the Fuehrer's confidence and even friendship and who subsequently became one of the Fuehrer's most intimate collaborators. Hitler is known to have remarked on a number of occasions that it was the duty of staff officers only to transmit orders to their subordinates and not to "communicate their own pessimism". He alone had the right to hold opinions upon which decisions could be based. But in contrast to his interference with the "Conservative Army" and the "Imperialist Navy", Hitler was always content to leave the "National Socialist Air Force" to be mis-managed by Goering in his own way.

116. In his dealings with the General Staff Hitler appears largely to have been governed by his obsession that, owing to their breeding, upbringing and traditions, the advice of professional soldiers (and for that matter sailors or airmen) was most likely to be wrong. This distrust tended to extend to anyone of aristocratic or even *bourgeois* origins who had not proved himself in the Nazi party. His experiences in the period

1938-40 appear to have convinced him more than ever of the soundness of this view and of the essential superiority of his own powers of judgment, which consequently required that he should pay only scant attention to "expert" advice.

117. He never allowed himself to think that any disaster might have been due to a mistake of his own. He considered that the Generals had lost their nerve over the first winter campaign in Russia and if it had not been for his own tenacity the misfortune would have been greater. In his opinion military leadership was a matter of intellect, tenacity and nerves of iron; he considered that he possessed these qualities to a much higher degree than any of his generals. He was so anxious to prove that he was always right that he gave orders that all the daily conferences on the military situation should be taken down in shorthand, because he wanted to prove to posterity how right he had always been. His unshakable faith in his lucky star was pathological, his escape on the 20th July, 1944, when an attempt was made on his life, made him all the more convinced that he had been pre-destined by Providence to achieve the goal which it had set him.

118. Although his dislike of the "professional" elements and their attitude of *non possumus* sometimes provoked the violent outbursts in conference, of which there are so many vindictive personal accounts, it would appear to have been equally common for Hitler to listen quietly and without comment, only to castigate them mercilessly and with considerable histrionic ability afterwards in his "private circle". Owing to this characteristic, the officer or official who had fallen from grace might be unaware of his lack of success until the news reached him by devious and indirect channels.

119. Hitler constantly emphasised that he had served and been wounded in the last war as a common soldier, and that the generals whom he has so disliked could not understand the feelings of the ranker. General Jodl has offered the interesting explanation of Hitler's constant refusal to yield ground to his conviction that, although it was easy for the High Command to order advance one day and retreat the next, the psychological effect on the private soldier, who had shed his blood to gain a few hundred yards of ground, might be disastrous. It is doubtful, however, whether, though he used the interests of the German private soldier as he did those of German racial unity as arguments to support his point of view, Hitler ever fully identified himself with the welfare of his troops.

120. As head of the State he would not have been expected to visit the front repeatedly, but the troops were entitled to expect it from the Commander-in-Chief

of the Army, particularly in view of his system of making personal decisions on all details. He also discouraged his military advisers from going, and during long months on the eastern front when the troops were suffering from intense hardship owing to inadequate equipment and transport, deficient clothing and lack of supplies, no one from headquarters went to visit them. Speer considers that Hitler's decision to make himself Commander-in-Chief in 1941 was the most unfortunate decision taken in the war. As Hitler had no time to carry out the important functions of a Commander-in-Chief, it meant that the post had been abolished and there was no one to iron out the differences between the army at home and the army at the front. He probably also kept away from the front because, with the beginning of the war, he became more and more concerned about the preservation of his own life, as he considered that he was essential to Germany. As a result he became increasingly out of touch with reality. According to one authority he never even visited a bombed city during the entire war.

121. On the civil side, only Speer had the courage to represent the truth to Hitler, however unpalatable, and Hitler, for a time, was prepared to listen quietly, possibly on the strength of a long-standing personal intimacy. But as Speer's forebodings became more and more grave, he too fell from favour and was unable to gain access to the Fuehrer, who preferred to hear the facile and irresponsible optimism of Speer's lieutenant, Saur. Nevertheless, in the last days of the régime, it was, according to Guderian (and confirmed by Speer himself), Speer who was, "the first person to tell Hitler plainly that the war was lost and must be stopped". He was considered by his colleagues to be the only man who could do so and escape with this life.

122. The fact that Hitler was a bad judge of character came home to him in the end. In March 1945 he despairingly admitted to his Secretaries that the choice he had made of the successors to himself had not turned out well; Hess had gone mad, Goering was lazy and extravagant and Himmler he believed to be an enemy of the Party, which was an idea probably suggested by Bormann.

123. Hitler's distrust of his professional advisers and confidence in his own capabilities and judgment was accompanied by an optimistic determination to ignore the possibility of defeat which far exceeded that required of a national leader, and which ran to extravagant lengths. This attitude did not confine itself to such relatively harmless matters as reiteration of the slogan "for us Germans there is no such word as impossible", the banning of all discussion of the possibilities of defeat, and the setting of "impossible" goals for war production programmes.

## *His Failure to Appreciate the Opinions and Reactions of Foreign Countries.*

124. Not only was Hitler untravelled and ignorant of other countries and peoples, but he chose his advisers not because they were experts but because they had worked well in the Party machine, or because he liked them. It was done, said Speer, as quickly and as intuitively as he made all his decisions; "What risk and irresponsibility were involved in this intuition," he added. Hitler relied a great deal on Ribbentrop for his appreciation of Britain and America. He thought that the terror tactics which had been effective in France (perhaps largely because France had so often been invaded) would also have the same effect in cowing Britain. There was the same ignorance with regard to Russia.

## *His Opportunism and the Ultimate Failure of his Plans.*

125. In the early part of Hitler's active policy it is possible to discern two character-istics which became increasingly dominant factors in his later strategy; firstly Hitler planned throughout with such confidence of success that when his plans failed he was unprepared with any alternative strategy; secondly though constantly aware, of his ultimate objective and ultimate programme, at no time, did he plan more than one step ahead. Only when that step had been successfully carried out did he call for detailed plans for the next.

126. The apparent gap between his ultimate programme and his step-by-step planning probably derived from his intense distrust of all his collaborators, and in particular the leading generals of the German army whom he instinctively suspected and disliked. In the early days, Hitler appreciated, rightly, that were he to expound to them in detail the whole of his grand design they would regard him as a madman, and the opposition to his policy would increase. He therefore withheld from them his later intentions until he thought the moment had come for them to start detailed planning. To this extent, therefore, the lack of a longer-term plan was more apparent than real. The fact, however, that he was disinclined to plan beyond the immediate phase on which he was engaged cost Hitler increasingly dear as one by one in the course of the war unexpected factors intervened to prevent the fulfilment of his strategy.

## *Overcentralisation and obsession with detail.*

127. Whereas before the war Hitler delegated work to others, and took considerable time off for recreation which included seeing two films every day, he decided at the beginning of the war that he must have no more amusements and see no more films. He became a slave to work and increasingly concerned himself with details. His grasp of detail, including mechanical and statistical detail, was astonishing, and he was clearly capable of detecting with great rapidity and clarity of perception the weaknesses in even the most detailed and carefully prepared arguments put before him by the most highly qualified technical experts. But, apart from certain personal enthusiasms, his excursions into matters of detail were unsystematic, sometimes with disastrous results and usually at the expense of the weightier matters of high policy which needed his attention much more urgently. General Dittmar has stated in this connexion that "the Fuehrer was interested in the very biggest questions and also in details. Everything in between was of little importance to him. But he overlooked the fact that important questions have to be decided in this intermediate sphere".

128. Thus, there seems to be little doubt that Hitler possessed an extensive knowledge of army weapons. This was coupled with an enthusiasm for the subject which, although it caused him to neglect the weapons of the other services and to pay far more attention than the subject warranted to new developments, seems on the whole to have been beneficial, despite the fact that he was often opposed by the professional soldiers. Thus his influence on army weapon development of tank and assault guns is said to have been both practical and imaginative. And he saved the Army General Staff from a major blunder when he stopped the introduction on a large scale of taper-bored anti-tank guns which could not have been supplied with ammunition owing to the shortage of tungsten with which to manufacture tungsten-carbide cores. In the air war his excursions into detail were nearly always disastrous to the G.A.F. Difficult tactical problems always excited his personal interest. He personally planned, in the last detail, the assault on Fort Eben Emael in 1940, and took a similar interest in the planning of the projected assault on Gibraltar by air power and heavy artillery, and in the bombardment of Sebastopol with mammoth mortars.

129. Apart from these special operations, Hitler's attention was from the very outbreak of the war taken up with details of the tactical situation at the front, to an extent which seriously interfered with the progress of future planning. As the Eastern

war began to go wrong he concerned himself increasingly with tactical matters and troop movements which were the proper province of his commanders and the Army General Staff. Preoccupation with current operations in this manner tended more and more to upset Hitler's judgment on the larger strategical issues, and after the bomb attack on the 20th July, 1944, this characteristic became still more marked. In the final months of the war he spent practically all his time in the detailed conduct of operations, ordering counter-attacks by units which had already been over-run, demanding the last-ditch defence of strong-points which had already fallen, and planning movements of troops which could not be carried out for lack of reinforcements. He rarely left his headquarters and was virtually inaccessible to all but his personal staff, convinced that he alone possessed clear conceptions regarding all fields of human endeavour. He condemned generals, staff officers, diplomats, officials and even, at the end, the Party, the S.S. and the whole German nation as incompetents, weaklings, cowards, and finally as criminals and traitors, who deserved only to perish.

130. As a result of his self-imposed mental isolation and his over-work he lost the gift of working intuitively. "Formerly", says Speer, "he had had the habit of reasoning out his problems only up to a certain point, after which he would rely on his intuition. After he had lost this capacity, he increasingly resorted instead to his abnormal faith in his lucky destiny, which was based on self-persuasion, and relied on it as an incontrovertible argument. The longer and more difficult the war, the more pronounced became this process". Before the war he had drawn vitality and confidence from the enthusiasm of mass meetings and those of his entourage, but, cut off from this, his irresponsible self-assurance "turned into uncertainty and tortured indecision". He could not see his way through the mass of detailed work with which he surrounded himself. Whereas before the war he had had the ability to extricate Germany from difficulties, he lost this capacity after 1942 and followed rigid lines of policy. He did not try to mitigate military set-backs by political means, such as attempting to win over the French and Russian occupied peoples by generous treatment rather than wholesale persecution and terrorism. To a certain extent he offset his mental and physical exhaustion by means of artificial stimulants, but it only increased his incapacity to take decisions, which he put off from day to day even when every hour was vital.

131. A man like Hitler, who depended to a great extent on his emotions and relied on his intuition, could not suddenly do regular work and try to absorb a mass of detail without disastrous consequences. The Hitler of 1945 was, as a result, a very different

man from the Hitler of 1938. His character became hardened and petrified as he shut himself off more and more from all problems and all reality. While the grand design of his policy at first followed the lines laid down in *Mein Kampf*, he gradually acquired his own precepts. It has been said that in *Mein Kampf* there are certain ideas with regard to the loss of war which make sense, and that many of Hitler's colleagues were astounded in the last months to see how he himself acquired those precepts.

132. This centralisation of ultimate authority in Hitler's hands had the effect of weakening at all lower levels any sense of responsibility for co-ordination of policy. This did no harm so long as Hitler himself actually supplied the necessary co-ordination, but in the course of the war this gradually ceased to be the case, as his time and attention were increasingly taken up with purely military matters. Some of the specialist Ministers in charge of civil departments, discussing the situation among themselves, agreed that what Germany needed was a second-in-command (for whom the title of "Reich Chancellor" was suggested) to provide the necessary co-ordination of civil policy, but it does not seem that anyone ever dared to make this suggestion to Hitler himself.

# Chapter II. –

# Machinery of Joint Command.

133. This chapter does not attempt to give a full description of the German system of Joint Command, but merely endeavours to provide sufficient detail to appreciate the principal weaknesses which contributed to the German failure. Annex IV to this report gives more detail and describes instances of mishandling with particular reference to the Army Staffs.

## *Supreme Command of the Armed Forces and Supreme Command of the Army (OKW and OKH).*

134. Until 1935 OKH was solely responsible for the mobilisation and organisation of Germany's entire war potential. This Staff was also responsible for all aspects of planning, and control was not confined to the Army only, but also included both the Navy and the Air Force within its scope. It is possible, therefore, to realise the immense power which was then wielded by the Staff of the Supreme Army Command and to understand that the Army, which was traditionally of first importance, considered the Navy and Air Force as "supporting services." It is not an exaggeration to say that Germany never fully appreciated the true value of having completely independent sea and air forces, and as a result the Naval Staff (OKM) and the Air Staff (OKL), though represented in OKW, had in practice less standing than OKH.

135. To a man of Hitler's temperament, beliefs and "intuition", the power enjoyed by the Army was dangerous, and in 1935, in order to curb this power and exercise the control he felt was necessary, he set up the Supreme Command of the Armed Forces (OKW). Apart from its responsibility for the co-ordination of the efforts of the three

services, the civil administration and the productive capacity of Germany, OKW was also responsible for reporting direct to Hitler on all matters of importance. In actual fact, both OKM and OKL, together with the views of the Services they represented, were virtually disregarded, and the focus of attention was centred on OKH and the OKW. OKL, which was headed by Goering, did enjoy a considerable independence, but this was only obtained through the personality of its leader and his close contact with the Fuehrer.

136. The conception of a Supreme Joint Command was well founded in theory, suited to the German mentality, and, if properly handled, could have been effective. After consultation with the Chiefs of the three Services the Fuehrer should have laid down the major strategic policy to be followed, OKW should then have issued the necessary directives to enable this policy to be effected, and the staffs of the three Services and of the civil Ministries should have undertaken the detailed planning. The plans, when completed, should then have been submitted to OKW for final approval and co-ordination. This system, however, demanded that OKW should not have an executive function, but Hitler's great fear of the power of the Army, together with his personal belief in himself, lead him to encourage OKW to interfere with the planning and "command" functions, which were the responsibilities of the Services. In particular, this led to OKW becoming overburdened by duties which should have been performed by OKH, thereby, gradually losing sight of the long-term strategical issues and being overwhelmed by a mass of detailed planning. Meanwhile the views of OKL and OKM were almost invariably disregarded.

137. Although OKW was designed to direct and co-ordinate, there were a number of factors which prevented such co-ordination from being entirely effective. One of the great draw-backs of OKW was its independent position as regards the Service Ministries. This was implicit in Hitler's conception of it as his own personal machine. Though it was staffed by officers from all three Services, they had no function as representatives of their own Ministries in which they had no status or responsibility. The only links with the Service Ministries took the form of small detachments which existed for liaison purposes. Thus, the independent position of OKW in relation to the Service staffs resulted in frequent divergencies of opinion and plans. This was a specially serious disadvantage because of the discord that existed not only between OKW and the Army, but also between the Air Force and both OKW and the Army. The Air Force under Goering had always endeavoured to maintain an independent position, while the Naval Staff were consistently subordinated to the Army element of the Supreme Command and was unable to press its views on or obtain its requirements from the G.A.F.

138. Another shortcoming was the lack of co-ordination between civil, political and military affairs. The example was largely set in Hitler's own daily conferences, where political figures were excluded from military conferences and military chiefs from political conferences. This enabled Hitler frequently to disregard his advisers, claiming in particular when debating strategy with his military chiefs, that a question was primarily one of political necessity.

139. When in 1941 Hitler assumed command of the Army, OKH as well as OKW came under his direct control. This represented a radical alteration to the structure of the Command Machine. Increased friction between the two Staffs resulted, and Hitler became increasingly involved in a mass of detailed work, thereby obscuring his vision and confusing his mind on long term issues.

140. As the war with Russia developed, Hitler made OKH directly responsible for operations on the Eastern Front, while OKW remained responsible for operations in all other theatres. Thereafter, relations between OKW and OKH progressively deteriorated until what was virtually a feud existed between the two staffs; both OKW and OKH jealously guarded their own interests at the expense of each other and, incidentally, of Germany.

## *Supreme Command of the Air Force (OKL).*

141. While Hitler realised the importance of air power, his conception of air strategy during the war was frequently at fault. Although there are indications that the need to mount a sustained and co-ordinated strategic bomber offensive was appreciated, at no time after 1941 was such a policy effectively implemented. Hitler left the employment of the Luftwaffe to Goering, who repeatedly boasted that it would accomplish things which were beyond its power. A salient weakness in Goering's direction of the G.A.F. was the failure to co-ordinate its use to the main war effort as a whole. This was a legacy from the lack of a well-balanced joint approach to all problems through the machinery of High Command, which was aggravated by the fact that Hitler and his unpredictable personality were superimposed on the German War Machine.

142. Following the failure of the Luftwaffe successfully to complete the preparatory air operations for the invasion of England, Germany suddenly found herself with no alternative means of concluding the war against this country except by strategic bombing and sea blockade; for the former she was not prepared and the latter suffered from lack of co-ordination. German strategy in devoting the main strength of the

Air Force to support of the Army also contributed to the lack of air support for the navy. As the war progressed Germany's commitments became so widespread, and the forces ranged against her grew to such overwhelming proportions, that the Luftwaffe was of quite insufficient strength to be able to undertake the many requirements which had to be faced. Nevertheless, it is considered that the High Command failed to make the best use possible of the air forces which were at their disposal.

## Supreme Command of the Navy (OKM).

143. The small rôle played by the OKM reflects a further weakness of the Joint Command. Sea communications were the life blood of the British Empire and of the United States Forces operating in the European theatre; but sufficient weight was never given to this vital factor by the Supreme Joint Command. Had war with Britain been avoided until the German Navy was adequate for the task, had Rommel's supplies across the Mediterranean been properly protected, had the greatest effort been given to the introduction of the improved type U-boats in large numbers, before it was too late to affect the issue, Germany might not have lost the War. Lack of naval authority in the High Command resulted in inadequate air support being given to the conduct of the War at sea. For instance, not only did the U-boat warfare suffer throughout from the lack of effective air reconnaissance and support but in addition, at a time when her main object was to strangle Great Britain by close blockade, bombing attacks, which might have been concentrated against British ports, unloading facilities and communications, in order to augment the efforts of submarines and surface ships, were diverted to other targets.

## Combined Italo-German Command.

144. We have already referred to the debatable question whether Italy's entry into the war in June 1940 was in accordance with a preconceived Axis plan. There is ample evidence, as the war developed, that no attempt was made to pool all Italo-German resources or achieve concerted Italo-German operational plans. The generally opportunist nature of the Rome-Berlin Axis and Hitler's mistrust of his Ally resulted in there being no prearranged machinery for Italy's participation in the War. Thus, at no stage was there an "Axis" combined staff having both Italian and German representatives, and in consequence there was no adequate co-ordination of effort between the two partners.

# Chapter III.-

# The Weakness of German Intelligence.

## Introduction.

145. In the following paragraphs we discuss the functions and work of the German Intelligence Service, outline its failures, and summarise its weaknesses together with the main causes for its lack of success.

146. The Intelligence Branch of the OKW, the OKW AMT ABWEHR was the principal German Intelligence Service. It was under the direction of Admiral Canaris, and its task was operational espionage, political and military subversion, counter-espionage and the provision of intelligence from secret sources.

147. In addition it controlled a parallel department of Amstgruppe Ausland which received reports from "non-secret" sources, both from service attachés and the Foreign Office.

148. In 1939-41 the reputation of the *German Intelligence Staff* stood very high, due probably to two factors, firstly, the material superiority of the German armies was so great that their success was not vitally dependent on a good intelligence service, and, secondly, the counter-espionage department of the Abwehr was remarkably effective in its operations against enemy agents.

149. It is now known that during this period the section of the Abwehr which dealt with operational espionage achieved little result. The section which dealt with political and military subversion and sabotage, however, was successful in areas where the Germans were able to exercise some form of control or to exert strong political pressure, notably in the Balkans and Spain.

## *Failure of German Intelligence.*

150. In 1942, when Germany lost the initiative, her dependence on good intelligence became much more important than before. The crucial period was between 1942 and 1944, for, after the allied landings in 1944 which coincided with the Russian advance on the Eastern front, allied strength had become so overwhelming that no amount of good intelligence could have affected the result of the war.

151. The record of the Abwehr during the crucial period was one of uniform failure on almost all major issues. As a result, partly because of its incompetence, and partly because so many of its members were involved in the plot to assassinate Hitler, the Intelligence Section was finally removed from the control of OKW and re-organised as the Military Branch of Himmler's Intelligence Department.

152. Broadly speaking, the Abwehr's major failure during 1942-44 was its inability to provide its share of the information on which reasonable forecasts of allied strategic intentions could be made. This was in some measure responsible for the inaccurate German appreciations regarding the landings in North Africa, Sicily, Italy and Normandy. Though Allied superiority would probably ultimately have caused Germany's defeat, accurate information regarding our amphibious operations during 1942-44 might have produced for us consequences of extreme gravity, and allied casualties would have undoubtedly been much higher than they were.

153. Inadequate and unreliable intelligence, however, gave rise to a fear of the unknown, with the result that Hitler was forced to disperse his strength throughout the periphery of his defences, and in spite of having the advantage of interior lines of communications, he kept large forces locked up in widespread areas since he was always uncertain where and when the allies would attack.

154. As regards Russia, factual military intelligence appears to have been fairly good. The faulty German appreciations of Russian capacity and intentions derived amongst other things, from a misjudgement of Russia's economic resources and internal political strength. In any case, once the attack on Russia had been launched, Hitler was unwilling to accept any intelligence about the country which did not conform to his own wishes.

## Causes of the Failure and its effects.

155. The main causes of the failure of German Intelligence were bound up with certain inherent weaknesses within the Abwehr itself, and with the inadequate

organisation in the high command for a joint and co-ordinated consideration of intelligence and intelligence problems and requirements.

156. Admiral Canaris, the director of the Abwehr, was a difficult personality, who lacked organising ability, and to some extent was handicapped in his activities by the competition of Himmler's S.S. intelligence service and the independent intelligence bureaux of other ministries. Several of the higher posts in the Abwehr were filled by Canaris's personal friends, some of whom were idle and corrupt. There is also firm evidence that financial corruption and political disaffection existed throughout the organisation. Furthermore, few Abwehr personnel were General Staff officers, and they therefore received little support or sympathy from the General Staff.

157. Within the Abwehr there was little or no centralised evaluation of intelligence, which was in itself nearly always derived from personal sources. OKW reports were often rejected on internal grounds by the service ministries, who lacked the means of assessing the reliability of the information which they received.

158. In addition to the internal weaknesses of the Abwehr, the salient weakness of German Intelligence, and one of the main causes of its failure, was the absence of any inter-service staff for the co-ordination and appreciation of intelligence. Both Keitel and Jodl have stated that no organisation comparable with the allied joint intelligence machinery was ever formed. Operational intelligence was supplied by each of the service ministries and by the AMT Abwehr direct to the planning staff of OKW where it was inadequately co-ordinated.

159. Every move of the Allies in the West was conditioned by maritime factors, but the final consideration of intelligence rested mainly in the hands of the Army. As might be expected, therefore, it was in their forecasts of our amphibious operations that the Germans were mainly at fault. The naval reports were received at OKM, which was not in possession of the necessary military and air background information to make them comprehensible. Furthermore, when comparatively simple measures could have been taken to check the OKW appreciations of allied intentions, such as the ordering of air reconnaissances, the OKM lacked the necessary authority to put these into effect. Even if these faults had been overcome, the constitution of the Supreme Command was such that it is doubtful whether OKM would have carried enough weight to enable it to obtain full recognition of its views concerning allied intentions.

# Conclusions.

160. Up to the middle of 1942 the military strength of the German Army was such that it was not vitally dependent on intelligence. The result of the battles would have been much the same if the intelligence services had been bad or good.

161. After the summer of 1944, equally, no amount of efficiency in intelligence work could have made any appreciable difference to the result, or perhaps even to the duration of the war, as allied strength was so overwhelming.

162. So far as the value of intelligence is concerned, the time of the allied invasions between 1942 and 1944 was therefore the crucial period during which the necessity for good intelligence was vital.

163. If the Germans had had good and accurate intelligence in regard to allied strategic intentions during this period, consequences of extreme gravity might have resulted to us, and allied casualties might have been incomparably higher than they were, though no doubt allied superiority would eventually have caused Germany's defeat.

164. The weaknesses and failures of German Intelligence were due to an ill-directed, badly organised and corrupt Abwehr, which was generally inefficient except in regard sabotage and counter-intelligence, and to the absence of any inter-service staff for the co-ordination and appreciation of intelligence.

# Chapter IV. –

# Organisation of German War Production.

## German rearmament before the outbreak of war.

165. In 1933 when the rebuilding of Germany's armed forces was put in hand, the High Command, realising that a large expansion in the basic resources of Germany's economy would be necessary in order to sustain a large army in war, accepted the fact that such an expansion, requiring heavy capital investment, would be slow. In the meantime, once idle resources in man-power and plant had been put to work, the ability of industry to produce military equipment and new divisions except at the expense of the standard of living of the civil population was limited. In these circumstances the High Command was prepared to accept the comparatively small annual increment of military equipment which could be made available without depressing civilian standards by achieving full employment. They considered that a reasonable goal on the basis of "rearmament in depth" would be a strength of 120 divisions by 1942. The High Command, therefore, did not consider that the army and production organisation behind it would be in a fit state to enter a major war before 1943 at the earliest.

166. This schedule was too slow for Hitler. In contrast to the High Command's programme of "Rearmament in depth", *i.e.*, the co-ordinated mobilisation of military man-power and Germany's own industrial resources, Hitler demanded "rearmament in width", which meant that he desired an immediate display of the maximum of military goods in the shop window, regardless of the state of the shelves within. In

1937, he set a goal of 180 divisions by 1942 and responsible German commentators surmise that Hitler counted on early conquests to acquire the basic resources necessary for their equipment and maintenance in war. While Hitler was probably aware of the risks involved in this policy, he preferred them to the more laborious and time-consuming alternatives of building up Germany's basic industries on their own capital sources.

167. The German success in nourishing their enormous army was paid for by their navy. Although it was clearly impossible for Germany to reach the agreed naval strength in the four years between 1935 and the outbreak of war, she could probably have approached it more closely, at any rate in cruisers and destroyers, had she given the matter priority. Moreover, she could have prepared the way for a more rapid expansion in submarines – in case of war – than she actually achieved in 1939 and 1940.

## *Organisation of production during the war.*

168. In the event, the speed with which the armed forces were assembled and equipped up to 1939, followed the High Command's schedule to a greater extent than Hitler's aspirations. The much publicised policy of guns before butter was in fact largely a myth. In the first phase of the war, however, there can be no question of production failures having played any part in preventing Germany from achieving her original strategical ends. At no time during this period, which included the initial months of the Russian campaign, were the German forces in the field hampered or even inconvenienced by shortages of supplies or equipment arising from deficiencies in production. Indeed, consumption was so far below the anticipated level that production in certain instances was too ample in relation to the requirements of Hitler's strategy and was therefore cut down.

169. Although the failure to defeat Russia before the winter of 1941-2 came as an unpleasant surprise, but did not call immediately for a major long-term readjustment in German economic plans, Germany's leaders had every confidence that where the German armies had failed in 1941 they would succeed in 1942, but they grossly under-estimated the vast scope of Russian war mobilisation. In order to supply the equipment and munitions needed it was, however, necessary to reverse the reconversion orders which had been issued in the previous year, and to introduce

more drastic restrictions on the provision of goods and services to civilians. Whereas previously industry had been producing with one eye on peace economy, the law in April 1942 prohibited any further planning for peace-time production. This was followed in October by an order introducing for the first time, on a large scale, utility standards in the manufacture of goods for civilian consumption. However, the administrative machinery for controlling war production displayed major defects in all departments. These were mainly the result of the complacency of the earlier years of the war. During the earlier period the inefficient organisation of production by the General Staff and the civilian bureaucracy had merely involved the wasteful utilisation of resources, but did not lead to any critical deficiencies in the supply. Hence, when events called for an all-out effort, the machine was handicapped and was unable to take even the easiest gradients in top gear.

170. Nevertheless, over the first six months of 1942 armaments production increased by about 50 per cent. and there was a further increase of about 25 per cent. by the end of the year. These increases were mainly the result of the measures introduced into the armament industry by Speer who in May 1942 took over the full responsibility for the control of land armaments production from the War Economy and Armaments Office of the OKW.

## *Failure of the organisation and its causes.*

171. In spite of these increases, from the beginning of 1942 onwards shortages of equipment and munitions at the front were chronic and the armed forces as a whole were getting less weapons and munitions than they would have been able to use. Once the tide had turned in Russia, industry was never able to keep pace with the enormous wastage suffered in the successive retreats. This was largely due to the inept policy of allocation of new equipment whereby, as a general rule, 90 per cent. of new production was to be given to units being formed and 10 per cent. to the field to replace the losses of formations in action. The result was that veteran formations in action were chronically short of equipment while new green units were committed to action with a complete or nearly complete establishment of equipment only to lose a fantastically high proportion in the first engagement. Moreover, the allocation of supplies between the Eastern and the other theatres was often unbalanced. This was partly due to personal decisions of Hitler, many of which seem to have been taken without knowing

the facts, and partly because OKH was responsible for the Eastern front but had no authority over allocation of material. Such allocations were the prerogative of OKW, who favoured the other theatres, for which they were directly responsible.

172. So slow were the Germans to realise the full extent of Russian strength that it was not until the 1942 campaign had failed with the defeat at Stalingrad that the drive for complete economic mobilisation was introduced with full severity. Even so, although there was a great increase in armament production, amounting in the summer of 1944 to an increase of 3½ times above the level of production at the beginning of 1942, it was never found possible to make the best use of Germany's resources. This was due to three main causes: -

(i) Production from 1942 onwards was imperfectly related to the development of the war. This was an inevitable result of a situation in which there were in effect no coherent strategy to which production could be called upon to conform. The hesitant and unsystematic manner in which adjustments in the armament programme were carried out was largely due to the virtual absence of effective machinery for thorough and systematic discussion of requirements. The decisions as to what should be produced were made by Hitler himself on his own judgment or as the result of advice from one or other of his advisers, and seldom as the result of free discussion of requirements by all interested parties. The discussions which decided the pattern of German war production consequently took the form of hole-in-corner conspiracies rather than of staff conferences. The adaptation in detail of the armament programme to the requirements of defensive strategy were therefore rather slow and irregular. The consistent failure to concentrate in time the resources of the aircraft industry on the production of defensive fighters is well known. In land armaments the "infantry" programme designed to increase the defensive fire power of field divisions did not begin to yield substantial results until the middle of 1944.

(ii) The increase in the power of Speer and of his non-political bureaucracy was watched with jealousy by the major and minor Party bosses. Quite apart from genuine disputes as to the best means of managing Germany's war production and economy, Party leaders were naturally opposed to Speer and many aspects of his policy on political and sometimes personal grounds. Both by frequent refusal, overt or covert, to co-operate and by persecution of his staff, Party bosses did much to hamper Speer in his efforts to obtain the maximum war production from the sources available.

(iii) Labour was a major bottleneck in war production. In spite of the notable success of Sauckel and the labour leaders in mobilising foreign labour for work in Germany, the fact remains that neither full nor the most efficient use was made of the resources in man-power available to Germany. One source of inefficiency was the lack of a unified system of planning between the production and the labour departments. Moreover, German women were never fully mobilised. They were in general most reluctant to work in industry and the confusion caused by Allied air attacks often made it impossible to compel them. Added to this, the Party men who controlled labour were unwilling to use strong measures to drive reluctant women into industry, for political reasons and for fear of interfering with the Nazi programme for promoting the increase of the German race.

# APPENDIX I.

# THE FORGING OF THE GERMAN WAR MACHINE.

## I.– INTRODUCTION

Contrary to common belief, the rapid expansion of the German armed forces after 1933 was only possible as the result of the careful preparations made during the preceding fourteen years. The paragraphs below give an account of what was accomplished before and after the seizure of power by Hitler. Though they do not tell the whole story, they are almost entirely based upon authentic and authoritative German sources.

## II.– GERMAN ARMY PREPARATIONS.

### Training of Higher Commanders and the General Staff.

2. Early in 1921 the Inter-Allied Military control Commission rightly demanded the German Government to state the real functions of the Reichswehr Ministry, but it never received a satisfactory reply. Actually von Seeckt was maturing it like a plant for the future, and "it would have been very difficult to do the work of 1935-39 if from 1920-34 this centre of leadership had corresponded to the needs of the small army".*

---

* *Seeckt, Aus Seinem Leben*, Vol. II, by Gen. Lt. Von Rabenau, Chef de Reichsarchiv. This official biography, which was published in 1940, has been drawn on considerably in compiling this account.

3. In June 1925 the Allied Powers presented a Collective Note demanding satisfaction on five important points, the chief of which was the removal from the Chef der Heeresleitung in the Reichswehr Ministry of the functions of a Commander-in-Chief, which was forbidden by the Treaty. The reason attributed for this action, which is largely correct, was because the Allies had recognised that von Seeckt "had learned how to withdraw from the poison of Versailles its last and deepest effect – the moral disarmament of the troops".

4. It was of the greatest importance for the success of the whole work of education and training to have a sound Officer Corps. But the reduction in the army under the Treaty meant a decrease in the Officer Corps from 34,000 to 4,000. Although this made rigid selection possible, von Seeckt nevertheless complained in 1922 that out of 4,000 officers 1,000 had not been trained in Staff College. Such a proportion would have been considered highly satisfactory elsewhere. However, despite the difficulties on account of control, he set up staff courses.

5. Indeed, the most important feature of training of all was that of the General Staff and higher commanders. In organising and training the General Staff, Allied pressure made it necessary at first to give up the idea of a single Staff College, and training could only be realised in a camouflaged way. Future General Staff officers were trained in a two years' course in Wehrkreise after passing the Wehrkreis entrance examination; the syllabus of the course was similar to that of the pre-war Staff College and continued to combine wide training with technical instruction. At first each Wehrkreis trained its own "staff learners", as these officers were called with the approval of the Control Commission, and each trained such officers in its own way. But later Seeckt issued uniform directions for all Wehrkreise. In the third year of training uniformity was achieved by attaching a selected proportion to the Reichswehr Ministry. To quote the words of von Seeckt's biographer again: "The enemy did his best to destroy the General Staff and was supported by political parties within. The I.A.M.C.C. had rightly from its standpoint tried for years to make the training in higher staffs so primitive that there could be no General Staff. They tried in the boldest ways to discover how General Staff officers were being trained, but we were able to give nothing away, neither the system nor what was taught.

"Seeckt never gave in, for had the General Staff been destroyed, it would have been difficult to recreate it. He wanted a General Staff Corps as before, and although the form had to be broken, the content was saved. This applied to the army generally. . . .

"The enemy could not forbid assistants for the commanders of formations and, in fact, only the Great General Staff was prohibited. Without Seeckt, there would to-day (1940) be no General Staff in the German sense, for which generations of development are required and which cannot be achieved in a day however gifted or industrious officers may be. Continuity of conception is imperative to safeguard leadership in the nervous trials of reality. Knowledge or capacity in individuals is not enough; in war the organically developed capacity of a majority is necessary, and for this decades are needed".

6. In developing training, Seeckt built completely on old foundations but he employed an entirely new approach. This applied specially to the progressive training of generals, at that time unknown in other armies. Before 1914 the last staff appointment was the last chance of strategic instruction. In a small 100,000 army, if the generals were not also to be small, it was imperative to create a great theoretical framework. To this end large-scale tactical exercises were introduced. Each of them considered a specific practical military problem for Germany. Their main aim was not so much to train the General Staff, but rather the higher commanders.

7. In the summer of 1926 Seeckt conducted his largest skeleton exercise for commanders with staffs and signals. The smallness of the army and other considerations did not permit troops to be present, and so it was the only way of staging an exercise with several corps on each side. This (and similar exercises) helped to school leaders of large formations. It included practically all the generals, commanding officers and General Staff officers of the army. Later the idea was often current that the "new Wehrmacht had, so to speak, been made from nothing. But if one surveys Seeckt's tireless work in organising and training, here, too, it must be recognised that he paved the way, and of this there can be no possible doubt".

## Training of Regimental Officers, N.C.O.s and Specialists.[*]

8. In the early years of the Republic, the German military commanders were faced with two problems: the need to create an army of leaders, which was the policy increasingly favoured and before long officially adopted, and the need for formations to be in constant readiness in view of the internal political situation. Thus only in 1923 could a long-term programme of training be got out and a commencement made with

---

[*] Much of what follows is taken from: *Der Wiederaufstieg des deutschen Heeres* by Major in O.K.W.G. Themee, published in 1939.

training of the smallest units before going on to divisional training. Before this the emphasis had been on the latter on account of the continual necessity to use troops in internal disorders. Thus from 1922 the prevailing idea of a normal yearly programme was abandoned and progressive training by stages of two years was introduced with the specific object of training leaders at least to the next higher rank. The whole rank and file, with few exceptions, were to become cadres of a non-commissioned officer Corps and of specialists of all kinds. From 1924 individual units commenced to carry out their winter training, no longer by platoons, sections, &., but according to classes of capacity. This idea was further developed and extended in the following years. By 1930 this system of grouping men for training according to their standards was regulated uniformly in the whole army. One great advantage of this system was to present something new every year to the long-service soldier, and thus preserve him from boredom, lethargy, and mental stagnation. At the same time an extremely effective and thorough training in the most varied and specialised fields was carried through and a not unimportant reserve of leaders was got ready. It is true that not everyone in the 100,000 army was a leader in the fullest sense of the word, but it was possible in 1934, without an appreciable decrease in the general standard, for lance-corporals and corporals to be promoted sergeants; sergeants to be promoted sergeant-majors, and sergeant-majors to be promoted officers and army officials.

9. The preceding years had been accompanied by a rising standard both in character and accomplishments. This resulted in much weeding out and opening up vacancies for younger and more capable officers. However, the small number of officers available caused senior N.C.O.s to be used for the work of the former to the greatest possible extent. According to plan the best sergeants in infantry and artillery regiments were trained to command companies, batteries, &c. It is stated that the correctness of this process of selection and the value of the system of training was completely vindicated when in 1934 Hitler paved the way for conscription. Then a single infantry regiment was able to recommend 15 sergeants to command companies, that is nearly one for each of its 16 companies.

## *The Evolution of Tactical Doctrine.*

10. With regard to theoretical training, von Seeckt insisted upon its importance in view of the danger of false doctrine growing up as a result of individual experiences

during the late war. One of his first steps was to ensure that all the lessons of that war were thoroughly and systematically studied. In the words of his biographer: "Seeckt laid the foundations of present tactics and strategy, and especially the admirable technique of command".

11. The method of introducing new principles of training consisted largely in instructional courses and new regulations. The number of the former made heavy calls on the few officers available. The new training regulations were got out under Seeckt's personal direction, all existing manuals were re-written and were not intended for the 100,000 army. Sections of them, which had to conform with the rôle of the Reichswehr as imposed by the Treaty, were to be regarded as purely theoretical and not applied in practice; they were printed in special type. Although based on the lessons of the past, they set out the doctrine of the future. Seeckt's *Führung und Gefecht* (corresponding to Field Service Regulations) laid down principles that were retained right up to the outbreak of war, and proved themselves in the campaigns of 1939 and 1940.

12. Already in 1919 the first fundamental training regulations had been issued and in May 1920 first drafts of all the new training manuals were issued for comments by the troops, for which a whole year was allowed. One of the lessons of the war that was particularly stressed was the need for the closest co-operation of *all* arms, not only the principal ones, and to this the German successes in the early part of the present war were largely attributed.

## *Weapons.*

13. The German struggle to preserve weapons from destruction was waged bitterly throughout the period of control. Every form of deception was practised. The author of *Der Wiederaufstieg des deutschen Heeres* complains of the lack of support in this and says that even the police were so misused by the Weimar Government as to check and even hold up transport of arms by the Army. He adds that the laws against treason were unsatisfactory, and that the only way to deal with traitors was for the proceedings not to be public. Nevertheless, considerable numbers of weapons were preserved, and they created the first stocks for the future national Army. In the first years this work of evasion was carried through more or less unplanned and spontaneously, but from 1923 it became thoroughly organised, and gradually the existing surpluses of

arms and equipment were brought on charge and controlled by the duly appointed administrative service. The wave of patriotic enthusiasm on the French entry into the Ruhr in that year enabled considerable progress to be made and under this pressure it became possible to stop intervention by the Police and to establish contact with all kinds of armed associations.

14. The principle was now laid down that Reichswehr stores of arms could not be touched by the Police, and the declaration by any army authority that any dump of arms was the property of the Reichswehr sufficed to remove them from Police interference. In addition, the Police were now bound to deliver weapons confiscated from civilians, &c., to the nearest army depot. All the work involved in planning, distributing and safeguarding this surplus armament fell upon the troops, principally the officers, on account of the need for secrecy.

15. At first the financial situation and the public investigation of army accounts by the Reichstag prevented Government resources from being made available. But the growing public resistance after the Ruhr occupation caused funds from private sources to flow in to an increasing extent. All this helped not only to get hold of the necessary war material, but also enabled civil assistants to be taken on, surplus to the army strength. Thus gradually there was established a widespread organisation to relieve the troops of this task.

16. Under the camouflage of a civil organisation known as Landesschutz (National Protection), a system, uniform in character and direction, was created. Its task was to safeguard arms and equipment, to administer reserves and to prepare plans for frontier defence. From April 1926 representatives of this organisation were set up all over Germany and they formed the first permanent organisation for planning the necessary preparatory work for mobilisation.

17. With the cessation of control in January 1927, events moved faster, particularly in providing war material and in preparing the army reserve. Thus when the first appreciable increases in strength took place in 1933-35, arms, equipment and clothing were available in adequate quantities, and the first beginnings of an organisation of reserves existed. In 1934 the development and trial of modern weapons was intensified, and what had slumbered for long years as a project on the writing desk, or had existed only in a few prototypes, was now developed and produced in greater quantities.

"On the introduction of conscription, it became the task of industry to provide the necessary arms and equipment despite the dispersal of armament machines by the

Control Commission. The capacity of German industrialists, engineers and workers proved equal to the new demands". Raw materials were similarly made available by cutting down civil requirements.

## The Stages of Expansion.

18. Already by 1924 von Seeckt had certain definite achievements to his credit; for example, he was well aware that the strength of the army was slowly increasing beyond the 100,000 limit. In the words of von Rabenau: "the fruits of this were borne only ten years later", and next year von Mackensen congratulated von Seeckt on his building up of the Reichswehr and compared him to Scharnhorst. At this point the writer asks: "was Germany really disarmed?" and answers: "the old fire burnt still and the I.A.M.C.C. had not destroyed any of the everlasting elements of German strength."

19. For several years short-service training of soldiers over establishment was practised. These men were known as "Black", *i.e.*, illegal. From 1925 onwards the whole sphere of "Black" work by the Reichswehr Ministry was centralised and extended to cover all Wehrkreise, and from now on the improving financial situation enabled the Ministry itself to provide the funds.

Based on von Seeckt's "Fundamental Considerations in Resurrecting Our Military Power" was the Truppenamt plan of 1925 for the maximum extension and improvement of the Army outside the Treaty limits. Von Seeckt's idea was to double and then to treble the existing 7 Infantry divisions, though his ultimate aim was a minimum of 63. The Truppenamt plan aimed in the first place at 21 divisions, though it was realised that these could not yet be formed. The annual rate of discharge permitted by the Treaty – and therefore of intake – was to be nearly doubled so as to build up a reserve despite the most watchful control. All preparations for mobilisation were to be under provincial Defence Councils, which included civil branches. Lastly, the general military preparation of the people was to be put in hand under a camouflaged central Reichssport Officer, which would replace the independent associations. Although the Government refused to sanction this plan, the soldiers nevertheless persevered and did a great deal, especially from 1926 onwards, but von Seeckt's biographer quotes him as saying even then that "the solution of the problem must be defective because the long service 100,000 army affords insufficient means of expansion, and it is necessary to strive to set aside the present impossible organisation by shortening service, increasing the number of officers and, lastly, by adopting a military system more suited to the German character."

The preparations for mobilisation entailed getting unofficial cover from the parties in the Reichstag supporting the Government, and from the States. This was the chief job of von Schleicher, *i.e.*, to make progress with the successive Governments for legalising the organisation of trained reserves and training the new annual classes. Till 1926 the main obstacle was the opposition of the Prussian Socialist Government.

20. On the 1st April, 1933, for the first time, the establishment of the 100,000 army was officially exceeded, though as already stated its strength had for some time risen steadily above that figure. The introduction of conscription in March 1935 was however attended by various difficulties. There was insufficient experience in planning and organising short service, so experiments were put in hand by incorporating men from the S.A. and para-military bodies. At the same time there was an enormous demand for technical personnel of all kinds, whose training had to be organised on a large scale.

21. In May 1935 the new military law was passed to give effect to the decision, which had been announced in March, to create an army of twelve corps totalling thirty-six divisions. By October the incorporation of police formations, provided for by this law, was completed, but the expansion to the above figure of the ten weak divisions, allowed under the Treaty, together with the provision of the necessary corps troops and of the strong detachments which had to be made to the new Air Force, could not be carried through in one stride. After allowing for the incorporation of the police, expansion was indeed fivefold. Special difficulty was met in organising new units, such as artillery, pioneer, and signal units, which had been disproportionately weak in the Reichswehr.

22. In order to increase the Officer Corps, retired officers were reinstated on the active list in the autumn of 1934. Besides promoting regular N.C.O.s in large numbers, the period of training of officers was cut down from four years to two. Thus promoted Sergeants, who had six years' service on the 1st October, were promoted to Oberleutnant and two years later some were promoted to Captain and were soon made company or equivalent commanders. The Corps of N.C.O.s was in the first place formed entirely from suitable other ranks of the 100,000 army, and here again the period of training was reduced to two years.

23. In order to facilitate the necessary accelerated intake on account of the above difficulties, it was only possible to organise ten Corps, and these not completely in October 1935. XI and XII Corps followed only a year later, and XIII Corps in October

1937. On the latter date they were complete with small exceptions: 100 infantry regiments, 43 artillery regiments, 11 armoured regiments, 14 mounted or cavalry regiments, 55 pioneer battalions, and in addition a considerable number of heavy artillery batteries and also specialised troops, such as motorised reconnaissance detachments, motor-cycle battalions, armoured car regiments, machine-gun battalions, motorised infantry, signal units, training units, &c. Apart from this a large number of academies and schools were created: a Military Academy for future staff officers, four new schools for officers, and others for N.C.O.s and specialists.

# III.– GERMAN NAVY PREPARATIONS.

## A.– 1919. The Year of Transition. (In Supreme Command: Admiral von Trotha.)

24. Under the Versailles Treaty Germany was permitted to retain a small Naval Force with a maximum personnel strength of 15,000 for defensive purposes. For manning this force she relied principally on personnel from former U-Boat and torpedo-boat flotillas and in order to preserve as many as possible of these valuable men as a homogenous body, Naval Brigades were also formed and used for the enrolment of officers and men for the future Navy. Mine clearance was the first and overt task of this newly constituted German Navy, which depended at that time on voluntary enlistment. Whilst minesweeping kept the personnel together and providing sea experience, delays in its completion held up the reconstruction of the post-war fleet. The old "Reichsmarineamt" was replaced by the "Admiralitaet" as the supreme Naval authority and the "Admiralstab" (an advisory body of naval officers who had had direct access to the Kaiser) was liquidated.

25. Attempts to circumvent the Versailles Treaty were quick to appear. They took two forms, namely, the incorporation of naval organisations covertly into the permitted Civil Ministries and the evasion of orders to destroy coastal defences and guns. For instance, personnel of the German "Sea-mark" system (responsible for the maintenance of lights, buoys and navigational aids) were incorporated in the Civil Transport Ministry and the Construction Directorate of the Admiralty was surreptitiously conducted as a department of the Berlin Technical High School. Despite the efforts of the Allied Control Commission the navy succeeded in strengthening the

North Sear fortifications with new batteries and modern guns and by taking over control of the fortresses of Pillau and Swinemuende, from the Army, the Navy succeeded in salving some 185 guns and mortars there.

26. The Torpedo and Mining Inspectorate and the Inspectorate of Naval Artillery were formed, German mine-sweepers paid visits to Memel, Gothenburg and Fredrikshavn, the German Navy continued to operate lake and river flotillas in East Prussia and on the Vistula; and the German Naval Officers were permitted to participate in the settlement of the Aaland Islands question.

## B.– 1920-1924. The re-birth of the German Navy. (In Supreme Command: Admiral Behnke).

27. The traditional German Navy became the permanent German Navy between 1920 and 1921, and a permanent system of area commands and administrative bodies was set up. It was the task of the newly created German Navy to deploy its permitted strength to the best advantage. Authorised warship construction was, however, hindered by inflation at home, foreign political difficulties and the French occupation of the Ruhr.

28. The fleet, however, began to carry out regular exercises and made attempts to strengthen German influence abroad by means of foreign visits. Ashore, the Navy took over Army coastal defences and formed detachments of naval artillerymen for their manning. Co-operation between Army and Navy developed, though the Navy was in almost all matters subordinated to the superior authority of the Army.

29. Throughout this period evasions of the Versailles Treaty, mainly in the following forms, continued: -

  (i) The dispersal of equipment and munitions, so that the Inter-Allied Control Commission should not take note of them.
 (ii) Evasion of the demolition work prescribed for Heligoland.
(iii) The covert increase in numbers of naval personnel beyond treaty limits.
(iv) Certain activities such as those directed by Kapitaen zur See Lohmann, who in September 1918 was put in charge of the newly-formed "See Transport Abteilung", which in 1919 was charged with the sale of semi-obsolete German war material to foreign countries. The large profits thus made were used for various illicit purposes, such as subsidising the Dornier Aircraft Company

and the development of new weapons in defiance of the Treaty. In addition, Lohmann embarked on a number of commercial enterprises for raising further funds to supplement existing funds for Naval rearmament. He was exposed by left-wing members of the Reichstag in 1928, when it was revealed he had used public funds supplied by the Ministry of Defence and he had to be retired.

(v)   The secret and illicit building of U-Boats in Finland, Japan, Turkey and Argentina.

(vi)   Participation in preparations for building up the Luftwaffe, *e.g.*, by instructing midshipmen in passive air defence, &c.

30. The promotion of "naval-mindedness" among the German people as a whole was encouraged through various civil organisations, such as youth clubs and labour unions.

## C. 1925-1932. German Naval re-construction. (In Supreme Command: Admiral Zenker, followed by Admiral Raeder.)

31. On the 7th January, 1925, the new light cruiser *Emden* was launched. This date marked the change-over from the old to the new German fleet. A large building programme was put into operation, which included 10,000-ton pocket battle-ships (a new type of vessel with triple turrets and novel propulsion), destroyers and torpedo-boats.

32. A number of re-armament measures were put into operation openly and with the approval of the Reich Government, and measures which the German Admiralty considered were not likely to find favour with the Reich Government were nevertheless carried on behind its back. These included: -

(i)   Further activities at Kapitaen zur See Lohmann (see also 37 (iv) above).

(ii)   Further efforts to build up a U-Boat arm, by building U-boats in Spain and Finland, the instruction of U-boat personnel in both these countries, and the formation in Germany in 1932 of a U-boat training school in the guise of an anti-submarine school.

(iii)   An active participation in the preparations for reconstruction of the Luftwaffe. These preparations included plans for a Fleet Air Arm (never brought into being), the founding of the Sevra Aircraft Company (later known as "Luftdienst, G.m.b.H."), the creation of a naval flying school at Warnemuende and an air station at List on Sylt, the training of sea cadet candidates, flying-boat and catapult aircraft development and the encouragement of interest in flying by such means as the Deutschland Flight of 1925 and the seaplane Race of 1926.

(iv) Economic rearmament. A company known as the TESEC ("Technische Beatung und Beschaffung G.m.b.H.") was founded in the guise of a technical advice and supply company. Its real object was to act on behalf of the Navy to investigate supplies of raw materials, industrial capacity and other matters of war economy.

(v) Naval attachés, forbidden by the Treaty, were established under cover. It was not until 1932-33 that they were openly reappointed.

## D. 1933-1939. The Navy during the Period of expansion. (In Supreme Command: Admiral Raeder.)

33. With the assumption of power by the Nazi Party in 1933 the Navy was assimilated into the National Socialist State. It was thus necessary for naval personnel to swear the oath of loyalty to the Fuehrer and for certain alterations in flag and uniform to take place.

34. In the years 1933-35, *i.e.*, while a pretence was still made at limiting armaments, C-in-C., Navy (Admiral Raeder), was given a free hand to press on with his plans for the reconstruction of the Navy, independently of any policy openly stated by the Reich Government. The Germans described this as the "sole attempt made to disguise their rearmament policy" at the time. Raeder made preparations for the construction of a strong fleet and coastal fortifications.

35. On the 16th March, 1935, Germany publicly repudiated the Versailles Treaty and announced her intention to abandon any limitation of armaments. The Anglo-German Naval Treaty limiting German Naval construction to 35 per cent. of British was signed on the 18th June, 1935, and Germany publicly denounced unrestricted U-boat warfare seven days later. The naval treaty was adhered to throughout 1936 and 1937, but was abrogated by Germany on the 28th April, 1939.

36. The first fruits of the Anglo-German Naval Treaty were a large increase in personnel, the open utilisation of the armaments industry for naval purposes, the

building of coastal fortifications, and the reincorporation of units into the German Navy which had previously been preserved covertly under civil ministries. The principal tasks of the German fleet during this period were the preservation of German interests in the Spanish sphere, the absorption of the Danube Flotilla following the seizure of Austria in 1938, and co-operation with other services in the seizure of Memel on the 28th March, 1939.

37. At home, the Navy started a policy of preparing the German merchant marine for its part in a possible war, and of encouraging the German people as a whole to become "sea-minded".

38. In planning her naval construction up to the 35 per cent. of British strength allowed her by the London Naval Treaty Germany had two alternative to consider: the naval staff could assume that war with England would take place within 5 years (*i.e.*, by 1940) and build up to their maximum strength by that date, or they could assume that war with England would not take place until 1942-45, in which case they could embark on a long-term programme aiming at maximum strength by 1942-45, and accepting a weaker fleet in the intervening years.

39. Assured by Hitler that war with England was unlikely before 1942-45, the Naval Staff embarked on the long-term plan for her main naval programme and a short-term plan in support of her continental policy which necessitated considering France as a possible enemy (*i.e.*, *Scharnhorst* and *Gneisenau* were built as a reply to *Dunkerque* and *Strassbourg*), as a result of this policy Germany's naval strength at the outbreak of war was below the maximum allowed under the Treaty.

40. At the time of the signature of the London Treaty the German Naval Staff decided that their permitted capital ship tonnage should be allocated as follows: three pocket battleships, two battle cruisers and three battleships. Immediately after abrogation of the Treaty in the Spring of 1939 a further four battleships were ordered. Thus it was not until this date that the Fuehrer ordered full-scale naval preparations for war against England, but it was then too late for these ships to be ready for such a war unless it could be postponed until 1942 at the earliest.

41. The failure to build a large force of destroyers was largely attributable to constant changes in design, arising from efforts to build types capable of fulfilling the many and diverse tasks which would fall to them. In addition great technical difficulties with high pressure steam, further delayed their construction programme.

42. Thus when war broke out in 1939 the German Navy was much less prepared for such a war than the German Army or Air Force.

## IV.– GERMAN AIR PREPARATIONS.

43. Von Seeckt's biography contains interesting information regarding the part he played in the development of the future Luftwaffe. The German Flying Corps was dissolved in May 1920, and in his farewell order to it, von Seeckt said he did not give up hope that it would again rise, and meanwhile its spirit would live. Although no expert in the subject, he was the mainstay in keeping this spirit alive. His first step was to form a special Air Group inside the Reichswehr Ministry under Captain Wilberg, an experienced ex-Flying Corps officer, and he used his authority to shield this Group in the face of most grave Cabinet pre-occupations. He strove therefore to keep at least a remnant of the former Flying Corps, as he believed that it would come to life again while those with practical air war experience were still available. In a short time he succeeded in building inside the "airforceless" Army a cohesive and well-led air force skeleton which could not be discerned from without. Inside the Reichswehr Ministry there were air cells in the various offices and inspectorates and a controlling air centre in the Truppenamt (General Staff) itself, while in the Wehrkreise there were air advisers and other bodies. Against the wishes of the Army still in process of development, and despite grave doubts by its Personnel Branch, von Seeckt ordered it to accept 180 ex-flying officers specially selected by former air force commanders. The building up of the air personnel of the Officer Corps was, however, on so narrow a basis that it had to be undertaken by an experienced hand, and it was necessary for these officers to receive exceptional treatment and to be promoted into other branches – for whose duties they were partly untrained – otherwise promotion in their own sphere would have been too slow. Von Seeckt prevented attempts to engulf the Air Group by the Inspectorate of Mechanised Troops, and his farsightedness led him to conclude in a memorandum in 1923 that the future air force must become an independent part of the Wehrmacht. Wilberg, his head air adviser, was actively sustained by a few other officers, and despite obstacles inside and outside the Army they, led by von Seeckt, succeeded in their task.

44. Another measure which Seeckt introduced was to get his nominee, an experienced war-time air officer, retired Captain Brandenburg, made head of the Civil Aviation Department of the Ministry of Transport, despite strong opposition. In this case too he succeeded, and from then onwards the control and development of civil aviation took place according to military direction and in closest agreement with the R.W.M. In fact, Wilberg and Brandenburg were always at one, both as regards the objective and the determination to bring it about.

45. The Civil Aviation Department, the Lufthausa and various camouflaged military or naval air establishments were to a great extent staffed by ex-Flying Corps officers, who had no knowledge of civil aviation or commercial experience. An allied work of von Seeckt was his support by every possible means of gliding under the then Captain Student, later Air General in this war, who became head of the air technical group in the Waffenamt of the R.W.M. in 1920. In 1923 Germany obtained freedom over her own air, but these remained restrictive rules to prevent the construction of military aircraft. So von Seeckt persevered to retain and build up civil aviation and its industry. In 1926 the Paris "Air Agreement" abolished the above rules, but severe limitations were placed on the numbers of service personnel permitted to fly. Nevertheless this was circumvented and, to quote the writer of his life: "special measures by von Seeckt and the Transport Ministry enabled the Army to fly to the extent he desired, in order to build up the "silent" flying Group and other foundations for military aviation; the development of an efficient industry and of air force equipment went on despite all hindrances and difficulties. Seeckt's sowings were reaped later".

46. On the Naval side the outline history referred to in the preceding paragraph is of value. In the portion covering the years 1920-24, the Chapter dealing with evasions of the Treaty refers to preparations of crews of the future Luftwaffe, obtaining airfields, aircraft construction, training of pilots and instructions in passive air defence. The next portion on the years 1925-32 specially refers to the preparatory work in establishing a Naval Air Arm. The steps taken included the founding of the Aircraft Company "Severa", later known as Luftdienst G.m.b.H. (supposed to be a commercial company); the setting up of the Naval Flying School at Warnemunde and the Air Station at List, the training of sea cadet candidates in aviation, air co-operation, so-called "air defence flights", technical developments, including planning experimental stations, trials, flying boat developments (D.O.X., &c), catapult aircraft, armament, engines, ground organisation, aircraft torpedoes, &c.

# APPENDIX II.

# THE GERMAN POLITICAL SCENE.

## THE MEN AROUND HITLER.

### Summary.

No changes in the constellation of leaders under Hitler exerted an obvious major influence on German strategy or foreign policy, because Hitler remained the dictator and undisputed ruler of National Socialist Germany right up to a few days before his death. This was much more so than was often assumed by Allied assessments made during the war. Even the most powerful of his subordinates acted only by Hitler's grace, and subject at any moment to arbitrary interference. Many of the policies attributed to Himmler, Goebbels or Ribbentrop originated from Hitler himself. The "technical" Ministers did not see Hitler for years at a time, and had no share in the making of current policy. Their influence was confined to the expression of their views, often on matters outside their competence, to those who had the ear of Hitler.

### The Position of Hitler.

2. The Centre of the National-Socialist régime throughout its existence was the person of Hitler. In the first place, the "Leader principle" made Hitler personally responsible for every act of State. It gave Hitler the right to intervene at will in every department, which he exercised much more often in some fields than in others, but everywhere often enough to make it clear to even the highest of his lieutenants that they could only carry out a policy of their own subject to the risk of being overruled at any moment. The way to achieve practical independence was, therefore, to win and

retain Hitler's confidence, and the greatest power belonged to those who were most in favour at the Fuehrer's Headquarters.

3. This centralisation of ultimate authority in Hitler's hands had the effect of weakening at all lower levels any sense of responsibility for co-ordination of policy. This did no harm so long as Hitler himself actually supplied the necessary co-ordination, but in the course of the war this gradually ceased to be the case, as his time and attention were increasingly taken up with purely military matters. Some of the specialist Ministers in charge of civilian departments, discussing the situation among themselves, agreed that what Germany needed was a second-in-command (for whom the title "Reich Chancellor" was suggested) to provide the necessary co-ordination of civil policy, but it does not seem that anyone dared to make this suggestion to Hitler himself. It had actually been intended at the beginning of the war that Goering should perform this function, but Goering seems to have lost interest in all his official duties except those of commander-in-chief of the Luftwaffe, and in the latter years of the war devoted himself increasingly to his art collections and luxurious private life.

4. Though every allowance must be made for the natural disposition of German leaders now in Allied captivity to seek to avoid retribution by shifting all possible blame to Hitler, it seems that many details of National-Socialist policy which had been commonly attributed to Goebbels may well in fact have been laid down personally by Hitler, who took a continuous interest in propaganda and conferred on the subject with Goebbels regularly. There is even more evidence suggesting that the systematic cruelty of the S.S., so often laid to Himmler's account, was actually encouraged by a sadistic streak in Hitler's character rather than in Himmler's, Himmler being essentially a "professional" with no sentimentality about the choice of means to achieve a given end but also with no love of cruelty for its own sake, but with extreme ruthlessness in action.

5. The "technical" Ministers (Food, Finance, Transport, Economics, Labour, Posts), with exception of Speer, seem not to have seen Hitler for years on end, after the practical suspension of the Cabinet system at the end of 1937 and particularly after the outbreak of war. These technical Ministers seem to have been kept in the dark about the future strategical plans and in April 1941, several months after the attack on Russia was decided, we find the Finance Minister deducing German designs on Russia from an article in the German press.

6. The tendency of Ribbentrop, Himmler, or other leaders to seek peace with either the West or Russia remained a factor of no significance right up to April 1945. All "peace-feelers" were put out without Hitler's knowledge, in the hope that Hitler would take the opportunity if it were offered to him through such an initiative of his subordinates who seem to have acted independently of, and in rivalry to, each other in favour of making a separate peace in the East. A tendency is believed to have prevailed among both SS. and Party Leaders after the Allied break-through in Normandy. This was decisively reversed by January 1945, but it is doubtful whether Hitler took this into account in April when ordering the switch of German forces from West to East. Hitler is not known to have despaired before the 22$^{nd}$ April, and even then he refused to consider negotiation with the West until the Battle of Berlin had been decided.

## *External and Internal Influences on "Palace Politics".*

7. High politics were palace-politics. The importance of individuals depended on their personal influence over Hitler and on the strength of the "private armies" which each controlled. Individuals with access to Hitler were able to speak on subjects other than those with which they dealt officially. There was nothing resembling a Cabinet system. As will be shown in Annex XIV below, dealing with the organisation of the German Government machine, the "Cabinet", the "Defence Committee" and the "Secret Cabinet Council" were little better than meaningless window dressing, and these bodies were without information and indeed hardly ever met after the outbreak of war.

8. The Régime was not inherently stable. Its existence needed to be maintained deliberately, and this put power into the hands of those who were essential to its maintenance. As soon as the Régime became generally unpopular, control of the security services (Gestapo, &c.) made Himmler inevitably the most important man in Germany after Hitler himself. The operation of the "Leader principle" not only united the whole system in subordination to Hitler, but at the same time divided it into a multiplicity of organisations and departments each owing personal loyalty to its own particular leader. This personal relation was cultivated on principle, by such devices as naming organisations after their leaders, as in the case of the "Organisation Todt" and the "Baustab Speer" and was applied not only to Party formations but even to the branches of the Wehrmacht, so that, just as the S.S. was encouraged in a special

devotion to Himmler, so the Navy was encouraged to look up to Raeder, and later, Doenitz, and (above all) the Luftwaffe to Goering. Each leader thus banded his own followers into a "private army", which (it was tacitly understood) would follow him in the event of an internal conflict. Though it was never known how far this would actually happen if the case arose, the threat was enough to give to those leaders who possessed such "private armies" a backing in their conflicts with rival leaders which was to some extent independent of their personal influence on Hitler. The standing of such leaders rose and fell with the standing of the organisations which they led. A striking case of this was the connection between the decline in prestige of the Luftwaffe, when German air raids on Britain ceased to fill the headlines and it was found impossible to prevent increasingly heavy air raids on Germany, and the decline of Goering's personal influence.

9. The expansion of the Waffen-S.S. into a separate armed service on a level with the Army, Navy and Air Force was justified by Hitler himself as a method of winning for the new police force, which Germany was to have after the war, that respect which the German people would only give to soldiers who had proved themselves. In fact it was plainly designed also to provide the nucleus of the new wholly National Socialist army which was to take the place of the old army with it Imperial traditions. Hitler clearly saw in it a force specially devoted to himself rather than to Himmler. Himmler perhaps came to think of it as his own private army, but, if so, this was one of his great mistakes, for he weakened the Allegemeine S.S., which was really devoted to him, by continuous transference of replacements to the Waffen-S.S., which in the stress of battle acquired a sense of comradeship with the Wehrmacht (increased by considerable dilution with conscripts who found themselves in the Waffen-S.S. purely by accident) and came to think of itself as non-political.

10. Though the hierarchy of Gauleiters and other local Party officials could hardly be described as a "private army", their central position in the political and governmental system gave them collectively such power that, by cultivating their support and making himself their spokesman, Bormann was able to provide himself with a backing similar to that afforded by a "private army". Inner circle observers have maintained that one of the weaknesses of Himmler's position was his inability, without the goodwill of Bormann, to control the actions of the Gauleiters in the field of administration. Himmler at first possessed this goodwill, but lost it later.

11. The survival of Goering as at least nominally the second personality of the Régime and designated successor to Hitler until the very last days seems to have been entirely due to his general popularity. At the Fuehrer's Headquarters his prestige sank to zero, because Hitler himself was so angry at the failure of the Luftwaffe that he is said to have treated Goering "like a guttersnipe", but S.D. home morale reports showed that, with the general public, he remained the most popular of all the National Socialist leaders, although, particularly in the heavily raided areas, his popularity declined in consequence of the failure of the Luftwaffe to prevent the steadily-increasing Allied attacks. Hitler was a semi-divine symbol, the other leaders mostly disliked, feared or despised – Goering alone was considered "human". He could not be publicly dismissed without excessive dangers to the stability of the Régime.

12. External influences operated only through their effect on the play of intrigue at the Fuehrer's Headquarters, and there were personalities whose authority depended upon nothing except Hitler's confidence. An outstanding example was Ribbentrop, who owed his position entirely to the fact that Hitler believed him to be the best available expert on foreign affairs, trusting an amateur who knew how to talk his language and flatter his preconceptions more than professional diplomats, whom he suspected of unreliability as a class. Goebbels also lived by his wits, which were sufficient to make him invaluable in a great variety of positions – as Minister of Propaganda, as Gauleiter of Berlin, as Chairman of the Inter-Ministerial Committee on Air Raid Damage Relief, and, finally, as instigator and director of the last "total war" drive after the 25th July, 1944. Rosenberg owed his authority to the influence of his philosophical ideas on Hitler. Todt and subsequently Speer enjoyed a political importance such as does not normally fall to the lot of technical experts because Hitler was always personally interested in grandiose technological projects, and because they impressed the Fuehrer with their honesty as well as competence. As usual at autocratic courts, there were also a number of figures at the Fuehrer's Headquarters who were important as favourites of Hitler, and had opportunities for exerting great political influence, although it is still obscure how far and in what directions that influence was actually exercised, because it was probably governed by no consistent principle except that of immediate personal advantage. One figure of this type was Hoffmann, Hitler's personal photographer, who was one of his intimates and with whom he is known to have spent long hours discussing the favourite post-war project of his later years, the erection of a gigantic museum at Linz. It does not appear that Hoffmann had any

political interests, but he was important as a channel through which Hitler could be reached. Another figure of the same kind was Hitler's personal physician, Morell, said to have been originally introduced to Hitler by Hoffmann.

## *Combination of Leaders.*

13. As at all autocratic courts, the political scene at the Fuehrer's Headquarters was a continually shifting kaleidoscope of temporary alliances between rivals for the autocrat's favour. But in most of these combinations it is impossible to trace any continuous line of development which affected the general course of the war or the fate of the Régime. A possible exception is to be found in the relations between Himmler and Bormann. Though it may be assumed that Bormann himself was consciously pursuing his own exclusive advancement from the first, he seems to have risen under Himmler's patronage, after the departure of Hess had given him the control of Hess's office but not Hess's title or prestige. A special connection with Himmler appeared in the fact that Bormann was the only high-ranking member of the Régime who in conversation with Himmler used the familiar "du". At the end of 1942 he was still generally believed to be in "Himmler's pocket". It seems not unlikely that Himmler thought that he could use Bormann as an instrument to win for himself control of the Party organisation. But Bormann played his own game, attached himself to Hitler rather than to Himmler, became Himmler's only real rival, and in the last weeks ousted him completely.

14. Combination with others was naturally most necessary to those whose position was not reinforced by any backing such as the possession of a "private army". A name which recurs continually in reports of temporary alliances is that of Goebbels, because Goebbels's ability made him always valuable as an ally, while he had no backing such as Goering derived from his command of the Luftwaffe and Himmler from his command of the S.S.

15. Major changes in the political constellation during the war were: the continuous decline of Goering to practical unimportance; the continuous rise of Bormann; and the rise of Himmler to the position of greatest power under Hitler, and his decline after November, 1944. The rise of Speer up to mid-1943 and his subsequent decline, though of great economic importance, was politically not important, except in so far as Speer sabotaged Hitler's scorched earth policy in the West during the last phase

of the war. Goebbels retained almost to the end, by dint of his intellectual ability, a position of great and constant influence. The power of Bormann and Goebbels was such that they were able to administer severe setbacks to Himmler, even at the height of his power.

16. In the last stages of the war it is clear that Himmler began to think of himself as a possible successor to Hitler. This was probably inspired by the belief that he alone was capable of dealing with a situation which had now apparently got beyond Hitler's control. His opportunity came after the abortive coup d'État of the 20th July, 1944. It will probably always be suspected, though perhaps never proved or disproved, that Himmler was aware of the conspiracy beforehand and allowed it to develop for the sake of the advantages which he hoped to obtain from it. Some of the conspirators certainly seem to have talked very freely about their intentions – they even sounded members of Himmler's own entourage as possible sympathisers – so that it would be a surprising failure of what was otherwise a very efficient security system if Himmler did not get wind of what was happening. Out of the suppression of the attempt Himmler got the post of Commander of the Replacement Army, which gave him for the first time a standing within the Wehrmacht. He was now at the summit of his power. Yet it would be quite mistaken to regard Himmler even at this period as the ruler of Germany. Hitler's position was unchallenged, and Bormann's influence unchanged, and Goebbels, on the very morrow of the 20th July, intrigued himself into the appointment of Commissioner for the Total War Effort. Himmler's resentment at this manoeuvre by Goebbels was extreme.

17. In October Himmler made the broadcast speech on the occasion of the establishment of the Volkssturm, which if it had happened in the earlier years of the regime, would certainly have been made by Hitler himself.

18. Here, however, Himmler had overreached himself. He did not allow for the fact that Hitler, always suspicious, had been made excessively so by the events of the 20th July and was now inclined to see disloyalty everywhere. It is also likely that Bormann pointed out that Himmler was now becoming dangerous. Himmler's name began to crop up everywhere in the last phase of the war. The new Volks-grenadier divisions were directly subject to his authority like units of the Waffen-S.S. He even ventured into the sphere of active military operations, taking personal command of the Army Group Oberrhein, and then of the Army Group Vistula, in an attempt to stem the Russian onslaught. It is known that Hitler did not like this, though it is not

clear whether his objection was to the mere fact of Himmler's assuming command, to the tactics which he adopted or simply to their failure. Himmler himself does not seem to have realised that he had made any mistake. He had taken into his own hands the task of saving Germany and seems by now to have thought of Hitler only as an obstacle to the achievement of a final settlement.

19. In the field of domestic policy, clashes between Himmler on the one hand and Bormann and Goebbels on the other, were threatening throughout the last 18 months of the war, but never came to a head. Here, lack of co-ordination by Hitler necessarily meant the triumph of the principles of Goebbels and Bormann, tending to conserve the character of the Party Régime with its corrupt "Bonzentum" and its technique of propaganda. There can be little doubt that this solution tended to postpone Germany's defeat, for if Himmler had achieved a radical change in these respects the immediate damage to the war effort would have been enormous. As it was, Himmler could never get beyond the preliminary stage of criticising details.

## *Independent peace-feelers.*

20. Not till mid-April, 1945, did Himmler, who considered himself Hitler's successor, decide that his oath of loyalty to Hitler must be broken and Hitler removed. In consequence he offered surrender to the Western Powers, but it does not seem that he was able, or had time, to do anything to hasten Hitler's disappearance. On the contrary, Hitler's distrust of Himmler, fanned by Bormann after Himmler's rise to eminence in 1944, now culminated in a total break, and the nomination of Doenitz, instead of Himmler, as the Fuehrer's successor. Himmler's bad reputation abroad on account of the association of his name with the Gestapo, the concentration camps, &c., was discussed and recognised by Himmler himself, who arranged for the liberation of a large number of Jews and connived at the escape of others, with the express intention of proving to the Allies that he was not what they believed him to be. When the telegram from Berlin was received in Flensburg announcing that Doenitz was chosen to be Hitler's successor, it clearly came as a complete surprise to Himmler, though he acquiesced and discussed the situation with Doenitz. But Goering was clearly better informed concerning the atmosphere at the Fuehrer's Headquarters, for his explanation of his unwillingness to abandon the position of designated successor is that he believed that otherwise Bormann (not Himmler) would be chosen.

## The Rise of Bormann.

21. Bormann seems to have been Hitler's real "evil genius". It does not seem that he would ever have been capable of taking command himself, as Himmler at the end proposed to do and could have done, for his influence was in the last resort always exerted through Hitler. But he represented at the Fuehrer's Headquarters the worst elements in the regime – the company of self-seeking gauleiters, &c. Having risen to power in Himmler's wake, he finally reached a position of equality with him. When Himmler took upon himself the actual direction of the last efforts in the North, Bormann was left alone to influence Hitler.

22. As Director of the Party Chancery he controlled the whole regional hierarchy of the Party, which became all-important in the last phase of the war, when Germany became in effect decentralised and all the most important administrative decisions were those taken by the Gauleiters. Bormann served also as Hitler's secretary, in which capacity he not only decided who could and who could not see Hitler but announced Hitler's decisions and was suspected of often attaching Hitler's name to what were actually decisions of his own.*

Germany's government was already described as a "Bormann dictatorship" in August 1943, but the description seems to have become increasingly accurate later. In the very last days Bormann seems to have combined with Goebbels in an effort to maintain their authority and that of the Party even after Hitler's death, for a telegram was sent to Doenitz requiring him to appoint Goebbels as Reich Chancellor, Bormann as Minister for the Party, and Seyss-Inquart as Foreign Minister; these instructions were disregarded by Doenitz.

## The Futility of the Men around Hitler.

23. Nearly all the important political figures with access to Hitler were astonishingly ignorant of Germany's true position and of realities in the outside world. This was no accident, since they owed their position in the system to qualities which made such defects inevitable. Similarly, the exclusive responsibility of Hitler for individual major decisions does not obscure the responsibility of the system as a whole for his decisions

---

* Bormann achieved immense advantage by adjusting his own hours of work and sleep to the extraordinary hours kept by the Fuehrer.

in the mass. In the long-term both Hitler and his lieutenants can be viewed only as parts of the whole National Socialist system.

24. Of the six important political figures who for a long period of time had serious influence with Hitler, one (Ribbentrop) was both of low calibre and ignorant of realities; one (Goering) was ignorant of the outside world and too indolent to apply his abilities on internal affairs; three (Himmler, Bormann and Goebbels) were outstandingly capable in their own spheres but were astonishingly blind to the realities of Germany's position: and only one (Speer) was both capable and aware of realities. It may be true that Hitler would not have tolerated men who were both able and courageous enough to tell him of realities. But Germany would have had a different kind of leadership if she had possessed a sufficient number of politicians both conscious of realities and courageous enough to speak out for them.

25. Goebbels, Himmler and the rest, dwelling within a system of palace-intrigue, conceived of government in the democracies as something similar, hampered only by the stupid interference of the crowd. Themselves actuated by considerations of power alone, they could hardly conceive the policy of other States in different terms. Because Germany was hostile to every other State, they believed in the hostility of all States to each other, and created the dogma of an "automatic" breach between Russia and the West. They had reached power in Germany by believing in their own propaganda, and they could not lose the habit. But in many cases, even if they had been able to approach intelligence with open minds, the intelligence which they received was tainted at the source, for in their system it was unwise to tell unpalatable truths.

# APPENDIX III.

# NAZI MACHINERY OF GOVERNMENT.*

## A – CONFUSION OF AUTHORITY.

### The Reich Cabinet (Reichskabinett).

The Reich Cabinet was never convoked by the Fuehrer during the war, either to advise, or to make decisions, or to receive information on new government policies from the Fuehrer. The Cabinet held its last meeting [in] November 1937. In early February 1938 there was a last brief conference of ministers, which was informed by the Fuehrer of personnel changes in the Reich Government. Legislation by the Cabinet was done by circulation of proposals in writing to the members (Schriftliches Umlaufverfahren) except where it had been replaced by other methods of legislation (such as decrees of the Ministerial Council of National Defence, Fuehrer Decrees, &c.).

### Consolidation of the Activities of Several Departments under Plenipotentiaries General (Generalbevollmächtigte).

2. In the interest of tighter control of government and administration, some Reich Departments were consolidated under one head at the outbreak of the war. The following consolidations occurred: -

---

* Information obtained by interrogation of Lammers, Chief of the Reich Chancery.

(a) Under the Plenipotentiary General for Administration (G.B.V. – Generalbevollmächtigten für die Verwaltung) were to co-operate: The Reich Ministers of the Interior, of Justice, of Science, Education and Popular Instruction, of Church affairs; further, the National Zoning Office (Reichsstelle für Raumordnung). The Minister of the Interior was the G.B.V.

(b) Under the Plenipotentiary General for Economic Affairs (G.B.W. – Generalbevollmächtigter für die Wirtschaft) were to operate: the Reich Minister of Labour, the Reich Minister of Food and Agriculture, the Reich Forestry Office, the Reich Minister of Finance (as far as war financing was concerned), and the Reich Minister of Transportation (as far as civilian traffic was concerned). The Minister of Economics was G.B.W.

(c) Under the Chief of the OKW were to operate, for military traffic problems only, the Reich Minister of Transportation and the Reich Postal Minister.

Unconsolidated remained: the Ministries of Foreign Affairs, of Popular Enlightenment and Propaganda, and of Finance (except for war financing).

## Ministerial Council for National Defence (Ministerrat für die Reichsverteidigung).

3. A Fuehrer decree created this Council at the outbreak of the war. It consisted of:-

Reich Marshal Goering, chairman.
Deputy of the Fuehrer, Hess, later replaced by the Chief of the Party Chancery, Bormann.
The Plenipotentiary-General for Administration.
The Plenipotentiary-General for Economic Affairs.
The Chief of the OKW.
The Chief of the Reich Chancery (executive member of the Council).

4. The Council's main task was the issue of legislative decrees. Unlike the Cabinet, this Council did not depend on the chairmanship of the Fuehrer; it was hoped that the small number of its members would expedite the creation of laws as required by the war. Lammers, as chief of the Reich Chancery, was made executive secretary (Geschaeftsfuehrer) of the Council, because in the Cabinet he also had to

look after the formal procedure of legislation, and could maintain liaison with the Cabinet and the Fuehrer.

5. During the first six or eight weeks of war, the Council met several times, did profitable work, and issued numerous decrees required by the outbreak of the war. These meetings did not concern themselves with major political questions. The Council especially abstained from major questions of foreign policy. According to Lammers, the Fuehrer omitted the Foreign Minister from the Council advisedly, and held it sufficient to have him consulted on topics which touched on foreign policy. (See also paragraph 8 below.) The same applied to the field of propaganda.

6. No purely military questions were considered by the Council. Only the chairman was authorised to convene it. During the later course of the war the Council did not meet. In its stead, however, the chairman convened several meetings of the members of the Council with large numbers of representatives of the government party, and business. These meetings, however, did not adequately replace meetings of the Council, and were later abandoned. The Council held its last meeting in December 1939. From then on it exercised its legislative powers only by circulation of proposals in writing (Schriftliches Umlaufverfahren). But even that was limited, as the Fuehrer did not like legislation by the Council and turned more and more frequently to regulation of war-essential problems through Fuehrer decrees. The Council's procedure in writing was considered too slow and dragging, and often did not satisfy war requirements.

7. The Chairman of the Council (Goering) had no personal authority to issue decrees by virtue of that office. However, he was able to handle alone many problems which should otherwise have come up before the Council, since he was simultaneously Commissioner for the Four-Year Plan and thus had extensive controlling and directive power over agencies of the Government and Party. These far-reaching powers of the Commissioner of the Four-Year Plan also prevented the office and duties of the Plenipotentiary General for Economic Affairs from having effect from the very beginning, and made them illusory. Goering, in fact, could give instructions to the ministries concerned either personally or through his subordinate Commissioners-General in the various business fields; thus he could countermand instructions of the Plenipotentiary General for Economic Affairs (Funk); and he could even give Funk instructions in the latter's capacity as Reich Minister of Economics and President of the Reichbank. Funk, inversely, had no influence over the Four-Year Plan. A possible

solution, which lay in appointing the Plenipotentiary General for Economic Affairs simultaneously Deputy Commissioner for the Four-Year Plan, did not materialise. As early as late 1939 it was therefore found necessary to restrict the jurisdiction of the Plenipotentiary General for Economic Affairs to two fields: the Ministry of Economics and the Presidency of the Reichbank. Funk, of course, enjoyed that jurisdiction any way, since he himself was the Minister of Economics and the President of the Reichbank, The balance of the former jurisdiction of the Plenipotentiary General for Economic Affairs was transferred to the Four-Year Plan. The office of the Plenipotentiary General for Economic Affairs thus virtually ceased to exist, although it was never expressly abolished, and remained *pro forma*.

## Secret Cabinet Council (Geheimer Kabinettsrat.)

8. This Cabinet Council was created in 1938 by a Fuehrer decree published in the Reich Law Gazette. Its chairman was von Neurath, who had just been relieved for the office of Foreign Minister. The Council was to advise the Fuehrer in foreign policy. Only the Fuehrer had the authority to convene it. He never did.

## Encroachment upon Governmental and Administrative Jurisdiction through the Appointment of Special Plenipotentiaries (Sonderbevollmächtigte), &c.

9. The Fuehrer had a tendency to eliminate Reich Ministers from certain fields which were close to this heart, and to appoint Reich Commissioners, Reich Plenipotentiaries-General, Inspectors-General, &c. This was appropriate to the attainment of specific purposes in certain cases – *e.g.*, the appointment of an Inspector-General for the Reich Capital. Yet these appointments had unpleasant results in one respect, particularly as their number grew in the course of the war. They disturbed the smooth operation of the governmental and administrative machinery, and caused numerous sharp jurisdictional disputes. The assignment of the special commissioner and plenipotentiaries usually cut across the jurisdiction of several ministers, and responsibilities were shifted. Clear jurisdictional boundaries were missing, sometimes impossible to establish. Furthermore, the special commissioners and plenipotentiaries were usually directly subordinate to the Fuehrer and therefore thought themselves above the need of acting in accord with the minister

concerned. They were actually in a position to do that, since they had regular access to the Fuehrer, which most of the ministers did not have. The shifts in responsibility and jurisdiction which accompanied the appointment of special plenipotentiaries were really known only to the initiated, and were never sufficiently apparent to the outsider. Lammers states that it is small wonder, therefore, that the occupying Allied powers blame responsibilities on former German governmental and administrative agencies, "where such responsibilities do not belong". Furthermore, shifts were even less apparent to the outsider; they were clear only to the initiated, who knew or suspected that the man who was *de jure* in charge was faced with a competitor, usually more influential than himself.

10. The most striking instance of a *de facto* shift in authority was the relation between the Reich Minister of the *Interior* and the Chief of the German Police, at the time when these two offices were held separately by Frick and Himmler respectively. Although normally the police force is part of the interior administration, and acts as its executive instrument, the moment of Himmler's appointment to be its Chief. It finally gained such independence that it was able to give instructions and dictate policies to the interior administration. While the Reich Minister of the Interior, Frick, had thus lost real control over the police, to the outside observer Himmler still appeared as a State Secretary in the Ministry of the Interior, *i.e.*, as Frick's subordinate. Himmler's independent position was in accordance with the Fuehrer's wishes. On several occasions when Himmler and Frick had differences of opinion, Hitler instructed Frick, through Lammers, not to concern himself with police matters or to interfere with Himmler's activities. Himmler's powers gradually increased as the regime came to depend more and more upon the efficiency of its security services. In August 1943 he became Minister of the Interior, after the fall of Mussolini had made Hitler increasingly suspicious of possible revolt and proportionately anxious to strengthen his security system still further. Another case where the real distribution of authority was not what it seemed to the outside world was that of the Plenipotentiary General for Economic Affairs (see paragraph 2 (*b*) above), whose essential functions had all been usurped by the Commissioner for the Four Year Plan before he ever had a chance of exercising them. In the field of jurisdiction of the Reich Minister for Science, Education, and Popular Instruction, matters pertaining to the text books were entrusted to the Chief of the Fuehrer's Chancery of the N.S.D.A.P., Reichsleiter Bouhler. There was, however, nothing to show the outside world that the

Minister of Education had lost his normal responsibility for this essential part of the school curriculum.

11. The Reich Minister of Economics had lost his jurisdiction in the field of armaments, which received special treatment. At first much of his power passed to the military authorities, then to the Commissioner for the Four-Year Plan, and to the Reich Minister of Armament and Munitions. When the latter Ministry was later expanded to become the Ministry of Armament and War Production, the Minister of Economics lost all control over commercial production, and maintained control only over distribution. His control over foreign commerce, was disputed by the Foreign Office, who established that such control was their sole concern, particularly in the field of foreign commerce. The Minister of Economics thereafter retained only the technical execution of the policy decided.

12. The Chief of the Reich Chancery (Lammers) found himself restricted by two competitors: first, the Chief of Hitler's Chancery of the N.S.D.A.P., Reichsleiter Bouhler, then the "Secretary to the Fuehrer", Reichsleiter Bormann. Both agencies caused Lammers many jurisdictional disputes, and blurred the boundaries of his responsibility. This applies particularly to the Secretary to the Fuehrer whose appointment largely put an end to Lammers' personal conferences with Hitler on matters pertaining to this field. The conferences were replaced by written instructions passed on by Reichsleiter Bormann. It was up to Lammers to defend these to outsiders as decisions of the Fuehrer, so that it was naturally assumed that he had personally obtained these decisions from Hitler.

## Government of Occupied Territories.

13. Although extensive powers in all fields seemed to be the prerogative of the Reich Commissioners and Chiefs of Civilian Administration in the occupied territories (Norway, Netherlands, Alsace, Lorraine, Luxembourg, &c.), they were successively and severely restricted by the following: -

(a) The Armed Forces.

(b) The Commissioner for the Four-Year Plan, who had extensive powers to issue decrees and instructions.

(c) The Chief of German Police, who acted independently and directly in his field, and frequently omitted the prescribed contact with the Reich

Commissioners and Administrative Chiefs. Himmler had similar authority in his capacity as Reich Commissioner for the Strengthening of Germanhood.

(d) The Plenipotentiary General for Man-power, Sauckel, who also operated independently in such territories, and often without reference to the Reich Commissioners and Administrative Chiefs.

(e) Reich Minister Speer, for technological problems of railroads and postal service.

In matters handled by the above agencies (*a-e*), the Reich Commissioners or Chief of the Civil Administration concerned had no say or responsibility. On the other hand, these officials were directly subordinate to the Fuehrer and thus independent of the Central Reich Authorities. Hence the latter could put through their measures, as pertaining to the whole German sphere of interest, only after negotiations with the Reich Commissioners or Administrative Chiefs, or by express order of the Fuehrer.

14. What has just been said about the Western occupied territories applies in like measure to the occupied Eastern territories, which were consolidated under the Reich Minister for the Occupied Eastern Territories, Rosenberg. His competence and responsibility were generally subject to the same restrictions as those of the Reich Commissioners or Chiefs of Civil Administration elsewhere.

15. The position which Himmler held since 1939 of "Commissioner for the Consolidation of the German Racial Element" was as much an acknowledgement of his special interest in racial questions as an off-shoot of his security duties, but the way in which he used in practice the indefinite powers which it gave him was in line with his policy elsewhere. He did not attempt to supersede or take over the regular German administration (civil or military) in German occupied Eastern Europe, but set up his own independent S.S. organisation, which was responsible only to himself, and carried out his policies without reference to the policy of the administrative authorities. Himmler could always justify this practice as a security check, to ensure that the local authorities were always aware that they were subordinates not sovereigns. "Consolidation of the German Racial Element" was always interpreted by Himmler as closely connected with police measures against the recalcitrant native population, as that it was seldom clear in which of his two capacities he was acting.

# B.– CO-OPERATION BETWEEN STATE AND PARTY CHANCERIES.

## *1933-end 1937.*

16. As long as meetings of the Reich Cabinet were still held (till late 1937), Hess, as Chief of the Party Chancery, had the right to participate in the Cabinet meetings but did not always use it. During that period co-operation between Reich and Party Chanceries was loose but difficult; Hess was hard to reach, there was no continuous connection, and liaison was mostly by correspondence.

## *1937-1945.*

17. From 1937 to 1941 (the year when Bormann took over the Party Chancery) there was increasing interference by the Party Chancery in administrative and personnel matters. With this the need for close co-operation increased, and when Bormann took over, Lammers tried to establish close co-operation with him. Bormann was in the stronger position of the two, since the Party had the right to interfere in State matters but not *vice versa*. *De jure* the Party had no right to anything beyond being heard in matters of State. In fact, however, it exceeded this right and interfered constantly in such matters as appointments, promotions of higher officials, &c. At times appeal was made to the Fuehrer's decision.

# C.– HOLDING OF OFFICES IN STATE AND PARTY.

18. The reasons for abolishing the simultaneous holding of offices in the State and in the Party, as presented by Lammers, are described below –

    (a) Hitler did not want complete union between Party and State. He considered the Party the dynamic and political force driving the State to action; the State and administration were static elements. A personal union was to exist in the Fuehrer himself, and down to Gauleiters (inclusive), who were simultaneously Oberpräsidenten. In practice, the Gauleiters took over all control of administrative matters and did not confine themselves to directing overall policy as intended by Hitler. Unification in fact, went further down than intended, and led to personal union of State and Party functions on such lower levels as those of Kreisleiters and Lanraete. This did not work out at all well, because the people in dual function could choose in any one instance whether to act as Party of State functionaries and thereby bypass Party and State as they wished. Further, the Party drove its men to radical and brutal measures. It produced, and even liked, friction between Party and State. If, in a district, Kreisleiter and Landrat harmonised, the Kreisleiter was likely to be kicked out.

(b) In the last months of the war many Party functionaries had lost their jobs in territories freed or occupied by the Allies, and many former Kreisleiters became Landraete.

(c) Generally speaking, the co-operation between State and Party agencies depended on personalities in individual districts. Since 1944 a number of changes took place among officer holders, but time was too short to observe in what way this affected co-operation between Party and State.

# APPENDIX IV.

# THE MACHINERY OF JOINT COMMAND.

## *The development of OKW and OKH throughout the war.*

The preparations for the campaign against Poland, as it was originally planned, brought out the difficulties of the organisation of the High Command. In the spring of 1939 Hitler ordered the OKW and the High Commands of the three services to complete by the middle or end of August their preparations for a campaign to reduce Poland and to take Danzig and the Corridor. The OKW then outlined the strategic objectives in accordance with Hitler's general directives and the three Service High Commands proceeded to make their plans. Later, the three services, in the presence of Keitel of the OKW, laid their plans before Hitler, who ordered several modifications. Halder has stated that the OKW directives were those formulated in the first place by the Chief of the Army General Staff, which were then written up by OKW. Thus, OKH received back the work done by the Army General Staff as an order, with the rubber stamp of the OKW. This procedure was followed until almost the end of 1941 and was the characteristic solution of the dispute between OKW and OKH on the responsibilities of direction.

2. Mobilisation was achieved smoothly. The zero-hour fixed by OKW for the crossing of the frontier was postponed by Hitler for some days, for political reasons, about eight hours before operations were due to start. This considerably embarrassed OKH and caused them to complain that the Supreme Command was not aware of the practical difficulties involved. The OKW and the High Commands of the services split into their forward and rear echelons and the campaign proceeded. Commander-in-Chief Army reported about twice a day by telephone to Hitler on the course of the

operations. Apart from this, the Ops. Staff of the OKW was kept informed morning and night by the operations Branch of the General Staff, and each day, the Army contributed its share to the OKW official communiqué.

3. Occasionally OKW interfered in the conduct of operations, as for example, when German troops were withdrawn before the entry of the Russians into East Poland. The OKH found it difficult to carry this out in areas where the troops were still fully engaged, and again ascribed the difficulties to OKW's ignorance of practical considerations.

4. During the last days of the Polish campaign the Higher Commands of Germany entered on the first of their many internal conflicts. The subject under dispute was the administration of occupied Polish territory. OKH had formulated a military administration for Poland. OKW steered a middle course between OKH and Hitler. The latter refused to allow a military administration, and set up the General Government under Frank, excluding both OKW and OKH from control of the occupied territories. Moreover, Hitler was able, by means of the Party machine, to deflect much of the credit resulting from the success of the Polish campaign from the Officer Corps and thus to prevent their power from increasing.

5. As soon as the Polish campaign was completed Hitler demanded that the campaign in the West should begin in October 1939. Brauchitsch, Commander-in-Chief, Army, opposed this demand for the following main reasons: -

(i)  the Army was neither sufficiently reconstituted nor well enough equipped for the war in the West;

(ii) there was no plan of operation in existence due to the fact that several important political factors, such as the neutrality of Holland and Belgium, had not been decided.

The process of planning began, and, as in the Polish campaign, it followed the now accepted course. The Army General Staff drew up the drafts, OKW amended them on the basis of Hitler's recommendations and the OKW issued them as directives to the services. It was characteristic of the relationship between OKW and OKH that so far as the "side-shows" in Norway and Denmark were concerned the Commander-in-Chief Army and the Army General Staff received no final notifications about the forthcoming attacks. They merely received an order to place the necessary personnel and equipment at the disposal of the OKW. The campaign in the West began, and was carried through, without any major change taking place in the structure or inter-relationship of OKW and OKH. At this time a much reduced forward echelon of OKW and OKH was with the Fuehrer in the Eifel. After the campaign was over, the form of administration in the areas occupied by the army was fixed by OKW upon Hitler's directives; in effect the military administration instituted by OKH was retained. The Army General Staff returned to Zossen from Fontainebleau in October 1940 and began at once to draft plans for the attack on Russia. Again, these plans, which were ready by about the end of January 1941, were accepted by the OKW and turned into OKW directives. This time, however, the directives went further than the General Staff plans, in that Finland became an "OKW theatre of war". OKH had to supply, equip and administer the requisite number of troops though the conduct of the operations in Finland was to be entirely an OKW concern.

6. When Italy attacked Greece in October 1940, the OKW were taken by sur-prise. Orders were given to OKH for armaments and equipment to be supplied to Italy. These were furnished by the Head of Army Supply in OKH, and Commander-in-Chief, Army, had little influence in what was undertaken. The German decision to attack Yugoslavia gave a new task to the General Staff already heavily engaged in the detailed planning of the campaign against Russia. Improvisation under pressure of time had to be undertaken. OKW accepted the hastily prepared plans of OKH and issued them as directives. The campaign was directed from the OKH Command Post at Wiener Neustadt, and the operations were strongly influenced by OKW. The occupation of Crete was entrusted by OKW to the G.A.F. and the Army scarcely came into the picture. Because of the political background and the necessity of co-operation with the Italians, the influence of OKW upon the military administration in Greece was very strong.

7. The campaign in North Africa had not absorbed much of the attention of OKH. It had been declared on OKW theatre from the beginning. Similarly, Norway was regarded as an OKW theatre. Thus, by the beginning of the campaign against Russia the elaborate machinery of command evolved at Hitler's instigation was already beginning to show signs of weakness. As the war spread and the thea-tres of war increased in number, the system, devised for a one-front war and so suc-cessful in the early stages against Poland and France, became less capable of dealing with developments. It was clear that the OKH would have its hands full with the direction of the Russian campaign. Therefore, operations in the subsidiary theatres

were controlled by the OKW, which, at the same time, continued to superimpose itself on the OKH on the Eastern Front.

8. Headquarters of OKH and OKW were transferred to East Prussia at the start of the Russian campaign. Still, there had been no major changes in the organisation of either command.

The differences between OKW and OKH began to mount as the Russian campaign progressed and Hitler played one off against the other, bringing especial pressure to bear upon Commander-in-Chief, Army. The ideas of the Operational Planning Staff OKW were essentially those of Hitler. Differences were frequently grave. The following provides an outstanding example of the difficulties thrown up by the system. Hitler, flushed with the successful opening stages of the Russian campaign, gave orders for about forty army divisions to be dissolved (the man-power to return to industry) and munitions production for the Army to be dramatically reduced. These orders were drafted without previous consultation with Commander-in-Chief, Army, and actually were announced by OKW direct to the head of Army Supply and Commander of the Home Army (Chef H. Rüst. u.B.d.E). This was a typical instance of the devastating effect of the application of the "Leader Principle", (Fuehrerprinzip). The dissolution of the divisions could not be carried out at all, and the order for reduction in munitions production was rescinded after about three weeks. In the short period that elapsed between the issuing of the order and its cancellation, the organisation for the production of munitions was thrown badly out of gear.

9. A series of military reverses set in soon after the early and unusually severe beginning of the winter. The Army General Staff attributed these reverses to the strategically wrong decisions of OKW and Hitler, the bitter weather conditions, the tired condition of the German troops and the large-scale Russian counter-measures. Rundstedt, Commanding Army Group South, asked for his retirement and was granted it, without Commander-in Chief, Army, being consulted. OKW interfered more and more in the OKH conduct of the war. Replacements for the Army were restricted by OKW, while the G.A.F. and the growing Waffen-S.S. were given the cream of what was available. Hitler's special plenipotentiaries (Sonderbeauftragte) became more and more numerous and intervened at Army and Army Group level without the authority of Commander-in-Chief, Army. On the 19th December, 1941, Brauchitsch was relieved of his position as Commander-in-Chief, Army, and Hitler himself took over the position in addition to that of Supreme Commander of the Armed Forces.

10. Halder was retained as Chief of the Army General Staff, now subordinate directly to Hitler as Commander-in-Chief, Army. Hitler told Halder that the most important task now was the National Socialist education of the Army, a task which he intended to carry out for himself. He is reported to have said "I have a National Socialist Air Force, a Conservative Army, and an Imperial Navy". The relations between OKW and OKH thus, at a single move, became fundamentally altered, Hitler's action being his second major move to acquire more direct military control, his first having been the removal of Blomberg and assumption of the Supreme Command of the Armed Forces. Now, however, that the offices of Commander-in-Chief, Armed Forces, and Commander-in-Chief, Army, had been combined, the OKH was no longer able as a homogenous headquarters to represent the interests of the army in dealing with the OKW.

11. Though no basic changes in the structure of either OKW or OKH took place at this time, the assumption by Hitler of the Command of the Army entailed a fundamental change in the lines of responsibility. The representation of the Army point of view in the direction of operations rested with the Chief of the Army General Staff, who now reported direct to Hitler. The Head of the Personnel Directorate and the Head of Army Supply and Commander of the Home Army reported to Keitel, as Head of OKW, who alone, decided whether they might report personally or not to Hitler. The OKW, as Hitler had always intended, was steadily sapping the independence of the OKH. The daily Armed Forces communiqué was still issued by OKW, for the OKW operational planning staff received morning and evening reports from the Operations Branch of the Army General Staff. Every day, at noon, however, the Chief of the Army General Staff reported directly to Hitler. The Fuehrer had thus succeeded in forcing his way into the OKH, and concentrating control both of the OKW and the OKH in his own hands.

12. In one respect – the acquisition of replacements – the Army benefited by this union of the offices of Commander-in-Chief, Army, and Head of the State. Large numbers of G.A.F. field formations and of Waffen-S.S. formations began to appear. Moreover, the necessary increases in armaments and munitions for a spring offensive in 1942 were speeded under pressure from Hitler, who had set up, under Keitel, a special Group under General Buhle. This Group, which soon became an organ of Hitler's personal interference in the production and distribution of armaments, brought with it grave disadvantages. Hitler frequently believed that he could eliminate tactical

tensions, as they arose on a very long front, by despatching special equipments, such as anti-tank guns, by the shortest possible route. This equipment was flown with the utmost priority direct from factories to the front line, without any regard for the plans made by the Head of Army Supply. The result was that Hitler's efforts in this respect were frequently quite unco-ordinated with the supply, for example, of the appropriate ammunition.

13. By July 1942 the Army General Staff found itself in daily conflict with Hitler and the Operational Planning Staff of OKW over many basic questions, the chief of which were the strategic conduct of operations, replacements for the Army and the organisation of the Army. Hitler's distrust of the Army General Staff grew constantly and in September 1942 he relieved Halder of his post as C.G.S. and replaced him by Zeitzler. Hitler's entourage regarded his move as the triumph of OKW over the bigoted and conservative Army General Staff. Zeitzler was warmly recommended by Goering, and it was considered unlikely that Hitler would henceforth encounter bitter opposition from his Army General Staff.

14. The dismissal, first of Brauchitsch and then of Halder, meant that Hitler himself had taken over the reins of the Army. All his efforts and those of his staffs were now concentrated upon the Eastern theatre of Operations. The immediate effect of his assumption of control of the Army was that the Operational Planning Staff of the OKW faded out of the picture as far as operations in the East were concerned, and the Army General Staff lost its control of the Army forces, in all theatres other than the East, to the Operational Planning Staff of the OKW. Thus OKW gradually abandoned its main task as the supreme staff for strategical planning and for the surveying of the entire field of operations, becoming instead a second army operations section. Warlimont, who was Deputy Chief of the OKW Operational Planning Staff and Head of its operational departments, under Jodl, claims to have written the last military survey of the overall situation in October 1942, and states that this was the last comprehensive strategical study to be developed in written form by any German staff.

15. One of the most troublesome results of these developments, and one which persisted until the end of the war, was that Hitler's personal approval was required for the transfer to or from the Eastern Front of any Army division. This was usually obtained only after long deliberations and difficulties between Hitler and the two Chiefs of Staff, Jodl and Zeitzler. Jodl never tried to restore the original position of the OKW Operational Planning Staff. In the autumn of 1943 he issued an

order prohibiting all officers of his staff from further discussion of how the Supreme Command of the Armed Forces should be organised.

16. The limitation of OKW's activities in the strategic field was accompanied by further restrictions, which followed the dismissal of Halder. Zeitzler became the temporary favourite, and Keitel and Jodl were in disfavour for many weeks. At about this time the major part of the Defence Economics Directorate in the OKW was removed to Speer's Ministry. Thus the OKW suffered the loss of an important branch, which had been one of the reasons for the creation of an OKW in the early stages.

In the old Reich Ministry of War there had been a Defence Economics Staff (Wehrwirtschaftsstab), which, early in 1938, on the disappearance of the War Ministry, became a department of OKW and was renamed the Defence Economy and Armaments Directorate (Wehrwirtschafts-und Rüstungsamt) under General Thomas. Its major functions were the working out of detailed plans for economic mobilisation for war, the co-ordination of the requirements of the three services and the preparation of detailed directives for the armaments industry. The directorate had a regional organisation of Armaments Inspectorates (Rüstungs-inspektionen) and Armaments Headquarters (Rüstungskommandos). In January 1940 a new Ministry, called the Ministry of Arms and Munitions, was created, under Todt. In February 1942 Todt was killed and Speer took over the Ministry. Then began the process of centralising Germany's armaments production in Speer's hands. On the 7th May, 1942, almost the whole of the Defence Economy and Armaments Directorate, together with its vast regional organisation, was transferred to Speer. The very small remnant left in the OKW was, in May 1944, renamed the Field Economics Directorate (Feldwirtschaftsamt) and was concerned almost solely with the collation of economic information on occupied and foreign territories.

17. Early in 1943 Hitler instituted the National Socialist Indoctrination Staff into the OKW. This staff, under General Reinecke, in no way strengthened the authority of the OKW, because Hitler directed its activities himself, over the head of Keitel. Its purpose was to ensure the political education and unification of the Army.

18. OKW suffered the amputation of another major part of its organisation when two of the three which comprised the Intelligence Directorate (Abt. Ausland/ Abwehr) were removed from Canaris's influence in 1944 and became the responsibility of the Security Service under Himmler.

19. It was not until the Allied invasion of France in June 1944 that the direction of the war became ridiculously lop-sided. It was already obvious that the OKH was fully taken up with the Eastern front, and as other fronts opened they became the responsibility of OKW. The East was the OKH theatre, and as long as activity in other theatres was principally at sea or in the air, the OKW was theoretically competent to control the conduct of operations in these theatres. Even the African campaign, owing to its special character and the comparatively small land forces involved, did not present any important anomaly. The view of the OKH about the desert war probably corresponded to that expressed by the German soldiers on the Eastern Front "In Russia it is the German Army doing the fighting, in Africa it is only the fire brigades" ("In Russland kämpft das deutsche Heer, in Afrika die Feuerwehr"). The system which had applied to the African war was inherited by the campaign in Italy, and the influence of OKW is perhaps reflected in the appointment of Kesselring, an airman, as Commander-in-Chief, South-West. When France was invaded, however, there was now a major land war on three fronts. From this time on, the Chief of Army Staff – first Zeitzler, then Guderian and, lastly, Krebs, under Guderian – directed operations in the East, and the Chief of the Operational Planning Staff of the OKW, Jodl, directed operations in the other theatres. In the East, there was no effective subordination of OKH to OKW. The direct control of Hitler with OKH in the East and Hitler with OKW over the West and South saved an echelon in each case, but at the cost of breaking the symmetry of the machine. In practice the Fuehrer's Headquarters was combined with the command post of OKH for the Eastern front and OKW for the Western and Southern fronts at once. The organisation, the reinforcement, the armament and, up to a point, the supply of the armies in the West and South continued to be the responsibility of the rear echelon of OKH, but its forward echelon had no command responsibility there.

20. Such other reorganisation within OKH and OKW not yet mentioned was largely a matter of brining inter-service administrative control into the OKW from OKH. This worked in a limited number of cases, usually where the relevant OKH organisation had always, in effect, been responsible for all three services, as in the case of Transport and Medical Services.

21. Another reorganisation which took place during the war was in connection with the system of mechanisation in the army, and, later, within the Armed Forces as a whole. In early 1941 there was, in the General Army Directorate of the OKH, the

Inspectorate of Armoured Troops (Jn. 6), which at that time was responsible also for mechanisation questions generally. In the OKW was the General of Mechanisation (General der Motorisierung) who looked after the problem form the combined services point of view, and controlled Inspectorate 6 in his dual capacity as Commander of Inspectorate 6 in the OKH and General Mechanisation in OKW. When in late 1941, Inspectorate 12 was formed and took over the responsibility for all unarmoured M.T. from Inspectorate 6, the General of Mechanisation took over the Inspectorate 12 instead. In August 1942 he was transferred wholly to OKW under the title of Head of Armed Forces M.T. system (Chef des Wehrmacht-kraftfahrwesens – Chef W.K.W.). At the same time the office of Inspector of M.T. System (Insp. d. Kraftfahrwesens) was set up between Chef W.K.W. and Inspectorate 12 and later, in 1943, the Inspector was renamed General of Mechanisation. In brief, this was simply an enlargement of scope and transference of the main weight of authority from OKH to OKW.

22. Similar reorganisations took place within the Replacement System. The original system within the General Army Directorate (A.H.A.) of the OKH was that there were two departments, the Department for Army Setting-up and Armed Forces Replacement System, and the Department of Army Affairs, which together constituted the Army and Replacement System (Heer und Ersatzwesen – H.E.W.). They were, in effect, one department, the main part of which looked after the replacement for the Armed Forces as a whole. In 1941 this department changed its name to Branch for Replacements and Troops (Amtsgruppe Ersatz und Truppen) without changing its essential functions and internal organisation. It comprised two main sections, one for replacement (Abt. Ersatzwesen) and the other for Army Affairs (Truppen Abt.). The Head of the General Army Directorate still controlled the Branch, the head of which was, however, answerable to OKW for the control of the Replacement Section but to the OKH for the Army Affairs Section. In the Autumn of 1943 the title Defence Replacement Branch (Wehrersatzamt) came into being. On the 21st July, 1944, the whole branch moved into the OKW, where it was placed under Keitel. On the 8th May, 1945, the branch (Amt) became a Department (Abteilung) and was placed in the General Armed Forces Directorate (A.W.A.) for demobilisation purposes.

23. After 1942, the increasing influence of Guderian is a factor worth noting. With the growing importance of the tank arm in the war, Hitler appeared dissatisfied with the position in regard to armoured training and the supply of tanks. The training of armoured troops was in the hands of the Director of Training and took

its place without precedence in the training of all other arms. Inspectorate 6 existed to further the technical development and training of the arm. The supply of tanks was included within the ordnance supply system and was controlled by the Field Ordnance Controller (Feldzeugmeister) under the Head of Army Supply. The creation of a Head of Mobile Troops (Chef der Schnellen Truppen) had helped to further technical training and development, but the situation in the East called for more energetic measures. The post of General Inspector of Armoured Troops (General Inspekteur der Panzertruppen) was created in March 1943, for General Guderian. He was made directly responsible to Hitler and was given complete control of equipment, organisation and training of tank, Panzer Grenadier, Motorised Infantry, Armoured Reconnaissance, Anti-tank, and Heavy Assault Gun Units. This, coupled with his direct approach to Hitler, gave Guderian an army of his own. The Inspector of Armoured Troops, at Inspectorate 6, still continued to exist and represented Guderian's demands within the rear echelon of OKH. Guderian also had his man in the forward echelon of OKH, in the form of the Armoured Fighting Vehicles (A.F.V.) officer with the General Staff (Panzer Offizer beim General Stabe des Heeres), who advised the C.G.S. on A.F.V. questions. Guderian's Chief of Staff was General Thomale and when, in July 1944, Guderian became Chief of the General Staff, Thomale did much of the work previously done by Guderian as General Inspector. Nevertheless, Guderian did not relinquish the title and continued to be known both as C.G.S. and General Inspector of Armoured Troops. At the last hour, therefore, Guderian not only controlled the whole of the armoured arm, but as Chief of the General Staff had a prime rôle in the strategic conduct of the war.

24. The Army General Staff itself underwent changes, but none of them radical. When Halder departed in 1942, the Central Department was split. A very small staff continued to exist, under the same name, to deal with certain minor staff matters connected with General Staff Organisation. The main body of the department, however, still organised as before, and still under the same head, was renamed Dept. P 3 of the Army Personnel Directorate, but remained at G.H.Q. and under the control of C.G.S. The Organisation Department, despite the fact that in operational control the Army General Staff was limited to the Eastern Front, continued, nominally at least, to cover the organisation of the whole German Army. Its duties were still to supervise and assist the work of the staffs, the setting up and reforming of formations and the drawing up of establishments. In connection with its work of supervision, a good

example of the Department's efforts was its intervention in the tank supply questions in the Spring of 1942. The distribution of A.F.V.s at that time was seriously deteriorating and the Organisation Department took the matter out of the hands of the Q.M.G. and for the remaining months of the year arranged the distribution directly with Hitler, working on two-monthly plans. This ceased in March 1943, when Guderian's position as General Inspector of Armoured Troops was set up and he took over every aspect of the General Staff work concerning Armoured troops, their training, organisation, employment and equipment. Although nominally the Organisation Department covered all fronts, there was, in fact, a distinction between the Eastern Front on the one hand, and France and the area of the Home Army on the other, both of which were handled by the Commander of the Home Army. This was due in part to the position of the new OKW Army Staff (Heeresstab) under Buhle. The normal course would have been for Commander-in-Chief, Army, to have controlled all setting-up and refitting through the C.G.S., using the Organisation Department for the purpose. It was at this point that Buhle as Head of the OKW Army Staff, intervened. His post had been created to advise Keitel (and thereby Hitler) on the requirements of the Army. In effect, Buhle attended upon Hitler, ascertained his wishes concerning the Army, and passed them on to OKH, or to OKW also, if it were a matter affecting the other services. His functions, even so, should have been confined to communicating Hitler's wishes to the Organisation Department in the General Staff of the OKH and, if necessary, to the Organisation Department in the Operational Planning Staff of the OKW. Buhle endeavoured to cut out the Organisation Department of the General Staff as far as possible by sending on Hitler's directives on organisation and refitting directly to the Commander of the Home Army and even down to the General Army Directorate where formations in Germany were concerned. As France came under the sphere of the Commander of the Home Army as far as these matters were concerned, Buhle followed the same route. In January 1945 Hitler abolished the title "Head of Army Supply and Commander of the Home Army" (Chef H. Rüst.u.B.d.E.) and replaced it by "Commander of the Home Army" (Ob.d.E.). At the same time he ordered that all requirements of the Army for weapons and equipment would be handled by the Chief of Army Staff with OKW, General Buhle, who, in this respect would be directly responsible to Hitler himself.

25. Viewing the progress of the OKH and OKW as a whole throughout the war, it is obvious that the greatest changes occurred at two culminating points. The first

was the dismissal of Brauchitsch in December 1941 and of Halder in September 1942, followed by a period in which the concept of a Combined Supreme Command went by the board, leaving OKH in charge of operations in the East and O.K.W. elsewhere. The second was after the 20th July, 1944, attempt on Hitler's life. This reshuffle which followed this was mainly of personalities; the machine was already breaking down. The period was characterised firstly by the emergence of Guderian as Chief of the General Staff as well as General-Inspector of Armoured Troops, a position much more powerful than that of Jodl, Chief of the OKW Operational Planning Staff or of Keitel, Head of the OKW itself, who had long since been by-passed in the chain of command. It was characterised secondly by the increasing scope and power of Himmler, who, already powerful enough in his capacity of Head of the SS, and Police, now became commander of the Home Army and thereby stood next to Hitler himself in power.

26. The fusion of OKW and OKH which took place in April 1945 was a mere expedient, forced upon the German Command by Allied pressure. It contained the principal elements of both commands in order to maintain some form of centralised control. Some of this "new organisation" was never, in fact, carried out. The proposed Armed Forces Armaments Directorate (Wehrmacht-rütungsamt), a combination of the Field Economic Directorate of the OKW and the Army Ordnance Directorate in the OKH, never had time to form, other than on paper. The splitting of this fused command into two parts, a northern part at Flensburg, a Southern part at Salzburg, was the last desperate effort to maintain some sort of control over the country, torn asunder by the Allied Armies.

27. So far, this Appendix has mentioned only the OKW and OKH. That this is so fairly reflects the constitution and consequent deficiency of the Machinery of Joint Command.

28. The OKW was, however, conceived as a supreme command to direct in general terms, and to co-ordinate the efforts of the three Services and the nation for total war. To fulfil this function satisfactorily necessitated the effective representation of the three services together with adequate representation of the political, economic and other departments of State. Not only was this representation never achieved, but it was part of Hitler's deliberate policy to keep his military chiefs apart from his political chiefs so that he could play one off against the other. Furthermore, the OKW exercised Supreme Command and yet fulfilled the rôle of Hitler's personal staff. It

comprised a joint planning staff composed of members of the three services. Hitler laid down the major strategic policy to be followed, the OKW issued the directives to enable the policy to be carried out, both to the Services and the necessary Civil Authorities. The staffs of the three services worked out detailed plans which were finally submitted to the OKW for co-ordination and approval.

29. Although the OKW was staffed by officers from all three services, they had no function as representatives of their own ministries in which they had no status or responsibility.

30. Herein lay the principal weakness in the Machinery of Joint Command – although theoretically the three Services, were represented, the representation was in fact not effective – what is more, the need for effective joint representation does not seem ever to have occurred to the German High Command. For this reason the correct co-relation of policy, both as to the object to be achieved, the correct employment of the armed forces to achieve it, and the consequent allocation of priorities as between the three services was impossible.

31. At certain stages, particularly in the early part of the war, the Air Force was to some extent able to overcome this deficiency by means of Goering's direct access to the Fuehrer and his high standing in the State and its Councils. The Navy, however, had little say in the policy to be pursued, accepted its directives from the OKW and did its best to fulfil them. On occasions both Raeder and Doenitz made direct representations to the Fuehrer, but problems were considered jointly by the Chiefs of Staff. Outstanding results of this deficiency were the naval unpreparedness in 1939, lack of co-ordination of German Naval and Air War at the height of the German concentration on Allied shipping and failure to appreciate the importance to the Allies of the Mediterranean theatre, and to adjust the German strategy accordingly.

32. The foregoing makes no more than an attempt to sketch this particular aspect of the weakness of the Machinery of Joint Command. Examination will show that it affected the German War effort in every way.

# APPEDIX V.

# THE GERMAN SECRET INTELLIGENCE SERVICE.

## I.- HISTORICAL ACCOUNT.

The history of the German Intelligence Services during Hitler's dictatorship reflects the same confusions, the same personal factors and the same struggle between Party and State as does that of the general machinery of Government and Command. The following paragraphs will attempt to explain more specifically the intelligence organisations of the Third Reich and give some examples of their insufficiency. Special attention must be drawn to the place which was allotted to them in their final form as departments of Kaltenbrunner's Reichssiehrheits-hauptamt, one of the main controlling and repressive forces of the party-State.

## A.- THE ABWEHR.

### *The Intelligence Service of the OKW.*

2. Developed from the counter-espionage bureau which was the only form of intelligence department permitted to Germany by the Versailles Treaty, the Abwehr became (and remained till 1944) the main secret intelligence service of the OKW. By constitution, organisation and character it was primarily a service institution answering to service needs, though these were in the German tradition interpreted to include the domain of Wehrwirtschaft (War Economics). It formed an Amtsgruppe of the OKW. Its main departments, numbered I, II and III, dealt respectively with espionage on operational and economic matters, sabotage and subversion, and counter-espionage,

including military and some phases of internal security. Through its parallel department, the Amtsgruppe (formerly Amt) Ausland Abwehr, also subordinated to Admiral
Canaris, and responsible for the collation of non-secret and semi-secret reports from
service attachés, the Abwehr had some dealings with the Auswaertiges Amt, but it
was not equipped to provide sound secret political intelligence, nor yet to undertake
the surveillance of Germans at home and abroad without which a totalitarian State,
even in Germany, could not hope to survive.

3. The three sections were further sub-divided into appropriate sub-sections.
Inside Germany, and in occupied territory, the regional organisation of the Abwehr
was dependent upon, and parallel to, that of the OKW; there was an Ast in every
Wehrkreis in the Reich, and an Abwehrleitstelle with every Heeresgruppe in the
occupied countries. In neutral countries the Abwehr was represented by so-called
K.O.s (Kriegsorganisationen) attached to the German diplomatic missions. In addition to this static organisation, the Abwehr had mobile Abwehr Kommandos and
Trupps operating with the armies in operational areas. The type of organisation in
occupied territory was mobile or static according to the strategic needs of the area.
The mobile formations were organised separately for the duties of Sections I, II and III
and performed some duties, such as technical interrogations, which were not really
the province of a secret intelligence unit. Abwehr Abteilung II also disposed of a private army, the Brandenburg Division, used both as a pool for linguists and other specialists and a task-force for sabotage and subversion. This was returned to the OKH in
September 1944, to be reconverted into an ordinary Wehrmacht formation.

## Achievements.

4. The reputation of the Abwehr in Germany stood, at the beginning of the war, very
high; and this reputation was not seriously questioned until after 1941. Although our
knowledge of its activities is less complete during that time than later, it is clear that
such a reputation was not really due to its achievements. In fact, if the achievements
of the G.I.S. are analysed functionally, it is clear that (except for certain kinds of
shipping information in the Mediterranean area) Abt I was largely unsuccessful as a
source of secret operational material, though it had some successes in obtaining and
collating Allied technical information from trade and scientific journals; that Abt
II had some successes in areas where the Germans had a degree of effective control

which the Allies had not (*e.g.*, especially in the Balkans in 1941) or diplomatic supe-riority (*e.g.*, in Spain 1939-43), but was regularly unsuccessful in areas where these advantages were with the Allies (*e.g.*, in the Middle East and in liberated areas); and that Abt III was generally successful. Between the work of Abw Abt III and R.S.H.A. Amt IV (*i.e.* the Gestapo), the Allied intelligence services in the Low Countries were deeply penetrated at the beginning of the war, and throughout the history of resist-ance movements in occupied territory there were many instances of effective German penetration, some of them on a large scale (*e.g.*, in Holland in 1944). It must be remembered, however, that this success was achieved mainly on the agent level, and that the G.I.S. learnt, or at least pieced together, very little about the higher level organisation of the Allied Intelligence Services.

5. In the early years of the war, the Abwehr lived on the success of the German armies (which was naturally taken to imply good intelligence), and on the success of its own counter-espionage, which, as stated above, was considerable. With the turn of the tide of war in 1942, the achievements of the G.I.S. assumed greater importance to the Germans, and its failures were submitted to greater criticism. These failures were reg-ular and conspicuous, and, aided by certain secondary causes, led to the complete col-lapse of the Abwehr, which was absorbed by Amt VI of the Reichssicherheitschauptamt (R.S.H.A.), or central office of Himmler's Sipo and S.D.

## B. – THE S.D. AND THE GESTAPO.

6. In the early years of its existence, the Nazi Party was concerned primarily with combating opposing political parties and with the penetration of State institutions, amongst them the Police. However, it was not until 1931 when the influence of the Party had become so great that its ultimate assumption of power seemed probable, that any steps were taken to form a centralised political intelligence service. In that year Himmler entrusted this task to Reinhard Heydrich, who by 1932 had organised a Press Information Service within the ranks of the S.S.: - an organisation which later assumed the title of Sicherheitsdienst.

7. The Sicherheitsdienst remained to the very end a Nazi Party institution, though with the passing of the years its rôle underwent a fundamental change. For after the assumption of power by the Nazis in 1933 the emphasis was no longer on intelligence

but on repression; and as a result of the taking over by the Nazis of all existing police services, a far more formidable organisation emerged in the shape of the Gestapo, originally the political police of Prussia under Goering and later to become under the direction of Himmler the most powerful organ of repression within the State.

8. By 1936 the position was more or less crystallised. Himmler, in his newly-appointed capacity of Chief of the German Police, had achieved his long-desired objective of forming a centralised Police Service under Party control. The Gestapo was fused with the Criminal Police to form the Sicherheitspolizei, which was placed under Heydrich, so that the Gestapo and S.D. were brought finally under unified control. The Gestapo was now responsible for the functions of all political police forces throughout Germany and a decree of February 1936 gave it authority to arrest and imprison persons without reference to the courts of law.

9. Although the Sipo and S.D. were now nominally under one head, their attempts at collaboration were far from harmonious. During the early years of power, when Himmler and Heydrich were striving to achieve mastery of the police services, little encouragement had been given to the S.D., and if the Party had achieved supremacy, it was not through the efforts of its own organisation. Formed to work on the same spheres of interest as the Gestapo, but yet without any executive power, the S.D. had by 1938 developed into a mere intelligence reporting agency, while at the same time it was developing a subsidiary interest in the establishment of an Auslandsnachrichtendienst (Foreign Intelligence Service). In spite of the efforts of Heydrich to merge the two departments into one, they remained stubbornly independent and each organised its own information service, which spread step by step over the fields of internal intelligence (Innere Gefner), counter-intelligence (both in the countries bordering Germany before the outbreak of war and subsequently in the occupied territories), and later foreign intelligence. Still further centralisation as a result of the creation of the R.S.H.A. in 1939 did nothing to dispel the atmosphere of rivalry arising out of the struggle between conflicting personalities for personal prestige and personal power. On the one hand the officials of the Gestapo were professional policemen, who doubted the ability of the amateurs of the S.D. to compete with them in police matters, while the "Alte Kaempfer" of the S.D. resented the intrusion of these outsiders, many of whom were not even members of the Party.

10. The division of functions at the time of setting up the R.S.H.A. in 1939 was along the following lines. Amt I was a central department dealing with administration

and personnel. The former S.D. Hauptamt was split up to form three new Aemter: - II, III and VI, of which Amt II was an unimportant research section, Amt III supervised all aspects of German life and Amt VI became a somewhat enlarged Auslandsnachrichtendienst. The Sicherheitspolizei on the other hand resolved itself into Amt IV (Gestapo) and Amt V (Kripo).

11. The authority of the R.S.H.A. was exercised in Germany through a chain of Stapostellen, Kripostellen and S.D. Abschnitte. The activities of these stations were co-ordinated by an I.d.S. (Inspekteur der Sipo und des S.D.) who was in turn subordinate to the Hohere SS and Polizeifuehrer, Himmler's personal representative in each Wehrkreis. In the occupied countries the power was vested in the person of a B.d.S. (Befehlshaber der Sipo und S.D.). Amt VI, however, remained independent of this organisation, and its stations abroad usually reported direct to Berlin. Only in exceptional cases was an Amt VI representative attached to the local S.D. Abschnitt.

12. The most interesting point in this reorganisation is the division of the S.D. into Amt III and Amt VI. With the executive power finally in the grasp of Amt IV, Amt III's functions were limited more and more to reflecting public opinion and enabling the regime to keep in touch with a public that had no other means of self-expression, for with gradual identification of Party and State, criticism of the State had become to all intents and purposes criticism of the Party and thus a matter within the sphere of Amt IV. On the other hand, considerable progress was made with the expansion of Amt VI, which, although continually hampered in matters of personnel through the jealousy of the other Amtschefs, developed rapidly after 1941, thanks to the energetic leadership of Schellenberg. The latter, who was to become the dominating figure in the intelligence world after Canaris' dismissal, had many grandiose schemes for setting up a unified German Intelligence Service (Geheime Meldedienst), but they matured too late and by the end of the war Amt VI had little to show for its efforts save a few ineffective networks in neutral countries and some interesting preparations for espionage work through commercial undertakings.

## *Achievements.*

13. Its achievements can be summed up under the following two headings. It had developed a technique superior to that of the Abwehr for penetrating Allied and neutral embassies, and it had gained a name for itself through the spectacular sabotage and

terrorist activities organised by Skorzeny. In all other respects, save that of repression and counter-espionage, the R.S.H.A. proved itself to be almost totally ineffective.

14. The successes of the Gestapo both in counter-intelligence and generally in the repression of conspiracy and unrest were considerable. As in the Abwehr, so on a much larger scale in the R.S.H.A., the natural advantages were all on the other side of the defensive, rather than of offensive espionage; and better information was in fact obtained by the use of penetrating agents than by the use of direct informers. As an example it is worth noting that the Gestapo, by questioning in the interest of security German workers and technicians returning from Russia, had a less inadequate picture of Russia's war potential in 1941 than either the Abwehr or Amt VI; in June 1944 both the Gestapo and the Military counter-espionage units in the field, by the penetration of French resistance movements, could infer in the imminence of D-day which Amt VI and the old Abwehr had failed to predict. Between 1941 and 1944 the Gestapo succeeded in penetrating many of the resistance movements in the West and in destroying by penetration at least one effective Russian espionage network. As will be explained later the combined units of the Sipo and S.D. in occupied countries were the most closely integrated and successfully organised of all R.S.H.A. Stations.

# C.- THE BREAKDOWN OF THE ABWEHR AND ITS FUSION WITH THE R.S.H.A.

15. The period of crisis which led to the fall of the Abwehr lasted from November 1942, when the Allies landed in North Africa (Torch), till June 1944, when they landed in France (Overlord), and was directly connected with its failure in respect of Allied strategic intentions over this period. After the summer of 1944, the relative strategic and material situation of the belligerents was such that good or bad intelligence could only have a tactical significance.

16. It is therefore significant that neither Torch, nor Husky, nor Overlord, was correctly forecast by the Abwehr, which, on the contrary, drowned the OKW with misinformation, sometimes invented, and often deliberately supplied by the Allies. This uniform record of failure was the prime cause of the collapse of the Abwehr, though it should be remembered that the responsibility for failing to appreciate Allied intentions lies most heavily upon the Planning Staff of OKW, who had many other

sources of intelligence at their disposal and should not have relied upon secret intelligence alone. Secondary causes were the growing and inescapable evidence of financial corruption and political disaffection among its members, and the competition of Himmler's S.S. intelligence service, which ultimately replaced it. The fall of the Abwehr was rendered slow and gradual by other secondary causes; and, in particular, the personal success of Canaris in Spain. These successes enabled Canaris to survive the preliminary purges of the Abwehr, and when he fell (February 1944) a change of policy in Spain was one of the immediate causes of his fall.

17. The Abwehr's record of sabotage in the same period was no higher. An elaborate plan to leave saboteurs in all evacuated areas in the Mediterranean, which was projected at this time, was afterwards admitted to have been a total failure.

18. At the same time the increasingly personal direction of the war and of internal German affairs by Hitler was intensifying the duplication of Party and State mechanisms; and amongst the Party directorate who advised him, Himmler succeeded for a time in gaining a preponderating influence which allowed him to interfere more and more in internal security and intelligence. The Services were increasingly penetrated and controlled by this SS nominees, backed by the Waffen SS; and in the administration of the Reich and occupied countries Himmler's plenipotentiaries, the Hohere SS and Polizeifuehrer, gradually achieved superiority over the regular administrative services. Some time before the R.S.H.A. was in a position to interfere in the fields of espionage and counter-sabotage, it had largely taken over security and counter-espionage activities and with them many of the personnel of Abwehr III in the Reich and in occupied countries. With his direct access to Hitler, Himmler was also able to report to him, often to the detriment of the Auswaertiges Amt, such political information as Schellenberg obtained through Amt VI: and in 1943 Amt VI under Schellenberg became an increasingly serious rival to the Abwehr in espionage and sabotage.

19. For the reasons explained below the Abwehr was incapable of resisting the pressure of competition and criticism from the R.S.H.A. With the collapse of Italy the R.S.H.A. services were at least more vigorous and better organised to cope with a political crisis, though they were singularly ineffective in action later. Research into Abwehr archives shows that the Abwehr was still writing up Badoglio, and the S.D. reports on the political situation were full and realistic. The prestige of the R.S.H.A. was further enhanced by Skorzeny's rescue of Mussolini. The arrest of Helmuth and the uncovering of Axis networks in the Argentine deprived the Abwehr of any little

remaining support it could expect from the Auswaertiges Amt; and the defection of Wermehren [sic] and others in Istanbul came soon after. The final downfall of Canaris followed his unsuccessful attempt to resist Allied counter-action in Spain, and in February 1944 he was replaced by Hansen.

20. The months immediately following the fall of Canaris were months of negotiation and compromise behind which unresolved conflict between the General Staff and SS was continued. In the negotiations, the SS held all the trump cards, and both sides acted on the assumption that Himmler would in fact take over the Abwehr, though some face-saving formula would be found. The General Staff's plans, however, were not confined to the field of these negotiations. They were planning the elimination of Hitler and Himmler and the whole Nazi leadership by political conspiracy, and it was therefore immaterial if the negotiations went against them.

21. Of these two parallel developments, the negotiations over the Abwehr and the political conspiracy of the General Staff, the former matured first. After a series of preliminary conferences in which the Abwehr was represented by Hansen and Engelhorn and Amt VI by Schellenberg and Sandberger, the representatives of the Abwehr and the R.S.H.A. were summoned to the Kursalon at Salzburg for a final session lasting from the 10th to the 15th May. There the decision was promulgated by Himmler. In a bombastic speech, he declared that the name Abwehr was "un-German", and the thing was to be abolished. A new organisation, the R.S.H.A. Militaerisches Amt, was to be founded. He would decide which of the Abwehr officers should have the privileges of being transferred to this new organisation, which would come officially into being on the 1st June.

22. The nature of the Salzburg decision, which preserved much of the original form of the Abwehr under the authority of the R.S.H.A., need not be specified, for it was short-lived. Within two months, the Generals' Putsch had taken place and failed; and its failure enabled the extremists of the SS to substitute for the Salzburg formula a far more radical solution.

23. Almost all the General Staff officers of the Abwehr, with the exception of those appertaining to military security, were either transferred to the appropriate sections of the Amt IV and Amt VI (this applied to economic espionage and counter-espionage in particular) or were carried on by the old personnel in the new Militaerisches Amt, as a subordinate formation of Amt VI. The chief positions in the Mil Amt were, however, held by Schellenberg's senior Amt VI officials in addition to their normal posts.

Thus Skorzeny was as head of Mil Amt D, responsible for the sabotage and subversion tasks still carried out by ex-Abwehr Kommandos in the Field and at the same time controlled Amt VI S, with its sabotage units and services. Though the Mil Amt was largely concerned with operational areas, it also maintained the former Abwehr Kos in neutral countries and static regional stations in Germany, both now under the name Kommando der Meldegebiet (KdM).

25. In the final stages, Schellenberg, working outwards from the centre, pressed on with his hopeless task of welding the whole unwieldy and unsound structure into the Geheime Meldedienst of his dreams. He had no time to investigate the old Abwehr's personnel and achievements nor opportunity to reorganise its methods and replace more than a few of its members; and there were worse difficulties inside Amt VI itself than he could hope to set right. With dissolution in sight the personal rivalries into which the party system inevitably declined set Schellenberg and Himmler and Kaltenbrunner and Skorzeny more than ever in different camps. Unable and unwilling to admit the possibility of defeat they could not plan effectively either resistance and sabotage behind the Allied lines or a final stand in a Wagnerian redoubt in the Bavarian mountains. Such efforts as were made served only to reveal the complete moral bankruptcy of Nazism in the time of crisis. The final defeat of Germany found almost all the main personalities intent on their private schemes of rehabilitation; and as a result it has been easy enough to draw from them the remaining facts necessary to complete the story of the German Intelligence Services.

# II. – THE REASONS FOR THE FAILURE.

26. From the historical summary of Section I above it will be clear that there was at no time during the Nazi regime a single intelligence service responsible for the provision of secret intelligence and for other secret duties to the various Government and service departments.

27. The paragraphs which follow will do something to explain why the services which existed failed so miserably to provide valuable intelligence at critical periods in the war; but it must be stressed that however good the German Secret Service might have been, the chaos which existed in the organisation of strategical and political planning would have made it difficult for it to exert a useful influence on the course

of the war. Uncontrolled by any organisation for collating the intelligence requirements of the service and other ministries in time of war, for assessing priorities and
for evaluating the general significance of intelligence received from all sources, both
overt and secret, the Abwehr and the S.D. alike were free to concentrate on whatever
objectives suited their directors or were easiest to attain, and they were not subject to
criticism except on particular issues.

## *Lack of Central Evaluation.*

28. Another result of the lack of a joint intelligence committee was that neither the
Abwehr and S.D. nor the Secret Intelligence departments had the necessary criteria
for the evaluation of secret reports, either on the strategical level or in matters of
detailed interest to service and economic departments. There appears to have been
little interchange of information between ministries and each major figure attempted
to make a corner in some type or other of intelligence. The Abwehr had no section
responsible for the circulation of reports to ministries. They seem to have been passed
on largely at random without attempt at critical evaluation, the comments of outsta-
tions or of the officer responsible for running the individual agent being generally
accepted by head office. This practice was especially dangerous in view of the inefficiency and unscrupulousness of many of the officers concerned. Only in the final
stage of the campaign in the West was any attempt made to provide such a circulation
section, and this functioned only for the western front.

29. In the R.S.H.A., Amts III and IV, whose functions were mainly repressive,
appear to have contributed little to outside departments. Such appreciations as they
made, mostly the result of the work of Amt III observers, were confined to party
officers and to the personal entourage of Hitler. They were mainly used by individuals
such as Himmler and Kaltenbrunner for their own ends in their frantic competition
with Goering, Bormann and the rest. Schellenberg's more professional instincts led
him to set up a sort of personal office to collate the work of the various subsections
of Amt VI and later of the Mil Amt. But Amt VI, like the Abwehr, worked in a void
without the responsibility of cross-checking its results against a wider general picture. Even internally, VI.S under Skorzeny and VI.E. (concerned with Balkan espionage) reported directly to Kaltenbrunner, and Schellenberg was often ignorant of
their work.

# Personnel.

30. All intelligence services depend largely for their success upon the quality of the higher personnel they employ; in addition to their technical abilities, their staffs must be capable of objective and disinterested appreciation of events and be as free as possible from political or social bias. In different ways the Abwehr and the S.D. fell so short of this ideal that on this one count alone their failure was inevitable.

## (a) Abwehr.

31. The Abwehr was staffed mainly by service personnel with the addition in time of war of "volunteer reservists" from the business and professional world. Instead of being the pick of the officer cadre, the regular Abwehr officers were generally second or third-rate men who had failed in regular service employment or were seconded to its obscurity as a punishment for irregular conduct. The reservists were sometimes able but unscrupulous, often tired and disillusioned. Further, as is usual in work of this kind, personal recommendation by those already inside the organisation was the main method of recruiting; and it is, therefore, not surprising that Admiral Canaris typified in many ways the outlook and capabilities of his subordinates.

32. Though an astute and even able man, Canaris lacked organising ability and was a bad judge of others, selecting his assistants more for their compatibility with his curious and restless temperament than for their suitability for intelligence work. They became, under his paternal eye, not an efficient and well organised department, but the "family Canaris", a self-interested and often corrupt body, largely alien in sentiment from, and disliked by, the General Staffs they purported to serve.

33. Like Canaris, who was a German nationalist of the old school, they were thoroughly out of sympathy with the Nazi Party and retained a code of "gentlemanly" conduct which gave them, in contrast to their S.D. colleagues, a superficial charm. Most of the senior officers, and especially those with General Staff connections, were prepared to push their hostility to the regime further than Canaris himself, and were directly involved in the 20th July Plot, to which Canaris lent only his moral support. Most noteworthy amongst these were Oberst Hansen (acting head of the Abwehr at the time of the plot), Freytag von Loringhofen and Lahousen (at different times in charge of the sabotage service) and Marogna-Redwitz, one of the few really able intelligence officers and head of the Vienna station. It is worth noting that Lahousen's

defence of the Abwehr's inefficiency was that it was part of the contribution of himself and his friends to the destruction of Nazism.

34. With this kind of leadership it is not surprising that the lower ranks of the Abwehr organisation were selected in their turn on personal grounds without regard to suitability or training. The absence of any proper system of selection opened the door to every kind of intrigue, corruption and nepotism. The ablest officers were to be found in the C.E. section and as heads of stations, but since no attempt was made to define their duties or limit their powers, even men like Cellarius in Finland, Kleyenstueber in Spain and Wagner in Bulgaria were gradually reduced to the same low level of efficiency as the rest. There was little to prevent an intelligence rogue from inventing both agents and reports and pocketing the proceeds – there are plenty of such cases on record – or from continuing to run an agent long since known to have been compromised to the enemy; and there was nothing to spur him to special effort, except personal ambition or personal gain.

35. As the war continued, the few young men were drafted away to combatant duties, and it was not until the Abwehr was absorbed by the Mil Amt that any real attempt was made to find better replacements. By this time the shortage of manpower was so great that there was little to be done and heavy casualties in the Mobile Field Units made worse an already hopeless situation.

## (b) *S.D. Personnel.*

36. At the outbreak of war the repressive departments of the R.S.H.A. were comparatively well staffed. Amt III consisted of old and trusted Party Members, whose experience in many cases began before 1933; Amt IV's personnel were all highly-trained police officers; and a large reserve of potential recruits was always to be found in the ranks of the Ordnungspolizei. Amt VI was much worse off.

37. Heydrich had apparently not realised the importance of a Foreign Intelligence Service in war, and peace. In any case he paid too little attention to Amt VI and gave it little support. Jost, the original Amtschef, was an ineffective man, with no foreign experience and only limited intellectual capacity, so that even in peace time he had no idea how to develop his department to its best advantage. In addition he made no preparations whatsoever for war-time expansion or against the possibility of S.D. personnel being called up for service in the Armed Forces.

38. A far more serious disadvantage was that in the early stages the principal qualities required in a candidate for the S.D. were political reliability and membership of the S.S. The S.S. was recruited largely from members of the *petit bourgeois* lower middle class, which in all countries is the least cosmopolitan, the most conventional and the most narrow minded.

39. In consequence the higher-ranking officers of the Amt VI were not intelligent, gifted men, full of energy and ideas, but men of mediocre intellect such as Daufeldt and Carstenn or else Nazi bullies like Naujocks. They had little aptitude for intelligence work and no knowledge whatsoever of foreign countries. In the stations abroad the situation was even worse, as the number employed was disgracefully small and the demand on the personnel correspondingly greater. Yet in no case was any effort made to introduce suitable personalities with a foreign background.

40. It was only after the appointment of Schellenberg as Amtschef VI in 1942 that efforts were finally made to strengthen the representation of the Amt in all spheres of its activity. The S.S. and Party qualifications on which Heydrich had insisted were modified, thus greatly widening the field of recruitment, and Schellenberg's newly appointed Gruppenleiter tried to obtain qualified personnel both from outside the R.S.H.A. and from other departments. However, owing to the prevailing jealousy between the different Amtschefs, little headway was made in the latter direction and owing to the complete mobilisation of man-power the available material outside the R.S.H.A. was strictly limited. When Sandberger took over the administration of Amt VI early in 1944, he made strenuous efforts to obtain the transfer of experienced officials from Amt III as Section heads and to recruit for Gruppe VI C experts on Eastern matters with knowledge of the Russian language and country. He was largely unsuccessful owing to the refusal of Amtschef III and the various B.d.S. in the occupied countries to release their key men. Amt I, the personnel department, had not the authority to overrule them.

41. A solitary exception is to be found in the case of Waneck, Gruppenleiter VI E. Owing to his good relations with Kaltenbrunner, he was frequently able to bring pressure to bear on Ehrlinger, Amtschef I and in fact did succeed in obtaining the transfer of a number of Amt III officers to Amt VI. This may in part account for the all-round superiority of Amt VI E over the other country sections, who were increasingly forced as time went on to send good men from Head Office to bolster up the stations abroad.

42. A striking feature about the R.S.H.A. was the continual rivalry and self-seeking of its personnel. Rival factions, led by Kaltenbrunner and Schellenberg respectively, continually strove to win the support of Hitler and Himmler. Waneck and the Austrian group in Amt VI E supported Kaltenbrunner, while Steimle of VI B and Paeffgen of VI D were the principal members of a Swabian group centred round Schellenberg. Indeed, not only did these rivalries greatly influence the effective contribution of Amt VI to the German war effort, but each faction had its own ideas about the future course of the war and the lines of German foreign policy. Thus while Hoettl was negotiating with the Americans in Switzerland, ostensibly on Kaltenbrunner's behalf, Schellenberg was acting as Himmler's representative in making overtures to the Western Allies through Count Bernadotte. The result was that in the closing stages of the war the gathering of intelligence was one of the last matters with which the S.D. was concerned. In so far as information was obtained at all, it was not co-ordinated to give a general picture of enemy plans, but jealously guarded by each department to support the labyrinthine intrigues of independent groups aiming at political power.

## *Overlapping of Functions inside the R.S.H.A.*

43. To personal rivalries must be added the mistrust of the Sicherheitspolizei and the S.D. at all levels, due mainly to differences in training and out-look. The internal overlapping which is a marked feature of the R.S.H.A. must be attributed to these two causes. For example, when Heydrich ordered the establishment of Amt IV of a Gegnernachrichtendienst in 1941, to operate against subversive elements inside Germany, Mueller, Amtschef IV, sought to develop lines outside Germany in direct competition with Amt VI.

44. The result was inevitably that each Amt maintained its own representation abroad and in the occupied countries, working often quite independently of one another and with little or no liaison. A fair example of this is to be found in Slovakia, where it was always uncertain which was the competent department, seeing that during the course of the war responsibility changed from Amt VI to Amt III and finally in 1944 to Amt VI again.

45. Yet it is clear that with a better organised system in Berlin the R.S.H.A. could still have achieved something of value. For in the operational areas of the occupied territories, where all intelligence and security work was centralized into Einsatzkommandos,

comprising both Stapo and S.D. personnel, the closest co-operation was achieved. These units were directly subordinated to the B.d.S., through whom all reports were submitted to the relevant departments of the R.S.H.A., thus ensuring some measure of uniformity.

## *Overlapping of functions within the Abwehr.*

46. The lack of central direction in the G.I.S. was reflected no less in the Abwehr than in the S.D. Centrally the situation was slightly improved by the fusion of the two services which took place in Summer of 1944, but by then no intelligence service, however efficient, could seriously affect the course of the war. The lack of centralised direction in the Abwehr was not as important as some of its other defects, but it was none the less a factor which did contribute in some degree to its failure.

47. The first feature which is obvious is the overlapping of the Asts themselves. Theoretically the Ast in each Wehrkreis had a separate territorial sphere of operation. In practice the area depended upon the whim or interests of the head of the station; and the officers of the Abwehr like those of many other services were adepts in the art of Empire building. The result was that the territorial commitments of the Asts bore no relation to logic or common sense or anything else except the ambition and capacity for intrigue displayed by their commanding officers. Ast Hamburg and Nest Cologne for example both ran groups of agents in South America, Ast Munich and Ast Vienna both had independent stay behind networks in North Italy and both endeavoured to parachute agents in the South, with practically no co-ordination. Even more serious was the confusion caused between the Asts and the KOs.

48. Since the Asts were allowed to operate in neutral territory and since they seldom troubled to keep the Kos informed of any details, it was difficult to prevent the two agencies trespassing on each other's activities, and even more difficult for the KO to cope with diplomatic protests resulting from the conduct of agents of whose bare existence even it might be ignorant. This situation became worse as the German diplomatic position grew weaker and it became less and less easy to defend the operations of agents in neutral countries. The lack of co-operation is well exemplified in Sofia, where Ast Vienna ran a special espionage office operating against Russia, constantly at loggerheads with KO Bulgaria, which had at least partially the same assignment. All neutral countries show in some degree the same confusion and lack of co-ordinated plan.

49. The creation of the mobile Frontaufklaerungs-Kommandos and Trupps (FAKs and FATs) which co-operated with the armies in the Field did nothing to reduce the general confusion. On the contrary it became even worse, as yet another class of agent-running unit was added to those already in existence. Italy is perhaps the most striking example. By the end of the Italian campaign, KdM Munich, KdM Vienna, FAK 150, FAK 190 Luft and Ast Italy, to name only the major units, were all running stay behind agents in North Italy, often apparently without any agreement or even knowledge of each other's plans. The confusion was scarcely less on the Western Front, where the major KdMs (the new name given to an Ast after the Abwehr was absorbed by the R.S.H.A.) were engaged in making plans for an elaborate stay behind network in Western Germany. The army-controlled FAKs and FATs were engaged in the same work and agents would be placed in the same town by different agencies with little or no regard for rational distribution or a sensible plan. By this time of course it made no difference to what the Germans did, and the most efficient service in the world could not affect the outcome of the war. The example is merely cited to show the sort of confusion that existed even after the R.S.H.A. had absorbed the Abwehr and Schellenberg was trying to make real his dream of a unified Meldedienst.

## *Technique.*

50. In view of the many deficiencies in organisation in both S.D. and Abwehr it is not surprising to find a corresponding weakness in the technique of intelligence production. No German service could hope to recruit agents for work abroad or in occupied countries except from amongst the ranks of Nazi sympathizers, from amongst those who could be blackmailed by threats into working against their convictions and from the international sludge of professional agents, touts, and ne'er-do-wells. Both organisations specialised in recruitment through blackmail, especially when they could threaten parents or friends in the Reich. At the best they received unwilling service from agents recruited this way: more often than not once they were beyond the reach of their spymasters, the victims invented reports or went over to the Allies. The Nazis and Nazi sympathisers were little more successful, for they were branded everywhere for their political sympathies and were unlikely to receive the confidence of the Allied and neutral authorities. The professionals perhaps provided the best material, but they soon discovered the inability of the Abwehr to check their reports and relied upon their invention rather than their industry to provide information.

These weaknesses were particularly evident in the post-occupational wireless networks set up both by Abwehr and S.D. to report on the Allied invasion of Europe from behind Allied lines. Many of the three hundred or so wireless and sabotage agents involved defected immediately to the Allies with their sets and instructions; others who were known as Nazis and were strangers in the district were rounded up by the Maquis long before the Allies arrived. Of the remainder the majority lay low until the interrogation of their comrades revealed their identity. The agents were trained very hurriedly in large classes and were equipped with W/T sets which were frequently unsuited for maintaining contact with their control. At no time were more than about twenty actively trying to keep in touch with their masters. This example is taken from a period when the defeat of Germany could be safely predicted, and when security and efficiency were sacrificed in a frantic effort to produce results; but in a lesser degree the practice of earlier years shows the same deficiencies.

51. If the methods of recruiting were unco-ordinated and based either on bribery or blackmail, training was no less chancy. Some Asts ran extremely efficient wireless and technical training schools, particularly Ast Hamburg. Others favoured training in neutral countries as a result of which agents were often blown before performing any real task. Briefing was often vague and inconsistent and cover stories ill prepared. In neutral countries local colour was easily provided; but agents intended for Allied territory were frequently detected early in their careers because they committed some obvious breach of custom.

52. It is only fair to add that the Germans were aware of their difficulties in selecting suitable agents and used them on a mass production system with the hope that a few at least would survive to pay eventual dividends. This practice made it all the easier for interrogators to learn about the habits and plans of the various despatching stations. It should also be noted that Reichsdeutsche, amongst whom were most of the best agents, were rarely despatched to enemy territory, so that from the German point of view the wastage was not serious.

# III. – CONCLUSIONS.

53. It is important when assessing the failure of the G.I.S. to consider what, if anything, an efficient Intelligence Service could have done to alter the course of the war. When the problem is viewed in this light it is clear that many of the errors of

the G.I.S., among them some of the most sensational, did not in fact matter since the result of the war was already settled beyond dispute. Up to the middle of 1942 the military strength of the German army rendered intelligence almost unnecessary in the sense that the result of the battles would have been much the same if the intelligence services had been good or bad. After Summer 1944, equally, no amount of efficiency in intelligence work could have made any real difference to the nature or duration of the war. This leaves 1942 to 1944, the period of the Allied invasions, as the vital time during which efficient intelligence could have contributed to the German cause. If any leakage had occurred over the invasions of North Africa, Sicily, Italy and, above all, Normandy, then consequences of extreme gravity might have followed, and, though no doubt the material superiority of the Allies would have eventually caused Germany's defeat, casualties might have been incomparably heavier, and the whole course of the war might have changed.

54. It remains to be decided whether in fact an efficient intelligence service could reasonably have been expected to discover Allied intentions during this period or whether the task was beyond the powers of any service, however capable. Secret Intelligence forms only a part of the data on which a General Staff bases its inferences about enemy plans, and it would not therefore be fair to expect a Secret Intelligence Service to serve up on its own account the sort of secret information which would have been needed for accurate prediction of the North African and European invasions. It is true that occasionally a brilliant *coup* may be brought off, and it is true also that, the more efficient and careful the preparations, the better chance there is of some such unexpected scoop occurring. Nevertheless it cannot reasonably be relied upon, and therefore the fact that the G.I.S. not only failed over this but failed abysmally, does not necessarily saddle them with complete responsibility for the ignorance of the OKW. A much better intelligence service might also have failed to prophesy Allied plans, though it would have given itself a much better chance of success than the G.I.S. ever did.

55. If, however, the G.I.S. cannot be blamed for not securing the vital information, and if the failure to appreciate Allied plans was largely due to completely inadequate machinery at the level of the OKW, nevertheless its responsibility is considerable. The G.I.S. might reasonably have been expected sometimes to produce reports that were not positively misleading or merely confusing. In fact over the whole of this crucial period the G.I.S. produced almost nothing that could have been of the slightest

assistance even to an intelligent and capable OKW, and this failure is one which did contribute considerably to the general failure of the German war effort.

56. The reasons for this failure will have emerged from the historical and critical sections of this paper. It must be attributed partly to the lack of organisation and control of intelligence work at Cabinet level, partly to the weakness of the personnel employed and in a great degree to the spiritual, moral and practical disadvantages of Nazism *vis-à-vis* the Allied and neutral Powers. Where Germany's stock was high or her credit good the Intelligence Services could command assistance and even respect; where it was low, or more real standards prevailed, they lacked the natural advantage of good will and resorted to force or blackmail without success. Their success in repressive counter-espionage work at home need cause neither surprise nor alarm. It is a commonplace of tyranny and was balanced in Germany's case by their increasing failure to prevent information reaching the Allies despite fierce counter-measures from those countries where the instincts of freedom and liberty were most deeply ingrained. The failure of the Abwehr, however, dates from long before the crisis of Nazism. If its final dissolution may be attributed to the pressure of Nazi politics, the responsibility for its long history of weakness and inefficiency between the wars must be shared by Admiral Canaris and his friends, who were themselves until 1941 virtually the German Intelligence Service.

# APPENDIX VI.

# GERMAN WAR PRODUCTION.

## I.- GERMAN POLICY.

The history of Nazi Germany's war production falls naturally into four phases:-

- (a) The period of preparation: 1933-September 1939.
- (b) War without tears: September 1939-1941.
- (c) The struggle for total mobilisation: 1942-July 1944.
- (d) The collapse: August 1944-May 1945.

2. Before proceeding to describe the measures which were adopted, it will be appropriate to indicate the main features of German policy with regard to war production in each phase.

### The period of preparation: 1933-September 1939.

3. On the accession to power of the Nazis, Germany was only just emerging from a violent depression and a substantial proportion of her man-power and productive capacity was unemployed. The creation of work for the population was one of the primary concerns of Nazi policy, but from the first the type of employment provided was to a large extent directed towards preparations for war. These preparations took the form, not only of producing armaments and building further factories to produce them, but also, with the introduction of the Four-Year Plan in 1936, of increasing indigenous production (for example, iron ore) and providing capacity for synthetic production (for example, oil, rubber and textile fibres) of strategic raw materials for which Germany was heavily dependent on imported supplies. Where self-sufficiency could not be achieved by such means, action was taken to lay in stocks, for which purpose a tight licensing

control was maintained on import and export trade in order to extract the maximum amount of foreign exchange for Government-directed purchases abroad.

4. In view of the low level of employment prevailing when the Nazis came into power much of the new production required for rearmament purposes was obtained without difficulty in the process of reactivating formerly idle capacity in the capital goods industries. It was not necessary to depress the level of consumers' expenditure, which was already at a depression level, in order to free additional resources. In fact, consumers' expenditure was permitted to rise somewhat. But sufficient controls were imposed to ensure, indirectly, that the natural tendency of consumers' expenditure, and hence of the production of consumer goods, to rise fairly sharply in a period of economic recovery was held in check. This was the meaning of the slogan "guns before butter". Thus although full employment had been virtually achieved by 1936 and the volume of production had been restored to the 1928 level, the distribution of industrial effort as between capital goods (including war equipment) and consumer goods was very much less favourable to the customer than it had been in 1928 as the following figures show: -

## Net production value of German industrial output in 1928 and 1936

(RM. Milliards).

| Production | 1928 | 1936. |
| --- | --- | --- |
| Mines | 3.4 | 2.2 |
| Building materials | 1.6 | 1.2 |
| Metal industries | 3.5 | 5.3 |
| Machine and vehicle construction | 2.8 | 4.0 |
| Electrical engineering | 1.6 | 1.5 |
| Building | 3.9 | 4.3 |
| Chemicals | 1.52.5 | |
| Total, production goods | 18.3 | 21.0 |

Consumer Goods –

| Textiles | 2.6 | 2.8 |
| --- | --- | --- |
| Paper industry | 2.0 | 1.5 |
| Leather industry | 0.6 | 0.6 |
| Woodworking industry | 1.9 | 1.0 |
| Food industry | 5.0 | 3.5 |
| Clothing industry | 2.00.8 | |
| Total, consumer goods | 14.410.7 | |
| Total industrial production | 32.7 | 31.7 |

5. The General Staff put in hand the rebuilding of Germany's Armed Forces as a matter of course, and regarded rearmament as an end in itself. As represented by General Thomas, however, who was made responsible for war production with OKW, they were not happy with the increase in war potential which would result from the reactivation of idle capacity and the implementation of the self-sufficiency programme provided by the Four-Year Plan. Thomas considered that in order to be certain of sustaining a large army in a long war it was necessary, in addition to the measures already in hand, to take such steps as expanding the existing steel production and fabricating capacity and to expand coal production by sinking new pits. He was influenced to a large extent by the heavy concentration of existing heavy industry in the vulnerable frontier area of Rhenish-Westphalia. Thomas and the General Staff realised that such expansions, in addition to the formidable measures already proposed, would require heavy capital expenditure over a number of years and could therefore only be achieved slowly unless the production of consumer goods was to be drastically curtailed, which they were not prepared to recommend.

6. In these circumstances the High Command were willing to base their rearmament plans on the annual increment of new military equipment which could be made available by achieving full employment and without depressing civilian consumption standards and to spread the investment necessary for the full development of industrial war potential over a number of years. In the meantime they proposed to use the accessions of new military equipment for the purpose of rebuilding the Armed Forces to a comparatively leisurely schedule, which would in addition permit sound planning and thorough training, especially in the replenishment of the sorely depleted cadre of officers and N.C.O.s. General Thomas accordingly considered that a reasonable goal, on the basis of "rearmament in depth", would be a strength of 120 fully-equipped divisions by 1942. The adoption of this comparatively modest goal would enable him to ensure a really high standard of equipment and mechanisation and to introduce simultaneously in industry a plan for expanding productive capacity in a manner and to the extent which he considered adequate. In view of these considerations the High Command did not consider that the Army and the production organisation behind it would be in a fit state to enter a major war before 1943.

7. This schedule was too dilatory to be satisfactory to Hitler. In contrast to the High Command's programme of "rearmament in depth", involving the co-ordinated mobilisation of military man-power and industrial resources, Hitler demanded

"rearmament in width". In other words, he desired the maximum and most immediate display of military goods in the shop window regardless of the state of the shelves within. He accordingly, in 1937, set a goal of 180 divisions by 1942 - 50 per cent. higher than General Thomas considered prudent. In the light of subsequent events, German commentators have surmised that Hitler was probably aware of the risks involved in this policy, but that he counted on securing the necessary broadening of the basic resources of an inflated military economy by cheap and early conquests of additional Lebensraum – a prospect which he preferred to the more laborious and time-consuming alternative of further building up Germany's basic industries from her own capital resources.

8. In the event, the speed with which the Armed Forces, excluding the Navy, were rebuilt and re-equipped up to 1939 followed the High Command's schedule to a greater extent than Hitler's aspirations. For his policy contained a fundamental contradiction. While urging the speediest possible construction of a large Army, Hitler refused to allow the depression in the civilian standard of living which this would have involved. In this he was supported by the Gauleiters and other Party functionaries who feared that any reverse in the new-found semi-prosperity of the masses would remove the chief foundation of the Party's popularity with the public. Hence the investment of capital permitted by the Government for strengthening the country's war potential, under the Four-Year Plan, was on a less ambitious scale than the High Command would have liked and mainly concerned with projects designed to ensure self-sufficiency in a number of important imported raw materials without which Germany could not contemplate a major war at all. To have gone further, simultaneously with the execution of the armaments production programme, could only have been done at the expense of the Party's building programme or by a substantial depression in the level of consumption in order to free additional productive resources for capital construction. But neither course of action was politically acceptable.

## War Without Tears: September 1939-41.

9. In the opinion of the High Command, Hitler's strategic aspirations greatly outran the military strength at his disposal and, more particularly, the ability of the economy to sustain, in a long war, the military strength which could be mobilised. At the time of the Munich crisis, OKW was filled with prognostications of military disaster if

war should come too soon and, when war did come in September 1939, the High Command considered itself to be, to a large extent, unprepared.

10. The mobilisation in the summer of 1939 followed the lines of Hitler's full "rearmament in width" and caused an immediate falling-off in industrial production within the Reich, due to the loss of man-power and disturbance of working schedules. It was planned to offset this by proceeding with the fuller mobilisation for war of the country's economic resources. For this purpose Reichswirtschaftsminister Funk had been appointed General Plenipotentiary for Economy, with supervisory powers over all the economic Ministers, and had drawn up plans to be introduced on the outbreak of war for the further limitation of civil consumption and the diversion of productive resources into armament production. A considerable number of decrees affecting this field were issued in the autumn of 1939 by the Ministerial Council for National Defence which Hitler had set up under Goering to co-ordinate policy on the home front. But these decrees do not seem to have been very strenuously enforced and there was, in practice, little decrease in civilian consumption or increase in armaments production for many months. It must be remembered that full employment had already been achieved as early as 1936 and that the existing controls, by holding consumers' expenditure in check, had already ensured that a substantial proportion of the nation's productive capacity was geared to war requirements. Moreover, an atmosphere of "business as usual" was encouraged by the rapid success, and small losses, of the Polish campaign. Party leaders and press explained that, with the Nazi method of making war, extreme privations on the part of the civil population were unnecessary; the thoroughness of pre-war preparations, the strength of Germany's invincible armies and the military genius of the Fuehrer would ensure quick and easy victories. The Ministerial Council for the National Defence had ceased to meet by the end of 1939 and never assembled again. In December, Funk was deprived, in effect, of his powers as General Plenipotentiary for Economics which were added to those of Goering in his capacity as Commissioner for the Four-Year Plan which they already largely duplicated. Goering put them into cold storage and paid progressively less attention to his co-ordinating responsibilities on the economic front. It is significant that the Economic General Council (Generalrat der Wirtschaft), with which he was provided, is never known to have met.

11. This policy received further encouragement from the success of the Norwegian and French campaigns in 1940, for which industry was called upon only for a brief

improvised spurt during the winter of 1939-1940, in order to build up the necessary stocks of ammunition. It was in order to facilitate this drive, by improving the organisation and technique of production within the war factories, that Todt was appointed Minister of Armaments and Munitions.

12. For the attempt to invade England, the German war production executive was given only three months to prepare, and in these circumstances its preparations were naturally, for the most part, improvisations. When the impracticability of the project was recognised in November 1940, industry was called upon to extemporise preparations for the Russian war. The demands made did not strain the productive capacity of the economy as then organised. Preparations followed the pattern of the "rearmament in width" of the summer of 1939. The number of divisions available was made up to 210 (of which 186 were first-line divisions) by a fresh call-up of man-power, but no measures were taken to ensure an equivalent long-term expansion in the production of weapons and munitions. Indeed, so great was the confidence in the rapid and successful conclusion of the Eastern campaign that the production of most classes of weapons and munitions was sharply reduced, on Hitler's orders. In the case of certain classes of ammunition, the reduction was ordered at the end of the French campaign in 1940. The reduction of armaments production was to be followed as soon as possible by a reduction in the size of the Army by 66 divisions. The continuation of the war with England would be mainly conducted in the air and at sea and would make relatively small demands on man-power and munitions production. German industry, backed by the vast conquered resources of the East, might even be able to revert to a large extent to conditions of peace-time economy.

## The struggle for total mobilisation: 1942-July 1944.

13. The setback on the Eastern front in the winter campaign of 1941-42 came as an unpleasant surprise. Germany's leaders, however, had every confidence that where the German Armies had failed in 1941, they would succeed in 1942. In order to supply the necessary equipment and munitions, it was necessary to reverse the "reconversion" orders which had been issued in the previous year and the restrictions on production for civilian consumption were considerably tightened and more strenuously enforced. Whereas previously industry had been encouraged to work with one eye on peace economy, a law passed in April 1942 prohibited any further planning

for peace-time production and was followed in October by a further order introducing the Kriegsauflagenprogramm which extended "utility" standards to the manufacture of most of the essential goods for civil consumption. In war production, however, the emphasis was still placed on the manufacture of offensive weapons with which the army could finish the Eastern campaign in the course of the war.

14. Over the first six months of 1942 armaments production increased by about 50 per cent. and there was a further increase of 25 per cent. by the end of the year. These increases were mainly the product of the rationalisation measures introduced into the armament industry by Speer who succeeded to the office of Minister of Armaments and Munitions on the death of Todt in February 1942 and in May took over responsibility for the control of armaments production from General Thomas of the Wehrwirtschafts –und Rüstungsamt (War Economy and Armaments Office) of the OKW.

15. The drive for total mobilisation was, however, not introduced with full severity until the 1942 campaign had failed with the defeat of Stalingrad. As long as there was any prospect that Germany would conquer and convert to her own use the agricultural, raw material, and industrial production of Western Russia, Speer confesses that he was not overawed by the superiority of Anglo-American economic resources. When it became apparent, after Stalingrad, that German plans for conquest in the East had failed, he believed that Germany could still fight a successful defensive war with her own resources and those of the territories which she had already conquered, provided that these were fully mobilised and that armaments production was organised with the fullest efficiency in the interests of maintaining the qualitative superiority in weapon performance which, he considered, Germany possessed at that time. The adaptation of the armament programme in detail to the requirements of defensive strategy was, however, rather slow, particularly in the field of aircraft production. The consistent failure to concentrate the resources of the aircraft industry on the production of defensive fighters is well known. In land armaments, the "Infantry Programme", designed to increase the defensive fire power of field divisions, did not begin to yield substantial fruit till the middle of 1944; this development was accompanied by the increasing conversion of tank factories to the production of assault guns.

16. For the fulfilment of Speer's plans, it was necessary to introduce unified control both of the means of production and of the armament programmes of the three Services. This aim was never fully realised. Considerable progress towards it was made

by instalments but in most cases action was taken too late to turn the tide of events which was setting irresistibly against Germany. Organisational reforms continued to be introduced right up to the end of the war, at which time still further reforms, recognised as necessary, were in preparation but had not been introduced. The political obstacles to total mobilisation remained formidable. Hitler himself was persuaded of the necessity for it with difficulty. The Party, personified by the Gauleiters, consistently resisted and sometimes endeavoured to undo its more unpopular manifestations.

17. Speer's control of raw material production (and through it of civilian consumption) was not made effective until September 1943 when he took over the responsibilities in this connection of the Ministry of Economics. The change was signalised by the change in his title to Minister of Armaments and War Production.

18. Control of the various branches of armaments production was only achieved by stages. Speer had already gained control of the production of army weapons in May 1942. The assumption of control of naval shipbuilding was negotiated with Doentiz early in 1943 when the latter succeeded Raeder in the High Command of the Navy. The G.A.F. relinquished control of fighter production in March 1944 but it was not until August 1944 that Speer acquired control over all branches of aircraft production. In the course of the Summer of 1944 Speer's control over armament production was extended into the field of armament design and development.

19. At no time did Speer control the allocation of labour which remained in the hands of Sauckel, who was appointed General Plenipotentiary for Labour Control under the Four-Year Plan early in 1942. Moreover, owing to personal and political differences, effective co-operation between the two was never secured and the failure to secure it was a constant source of inefficiency.

20. In the two-and-a-half years following his assumption of officer, Speer succeeded in more than tripling Germany's production of armaments. This achievement was the more remarkable in that it was accompanied by hardly any increase in raw material production and by a decline of only 25 per cent. in the production of consumer goods (other than food). For, to a large extent, the increase in weapon production was made possible by eliminating waste in the utilisation of raw materials and technical improvements in production methods designed to economise skilled labour. By this means the inevitable consequences of Germany's inferiority in economic resources were held at bay for many months and adequate working stocks of all vital materials were maintained.

21. Without the assistance provided by the Occupied Territories these results could never have been achieved. Their greatest contribution was in foreign workers for German industry, which enabled the strength of the industrial labour force to be maintained despite the withdrawal of native Germans for the armed forces. By the summer of 1944 more than 7 million of foreign workers, including prisoners of war, were employed in German industry, constituting 20 per cent. of the total industrial labour force. In addition, the manufacture for Germany of armament components, miscellaneous war equipment and consumption goods was organised on a large scale in the factories of the Occupied Territories, particularly in the West. In a number of strategic raw materials, the contribution of the Occupied Territories was decisive in maintaining total German supplies at the level required by the armament production programme. To a substantial extent, especially in the West, this assistance was exacted without equivalent payment and represented in a pure gain to the German war effort.

22. Speer alleges that his achievements in the field of production could have been greater but for interference by Service agencies bent on introducing modifications in designs already in quantity production. He also considers that the benefits of the increased flow of armaments from the factories were partly dissipated by inefficient distribution policy on the part of the Wehrmacht. He cites the excessive allocation of new production to new and untried units, which resulted in the diversion of new supplies to training grounds at times when seasoned units at the front were crying out for replacements and were forced to retreat for lack of them; this policy also, in his view, led to unnecessarily high battle wastage. At the same time he criticises the Wehrmacht for "sterilising" an excessively large proportion of the total armaments production in the form of holdings in the elaborate system of Ordnance Depots. He would have preferred to introduce the Russian system of linking formations direct to specified groups of factories for the purpose of obtaining replacements, but the Army traditions of supply organisation were too strong to enable this to be done.

## The Collapse: August 1944-May 1945.

23. German armaments production reached its maximum in the middle of 1944 at about 3½ times the level of the beginning of 1942. Nevertheless, Speer had planned during the spring of 1944 for further increases which would have carried production

by the end of the year to about five times the level of the beginning of 1942. This increase was considered to be attainable given the full mobilisation of man-power for war production, which had been far from completely obtained even by the spring of 1944. There had, in fact, been a net decline of about 700,000 persons (2 per cent.) over the previous twelve months in the numbers employed in industry, due to the failure to recruit sufficient new labour to offset the call-up of further workers for the Armed Forces.

24. A renewed call for maximum sacrifices in the interests of total mobilisation was issued at the end of July 1944, a suitable opportunity having been created by the attempted assassination of Hitler. Realisation of the programme depended essentially on the further mobilisation of the labour of German women, who had hitherto come forward for industrial employment in altogether unsatisfactory numbers. In practice, however, practically no net increase in the female labour force was secured, and from August 1944 onwards the industrial labour force actually declined, due to the removal for the Armed forces of a million of the remaining able-bodied men. In facing the problem of providing continual reinforcements of labour to make good the withdrawal of native man-power from industry for the Armed Forces, Sauckel relied to a large extent on the resources provided by the Occupied Territories. During his first two years of office energetic measures of recruitment succeeded in producing very considerable numbers of workers of good quality. In the later stages of the war the flow could only be maintained at the expense of firms in the Occupied Territories which were already at work on important German orders. This was one of the causes of the many clashes between Speer and Sauckel. Hitler and the Party were, on principle, reluctant to use compulsion to force German women into industry, on "biological grounds", and, in view of the strong reluctance of the women themselves to take up such work, it may well have been that the disturbance to popular morale would have been greater than the material benefit to industry. When the situation became so desperate as to acquire more drastic measures, the breakdown in administrative machinery promoted by bombing, evacuation, and other causes, made it hopeless to expect that they could be effectively enforced.

25. Difficulties of labour supply were, however, rapidly overtaken by other forces as the main factor in the spread of economic collapse. By the end of the year there were, in fact, considerable numbers of workers for whom productive employment could not be found owing to the progressive loss of manufacturing capacity and

dislocation of industrial schedules. The main factors which operated prior to the loss of Silesia in January 1945 may be summarised as follows:

(a) Transportation, which had stood up well to all demands hitherto, began to wilt under the pressure of Allied air attack in September. The average number of wagons loaded per day fell from 133,000 in August 1944 to 87,000 in December, and to 70,000 in January 1945. Attempts to obtain relief by intensified use of inland waterways were frustrated by the air attacks on the canal and river transport systems.

(b) The production of coal, which had been barely adequate to meet essential requirements, was immediately affected by deterioration of the transport situation owing to inability to remove current output from the pits. Production of hard coal fell from 26.3 millon tons in July 1944 to 14.3 million tons in December and 11.8 million tons in January 1945. Supplies of brown coal were less seriously affected by transport difficulties, but the effective loss of the production West of the Rhine was an aggravating factor.

(c) The production of electric power and gas declined, due to air-raid damage to producing plants and failure to keep pace with wear and tear. The electricity generating capacity available in mid-1944 was already insufficient to meet peak-load requirements by about 20 per cent. By the end of the year the effective capacity available had been reduced by one-third, air-raid damage being the principal factor. At this time only 3½ per cent. of the total capacity was shut down through lack of coal, but in January it was necessary to reduce fuel supplies to hard-coal generating stations by 50 per cent. By October supplies of gas had been reduced by about 25 per cent., due to air-raid damage (principally in the Ruhr) and by February the Ruhr grid was delivering only one-third of its former supply, while town gasworks elsewhere in Germany were being progressively shut down through lack of coal.

(d) Raw material production had already been flagging in the early months of 1944, and, although the declines from the peak output of 1943 were nowhere large, production was running some 15 per cent. below the (increased) figure demanded by the programme. Damage to productive capacity inflicted in air attacks caused a drastic and progressive decline in oil, chemical and steel production from the middle of 1944 onwards. Chemical and steel production were also affected to a significant degree at a comparatively early stage by loss of territory in the West. Raw material production as a whole fell by 50 per cent. between July 1944 and January 1945.

(e) The loss of the Western Occupied Territories and the invasion of Germany west of the Rhine seriously affected the programmes for certain important classes of raw material production and deprived certain industries of a significant fraction of their total production capacity. The operations of certain branches of manufacturing industry (*e.g.* motor vehicle production) which had relied on the Western Occupied Territories to a large extent for supplies of components were seriously disturbed and the supply of consumption goods (for which heavy reliance had been placed on the Occupied Territories) was severely affected.

(f) The manufacture of components for the armaments industry was sustained for a time by the use of working stocks and reserves of material in the factories, though these failed to avert a considerable fall in the production of particular items by the beginning of 1945. The smooth flow component supplies to the assembly plants was, however, seriously dislocated by the deterioration of the transportation system on which this branch of industry was highly dependent, due to the very large number of individual factories involved and their wide geographical dispersion.

(g) The output of end-products in the armaments industry held up fairly well in the autumn of 1944, in the course of which it was able to live in part on its working stocks. But there was some loss of productive capacity due to air attack and by the end of the year the other factors were beginning to take effect. Thus, from the peak level achieved in July, production had declined only by 7 per cent. in September, by 20 per cent. in December and by 30 per cent. in January 1945.

26. The overall decline in the net product of industry by January 1945 due to these factors and to the losses of territory suffered up to that time has been calculated by a leading German statistician from official records as 32 per cent. of the level of production in May 1944.* The wide divergence of experience between districts is worth citing in order to illustrate the special influence of air attack and loss of territory in the West:-

---

* Losses of territory up to January 1945 (*i.e.*, mainly losses in the West) have been calculated as involving the loss of about 15 per cent. of the industrial production capacity available in May 1944.

# Industrial Output† of Regions of Germany in January 1945.

(May 1944 = 100)

*Regions showing more than average decline —*

*Regions showing less than average decline —*

| | |
|---|---|
| South-West Germany . . . . . . . . . . . . . . . . | 42 |

| | |
|---|---|
| Ruhr-Rhineland . . . . . . . . . . . . . . . . . | 57 |
| North-West Germany . . . . . . . . . . . . . . . | 62 |
| *Total Reich* . . . . . . . . . . . . . . . . . . . . . . . | 68 |

| | |
|---|---|
| North Germany . . . . . . . . . . . . . . . . . . | 68 |

| | |
|---|---|
| Silesia, Sudetenland and Protectorate . . . . . . . . | 70 |
| Bavaria . . . . . . . . . . . . . . . . . . . . . | 72 |
| Central Germany . . . . . . . . . . . . . . . . . . | 80 |
| Danube-Alpine Region . . . . . . . . . . . . . . . | 91 |

† Net Production value.

27. The Ministry of Armaments and War Production reacted to these developments with a series of characteristic improvisations. Projects of capital construction, the completion of which could not contribute to armament production potential for many months, were stopped. Similarly Speer, through his so-called Concentration Programme, laid his hands on research and development activities and suppressed all development work on weapon design, &c., which did not promise significant results at an early date. In the field of weapon production, programmes were revised in a manner calculated to secure concentration of effort on the manufacture of weapons which were either easy to produce or which held out some promise of achieving for Germany tactical superiority in particular fields of operations. Finally, in many branches of production, effort was concentrated on producing spares in order to keep existing equipment in service and programmes for the production of new equipment were largely abandoned. On this basis, plans were drawn up at the end of December 1944 which promised steep rises in the course of 1945 in the production of the classes of equipment selected for priority treatment.

28. In view of the intensification of all the factors which had already been operating to reduce the performance of the German economy it is not surprising that

production of nearly all armament items in January 1945 fell well below the programmes set in the previous month. At the end of the month came the Russian break-
through into Silesia. The loss of this heavy-industry area, coming on top of the virtual
incapacitation of the Ruhr, convinced Speer that the final defeat of Germany was
now a foregone conclusion and thereafter his personal activities were mainly concerned with attempts to frustrate the destruction of all the basic facilities of economic
life as enjoined by Hitler's scorched earth directives. It was, however, necessary to
preserve an official façade of optimism, and the Ministry of Armaments and War
Production, which retained to the end its capacity to produce new programmes, set
about adjusting production plans to the new situation. The "Emergency Programme"
which resulted, in March, aimed at securing the maximum immediate production of
selected weapons and munitions by the assembly of working stocks of components
already available, that is to say by sucking the industrial pipe-line dry, until such time
as the reconquest of the heavy-industry area would enable long-term planning to be
reintroduced.

29. Nothing, however, was capable, in the last three months of the war, of avert-
ing the precipitate fall in all classes of production resulting from the cumulative and
interlocking effects of the adverse factors which had been developing in the previous
six months. The extent of the decline by March (the last month for which coherent
statistics are available) can be simply illustrated by the following representative statistics: -

|                                              | *July 1944.*           | *March 1945*  |      |
| -------------------------------------------- | ---------------------- | ------------- | ---- |
| Wagon loadings (daily average) . . .         | 136,000                | 15,000        |      |
| Hard-coal production (million tons) . . .    | 26.3                   | 7.0*          |      |
| Raw material production (1942=100)           | 100                    | 37*           |      |
| Armament production                          | (Jan./Feb. 1942=100)   | 322           | 145  |

* February: figures for March not available.


## Conclusions and Reflections.

30. That Germany would ultimately succumb to the combination of industrial
resources which was arrayed against her after the middle of 1941 was, from the

economic point of view, inevitable, granted anything like parity in the military skill, technical ingenuity and moral endurance of the opposing belligerents. No production executive can do more than make the best use of the available resources; the best may nevertheless be of no avail in support of a misguided strategy. Judgment of the effectiveness of Germany's industrial war effort can, therefore, only be made in relative terms and with the limited aims of establishing:-

(a) whether deficiencies in production caused, or contributed to, Germany's failure to win the war before the end of 1941;

(b) whether, thereafter, Germany's resistance was on balance prolonged or shortened by the performance of the industrial section of her war effort.

These questions can usefully be considered in the light of three criteria:-

(i) the efficiency with which production was geared to strategy;

(ii) the extent to which available resources were mobilised;

(iii) the adequacy and flexibility of the machinery for enrolling their use.

31. In the first phase there can be no question of production failures having played any part in preventing Germany from achieving her strategic aims. At no time, including the initial months of the Russian campaigns, were the German forces in the field hampered or even inconvenienced by shortages of supplies or equipment arising from deficiencies in production. Indeed, consumption was so far below the anticipated level that production in certain instances was too ample in relation to the requirements of Hitler's strategy and was therefore cut down. For the level of production required, only a relatively modest mobilisation of resources was necessary. The situation in regard to the control of their allocation may be described without injustice as one of free competition between Departments but although this resulted in very wasteful utilisation of resources it did not prevent the stated requirements from being met. Germany's failure was, in fact, Hitler's failure to appreciate the strength, physical and moral, of the forces with which he was faced and to prepare his own forces on a scale adequate to achieve his aims.

32. From the beginning of 1942 onwards the Armed Forces were in an almost chronic state of being able to obtain less weapons and munitions than they would have been able to use. Once the tide had turned in Russia, industry was never able to keep pace with the enormous wastage suffered in successive retreats. This factor is

well illustrated by the "gearing" between production and holdings at different times of typical weapons and munitions. It has been calculated by a leading German statistician that while, between January 1942 and June 1944, the monthly rate of production of the principal army weapons and ammunition increased by six-and-a-half times, wastage at the front was so great that net increase in holdings amounted only to 50 per cent. At the beginning of 1942, the ration of monthly production to total holdings had been 1:26. By June 1944 the ratio of production to holdings was raised to 1:6, but most of the benefit of the higher ratio was swallowed up by the increase in wastage. The position in the G.A.F. was even more striking. In the first six months of 1944 the input of fighters from new production and repair amounted to 12,675 aircraft, compared with 7,098 aircraft in the last six months of 1943. Yet average holdings declined from 8,298 aircraft in the second half of 1943 to 5947 in the first half of 1944. In the latter period the ratio between production and holdings had become 1:1 — that is to say, industry was being called upon to replace the entire front-line strength every month. When, in the early months of 1945, armaments production could no longer be maintained, the monthly input of new supplies of almost all classes of weapons and munitions fell below the current rate of wastage and it was seen that the destruction of the German Army and all its equipment could only be a matter of time.

33. It is therefore clear that from 1943 onwards the defeat of the German Armed Forces was hastened by the inability of industry to meet the requirements of the Armed Forces for weapons and equipment. But in reaching this conclusion it must be remembered that the growing disparity between supplies and requirements was the product of a considerable increase in production, overtaken by an astronomical increase in wastage. Although the production administration cannot be held to have made the most of their own opportunities, there is much to be said for their view that the equipment shortages of the Armed Forces were more often due to the colossal wastage promoted by a faulty distribution policy than to any basic insufficiency of production. Speer has claimed, in official print, that in the course of 1944 German industry produced insufficient equipment to fit out 225 infantry divisions and 45 Panzer divisions with their full complement of weapons.

34. That production was very imperfectly related to strategy in the second phase of the war was an inevitable result of a situation in which there was, in effect, no coherent strategy to which production could be called upon to conform. In spite of the fact that the defeat before Stalingrad spelt the irrevocable failure of Hitler's original strategic

plans, no general overhaul of strategy appears to have been undertaken and adjustments to the production programmes only occurred piecemeal. After the beginning of 1942, the armament production programme was, in its essentials, the outcome of Hitler's personal decisions, promulgated in the form of "Fuehrerforderungen". The requirements which were stated at the beginning of 1942 not unreasonably emphasised the need for increased production of offensive weapons – since German strategy still contemplated the defeat of Russia before the end of the year. After Stalingrad adjustments occurred which gave more prominence to defensive weapons. There were, for instance, notable increases in the production programmes for anti-aircraft and anti-tank guns; and the large-scale development of single-engine Fighter production dates from the beginning of 1943. But such adjustments were made piecemeal. It was not until 1944 that the Infantry Programme was introduced with a view to carrying out the comprehensive re-equipment of the German Army for a defensive rôle. The hesitant and unsystematic manner in which these adjustments were carried out was largely due to the virtual absence of effective machinery for thorough and systematic discussions of requirements. The decisions as to what should be produced were made by Hitler himself, on his own judgment or as the result of advice from one or other of his advisers, but seldom as the result of free discussion of the requirements by all interested parties. The discussions which decided the pattern of German war production consequently took the form of hole-in-corner conspiracies, rather than staff conferences.

35. The failure to achieve total mobilisation, even when it was belatedly recognised to be essential, was rooted in political causes. Its most persistent and consistent advocates, who finally succeeded in convincing the reluctant Führer, were Speer and his associates, none of whom occupied prominent positions in the Party. The increase in the power of Speer and his bureaucracy of non-political technicians was watched jealously by the major and minor Party bosses and obstructed by all possible means. His methods and personal appointments violated some of the most precious dogmas of the Party, and his policies required increasing personal sacrifices by the masses. The Gauleiters and other Party officials found in this situation what they imagined to be a good opportunity to earn cheap popularity in the rôle of protectors of the people.

36. The administrative machinery for controlling war production displayed major defects in all departments. These were mainly the result of the complacency of the earlier years of the war, during which the inefficiency in the organisation of

production by the General Staff, and by the civilian bureaucracy merely involved the wasteful utilisation of resources, but did not lead to any critical deficiencies in supply. Hence when events called for an all-out effort, the machine was incapable of taking even the easiest gradients in top gear. In this respect it may be said that at the end of 1942 the German administrative machine was no better conditioned to the economic implications of total war than was the government machinery of Whitehall in the spring of 1940.

37. Although Speer and his associates fully appreciated the weaknesses of the administrative machine from the very beginning of their tenure in office, political factors delayed the introduction of the appropriate remedies and the necessary reforms were spread over two and a half years. Consequently the principles which Germany's most capable executives had long since recognised as essential were still very imperfectly reflected in the practical organisation of the administrative machine at the end of the war. The recovery from the years which the locusts had eaten was never complete and was much too late to affect the issue.

38. Thus, right up to the end of the war, major defects continued to hamper the efficiency of all the major branches of the administration of production.

(a) The information services available to Germany's production executive failed to provide many of the data required for efficient central planning and production control. In particular there appear to have been available practically no information on man-hour costs and machine-loading by means of which Germany's economic planners could see the manner in which, and the extent to which, the various factors of production were being utilised.

(b) Planning was gravely handicapped, both by the inadequacy of the information services, and by the knowledge that the absence of adequate control over the factors of production rendered fruitless any attempt to plan beyond a certain point. In consequence the history of Germany's war production planning is, in practice, the history of a series of major improvisations. The German war production administration has aptly been compared, by a German commentator, to a boat leaking from twelve holes with only eleven plugs to stop them. In order to stop one hole it was necessary to remove the plug from another and start a fresh leak. This has earned for Speer among the older and more conservative industrialists the reputation of a "technical tight-rope walker", whose planning consisted in deluding the Fuehrer with empty promises and peremptorily placing on industry absurd demands which they could not possibly fulfil. In fact, contemporary documents show that the officials concerned seldom suffered from illusions regarding the inadequacy of the measures which they were forced to adopt, or were unaware of the real requirements of the situation. In discussion, under interrogation, of the obvious alternatives which they failed to adopt they have usually given the significant reply, "That, in our country, was politically impossible". Thus, one of the most striking failures of the Nazi system of government was the manner in which it confounded and utterly destroyed the traditional genius of the German nation for planning. On the other hand, many of the most remarkable and successful feats of improvisation on the part of any of the belligerents are to be found in the performances of the German production administration during 1943-44.

(c) Effective production control was rendered difficult by the inadequacy of information services, but the main obstacle was the impasse regarding the regulation of labour. Since labour was the factor of production which was in shortest supply, efficiency demanded that the control of production should be administered through the allocation of labour. The failure, partly for the political reasons already mentioned, of the Commissioner-General for Armament Tasks of the Four-Year Plan to work in unison with the Four-Year Plan Plenipotentiary for the Allocation of Labour made this impossible. In practice, the policy decisions of the Zentrale Planung were implemented mainly through the medium of steel allocations. But although the supply of high grade steel was probably the major limiting factor in the production of major items of land armament, it was not the limiting factor in German war production as a whole.

39. In assessing the shortcomings of the German war production organisation, how-ever, due regard must be paid to the fact that, in the last twelve months of the war it was prevented from functioning with the efficiency of which it would otherwise have been capable by Allied action. By the autumn of 1944, the necessarily com-plicated network of the statistical reporting service had largely broken down under

the pressure of the Allied air offensive and the central government agencies were deprived of much of the information necessary for planning. Long before this the uncertainty produced by continued air-raid damage to the productive capacity of industry had rendered long-term planning impossible. In 1942, Speer had been able to make confident and accurate forecasts of production, for the purpose of planning by the Armed forces, as much as 1½ years ahead. By the middle of 1944 he was unable to commit himself for more than 1½ months ahead. In the final phases, the dislocation of transport and communications deprived the administration of effective control over large sectors of production. It was impossible to make full use of the decreasing resources available because uncertainties of transport prevented the various factors of production from being brought together in the right quantities at the right times and places. And it was impossible to obtain reliable information as to what was happening. In these ways the administrative machine received a series of shattering blows at the very time when it was beginning to emerge from its earlier organisational difficulties and to attain a shape which would have rendered it a more efficient instrument of policy.

# II. – DEVELOPMENT OF ADMINISTRATIVE MEASURES.

## A.- Central Government Administration.

### General Features and Early History of Nazi Economic Administration.

40. The administrative machinery which regulated Germany's production suffered many changes, was at all times extremely complicated, and contained many apparent duplications and contradictions. Before proceeding to describe its development, it is necessary to touch upon certain basic features of the Nazi system of Government which explain some of the complications.

(a) The "leadership principle" which was the central feature of Nazi administrative doctrine frowned upon the democratic method of vesting collective responsibility for policy in a Cabinet of Ministers and supported the authority and initiative of individual Ministers within their respective spheres all of whom were directly and personally responsible to the Fuehrer. Thus consultation between Ministers for the purpose of co-ordinating policy was not only rare and difficult but was even discouraged in the belief that competition was healthy and would spur the individual leaders to greater efficiency. An important consequence of the observation of this principle was the readiness with which Commissioners and Plenipotentiaries were created to deal with particular problems *ad hoc* under powers delegated from Hitler himself, irrespective of the administrative machinery already in existence. By this process Ministers (except in so far as they were successful in obtaining the special appointments for themselves) tended to lose responsibility for policy and to be relegated to the position of supervisors of the administrative bureaucracy.

(*b*) By another manifestation of the "leadership principle" executive action was left to the various branches of industry, commerce and the professions which were compulsorily organised for the purpose into "self-administering" associations.

(*c*) The whole Nazi system of government was permeated by an element of dualism resulting from the co-existence of an elaborate Party organisation with the administrative bureaucracy. The Party as such was empowered to interfere at all levels with the administrative actions of the bureaucracy in the interests of preserving the purity of Nazi policy.

41. The setting up of a self-administering organisation of the national economy which would be capable of translating into action the Government's policy in the economic field was one of the first acts of the Nazi Government on coming into power.

Every aspect of the nation's economic life was represented in one of the four "Estates":-

Reichsnahrstand (Reich Food Estate).

Organisation der Gewerblicher Wirtschaft (Organisation of Industry and Trade).

Deutsche Arbeitsfront (German Labour Front).

Aufbau des Verkehrs (Corporate Organisation of Transport).

Of the seven branches of business covered by the Organisation of Industry and Trade, the largest (Reichsgruppe Industrie) covered all classes of industrial production organised in a large number of trade groups (Wirtschaftsgruppe) with subsidiary sections. The formation of the Wirtschaftsgruppe was greatly facilitated by the previous existence of numerous Trade Associations (Fachverbande) which had come together voluntarily to protect or advance the private interests of their members, often by means of cartel agreements involving a high degree of centralised control of the industries affected. These associations were often accommodated practically intact within the framework of the Reichsgruppe Industrie but the Party was hostile to private cartel agreements and, while it hesitated to interfere with them openly, the interests of the State gradually superseded the private profit motive as the driving force within the Organisation of Industry and Trade.

42. The Organisation of Industry and Trade was subordinated, for policy purposes, to the Reichswirtschaftsministerium (Ministry of Economics). In the early years of the regime, the interference of the Ministry with the freedom of industry was confined to the regulation of import and export trade in the interests of conserving foreign exchange resources. For this purpose the Ministry set up in 1934, for each raw material or group of industrial products, Reich Offices(Reichsstelle)* to scrutinise applications for allocations of foreign exchange and to issue permits.

43. While the three Service Departments placed their contracts separately, machinery was provided within the High Command (OKW) for co-ordinating their requirements and for overall planning of the necessary economic mobilisation measures. This was the special responsibility of the Wirtschafts- und Rustungsamt of OKW which was headed by General Thomas, the German General Staff's chief expert on economic matters. In furtherance of its planning and co-ordinating functions in the field of armament production, Wi-Ru also controlled the Armaments Inspectorate which was responsible for supervising progress with the contracting firms. It was, in addition, responsible for intelligence on the war potential of foreign countries.

44. The most important functions of Wi-Ru in the field of war production were:-

(*a*) to co-ordinate Service production programmes in the light of common strategy and to prevent inter-Service competition for resources;

(*b*) to work out and control in conjunction with the Ministry of Economics the raw material and other requirements raised by Service programmes;

(*c*) to represent to higher authority the necessary programmes of economic development for meeting future armament requirements.

In all three respects Wi-Ru performed indifferently.

---

* Originally called Supervisory Boards (Uberwachungstelle).

45. From 1935 to 1938 Blomberg attempted to make the High Command a reality and to insist on full co-operation between the three Services. After Blomberg's dismissal in 1938, Keitel did nothing to support his subordinates in their attempt to secure effective co-ordination of production programmes and since, for instance, Thomas was unable to resist G.A.F. programmes backed by the authority of Goering, Wi-Ru became in practice a purchasing officer for the Army alone.

46. In elaborating the Service armament programmes into detailed programmes of raw material requirements, the work of Wi-Ru was superficial and amateurish. The individual Services greatly overstated their raw material requirements as a matter of course in order to secure for themselves the largest possible allocations. In pruning these statements in order to bring allocations more into line with the available resources, Wi-Ru continued to over-estimate requirements through native incompetence and inability to detect possibilities of economies through simple and minor alterations in design. This weakness had two consequences. It was always difficult to fit the Service programmes into the Procustean bed of the available resources, and in course of time commodity cheques were issued to armament contractors to an extent considerably in excess of the Ministry of Economics' ability to cover them with raw materials. However, the execution of the armament contracts was never in practice impeded by raw material shortages because the requirements had been initially over-estimated; indeed, the main armament factories were even, in practice, able to build up substantial hidden stocks of raw materials out of the excessive quantities allocated to them. It may be observed, at this point, that a somewhat similar combination of circumstances dogged the footsteps of Germany's production executive throughout the war. The minutes of official conferences are filled with discussions of anticipated difficulties in providing sufficient raw materials to cover projected programmes. Yet raw material shortage has seldom been instanced as the main factor limiting production in practice; in the event some other limiting factor operated to prevent the achievement of the programme and the raw material situation remained in reasonable balance.

47. On the larger question of shaping Germany's economic development in the light of strategic requirements, Thomas was never able to make much headway. As already stated, his belief in the necessity for "rearmament in depth" conflicted abruptly with Hitler's own ideas on the subject, and Thomas was known to be a member of that section of the German General Staff which was most vocal in disapproval of Hitler's strategy in general. Any proposals which Wi-Ru might make were, therefore, subject

to a heavy political discount, and other agencies, such as the Four-Year Plan Office, saw no particular necessity to listen attentively.

48. The Four-Year Plan Office itself was mainly concerned with advancing German self-sufficiency in raw materials of major strategic significance and thereby avoiding one of Germany's gravest mistakes in the war of 1914-18. Its principal achievements were the construction of the synthetic oil and synthetic rubber plants. In addition it was responsible for the considerable expansion in the production of artificial fibres and for the stock-piling of imported materials which could not be synthesised or produced from domestic resources. In the further development of existing domestic resources its activities were on a more modest scale than Thomas considered necessary, though it did put in hand a large scheme of electric power development and, in the face of strong opposition from the Ruhr steelmakers, commence the development of the iron ore resources of Central Germany. In general, however, the Four-Year Plan was content with somewhat limited objectives even in its main field of advancing self-sufficiency, though even these objectives involved a vast outlay in capital construction. Fulfilment of the projects fell further and further behind schedule after the first few years, chiefly on account of difficulty in securing sufficient allocations of steel in competition with the immediate demands of armament production. The impression is gained that they were not pressed with much enthusiasm owing to the feeling, born of the military successes of 1939 and 1940, that they had become unnecessary extravagances.

49. Apart from its activities in planning the expansion of production of strategic raw materials, the Four-Year Plan Office nominally possessed all the functions of a supreme economic planning authority, through the delegation to Goering, as Reich Plenipotentiary, of all Hitler's powers in this field. In practice, however, the Four-Year Plan Office never seems to have functioned in this way and its General Council existed only on paper. Instead, as the course of the war gave rise to particular economic problems which exceeded the competence of the particular Ministry concerned, the authority which had been delegated by Hitler to Goering was delegated by him to turn to a further crop of Plenipotentiaries and Special Commissioners with their own staffs and super-Ministerial authority. It was usual to appoint prominent Party members to such posts. Among a list of such special appointments were: -

Plenipotentiary for Armaments and War Production: Speer.
Plenipotentiary for Building: Speer.

Plenipotentiary for Control of Labour: Sauckel.

Commissioner for Control of Prices: Fishböck.

To these must be added: -

Reich Housing Commissioner: Ley

Reich Commissioner for Shipping: Kaufmann.

who derived their authority direct from Hitler.

These appointments were not, however, made for the most part until a much later stage when the regular administrative organs of the State had shown themselves to be incapable of meeting contemporary requirements.

50. The outbreak of war in September 1939 necessitated few administrative changes of importance. The necessary powers for the mobilisation of the economy had been placed in the hands of the Minister of Economics (Funk) who had been vested for this purpose with the additional powers of a Plenipotentiary for Economics. In November, Thomas laid before the Reichsgruppe Industrie a plan containing most of the essential measures for total mobilisation of industrial resources and man-power but was rebuked by Goering for making suggestions which would cause alarm and despondency and which were not necessitated by the strategic situation. It was probably in order to prevent further manifestations of Thomas's urge to mobilise Germany's war economy that Funk's powers as Plenipotentiary for Economics were transferred to Goering in December and put into cold storage. Funk shared the general optimism and did not protest; Thomas made one of his many unsuccessful attempts to resign and thenceforth lost much of his remaining influence in matters of general economic policy.

51. The only other significant administrative changes up to the end of 1941 were: -

(*a*) the extension of the powers of the Reichsstelle to cover control of all raw material allocations.

(*b*) the appointment of Fritz Todt as Minister of Armaments and Munitions.

The former measure was a natural war-time development of the control of the Reichsstelle over imports and exports. The latter was less important than it appears at first sight owing to the limitation of the Minister's functions, as will be shown below.

52. During the period 1939-41 the administrative structure of war production may be summarised as follows:-

(*a*) Armament production programmes were drawn up, and the contracts allocated, by the individual Service Departments, subject to the co-ordination of OKW/Wi-Ru, which was in practice largely nominal. The contracts were placed with the main armament firms, the so-called A-Betriebe, numbering about 5,000 individual concerns, which were "nursed" by the local Armament Inspectorates.

(*b*) The main armament contractors were left in effect to sub-contract and to obtain supplies of components on their own initiative from the smaller firms (C-Betriebe) numbering some 60,000. These firms remained under the control of the Ministry of Economics working through its regional offices.

(*c*) The allocation of raw materials for armaments contracts was the responsibility of OKW/Wi-Ru, in consultation with the Ministry of Economics, which, through the Reichsstelle controlled the raw material producers.

(*d*) The overall supply of labour was determined centrally by the Ministry of Labour which met the demands of the Services by calling up men on an age-group basis and the demands of industry by reservations on the basis of individual indispensability in their current occupations. It was the function of the Armament Inspectorate to ensure, by negotiation with the Regional Labour Offices, that A-Betriebe retained sufficient labour. The interests in this connection of other firms were in the hands of the regional offices of the Ministry of Economics.

(*e*) In view of this set-up, the activities of the Minister of Armaments and Munitions were in effect restricted to the supply of efficiency experts to tackle production engineering problems within the armaments industry in order to make the best use of the raw materials and labour allocated by other authorities in the execution of the contracts placed by the Services. Otherwise his functions were purely consultative. This limited task suited the personality of Todt, who is said to have been more interested in his building organisation than in his functions as Minister of Armaments and Munitions.

53. Some of the deficiencies of this machinery have already been mentioned. There was no effective co-ordination of Service production programmes. There was little

examination of and planning for the subsidiary requirements of the main armament programmes, which was left to sub-contracting on a commercial basis. Raw materials were wastefully allocated. And there was little or no attempt above the regional level to secure co-ordination of the labour supply with the supply of other resources. But although the system operated inefficiently and wastefully and produced no significant increase in armaments output in the first two years of war, it served to supply the Armed Forces with their requirements up to the level demanded by contemporary German strategy.

## *The Speer Era.*

54. The inadequacy of the existing machinery became a handicap only when, in 1942, there were simultaneous demands for the mobilisation of more man-power for the armed forces and for increased armament production to replace the heavy losses of the first winter campaign in Russia. In the course of the year there were three significant developments:-

55. At the end of March 1942 Fritz Sauckel was appointed Plenipotentiary for Allocation of Labour under the Four-Year Plan for the purpose of –

(i)   recruiting new labour at home and abroad;

(ii)  allocating labour to industry;

(iii) freeing man-power for the Armed Forces from redundant industrial activities and by a "comb-out".

With Sauckel's appointment the Ministry of Labour lost all effective control of labour policy but remained as the administrative agency through which Sauckel's policies were enforced.

56. In the early part of 1942 Hans Kehrl, an industrialist turned civil servant in the Ministry of Economics, took in hand the reorganisation of the raw material controls. By that time the multiplication of Reichsstelle had led to a situation in which armament-contracting firms were compelled to seek permits from as many as a dozen different offices for the materials required in the execution of one contract. The divergence of methods and policies as between the different offices sometimes led to hold-ups in production through lack of one material; at other times it enabled manufacturers to obtain excessive allocations which either disappeared into hidden

stocks or were used for the manufacture of consumer goods. Moreover, the existence of so many separate controls made it much more difficult to impose upon industry any policy regarding the use of substitute materials. Kehrl's solution was to combine the existing Reichsstelle into larger groups. For instance, in February 1942 the Reich Office for Cotton, Cotton Yarns and Fibres and the Reich Office of Silk, Rayon and Staple Fibre were merged into a single Reich Office for Textile Economy which later also absorbed the Reich Office for Wool and Hair and the Reich Office for Bast Fibres. In the second place, Kehrl introduced an innovation in forming Reich Associations for certain products in which it was desirable that official control of production and allocation should be much more closely linked with the direction of the producing firms. In such cases control of the Reichsstelle was virtually handed over to the appropriate self-administering industrial association and the personnel engaged in the activities of the Reich Association and the Wirtschaftsgruppe were largely identical.

57. Having reorganised the raw material controls on these lines, Kehrl sought to improve their efficiency in the planning and execution of allocations by associating them more closely with their customers. To this end, he outlined a number of "spheres of control" (Lenkungsbereiche), each of which was put in the charge of a Special Commissioner (Reichsbeauftragte), who presided over all firms producing a given material together with the principal firms consuming the material and the relevant trade associations. The important feature of this form of organisation was the rule that every manufacturing firm should belong to one "sphere of control", and one only; this being the sphere from which it drew its principal raw material. Subsidiary materials were provided by block allocations between one "sphere of control" and another out of which all the requirements of member firms were to be met. This reform was an endeavour to relieve individual firms of much of their former papers work. Whether the bureaucracy would have proved capable of handling the extremely intricate problems of inter-control allocations in the absence of a central plan to guide them is difficult to say as the system never fully came into operation before the control of raw material production was taken over by Speer.

58. The third important event of the spring of 1942 was Speer's appointment as Minister of Armaments and Munitions in February, in succession to Todt, on the latter's death in an air accident. Albert Speer, whose age at the time was 37, was an architect by profession and a protégé of Todt. He had gained distinction

by his work in the design of many of the Nazi public buildings and had become Hitler's private architect. Since the outbreak of war he had been doing good work with his building organisation in the erection of armament factories. The call to office came as a surprise to Speer, who had no illusions regarding the imperfections of the existing production machinery and accepted his post only on condition that he received Hitler's full backing in the event of inter-departmental controversies. Within a few days he was given much of the necessary authority by his appointment as Commissioner-General for Armaments Tasks under the Four-Year Plan. It is of interest that Goering, from whom Speer nominally derived his powers, was not consulted in the appointment.

59. Speer's policy over the next three years can be easily described. He saw that a considerable immediate increase in armament production could be achieved merely by eliminating the inefficiencies tolerated by his predecessors and rationalising methods of production. To this end he worked to place effective control of production in the hands of properly qualified technicians regardless of their political background or official status. At the same time, he realised that to push the increase in armament production beyond a certain point would require fuller mobilisation of German economic resources, and that the approach to total mobilisation could only be achieved by concentrating the control of resources in the hands of a small executive who knew what they wanted and had a central plan for getting it.

60. Speer's first and most notable contribution to German administrative organisation was his creation of the Committees (Ausschusse) and Rings (Ringe). From the standpoint of securing increased efficiency in armaments production, the multiplicity of existing industrial organisations suffered from one simple defect – that none of them dealt exclusively with weapon and munitions production. Thus the Wirtschaftsgruppe of the Reichsgruppe Industrie were organised on a professional or occupational basis: that is to say all iron-founders were grouped together as being equally engaged in casting iron, whether for the purpose of producing kitchen stoves or bombs. The Reich Associations evolved by Kehrl showed a similar width of competence. By 1942 the resultant confusion had been further confounded by the effect of an order of 1939, intended to economise man-power in the bureaucracy, which had forbidden changes in the professional affiliations of firms. Thus a piano factory which had been converted to the manufacture of aircraft wings had to transact its official business through the Wirtschaftsgruppe dealing with musical instruments

and a chocolate firm engaged on the manufacture of small arms ammunition still remained, for purposes of administration, a member of the confectionery trade.

61. The Ausschusse created by Speer were formed for the purpose of dealing with particular end-products in the field of armaments production, such as tanks, aero-engines, guns, ammunition, &c. On each Ausschuss were represented all the firms engaged in the production of a particular weapon, regardless of their other activities and affiliations. In each case, one firm, chosen for its technical efficiency, was selected as the leader and its representative became chairman of the Ausschuss. All the representatives were technicians – proprietors or directors were specifically debarred unless possessing the requisite technical qualifications – and were all under 40 in the absence of a special dispensation from Speer himself. There were no "official" representatives and the leader firm provided the necessary office staff from its own resources; all the members were unpaid. Under the direction of their leader, the members of the Ausschusse were enjoined to pool patents, production processes and working experience with the object of securing within the industry maximum utilisation of capacity, maximum economy of materials and labour, simplification of production technique and the raising of average levels of efficiency to the standard of the most efficient firm.

62. The Ringe were similarly organised and performed similar functions in fields of raw material or components production which were of vital importance to the armaments industry. Here, in some cases, the departure from the previous administrative pattern was less abrupt in that, for instance, the Ring of the iron and steel fabricating industry was not performing functions markedly different from the Reich Association for Iron.

63. In spite of such duplications in some directions and of redundancies in others, no existing organisations were wound up on the formation of the Ausschusse and Ringe, or on further intrusions into their fields of competence, by Speer's subsequent organisational innovations. Throughout the war the German bureaucracy showed itself extremely tenacious of office and Speer, who had to contend with constant jealousy and opposition from Party circles, did not make enemies gratuitously. Thus, while he was interested in acquiring and combining under his own hand the controlling functions and authority of key offices under the jurisdiction of other Ministries, he was usually content either to take over the existing staff and use it in administrative capacities or to leave it in peace to perform residual functions. In some cases

these were of some usefulness – for example, in the distribution of goods for civilian consumption or in the compilation of statistics – but, in general, the process of reorganisation left an inflated bureaucracy which exercised a drain on the nation's manpower out of all proportion to its effectiveness.

64. Speer's acquisition of full controlling powers in the field of industrial production was, however, a gradual one. Although his authority as Commissioner-General enabled him to set up Ausschusse and Ringe in fields of production which he did not directly control, their authority in the first instance did not extend beyond the responsibilities for rationalisation of production methods, which the Ministry of Armaments and Munitions had already possessed under Todt. It was, however, Speer's intention to remove from the Service Departments all responsibility for armaments production other than the initial statement of requirements and to transfer from the Ministry of Economics the responsibility from controlling and allocating raw materials. Centralisation of the control of programmes and allocations under a higher planning staff was, in fact, an essential accompaniment to the investment of Ausschusse and Ringe with the responsibility for executing particular programmes. The Ausschusse and Ringe were set up to perform particular specialised tasks and were encouraged to develop "one-track minds". But without higher authority to hold the balance between them the experiment could only have ended in competition for resources between them without regard to strategic requirements. As it was, the necessary central control was only imposed by degrees. The steps in the process were as follows:-

65. In the absence of a centralised planning and co-ordinating organisation Speer managed to set up the Zentrale Planung, nominally within the Four-Year-Plan Office, to secure co-operation on an informal basis – one of the few effective examples of voluntary inter-Ministerial co-operation in Germany which has come to light. The principal members were Speer, Milch and Koerner of the Four-Year-Plan Office. The ready co-operation of Milch was particularly valuable in securing central co-ordination of the aircraft production programmes since Goering was opposed to Speer's interference with aircraft production in any way. The decisions of ZP were, moreover, made effective through the control of raw material allocations exercised by the Ministry of Economics. Although Funk was not represented on ZP, he always seems to have been amenable to dictation from Speer, who, in addition, built up a close connection with Kehrl. It is, however, noteworthy that Sauckel, the Labour Controller,

was not a member of ZP and would only accept its decisions as "advisory". Central planning decisions were never implemented through allocations of labour in spite of the fact that this was the major economic factor in shortest supply and therefore, theoretically, the factor around which production plans should have been built.

66. Speer's control over armament production was advanced in May 1942 by the transfer to his Ministry of the Rüstungsamt of Wi-Ru, which brought with it the control of production of army equipment and the ownership of the Armaments Inspectorate. This transfer was negotiated amicably with Thomas, who continued temporarily as head of the Rüstungsamt, but eventually retired into private life. The other half of Wi-Ru, the Wehrwirtschaftsamt, remained in OKW to continue its work on foreign economic intelligence, its name being changed later to Feldwirtschaftsamt.

67. In handling the problem of production of land armaments Speer adopted a policy which he later applied generally to all armaments. He insisted on confining the competence of the Wehrmacht to the specification of their requirements. The choice of factories and of methods of production for meeting them was claimed as the exclusive concern of the Speer Ministry for discussion, particularly, between the Ministry and the Aussschusse concerned. In practice, the requirements of the Wehrmacht were often Fuhrerforderungen drawn up by Hitler himself and transmitted uncritically and without alteration by Keitel and the General Staff. In practice, they were also in many cases discussed between Hitler and Speer, without the participation of the soldiers, before transmission. The Ministry retained the right to suggest modifications in the specifications in the interests of greater efficiency in production, after the discussion with the Ausschusse, and frequently exercised this right with great effect.

68. The transfer to Speer of the control of naval production proceeded with equal smoothness after the appointment as head of OKM of Doenitz, with whom Speer was on intimate terms. Doenitz did not share the views of Raeder, who, like Goering, insisted on the principle that his Service should be self-contained in every respect. Doenitz allowed himself to be convinced that Speer's experts would make much more effective use of the materials allocated to the Navy than had been the case under the Raeder regime. He was rewarded by the rapidity with which the new-type U-boats were developed and put into mass-production in 1943-44.

69. Speer's control over raw material allocations, which he had hitherto only been able to influence directly by representations made through the Zentrale Planung, was made absolute in September 1943. For some time past he had been exerting an

increasing influence in the affairs of the Ministry of Economics; for instance, he had regarded with approval the efforts of Kehrl to rationalise the raw material controls and had been able to secure his preferment at the expense of General Hanneken, who had hitherto had charge of allocations for the armaments programme. He now negotiated the transfer to himself of all the Ministry of Economics' powers of control of production by amicable agreement with the amiable and unambitious Funk. This brought with it the responsibility of ensuring essential supplies for the civilian population (which Speer tackled with characteristic energy and enthusiasm) as well as the opportunity to divert an increasing proportion of the available raw material supplies to armaments production. Funk henceforth was a figure of little importance in the economic field, his major responsibilities being confined to the control of foreign trade and the regulation of the distributive trades within Germany. With this transfer of powers, Speer's Ministry was renamed the Ministry of Armaments and War Production (Reichsministerium für Rüstungs-und Kriegsproduktion).

70. The combination under one hand of the responsibility for executing land and naval armament programmes and of the control of allocation of raw materials enabled Speer to create a balanced administrative machine for the control of German war production as a whole, with the one exception of aircraft production. The principal departments which he created within the Ministry* to this end and their main functions were as follows:-

(a) Negotiations with the Service Departments on matters of design and specifications were in the hands of the *Technisches Amt* under Saur. The principal function of the Department was to examine the requirements stated by the Services in the light of the technical possibilities of production and to suggest to the Services modifications in design and specification which would eliminate production problems without necessarily affecting the performance of the weapons. For this purpose the *Technisches Amt* became administratively responsible for most of the Ausschusse dealing with armament end-products, which were naturally involved in the detailed discussions with the Service weapon experts. Saur also controlled the Development Commissions (Entwicklungskommissionen)

---

* From the time of its creation in September 1943 until the end of the war the Speer Ministry and its dependent Ausschusse and Ringe were repeatedly reorganised. Only the main features of the organisation are considered here, and not necessarily in chronological sequence.

which were set up increasing numbers to control the development of new types of weapons. The object of these commissions was to bring industry and the Service Research establishments into contact at the early stages of development in order that new weapon designs might be developed from the start with an eye to the practical production possibilities. For this reason the heads of the Development Commissions were invariably production experts, drawn from the appropriate Ausschusse.

(*b*) The control of raw material production and allocations (and hence of most of the Ringe) was in the hands of the *Rohstoffamt*, under Kehrl who was imported from the Ministry of Economics and brought with him control of the Reichsstelle, Reichsvereinigungen and other relevant agencies formerly under the authority of Funk.

(*c*) Responsibility for the organisation of the flow of components and auxiliary equipment requirements with the *Rüstungslieferungsamt* (Schrieber). This department had originally been set up by Speer in an attempt to secure some co-ordination between armament production planning and the production of the vast variety of components and auxiliary equipment by sub-contractors. These numbered over 50,000 separate firms which prior to September 1943 remained under the control of the Ministry of Economics and were for the most part organised only within the framework of the Reichsgruppe Industrie and not according to the system of Ausschüsse and Ringe. With the extension of Speer's powers in September 1943 it became possible to organise the more important branches of the Zulieferungsindustrie increasingly as sub-sections of the Ausschüsse which they principally served. The Rüstungslieferungsamt therefore became an anachronism, but it was not wound up until the autumn of 1944, and then only because Schieber became the object of Party attacks. Its functions were subsequently transferred to the Technisches Amt.

(*d*) Co-ordination of the results of the activities of the three departments named above for the purpose of overall planning was in the hands of the *Planungsamt*. Officially this department was the executive office of the Zentrale Planung, but in practice it may be considered part of the Speer Ministry. Since its decisions were mainly enforced through the allocation of raw materials, it was appropriately headed by Kehrl, the chief of the Rohstoffamt. It possessed its own statistical office, under Wagenfuhr of the Institut für Konjunkturforschung, for the collation and presentation of statistics in the form required for central planning.

(*e*) The processing of armament orders was in the hands of the *Rüstungsamt*, the OKW's supervisory organisation which had been taken over from Wi-Ru in 1942. The duties of the Rüstungsamt were therefore entirely executive, in which connection it controlled the regional organisation of the Armaments Inspectorate and of the Maschinelles Berichtwesen – the organisation for collecting from firms and processing all statistics relating to production, costs, deliveries, employment, &c. One section of the Rüstungsamt (Arbeitseinsatz), however, had the important function of negotiating the labour requirements of the armaments industry with Sauckel, the Labour Controller. The *Rüstungsamt* ceased to have a separate existence in November 1944 when it was merged with the *Zentralamt* as the first part of a programme for concentrating and reducing the unwieldly subsidiary bureaucracy of the Ministry. The immediate occasion for the change was the desire of the head of the Rüstungsamt (General Waeger) to return to active service.

(*f*) The *Produktionsamt* (Seebauer) had the straightforward task of making the most of the residual productive capacity of the consumer goods industries, both for the supply of essential goods to the civil population and, by concentration and increased technical efficiency, with the object of releasing additional productive capacity for armaments production. In the latter capacity it was in practice allowed to supervise the production of a number of subsidiary armament items and materials.

(*g*) The *Zentralamt* was initially responsible only for general administration, including the regional organisation of the Ministry, but became the nucleus round which most of the subsidiary administrative functions were concentrated in the reorganisations of the autumn of 1944. Thus it absorbed, as well as the Rüstungsamt, the Generalreferat Wirtschaft und Finanzen, the office which transacted the Ministry's financial business. The change was precipitated by Party attacks on the Speer Ministry within which Liebel, the head of the Zentralamt, was the principal target. Speer replaced him by Hupfauer, an official of the Labour Front, in order to frustrate an attempt by Himmler to infiltrate a representative of the S.D., and in the hope of lessening the opposition from Sauckel and the Gauleiters who, by their influence on labour allocations, were able seriously to obstruct the fulfilment of Speer's armament production plans. In this connection, it will be observed that, with the transfer of the Rüstungsamt, Hupfauer became responsible for Arbeitseinsatz.

(*h*) The remaining departments of the Ministry were the *Amt Bau – Organization Todt* (Dorsch) and the *Amt Energie* (Schulze-Fielitz) which, as their titles denote, were responsible respectively for the constructional industries and for power and gas supplies.

71. At the time of the creation of the Ministry of Armaments and War Production in September 1943, Goering was successful in retaining for himself control of all aircraft production and equipment. The decree setting out Speer's increased powers specifically stated that "responsibility for end-product manufacture for the Luftwaffe remains with the Air Ministry, Director of Air Ordnance". The responsibility of the Speer Ministry as a whole was to supply raw materials and components, and the propensity of the Technisches Amt to interfere in production matters was curbed by an instruction that its function was "to render material assistance". Consequently the Ministry's influence on aircraft production continued to be slight, though the worst excesses of inter-Service competition for materials were curbed by Speer's success in securing the collaboration of Milch on the Zentrale Planung.

72. The transfer of the responsibility for aircraft production to Speer was precipitated by the American strategic bombers which, at the end of February 1944, inflicted such damage on the fighter assembly factories that Milch felt unable to cope with the situation and appealed to Speer for help. Speer immediately formed Saur and a team of trouble-breakers from each department of the Ministry into the "Jaegerstab" which (partly by reason of the inertia and inefficiency of the previous regime) produced a remarkable recovery in production almost immediately. The logic of this achievement did not fail to penetrate even Goering who in June 1944 was persuaded to transfer responsibilities for all classes of aircraft production (together with Milch) to Speer, retaining for the Luftwaffe only the right to specify their design and quantity requirements, in conformity with the position of the other Services. The Jaegerstabe then ceased to exist.

73. Although Speer had, by the Summer of 1944 obtained control of all branches of raw material production and manufacturing industry, the administrative machinery of his Ministry was still far from being adequately organised for the efficient exercise of the powers acquired. Since these powers had been acquired piecemeal, considerable differences existed between the methods and thoroughness of the organisation of those aspects of war production which had been brought under Speer's control early and those which had been assimilated later. Moreover, as has already been explained, the acquisition of powers had carried with it the acquisition of complete sections of the previous bureaucracy which required reorganisation and assimilation to the totally different forms of administrative control preferred by Speer. A long programme of administrative reform was therefore required, and was envisaged in order to shape the amorphous collection of agencies and appendages of RMfRuK into a compact administrative machine. The war did not, however, last long enough to permit more than a proportion of the necessary reforms to be introduced. Two of these are of sufficient interest to be considered in some detail.

74. Under the OKW administration of armaments production, no attempt was made to plan the stages of production behind the end-products and their major components. Thus, although the allocations of raw materials required for the achievement of a particular programme of weapon production were worked out and made to main contractors, no inquiry was made into the capacity of manufacturers of intermediate products to meet the requirements of the main contractors in time and quantity. As long as the level of armaments production was too low to place any serious strain on the capacity of German industry as a whole, this omission did not lead to any serious bottlenecks in production, though at all times the capacity of the basic industries, such as steel, to deliver primary materials (Vorlieferungen) in the form of particular semi-products such as forgings, plates, sections &c., appears to have acted as a limiting factor in fixing programmes. But once the basic materials had been secured by the main contractor there were plenty of firms to which work could be let out for machining, &c. (Unterlieferungen). And the capacity of the industries supplying auxiliary equipment (Zulieferungen) which is usually "bought out" (*e.g.* sparking-plugs and carburettors) was sufficient to be able to meet the demands coming forward on the normal commercial basis.

75. With the large and rapid rise in armaments production from the beginning of 1942 onwards, the ability of the components industries to keep pace became a matter

of great importance. But owing to the lack of unity and co-ordination in the control of programmes for the production of end-products during this period, planning of the production of intermediate products was rendered impossible. It was impossible even to obtain the information on which planning could have been based. The problem was further complicated by the direct demand of the Services and of other Government departments for most of the products of the Zulieferungsindustrie as spare parts and by the practice which the Services developed of buying some products direct and issuing them to contractors as "embodiment loans".

76. As long as Speer enjoyed full control of only limited sectors of the total field of production no comprehensive solution of the problem could be produced. The best which could be done in practice was to create the Rustungslieferungsamt and subordinate organisations in the Zulieferungsindustrie in order to secure the greatest increase in production which the circumstances would permit in the industries concerned. In these circumstances some of the Ausschusse which were earliest in the field with full administrative functions succeeded in solving their own difficulties at the expense of others by the expedient of including their principal component suppliers in their membership. But, more often, the firms represented on the Ausschusse pressed for ever higher production achievements, tended to concentrate more and more on assembly, and to rely more and more on outside firms to supply components and auxiliary equipment. But as co-ordination between the Ausschusse and Ringe was deficient, production plans frequently failed to provide for a properly co-ordinated flow of components and sub-assemblies, with the result that bottlenecks and hold-ups in the later processes of production were increasingly frequent.

77. During the latter part of 1944, when control of all branches of weapon production had finally passed to Speer, an extensive reorganisation of the Ausschusse and Ringe was put in hand in order to facilitate more coherent central planning. For instance, the acquisition of control over aircraft production enabled Speer to take the Hauptausschuss Triebwerke, which was hitherto responsible for aero-engine production, and subordinate it, as the Hauptgruppe Triebwerke, to the Hauptausschuss Motoren & Getriebe. This administrative change signalised the achievement of a position, after five years of internecine competition, in which the aero-engine manufacturers and the manufacturers of other types of engines, who employed much the same range of component and equipment suppliers, would at last be subject to the control of the same planning authority. In order to assist in securing the fruits of these

reforms, new statistical machinery was in preparation during 1944 based upon a system of code numbers for all classes of goods entering into production, which would have enabled accurate data to be obtained of the relationships between the producers of end-products and their various suppliers. The war, however, ended before the new system could be introduced, and it is indicative of the general shortcomings of the German administrative machine that the highly important problem of co-ordinating component production with end-product manufacture was, throughout the war, planned on a rule-of-thumb basis, if at all. In consequence, the leaders of the German production executive have to this day only the vaguest ideas of the overall man-hour costs of the various items produced and of their breakdown. Hans Kehrl, probably the shrewdest and steadiest of Germany's war-time economic administrators, has gone so far as to say that he regards this problem as incapable of any satisfactory and radical solution in time of war and that, in effect, it is better to trust to luck.

78. While these and other basic reforms in the administrative structure were being planned, there began the deterioration in the productive capacity of the German war industry and simultaneously the deterioration in Germany's strategic position which followed the Battle of France. In view of the highly sectionalised organisation of production at the time, adjustment to the requirements of the new situation could not be expected to follow automatically and required drastic action by higher authority. This, characteristically, took the form of a further crop of improvisations, which resulted in the insertion of a fresh horizontal layer of controlling authority into the administrative machinery. Speer realised that activities which would not contribute to the supply of finished equipment within the next six months were now of doubtful value. One manifestation of this was the cessation of all projects of construction and capital development, the abandonment of repairs to damaged factories engaged in producing capital equipment, and the increasing diversion of productive capacity in the armaments industry to the production of spare parts and repair work at the expense of the production of new equipment. In addition drastic action was taken to remove unnecessary obstacles to the maximum production of the superior types of equipment which had been singled out for priority, by means of administrative measures which were known collectively as the Concentration Programme. This involved, in each major class of weapon production, the appointment of a Programme Commissioner (a production expert from the Ausschuss) with powers to rationalise the activities of the Development Commissions. The Programme Commissioner was able to stop work on

developments which did not promise to produce practicable improvements on existing weapon designs within a significant period of time, and to concentrate further
activities on the most practicable and promising of the new developments. There were
designated as "Schwerpunkte". At the same time the Commissioner was able in the
interests of maximum output to enforce the cessation of modifications to equipment
already in mass production, the argument being that if the equipment was good enough
for mass production in the first instance, the balance of advantage now lay in obtaining
the maximum production of it rather than in seeking further minor improvements.
In practice, a time limit was set for the introduction of modifications to particular
designs, after which they became "frozen" and were declared "Fertigtypen" for unim-
peded mass production. By this means an attempt was made to curb the enthusiasm of
Service weapon experts, and the design staffs of manufacturers, for continually introducing modifications to designs already in production, which had for so long acted as
an obstacle to optimum utilisation of the productive capacity available.

79. The most important and in many ways the most characteristic of Speer's improvisations at this time was, however, the creation of the Rustungsstab (Armaments
Staff). This was a bigger and better Jaegerstab. The success of the latter in tackling
the emergency in fighter production in the spring of 1944 convinced Speer that a
similar organisation might now do useful work in the entire field of armament production. From officials within the Ministry or members of industry, Speer selected
a Commissioner for each major branch of production. These, together with representatives of the Amt Bau, Power Controller, Railways, Post Office, Civil Defence,
and with the Zentral Amt handling responsibility for labour supplies, were formed
into the Rustungsstab, which became an informal board of directors for the whole
industrial effort. The Rüstungsstab held daily meetings, usually conducted by Saur,
at which the latest misfortunes and difficulties of the various Ausschusse and Ringe
would be brought forward, discussed and, as far as possible, solved with the assistance
of the various interests represented. As in the case of the Jaegerstab, the Rustüngsstab
was the Speer Ministry in miniature, authorised to make immediate dispositions to
meet the new emergencies which were arising from day to day. It survived to the end,
being evacuated in turn to Blankenburg, Nordhausen and Bayreuth, and was finally
established in a special train.

80. The final reorganisations of the administrative machinery of the Speer Ministry
had hardly time to become effective before the loss of territory and the growing

dislocation of production and communications due to air attack virtually deprived the central Government of ability to plan coherently or control effectively the activities of its executive agencies. An abortive attempt was made to deal with the situation by decentralisation. This concluding episode may, however, best be considered in conjunction with other aspects of the regional organisation of administration. It remains, under the heading of Central Government Organisation, to consider the manner in which the central control of labour was operated and to examine the adequacy of the auxiliary machinery for facilitating planning and production control.

## *The Machinery of Labour Control.*

81. There was no registration of labour for national service in Germany before 1943. This was, to some extent, unnecessary since the introduction of "labour books" in 1935 had, in practice, already provided the Government with the necessary information for the classification of the working population for mobilisation purposes. Early in 1939 the Government took powers by decree to conscript or direct any adult inhabitant of the Reich for any purpose of national importance. This was, however, to a large extent a precautionary measure and the powers were at first used only sparingly for the direction of industrial labour. In the early years of the war persuasion and ordinary commercial incentives were relied upon to a large extent to provide labour for war-essential purposes. Official control was introduced (by a decree of September 1939) only to the extent of making changes of employment conditional on the consent of a Labour Office.

82. The call-up for the Armed Forces was operated by the traditional Continental method of mobilising classes according to age-groups. Reservations in the interests of essential work were from the first made on an individual basis, and there was no official schedule of industrial occupations which ensured automatic exemption. In each Wehrkreis, Commissions representative of the civil authorities, as well as the military, periodically visited factories and, after examining the personnel employed in relation to the work undertaken, negotiated with the management the release of redundant labour. That, at least, was the manner in which the system worked in theory. In practice employers were often called upon to surrender a certain number of workers from certain categories and were left to decide for themselves which men they could most easily spare.

83. The procurement of additional labour for essential war work (for example, for A-Betriebe with armament contracts) was left entirely to negotiation on a regional level. The firm concerned would apply to its Regional Labour Office (usually with the support of the Rüstungskommando), and the Regional Labour Office would endeavour to meet the demand out of the pool of labour becoming available within the region. The principal means of replenishing the pool were the activities of the Comb-out Commissions. These (which were later supplemented by Investigating Commissions appointed by the Ministry of Armaments and Munitions) toured the factories for the purpose of combing-out redundant workers in the same manner as the call-up Commissions, with whom they co-operated, the personnel being in many cases virtually identical. The labour so combed-out was notified to the Labour Offices for redirection. If a sufficient pool was not created by these means, the Regional Labour Offices could use their powers of conscription to fill the gap. These powers were not often used and there was rarely any inter-regional transfer of conscripted labour. By September 1942 the number of workers who had been compulsorily directed in this manner in the whole of Germany was less than 700,000. This figure does not include workers called up compulsorily for Emergency service (*e.g.*, clearance of air-raid debris and other temporary duties); more extensive use was made of the Emergency Service Decree to meet exceptional demands of this kind.

84. Although the Labour Offices possessed, in the last resort, full powers of compulsion and were placed in a position to exercise it by reason of the necessity to notify proposed changes of employment, their authority was in practice seriously undermined by a clause in the Change of Employment Order which enabled workers to leave their jobs by mutual consent of employer and employed. Under this provision workers were even able to leave war industries with the consent of their employers until June 1942, when the Order was amended. Even then opportunities for evasion remained and the Labour Offices were sometimes left with no alternative but to agree to accomplished facts with which they were confronted by collusion between employers and employed.

85. This system worked well enough as long as the combined demands of the Armed Forces for man-power and or armament production for essential workers did not exceed the total pool of labour formed by the pre-war working population and by the increment of new labour recruited from the Occupied Territories and from previously unoccupied persons attracted into employment by normal incentives.

Moreover, the regional machinery for combing-out redundant labour and reallocating it locally was adequate to meet essential demands without the necessity of planning reallocation on a national level. The situation changed only with the protraction of the Eastern war and with the growth during 1942 of a simultaneous demand for more man-power for the Armed Forces and more labour for war industry. The position became acute after Stalingrad. Thereafter the Government was faced with a chronic man-power shortage and with the necessity both of calling out all possible reserves of man-power and of practising the utmost economy in its utilisation.

86. The situation was taken in hand in a characteristic manner. Sauckel, a rising figure in the Party, and formerly Gauleiter of Silesia, was appointed General Plenipotentiary for Labour Control under the Five-Year Plan. The Ministry of Labour was subordinated to him and became in effect purely an administrative organ. He was given the task of combing out labour from German industry, both to provide more man-power for the forces and for reallocation to essential work, and of recruiting allocating new labour both from the Occupied Territories and from reserves of hitherto unoccupied labour at home. One of the first acts was to nominate the Gauleiters as his local deputies, though the Regional Labour Offices of the Ministry of Labour remained the channels through which regional control of labour was exercised.

87. Under the Sauckel regime the Regional Offices remained the focal points from which the concentration and reallocation of surplus labour was directed. Sauckel was concerned with overall measures designed to replenish their reserves and, to some extent, with overall planning of labour utilisation. Recruitment in the Occupied Territories was the chief source of new labour for industry. The native labour force available for home employment fell steadily owing to the withdrawal of man-power for the forces and it was only possible to retard the decline by mobilising the remaining reserves of unoccupied persons as far as possible. To this end compulsory registration of all men (ages 16-65) and women (ages 17-45) was ordered for the first time in January 1943.

88. The allocation of the new labour mobilised by Sauckel in the best interests of the national war effort obviously required the closest collaboration between Sauckel and Speer. This collaboration was not forthcoming, and it is obvious that there was much personal antipathy between the two men. For the account of their differences we are mainly dependent upon the statements of Speer and his associates

who cannot be considered disinterested parties. One may imagine that the griev-
ances were not entirely on their side. For instance, the Ministry of Armaments and
Munitions had long since been dabbling in the comb-out business. It had set up its
own Investigating Commissions (Prufungskommissionen) which tended to work in
competition with the Comb-out Commissions of the Ministry of Labour in search
of redundant workers, and claimed the right to reallocate these within the armaments industry through the machinery of the Regional Armament Commissions.
The Ministry was also engaged in endeavouring to free complete factories in the
consumer goods industries for transfer to war work by concentration of production
in selected firms (the so-called Wissmanaktion, carried on by Wissman in his capacity as Speer's Chief Commissioner for Transfer Industries – Generalbeauftragter
für Betriebsumsetzung) and it was Speer's intention to hand over the released
labour forces and executives *en bloc* to favoured armaments firms. Both these activities seem to have been flagrant infringements of the responsibilities of the Labour
Offices and if they had been allowed to develop unchecked the normal machinery of labour control might well have broken down. Sauckel accordingly cannot
be blamed for insisting that they should be brought under his control. Similarly,
he cannot be considered unreasonable in resisting Speer's claim to authority, as
General Plenipotentiary for Armaments Tasks under the Four-Year Plan, to dictate
economic policy to all the other commissioners and Plenipotentiaries appointed
under the Four-Year Plan. On the other hand, Sauckel appears to have allowed
political jealousy to get the better of his common sense in refusing to co-operate
with the Zentrale Planung. His presence and co-operation on this body would, for
the first time, have given Germany the effective overall economic planning authority, the absence of which had so markedly affected the efficiency of her war effort
hitherto. Sauckel, however, considered that the Zentrale Planung had no authority
over economic policy outside the field of industrial production and treated its decisions as recommendations which he was free to disregard rather than injunctions to
be fulfilled. Sauckel, in turn, seems to have exceeded his own rights in disputing
the authority of the Regional Armament Commissions to decide which were the
classes of production deserving priority for the supply of labour in their districts.

89. Since the effective control of labour allocations lay with the Regional Labour
Offices very close co-operation was clearly necessary between the Speer Ministry and
Sauckel's office in order that priority demands for labour within regions arising from

particular developments of armament production should be notified by RMfRuK in time for the Labour Controller to instruct the Regional Labour Offices accordingly. Within the Speer Ministry it was the duty of the Arbeitseinsatz in the Rüstungsamt (later transferred to the Zentralamt) to collect estimates of requirements from the Ausschusse, Ringe, Regional Armament Commissions and other subsidiary offices of the Ministry and present these to the Labour Controller as notifications of the labour requirements of the armaments industry. Close collaboration was most of all necessary in order to secure the prompt provision of additional labour for the special programmes and production drives which were continually occurring in one branch or another of armament production, usually on the orders of the Fuehrer. In the interests of priority programmes, the ordinary allocation system was refined by the use of teh Rotzettel (Red Label) machinery. Demands for labour put forward on Rotzettel received priority over all other applications. Firms engaged on priority work requiring extra labour put in a request for it on Rotzettel. These, after approval by the local Armaments Inspectorate, arrived at Arbeitseinsatz where they were collated and the aggregates laid before the Zentrale Planung. If the requirements were approved the Rotzettel were endorsed and returned via the Ausschüsse and Ringe to the firms, who presented them to the Labour Offices. The Labour Controller was simultaneously notified in order that he might make the necessary arrangements to ensure that that Rotzettel were met by the Labour Offices. One of the bitterest complaints of Speer and his officials against Sauckel is that the latter never made adequate arrangements for meeting his promises on Rotzettel, which remained, to a large extent, unhonoured, and were consequently in course of time seriously over-issued. In this and other failures to meet the labour requirements of the armaments industry, Sauckel was not necessarily activated entirely by ill-will, as Speer and his associates now commonly suppose. It is conceivable that at times his own honest expectations in regard to new labour supplies could not be fulfilled for reasons beyond his control, and it is known that repeated military crises caused ever-increasing demands on man-power for incorporation into the Armed Forces. It is, however, quite clear on the available evidence that the allocation of man-power was very badly co-ordinated with the allocation of the other factors of production at the time when German industry was called upon to make its greatest effort.

90. The administration of labour also gave rise to continual difficulties at the factory level owing to conflicts of authority. As the agency responsible for obtaining

production, the Speer Ministry was insistent on its right to vary the conditions of work in war factories in the manner required to ensure the most economical utilisation of the man-power available and to secure the most economical utilisation of the man-power available and to secure maximum efficiency of labour on the job in hand. For this purpose every war factory had its Arbeitseinsatzingenieur (Labour Control Engineer) and the Arbeitseinsatz maintained a special department (Leistungsanerkennung) to administer the distribution of special inducements to efficiency on the Stakhanovite principle. Sauckel, however, could not afford to be indifferent to conditions of work in the factories in so far as these affected the inducement offered to labour reserves enter industrial employment and reserved for himself questions of wages, and food and clothing allowances. The third factor in the situation was the German Labour Front, the organisation which, under the Nazi system of self-administration of the economy, was responsible for watching the interests and advancing the welfare of the workers in place of the suppressed Trade Unions. It is not surprising that measures introduced by one or other of these authorities conflicted from time to time with the interests of another interested party, and that disputes consequently arose, requiring high-level action. In consequence, most regulations concerning conditions of work required the joint authority of Speer, Sauckel and Ley.

## *Statistical Services.*

91. In all branches of administration, efficient planning demands adequate information services. The information required for production planning is mainly statistical and an efficient statistical service is therefore not by any means the least important of the weapons of total war. In this department German pre-war preparations were extremely thorough, and at the outbreak of war Germany's economic planners were far better equipped with essential data, if they had care to use it, than their opposite numbers in any of the other belligerent nations. However, full use was not made of the services available, and under the stress of war the performance of the machine steadily deteriorated.

92. The foundations of this system were laid by private enterprise. Very detailed statistics were exacted from their members by the cartels and trade associations which controlled the main branches of German industry in the inter-war period. These also

supported a number of special organisations, of which the following may be mentioned: -

(*a*) The National Institute for Rationalization (Reichskuratorium für Wirtschaftlichkeit) which had, since 1921, been engaged on research into such subjects as:-

    scientific methods of management;

    introduction of labour-saving devices;

    standardisation of production and distribution methods;

    evolution of efficiency standards;

    improvement of production control methods;

    standardisations of cost accounting and other reporting media.

(*b*) The Normenausschuss which was continuously engaged in the study of standardisation of components and products in industry.

(*c*) The Institute for Business Research (Institut für Konjunkturforschung) which was engaged in the overall study of economic trends and statistics for the purpose of producing estimates of national income distribution, &c.

The work of these bodies was made available in the form of a steady stream of recommendations for the improvement of methods of industrial control and management. The statistical data was often co-ordinated by the Statistisches Reichsamt.

93. On coming into power, the Nazis immediately took steps not only to make use of the data already available but also to secure the additional data necessary to facilitate economic planning for war. Thus, with the development of the self-administering organisation of industry, all firms were compelled to furnish detailed monthly statistical returns (Industrieberichte) to the Reichsgruppe Industrie. A Census of Production (including Agriculture) was taken by the Statistisches Reichsamt in 1933 and repeated in 1936. This provided the data for the elaboration of the Four-Year Plan and for considering measures of industrial mobilisation. In 1937 an inventory was taken of all machine capacity in German industry. In 1939 an important decree gave legal force to all the recommendations issued by the Reichskuratorium since 1921. This, among other things, imposed a standardised system of cost accounting on all German industry, which greatly facilitated the analysis of date for overall planning purposes. The resultant information was not only analysed on the national level. Detailed records were kept on a regional basis,

which included, among other things, registers of the performance of individual model test firms which were under continuous study for the purpose of evolving efficiency standards.

94. As armament output gathered strength, a separate organisation was set up to collect the data necessary for the planning and control of armament production. Further monthly returns (Beschachtigtenmeldung) were exacted from firms and were analysed by an elaborate mechanical accounting organisation known as the Maschinelles Berichtwesen, which was subordinated to the Wehrwirtschafts- und Rüstungsamt of OKW. This passed over to the Speer Ministry in 1942 with the break-up of Wi-Ru. The data collected by the Reichsgruppe Industrie and the Maschinelles Berichtwesen included the relevant employment statistics. Labour statistics were also compiled by the Ministry of Labour, on the basis of Labour Books, through the Regional Labour Offices.

95. While the information collected for planning purposes before the war had been organised on a rational and comprehensive system, the situation regarding the reporting of current data had therefore already, by the outbreak of war, become extremely complicated and a heavy burden of paper work had already been imposed on the management of firms who were called upon each month to present the same information on a great number of different forms for different purposes. Moreover, the efficient collation and analysis of the data at regional levels required the employment of a vast army of skilled subordinate officials and of specialised machinery. The former requirement was never adequately met and as the war developed was increasingly hampered by the call-up of personnel. As for the latter it is enough to state that, on the invasion of France, Hollerith accounting machines were allotted the No. 1 priority for organised looting activities.

96. Consequently, in the course of the war, the following weaknesses developed:-

(*a*) The Maschinelles Berichtwesen fell increasingly into arrears with its reporting, so that the information provided by it became less and less valuable for planning purposes. Its collated returns were liable to embody gross errors due to lack of sufficient staff at the lower levels with adequate training in mechanical accounting methods.

(*b*) The utility for war planning of the statistics collected by the Reichsgruppe Industrie was affected by the form of organisation of that institution into subsidiary associations grouped on a professional basis rather than with reference to end-products. Their validity was further affected by the "organisational stop" of 1939 which forbade the adjustment of the affiliations of firms in accordance with the war-time changes in their occupation.

(c) The statistics produced by Ausschusse and Ringe, which grew up independently of each other and without permanent staffs, were often rudimentary and, being compiled by a variety of different methods, were incapable of being combined to produce overall returns.

(d) The labour statistics rendered by the Reichsgruppe Industrie and the M.B., being compiled on the basis of actual employment, could not be reconciled with the labour statistics collected by the Ministry of Labour which were classified according to occupations. There were therefore no uniform statistics of labour which were acceptable for planning purposes both to the Ministry of Armaments and to the Controller.

(e) As firms learnt the uses to which the returns made by them were put, falsification of certain data became widespread. For instance, it was not in the interests of a firm to acknowledge (*e.g.*, after an air raid) that any of its labour force was "not productively engaged". It would have been promptly redirected elsewhere and would be difficult to recover.

(f) As air attacks necessitated the dispersal of head officer and disorganised administrative routine, the returns received by regional collecting offices were subject to delays and became progressively more incomplete. In order to "go to press" at the appointed time, they were increasingly compelled to incorporate estimates or old data in the place of the missing reports. In the course of 1944 with the growing pressure of air attacks on all forms of communication, the whole elaborate machinery of reporting gradually broke down.

97. The Statistical Office of Speer's Planungsamt did its best to draw out the lessons of the information available from the various sources. But by the last two years of the war the official information services had fallen into such disrepute with the planning agencies which they were supposed to serve that they were mostly in the nature of academic exercises to which little attention was paid in planning circles. During 1943 and for as much of 1944 as the communications situation allowed, the production statistics which were actually used for the purpose of deciding allocations in the

Zentrale Planung and Planungsamt were improvisations on the part of Saur's personal assistant who spent the last two nights of each month in telephoning the heads of all the Ausschusse and Ringe and obtaining their estimates of the current performance of industry.

## *Priorities and Programmes.*

98. There are two main alternative methods of control which the production executive of a Government can adopt for regulating the purchases of the State from private contractors. On the other hand, contracts can be classified by a central authority according to priority ratings and the demands of the various contractors for raw material, labour and other factors of production can then be met out of the available supplies in the order of priority attached to their contracts. On the other hand, the central authority can itself work out the necessary requirements of labour, raw materials, &c., for the execution of a particular contract and allocate claims to the requisite amounts along with the contracts. The two systems do not mix well; in Germany they were in effect, employed simultaneously throughout the war.

99. Labour was consistently allocated on a "priority" basis, by the attachment of various degrees of urgency to particular contracts which were to be observed by the Regional Labour Offices in directing labour to individual firms. At no time was the allocation of labour used as the control factor in central planning. There was merely a tendency to develop additional classes of super-priority (*e.g.* the Rotzettel system) in order to oil the wheels of particular classes of urgent work.

100. On the other hand, the supply of raw materials to contractors was always, in theory, arranged by means of allocations worked out beforehand on the basis of the calculated requirements of the programme and issued together with the contract. It is true that, in the early years of the war, the system worked imperfectly and in practice developed hybrid characteristics. As the raw material supplies were consistently over-allocated by the central planning authorities the raw material controls were consistently confronted with claims larger than they could meet and were therefore forced to take notice of priority ratings in allocating the amounts available. After Kehrl had taken the situation in hand, however, the supply of raw materials was regulated strictly in accordance with the system of allocating quotas together with the contracts. In fixing these quotas, the allocation of steel was in practice the control

factor in the case of land and naval armaments. In this field, steel was the essential material in shortest supply and programmes were examined initially in terms of the steel which they would require. After the allocation of steel had been fixed, the requirements of the other materials were adjusted in the light of it and the allocations made accordingly. In the case of aircraft production, the control factor was, inevitably, the allocation of aluminium.

101. Both methods, of course, require constant review by the central planning authorities of the relative importance and urgency of the different contracts. In so far as this involved fixing priorities between different classes of weapon and munitions production for the same service, these could be settled, in the first instance by the Waffenamt of the Service concerned. In so far as it involved allocating priorities between production for the three Services, OKW was nominally the authority. In so far as the needs of other Government Departments were concerned, the Four-Year Plan office was also involved. In the early years of the war, the combined programmes of the three Services were not sufficiently formidable in relation to the resources available to render the question of inter-Service priorities either difficult or important. All the requirements to which the Services attached importance could be met, and it was only necessary to curb the more exotic developments, such as the desire of Admiral Raeder to build battleships.

102. From early 1942 onwards, the control of priorities passed effectively into the hands of the Führer who in this, as in other matters, took upon himself the controlling authority of OKW. His interference was not confined to the decision of priorities between different classes of production. Hitler was dissatisfied with the level of armament production generally and more particularly with the "Conservative" views of the Heereswaffenamt as to the level of weapon and munitions production required for the supply of the army. Hence, from the early months of 1942 the programmes for most classes of weapon and munitions production were set by Führerforderungen, drawn up by Hitler himself. In all cases the requirements stated in these programmes were very much above the current levels of production and were widely regarded as impossible of achievement, though not by Speer and his technical assistants. Adjustments in priorities between the various items of the programmes were made at almost weekly intervals. These, again, emanated from the Fuehrer, though they were communicated as OKW orders. Since they were "Fuehrer decisions" there was no disposition to criticise them, except on the part of Speer who was not afraid to express himself frankly

to the Fuehrer. They were usually provoked by some development at the front which had come to Hitler's personal notice, or by the personal ideas or interests of one of the many generals or production chiefs who had been fortunate in momentarily securing the Fuehrer's attention. In view of this situation it is not surprising that officials with axes to grind contrived, on the slenderest pretexts, to get their *desiderata* embodied and issued as Fuehrer decisions in order to secure priority for them.

103. Since the Fuehrerforderungen were ambitious goals to be striven for by long-term endeavour, it was necessary to have some more realistic forecast of the actual production possibilities for the guidance of Wehrmacht planning. The forecasts produced by the Ausschusse hardly fell within this definition since they indulged in fanciful projections of the existing trend of production with the main object of showing that the Fuehrerforderungen would eventually be met. More realistic estimates were produced by the Planungsamt on the basis largely of its raw material allocation decisions. Initially, the Speer Ministry was able to provide accurate forecasts for the production of certain classes of equipment as much as 12 to 18 months in advance. By mid-1944, however, the interference of air raids and other factors with production had reached the point at which it was impossible to make firm commitments more than 4 to 6 weeks ahead.

## Finance.

104. Although the Ministry of Armaments and War Production became solely responsible for armaments production in the latter part of the war, the financing of armament contracts remained with the Services throughout for all normal purposes. The Service appropriations were taken outside the Reich budget as early as 1936 and thereafter the Finance Ministry had no authority to scrutinise and control Service expenditure.

105. Up till 1943, the procurement departments of the Wehrmacht customarily made advance payments to contracting firms at the time of allocation of the contracts, in order to provide working capital. The practice was discontinued in 1943 as liable to endanger the stability of the currency and thereafter firms were encouraged to finance contracts out of their own funds, which most of them were well able to do. Indigent firms, however, were given the benefit of a Reich guarantee for borrowings up to 30 per cent. of the value of the contracts placed, in order to assist

them in obtaining bank credits, but this assistance was seldom called for. The Service Departments also made considerable use in the later stages of the war of the system of "free issues" – corresponding to the British system of "embodiment loans". Under this system the Departments negotiated directly with suppliers the manufacturer of specific components, which were delivered free to assembly plants. One German investigator has estimated that 70 per cent. of the completed cost of a tank was covered by material and components provided in this manner. Extensive use of this system was also made in the aircraft industry.

106. The financing of plant extensions was also carried out for the most part by the Services but a variety of methods were employed, the following being the commonest:-

(a) The firm undertook to finance construction out of its own funds under a war-risk guarantee from the Reich to refund the book values of any assets left over at the end of the war which could not be converted to peace-time use.

(b) The firm received a Reich loan to cover the cost of construction and prices under subsequent delivery contracts were adjusted to allow for interest and amortisation charges on the capital advanced, the new plant and equipment becoming the property of the contractor. It was understood that any debit balance outstanding at the end of the war would be cancelled.

(c) Plants were built by the Reich and either operated directly by the Services as B-Betriebe (which was common only in the case of naval dockyards and ammunition filling and assembly plants) or, much more often, leased on completion for operation by private concerns.

(d) Plants were built and operated by Reich-owned companies specially floated for the purpose, though the bulk of the funds were often provided by the banks who were "invited" to contribute working capital. The Reichswerke Hermann Goering are the best-known example, but the innocently-named Wirtschaftliche Forschungs G.m.b.H. was hardly less important, being responsible for the construction and operation of the very extensive system of under-ground oil storage installations.

107. OKH and OKL operated special companies to carry out the financing activities described above. OKM does not appear to have done so and, from the nature of its

requirements, probably had no need to develop special arrangements of this kind. The institutions maintained by the other two services were as follows:-

(*a*) OKH's industrial trust was named Verwertungsgesellschaft für Montanindustrie G.m.b.H. This concern used OKH budget funds to finance the construction of plants required for the manufacture of army weapons and munitions. On completion the plants were usually leased either to individual concerns or to special holding companies created by the participation of several concerns. The lessee usually paid amortisation charges to Montan and profits were divided equally between Montan and the lessee. By the end of the war Montan had been responsible for the construction and leasing of 106 plants at an initial cost of Rm. 3,000 million, which stood in the balance sheet at a book value of Rm. 1,000 million. More than two-thirds of these investments were concerned with the production of munitions and explosives, the plants being operated by holding companies such as Sprengchemie and G.m.b.H. zur Verwertung Chemischer Erzeugnisse. Montan were not, however, permitted to handle the leasing of chemical warfare projects, which were transferred on completion to a special department of OKH which dealt directly with the firms operating the plants. Although Montan remained an OKH institution to the end, its finances were supervised in the latter years of the war by Rüstungskontor, a Speer institution which is described below.

(*b*) O.K.L. maintained, for similar purposes, the Luftfahrtanlagen G.m.b.H., which was a direct subsidiary of the Bank der Luftfahrt. Its total investments by the end of the war amounted to Rm. 3,500 to Rm. 4,000 million. The Bank der Luftfahrt also participated directly in the financing of aircraft concerns. Initially it was mainly engaged in providing working capital by way of credits but in course of time these were often consolidated and exchanged for shareholdings in the firms concerned. By this process, some well-known companies, such as Junkers, became in practice government-owned concerns while in others, such as Messerschimdt, Famo, and Rheinmetall Borsig, the Reich acquired majority holdings. In addition, the Bank der Luftfahrt maintained another subsidiary, the Ges. für Luftfahrtbedarf, which was exclusively concerned with the financing of the production and supply of spare parts and components, whether for direct use by the Luftwaffe or for "free issues" to aircraft firms.

108. Although the above institutions carried the financing of the vast majority of the construction projects in the armaments industry, the Speer Ministry found it necessary to maintain a similar financial trust of its own: this was called the Rüstungskontor G.m.b.H. The Service financial institutions understandably refused to touch the financing of projects which they considered to be too uncertainly or too remotely associated with Service interests. The most notable example was the financing of the production of producer-gas generators for fitting to motor vehicles. The Services considered the project as being of doubtful military value and the large engineering concerns would not touch it as a commercial proposition in view of its limited post-war value. The Rüstungskontor accordingly took on, through subsidiaries, the financing not only of the manufacture of generators by firms such as Imbert, which had been unable to raise the necessary capital by orthodox means, but also the production and distribution of the necessary fuels.

109. In course of time the Rüstungskontor floated off or acquired interests in a number of other institutions to handle special projects. The more important of these are described briefly below:-

(*a*) The *Industriekontor G.m.b.H.* was founded in the summer of 1944 to finance the construction of the dispersed and underground oil plants called for by the Geilenberg programme. Previously, the expansion of the oil industry had been financed by the private co-operation of large concerns in the formation of special holding companies, such as Brabag, at the "invitation" of the Government. But the Geilenberg programme was obviously not a commercial proposition and the private firms would not take it on.

(*b*) Rüstungskontor financed an office known by the code name of Pimetax, which was engaged in black-market operations in Occupied Territories (notably France and Belgium) for the purpose of special materials (such as precious metals, diamonds and machine tools) which were not forthcoming in adequate quantities on the open market at the controlled prices. Such goods were in great demand, but could easily be concealed, and in the course of time each Service became conscious that the official channels were not succeeding in tapping all the available supplies and clandestinely despatched their own confidential agents with a blank cheque to buy illicitly to cover their own urgent requirements. By 1945 the authorities had not only become aware of the activities of these privateers but had also discovered that the French black-market operators were very successfully playing them off against each other. Pimetex was therefore set up to be the sole official channel for black-market dealings! It was entitled to pay up to seven times the controlled prices, but was supposed to confine its transactions strictly to trafficking in good which could not be obtained by other means.

(c) Rüstungskontor was also responsible for the financial supervision of the company known as Roges (Rohstoffhandelgesellschaft), though this was under the direction of the Ministry of Economics and was financed (unusually) by OKW. Roges was provided with a standing credit of Rm. 150 million for the purchase on the open market of raw materials and machinery in Occupied Territories which were of value for war production in Germany. By 1945, when its annual turnover was Rm. 200 million, it had unintentionally accumulated a profit of Rm. 9 million, which was converted by increasing the normal capital of the company from Rm. 1 million to Rm. 10 million.

(d) In addition, Rüstungskontor directly financed a number of research and development projects, including those which the Services regarded as too academic or unpromising to warrant the expenditure of service funds, and a "lunatic fringe" which was wished upon it by political personages anxious to provide patronage for their tame quacks. In the former category was the "Talstation Loofer" at which Professor Barrisani expended Government funds in research into the lethal properties of high-frequency sound waves, as well as on the consumption of cognac. In the latter category were the activities of Professor Morell, a physician of doubtful antecedents who enjoyed the position of one of Hitler's medical advisers, and upon whom the Fuehrer wished to bestow an electron microscope as a birthday present. Rüstungskontor was called upon to pay.

# B. – REGIONAL GOVERNMENT MACHINERY.

110. The machinery of regional government administration was highly developed in Germany but did not display any particularly interesting features. A very large

bureaucracy was employed, the work of which was not facilitated by the fact that different regional boundaries were observed for different purposes. However the bureaucratic inflation was less than might be imagined at first sight owing to the multiplicity of offices which were often filled by the same individual.

111. In the field of war production, the regional organisation corresponded to the Wehrkreis (Army Command) organisation. The three principal offices responsible for war production were:-

(*a*) The Armaments Inspectorate (Rüstungsinspektion) sub-divided in Armaments Commands (Rüstungskommandos). This was staffed by Service officers and was responsible for the sponsorship and protection of armament firms (A-Betriebe) and armament production generally in each Wehrkreis, chiefly in the procurement of labour and transport. Originally depending from OKW, it was transferred, with the Rüstungsamt, to the Speer Ministry in 1942.

(*b*) The Ministry of Armaments and War Production in addition had its own Regional Commissioners (Wehrkreisbeauftragten). These were, in essence, the representatives of the Technisches Amt and were responsible for keeping firms up to the mark in technical matters and pushing the Ministry's priority programmes.

(*c*) Each of the Hauptausschusse and Hauptringe had regional representatives (Bezirksbeauftragten) to look after the interests of the particular industry concerned. The various Bezirksbeauftragten were answerable to one of their number who was designated Armaments Super-intendent (Rüstungsobmann) for the district. He was usually a prominent local business man and often combined his office with a similar office in the Gauwirtschaftkammer thus securing co-ordination between armaments production and other classes of industrial production.

112. In addition, the professional and industrial activities depending from the Ministry of Economics were organised by Regional Economic Offices (Landwirtschaftsamter) to which were answerable the Chambers of Industry (Gauwirtschaftskammer) representing the local organisations of business. The Ministry of Labour maintained Gauarbeitsamter for regulating the activities of the labour exchanges. There were also regional offices of the Power and Transport authorities.

113. All the above organisations were represented on the Regional Armaments Commissions (Rüstungskommissionen) of which the chairman, appointed by the Minister of Armaments and War Production, was usually the Rüstungsinspekteur, Wehrkreisbeauftragte or Rüstungsobmann. This body had no executive powers but was, in effect, a consultative assembly before which the various representatives could table their difficulties and problems and invite the co-operation of the other regional authorities in their solution. Its functions in this connection were of considerable importance in dealing with local emergencies, and particularly in fostering the recovery of vital armament production activities following air raids.

114. A usual, however, the normal structure was overlaid by improvisations to meet particular emergencies. The most notable was the Ruhrstab, appointed in the early summer of 1943, with the initial task of taking the necessary local action in the Gau concerned to mitigate the effects on war production which were expected to result from water supply shortage following the breaching of the Mohne dam. Its successful performance of this task caused its retention as a permanent institution to handle the special problems created by the sustained air attacks on the Ruhr industrial area.

115. A much larger improvisation was in course of introduction in the concluding months of war. With the breakdown in the centralised control of administration Speer planned to create eight Armaments Plenipotentiaries (Rüstungsbevollmachtigten) to assume dictatorial control of production matters in the various areas into which military operations threatened to partition the Reich. The incumbents, of whom only six were actually appointed, were prominent local industrialists or high officials of the Ministry from Berlin. Few had much opportunity to exercise their authority or even to reach their posts. If they had done so it is likely that the clash of authority between them and the Gauleiters would have produced some lively conflicts.

# APPENDIX VII.

# THE ORGANISATION OF GERMAN MILITARY SUPPLY.

## I.- MAIN REASONS FOR SHORTAGES IN THE FIELD.

That the Armaments Industry of Germany produced huge quantities of war materials is undoubted. It is equally true, however, that the Army in the field was almost invariably short of equipment of all kinds, especially after 1942, and particularly in M.T., ammunition and tanks. The wastage rates in the German Army far exceeded anything calculated by the Allies throughout the war. British and American wastage rates had hitherto to be employed as a criterion. The Tables 1 to 20 attached to this Annex show that wastage rates were often many times in excess of production. The wastage figures given in these tables include, however, all forms of wastage known, including battle casualties, normal wear and tear, issue to other services or allied States, &c., but do not take account of returns from repair. They are given in total figures in the tables, but there are sufficient examples available to show that this figure was made up of a rough monthly average of 90 per cent. battle and wear wastage, and 10 per cent. "other causes" chief of which was distribution and allocation to organisations outside the Army. It is certain enough, therefore, that wastage of equipment in the German Army was extraordinarily high. It is also reported that German training methods were very wasteful of equipment. It is known, indeed, that the realistic methods employed in German Army training must have used up much equipment, but there are no reliable statistics on the subject.

2. The reasons for the high wastage figures in action must be many, but it is obvious, and it can be checked from a scrutiny of the tables, that Germany suffered numerous

defeats in which losses of equipment were extremely high, such as Stalingrad, the Falaise pocket, Tunisia, and the various retreats in Russia. Ground attacks by Allied aircraft are known to have caused relatively high tactical losses of equipment. Strategic bombing scarcely enters into consideration here, although the attacks upon the Ordnance Depots caused a certain loss of stocks which at the moment it is impossible to assess. Interrogations of the higher personalities involved, however, confirm the impression that such losses played a very small part indeed in the overall position.

3. Chief among the causes, according to Speer, Minister of Armament and War Production, Halder, former Chief of the General Staff of the Army, Jodl, Head of the Operational Planning Staff of the OKW, and others, was the policy of distribution. Speer declares that this inept policy was decided by OKW, Halder says that OKW was giving effect to Hitler's demands, with which statement Jodl agrees. There is, indeed, no doubt that, especially towards the end of the war, Hitler himself decided allocations, frequently with fantastic results. The basic policy of allocation was that 90 per cent. of new production was to be given to units being formed, for new setting-up, while 10 per cent. went to the field to replace the losses of formations in action. There is abundant evidence from the field throughout the war that this was so. The result that veteran formations in action were chronically short of equipment, while new "green" units were committed to action with complete or nearly complete establishment of equipment only to lose a fantastically high proportion of it in the first engagement.

4. Yet a third cause of shortages in the field was the policy of trying to allocate existing stocks between the Eastern and Western theatres. This was almost entirely the affair of Hitler, and was at times extraordinarily unbalanced. In February 1945, for example, out of the total February allocation of 667 tanks, one only (a Panther tank) was allocated to the West, while 666 went to the East. Frequently Hitler's allocations bore no relationship to the numbers of equipments actually available; this was probably a matter of the deliberate misinforming of Hitler by his staff.

## II.– THE DISTRIBUTION SITUATION IN LAND ARMAMENTS.

5. In the following paragraphs a few brief instances are given of the typical distribution situation in each of the main categories of Land Armaments:-

# Tanks.

By February 1945 Germany had only 2,013 A.F.V.s (including assault guns of all types) in the West (of which 1.323 were "runners"). In February 1944 there had been 1, 233 runners in the West and 1,519 in the East. An almost equal number in each case were being repaired, *i.e.* were available as "non-runners" in the Reich. The A.F.V. distribution between East and West between November 1944 and March 1945 was as follows:-

| | West. | | | | | East. | | | | |
|---|---|---|---|---|---|---|---|---|---|---|
| | Nov. 1944. | Dee. 1944. | Jan. 1945. | Feb. 1945. | March 1945. | Nov. 1944. | Dec. 1944. | Jan. 1945. | Feb. 1945. | March 1945. |
| Type of A.F.V.— | | | | | | | | | | |
| IV | 205 | 47 | 58 | ... | ... | 10 | 65 | 120 | 194 | 53 |
| IV lg (A) | 49 | ... | 25 | ... | ... | ... | 24 | 37 | 49 | 16 |
| Panther | 281 | 191 | 85 | 1 | ... | 85 | 48 | 154 | 378 | 50 |
| Tiger | 26 | 6 | 6 | ... | 13 | 20 | 46 | 55 | 45 | 15 |
| Stu. Gesch | 382 | 361 | 82 | ... | 80 | 102 | 231 | 431 | 382 | 122 |
| IV lg (V) | 135 | 126 | 18 | ... | ... | ... | 82 | 92 | 227 | 28 |
| Jagdpanther | 20 | 49 | 36 | 20 | 5 | ... | ... | 42 | 48 | ... |
| Jagdpz 38t | 212 | 137 | 24 | 40 | ... | 73 | 135 | 327 | 352 | 83 |
| Jagdtiger | 9 | 16 | 6 | 6 | 14 | ... | ... | ... | ... | ... |
| Stu. Pz. | 20 | 17 | 4 | ... | 14 | ... | ... | ... | ... | ... |
| Totals | 1,345 | 932 | 443 | 67 | 134 | 288 | 631 | 1,244 | 2,555 | 357 |

In December 1943 the General Inspector for Armoured Troops estimated that of all A.F.V.s committed he could expect a total loss of 10 per cent. per month. That even for this period this was too low is proved by the wastage figures in the attached tables. A further 20 per cent. it was estimated would need long-term repair. Even this total of 30 per cent. wastage was usually exceeded by a further 20-30 per cent.

6. In March 1944 Guderian complained that the repair of tanks was becoming more and more difficult and the total stock of A.F.V.s was sinking because of lack of means of recovery and spare parts. At Uman, he said, 300 tanks fell into Russian hands, according to Army Group, South, because of lack of spare parts and means of taking tanks away.

7. On the 15th January, 1945, Guderian presented to the Führer a reply to the Russian-published claim to have destroyed 70,336 German tanks in the East between

the 22$^{nd}$ June, 1941 and 31$^{st}$ December 1944. Guderian said that the actual *total* losses in the East for this period had been supplied by Q.M.G. of the General Staff of the Army and were as follows, though even these figures are undoubtedly much too low:-

| Date. | Tanks. | Assault Guns (Stu. Gesch.). | Pack S.F. Art. S.F. | SPWu, Pz. Sp. Wg. | Others. | Total. |
|---|---|---|---|---|---|---|
| 22nd June, 1941, to 30th November, 1941 ... | 2,403 | 85 | 27 | 759 | ... | 3,274 |
| 1st December, 1941, to 31st December, 1942 ... | 3,195 | 219 | 91 | 972 | ... | 4,477 |
| 1943 ... ... ... | 5,637 | 1,459 | 1,111 | 2,676 | 153 | 11,036 |
| 1944 (not complete for December) ... ... | 4,438 | 3,468 | 1,669 | 4,746 | 216 | 14,537 |
| Totals ... ... | 15,673 | 5,231 | 2,898 | 9,153 | 369 | 33,324 |

## *M.T.*

8. M.T. throughout the whole war was probably the greatest single category of equipment in which shortage was felt. Even as early as May 1940 units in the West were 9,737 vehicles below reduced establishment. Establishments were reduced time and time again throughout the war. Even in tractors, for example, at the end of 1943 the relationship between supply and wastage was such that the following was the percentage held, in each type, of the establishment of total holdings:-

| | | | | | | Per cent. |
|---|---|---|---|---|---|---|
| 1 ton ... | ... | ... | ... | ... | ... | 59 |
| 3 tons ... | ... | ... | ... | ... | ... | 77 |
| 5 and 8 tons | ... | ... | ... | ... | ... | 81 |
| 12 tons ... | ... | ... | ... | ... | ... | 62 |
| 18 tons ... | ... | ... | ... | ... | ... | 64 |

Of the total holdings at this time (12,838 tractors), more than a third (4,385), were undergoing long-term repair. At the end of 1943 the OKW had this to say on the M.T. situation. The monthly production for the Army has been for some months about 4,000 M.T. It is planned in 1944 to raise this allocation to 9,000 per month. It is unlikely that more than 7,000 will be achieved in view of the growing threat of Allied air attacks. The Army proposes to employ this (hypothetical) allocation of 7,000 M.T. per month, in the following way:-

|  |  |  |  |  |  | M.T. |
|---|---|---|---|---|---|---|
| (i) | New setting up | ... | ... | ... | ... | 3,780 |
| (ii) | Supply— | | ... | ... | ... | |
| | Mobile formations | | ... | ... | ... | 2,080 |
| | Transport | ... | ... | ... | ... | 240 |
| | Re-equipment | | ... | ... | ... | 900 |
| | Total | | ... | ... | ... | 7,000 per month. |

In addition, the Army reckons on about 1,000 M.T. a month coming back from repair at home. This would bring supply up to about 4,000 per month, total allocations to 8,000 per month. The stock held by the Field Army at the time was 225,000 M.T., and the monthly wastage was 8,000. Supply therefore covered only 50 per cent. and the Army stocks would sink yearly by 48,000 M.T. Even this pessimistic picture only holds good if the planned allocation reaches 7,000 per month. In fact, the allocation never reached even 6,000.

9. The successive results of this constant drain were shown in the reductions in War Establishments of M.T. with the formations. The G.A.F. and the Navy suffered particularly in these cuts. On the 4th November, 1944, for example, M.T. in the G.A.F. and Navy was cut to 30 per cent. of the previous reduced War Establishment.

In January 1945, the Organisation Branch of the Army General Staff declared that M.T. production throughout the last year had covered less than 50 per cent. of losses and that the problem was unsolved. They declared that, despite rationalisation, decentralised production and evacuation of factories there had been a gradual drop in the production of M.T. and M.T. accessories. The Fuehrer had ordered the equipment to go to units being newly set up. This took the whole of new production plus all the repaired M.T. which could thus not be returned to the front. The only course to follow was to reduce the war establishments of M.T. of the Field Army still further.

# Ordnance Equipment (other than M.T. and Tanks).

10. In many categories of equipment for the Army there was never a radical shortage. Artillery, for example, was usually adequate enough in relation to the supply of ammunition. In the matter of small arms a serious shortage did not begin until after Stalingrad, but the establishments of field formations were not seriously affected until the beginning of 1944. After this date, war establishments were successively reduced. On the 4th November, 1944, for example, OKW reduced the war establishment of all active Armed Forces and Waffen SS units to 70 per cent. of previous WE. in rifles and pistols, 33 per cent. in M.P.s. and 50 per cent. in MGs., while units at home were reduced to 45 per cent., 15 per cent. and 0 per cent. respectively. There were, of course, exceptions to this rule, established by special OKW injunction. In February 1945 the Organisation Branch of the Army General Staff said that the losses of infantry and artillery weapons in the summer and autumn battles of 1944 could not even be approached by supply, and the Branch anticipated even higher losses in the winter in the East. In October 1944, even with reduced establishments, the weapon states of the East and West fronts were without exception well below establishment, as the following figures show:-

| | East. | | | West. | | |
|---|---|---|---|---|---|---|
| Weapon Type. | Establishment. | Actual State. | Shortage. | Establishment. | Actual State. | Shortage. |
| Rifles ... ... ... | 1,750,689 | 1,223,480 | 527,209 | 597,710 | 390,039 | 207,671 |
| L.M.Gs. ... ... ... | 116,851 | 52,767 | 64,084 | 43,859 | 17,353 | 26,506 |
| M.M.Gs. ... ... ... | 13,010 | 6,152 | 6,858 | 5,877 | 2,740 | 3,137 |
| 7·5-cm. A. Tk. guns ... | 3,859 | 1,779 | 2,080 | 1,331 | 669 | 662 |
| 8-8-cm. guns ... ... | 329 | 296 | 33 | 197 | 136 | 61 |
| 5-cm. mortars ... ... | 368 | 221 | 147 | 559 | 386 | 173 |
| 8-cm. mortars ... ... | 1,720 | 5,220 | 2,500 | 3,584 | 2,045 | 1,539 |
| 12-cm. mortars ... ... | 2,530 | 1,851 | 1,679 | 1,235 | 323 | 912 |
| 7·5-cm. inf. guns ... ... | 2,969 | 1,825 | 1,144 | 1,039 | 513 | 526 |
| 15-cm. inf. guns ... ... | 563 | 379 | 184 | 513 | 91 | 422 |
| 7.5-cm. guns ... ... | 1,899 | 1,269 | 630 | 360 | 163 | 197 |
| 10.5-cm. gun hows. ... | 3,578 | 3,030 | 548 | 223 | 151 | 72 |
| 2-cm. guns ... ... ... | 2,864 | 1,926 | 938 | 1,950 | 1,611 | 339 |

11. On the 30th June, 1944, Q.M.Q. of the Army reported that the totally insufficient supplies of M.T., equipment and weapons had until just previously to be sent almost exclusively to the East. The high losses in the South-West and Western theatres

now compelled a greater allocation there. The enormous losses of Army Group Centre could not be covered. He proposed for July 1944 the following measures:-

(i) Complete allocation of all production of weapons and M.T. to the Army.

(ii) No hand weapons or M.G.s for parachute units.

(iii) No allocations to the police or other para-military bodies.

(iv) Postponement of the equipping of the Italian divisions for a month.

(v) Cancellation of all allocations to Germany's allies.

On the same date an even more radical programme was devised by the Army General Staff to overcome the shortages of M.T. weapons and equipment. This was drawn up as follows:-

## *Army-*

(i) Field Army –

New setting-up to be only in the form of refitting of battered divisions. Combing out of all units for superfluous equipment. Equipment for newly-set-up non-combatant units to be cut down to 50 per cent.

(ii) Home Army –

Cutting down of reserve units in those arms which are already well supplied with reserves.

Combing out of all units.

Checking of W.E.s. of all Home Army installations.

Checking of W.E.s. of field units in the Home Army area.

Acceleration of production of horse-drawn vehicles.

Exchange of German guns in the Home Army with captured equipment.

## *Armed Forces –*

(i) Postponement of setting up of all units planned except Army Combat divisions.

(ii) Lowering of weapon and M.T. holdings of all other services and units to 60 per cent. weapons, 70 per cent. guns, 70 per cent. M.T.

(iii)  Giving up by all non-combatant staffs of weapons and M.T.

(iv)  Combing out of all parks and depots of G.A.F., Navy and S.S.

(v)  All Armed Forces M.T. in the areas of Army Groups to be at the disposal of Army Groups.

(vi)  Dissolution of all staffs not essential for the conduct of operations.

(vii)  Dissolution of Economic Staff, East.

(viii)  Combing of industry of all outstanding deliveries of M.T. and weapons.


## Para-Military Formations (including Police, Reich Railways, &c.).

(i)  Collection of firearms.

(ii)  Release of M.T., weapons and equipment in Staffs, Schools, &c.

(iii)  Giving up of holdings in parks and depots of all organisations.

(iv)  Combing out of all formations.

(v)  Reduction of W.E.s.

(vi)  Drastic reduction of P.O.L. allocations to all organisations, and only sufficient M.T. to be retained to use it.

(vii)  Dissolution of all organisations and staffs which became redundant in abandoning occupied territories.


## Exports and Purchase.

(i)  Cessation of exports to Germany's allies except to those where an equally rigid economy is practised.

(ii)  Large-Scale purchases in the West and in Italy of M.T. and equipment of all types.


## Ammunition.

12. The ammunition situation at the beginning of the war was fairly sound, though even after one year of war the Defence Economics Directorate published, on the 1st September, 1940, the following figures of shortages in ammunition. The figures

represent the amounts, in rounds, lacking to bring all field and home units up to establishment. It is not possible to relate these figures of amounts lacking to the total amounts required (*i.e.*, what percentage was actually lacking), save that it varied from 3 per cent. to 78 per cent. The numbers of rounds lacking were as follows:-

By October 1944, monthly output of ammunition was reckoned by Army Q.M.Q. to cover roughly only 48 per cent. of monthly consumption. As can be seen from Table 20 this is shown in the way the Army stocks of ammunition fell, year by year.

| S.A.A. ... ... | 136,575,000 |
| --- | --- |
| Anti-tank rifle amm ... | 27,416,000 |
| 5-cm. tank gun ... ... | 4,335,000 |
| 7·5-cm. ... ... | 837,000 |
| 5-cm. anti-tank gun ... | 1,275,000 |
| 8-cm. mortar ... ... | 2,095,000 |
| 15-cm. infantry gun ... | 1,403,000 |
| 10.5-cm. gun howitzer ... | 1,396,000 |
| 10-cm. gun ... ... | 887,200 |
| 15-cm. howitzer ... | 7,529,000 |
| 21-cm. howitzer ... | 584,310 |
| Tank mines ... ... | 46,000 |

13. In February 1945, the Operational Planning Staff of the OKW summed up the ammunition situation as follows, in a message to Commanders-in-Chief theatres of war.

"The current enemy air attacks on German industry and the constantly increasing shortage of coal, evoked especially by the loss of the Upper Silesian coal areas and the ever-increasing difficulties of the transport situation, have a very serious effect on the production of ammunition.

The steel contingent hitherto set aside for the manufacture of munitions can only be filled up to 65 per cent. Artillery ammunition output must, therefore, sink further by 35 per cent. While, in the last quarter of 1944, 18 ammunition trains of all types were available daily, this number sank to 11.6 in January 1945 and 9.5 in February. The enormous quantities of ammunition lost because of the Russian break-through means that emphasis must be placed upon replacing at least the initial issue of ammunition with units in the East. The situation is especially tight in respect of 12-cm.

mortar ammunition and ammunition for the 10.5-cm. gun howitzer and the 15-cm. howitzer. The Commanders-in-Chief theatres are, therefore, to practice the utmost economy".

It had been noticeable for a long time that there had been a grave shortage of staple munition types in the field, and tactical use of German artillery was undoubtedly limited by these increasing shortages. In the case of munitions, consumption was definitely limited by shortage of production.

TABLE 1.

*Acceptance of Lorries by the Army Ordnance Directorate in the OKH and Wastage Returns submitted by Q.M.G. and A.H.A. in the Field and at Home, September 1939–May 1945.*

| | | Accepted by Army Ordnance Directorate from Production. | Wastage. | | | Accepted by Army Ordnance Directorate from Production. | Wastage. |
|---|---|---|---|---|---|---|---|
| **1939—** | | | | **1942—** | | | |
| September | ... | 1,195 | 1,035 | May ... | ... | 4,582 | 1,649 |
| October | ... | 1,451 | 1,012 | June | ... | 4,355 | 3,321 |
| November | ... | 1,620 | 1,153 | July | ... | 5,126 | 2,168 |
| December | ... | 2,062 | 1,805 | August | ... | 3,674 | 2,549 |
| **1940—** | | | | September | ... | 4,177 | 6,477 |
| January | ... | 1,842 | 789 | October | ... | 4,505 | 6,238 |
| February | ... | 1,668 | 1,460 | November | ... | 4,151 | 8,909 |
| March | ... | 3,673 | 1,420 | December | ... | 4,044 | 6,788 |
| April | ... | 3,909 | 2,610 | **1943—** | | | |
| May | ... | 4,815 | 1,324 | January | ... | 3,946 | 49,894 |
| June | ... | 4,076 | 1,897 | February | ... | 4,407 | 16,035 |
| July | ... | 4,655 | 1,941 | March | ... | 4,913 | 6,077 |
| August | ... | 3,508 | 2,310 | April | ... | 4,783 | 7,769 |
| September | ... | 3,342 | 2,342 | May | ... | 4,921 | 12,849 |
| October | ... | 4,896 | 1,051 | June | ... | 5,043 | 6,546 |
| November | ... | 4,202 | 2,206 | * July | ... | 4,626 | 6,343 |
| December | ... | 4,150 | 1,421 | August | ... | 4,263 | 7,853 |
| **1941—** | | | | September | ... | 4,159 | 12,766 |
| January | ... | 4,310 | 1,665 | October | ... | 4,192 | 14,881 |
| February | ... | 4,167 | 1,418 | November | ... | 4,038 | 9,088 |
| March | ... | 5,287 | 1,740 | December | ... | 3,605 | 10,924 |
| April | ... | 4,033 | 1,516 | **1944—** | | | |
| May | ... | 3,644 | 1,627 | January | ... | 4,483 | 11,432 |
| June | ... | 3,478 | 1,054 | February | ... | 4,269 | 10,920 |
| July | ... | 3,944 | 1,477 | March | ... | 4,665 | 30,583 |
| August | ... | 3,174 | 1,354 | April | ... | 5,159 | 21,208 |
| September | ... | 2,905 | 1,507 | May | ... | 4,113 | 3,757 |
| October | ... | 3,741 | 1,438 | June | ... | 5,703 | 8,184 |
| November | ... | 4,137 | 1,511 | July | ... | 5,110 | 12,850 |
| December | ... | 2,858 | 1,250 | August | ... | 4,465 | 13,580 |
| **1942—** | | | | September | ... | 4,168 | 10,635 |
| January | ... | 3,210 | 5,985 | October | ... | 3,787 | 4,570 |
| February | ... | 2,843 | 8,123 | November | ... | 2,440 | ... |
| March | ... | 4,434 | 5,027 | December | ... | No subsequent figures. | |
| April | ... | 4,602 | 2,545 | **1945 ...** | ... | No subsequent figures. | |

    * All wastage figures from September 1939 to December 191 inclusive, comprise only lorries sent for repair or given by the Army to the other services, including the SS. These figures do not include battle wastage, which is not included in the monthly calculations until January 1942. The wastage figures for September 1939–December 1941, therefore, represent only about one quarter or one third of total wastage. Wastage figures from January 1942 onwards are complete.

**Table 2.** Acceptance of Cars by the Army Ordnance Directorate in the OKH and Wastage Returns submitted by Q.M.G. and A.H.A. in the Field and at Home, September 1939–May 1945.

| Stocks at the end of 1941 ... | 199,402 | No wastage figures available before 1942 | | | | |
|---|---|---|---|---|---|---|
| **1942—** | | | July ... | ... | 1,462 | 4,413 |
| January | ... | 1,712 | 3,545 | August | ... | 2,021 | 6,067 |
| February | ... | 1,906 | 4,090 | September | ... | 2,143 | 8,447 |
| March | ... | 2,492 | 1,989 | October | ... | 1,980 | 10,784 |
| April | ... | 2,328 | 761 | November | ... | 1,917 | 8,500 |
| May ... | ... | 1,850 | 1,093 | December | ... | 1,798 | 7,530 |
| June ... | ... | 2,118 | 2,712 | **1944—** | | | |
| July ... | ... | 2,212 | 4,918 | January | ... | 1,604 | 7,380 |
| August | ... | 2,242 | 6,505 | February | ... | 787 | 8,196 |
| September | ... | 2,106 | 5,790 | March | ... | 1,526 | 17,723 |
| October | ... | 1,469 | 5,680 | April | ... | 1,310 | 12, 564 |
| November | ... | 1,632 | 4,454 | May ... | ... | 1,731 | 13, 724 |
| December | ... | 1,606 | 5,620 | June ... | ... | 1,385 | 3, 499 |
| **1943—** | | | July ... | ... | 482 | 6, 272 |
| January | ... | 1,978 | 27,751 | August | ... | 427 | 7, 687 |
| February | ... | 2,227 | 10,391 | September | ... | 756 | 11,744 |
| March | ... | 2,461 | 4,663 | October | ... | 1,280 | 4,966 |
| April | ... | 1,805 | 4,657 | November | ... | 1,758 | ... |
| May ... | ... | 3,070 | 6,996 | December | ... | No subsequent figures. |
| June ... | ... | 2,221 | 4,050 | **1945 ...** | ... | No subsequent figures. |

**Table 3.** Acceptance of Rifles by the Army Ordnance Directorate in the OKH and Wastage Returns submitted by Q.M.G. and A.M.A. in the Field and at Home, September 1939-May 1945.

| **1939—** | | | | **1942—** | | | |
|---|---|---|---|---|---|---|---|
| September | ... | 62,100 | 7,900 | May ... | ... | 106,766 | 17,508 |
| October | ... | 80,600 | 0 | June ... | ... | 81,197 | 17,458 |
| November | ... | 68,000 | 4 | July ... | ... | 91,602 | 17,767 |
| December | ... | 69,100 | 4 | August | ... | 84,873 | 20,211 |
| **1940—** | | | | September | ... | 91,362 | 18,055 |
| January | ... | 68,400 | 0 | October | ... | 102,537 | 28,837 |
| February | ... | 61,400 | 0 | November | ... | 92,757 | 45,277 |
| March | ... | 86,100 | 82,400 | December | ... | 96,415 | 42,269 |
| April | ... | 94,800 | 7,000 | **1943—** | | | |
| May ... | ... | 101,600 | 10,800 | January | ... | 89,708 | 32,165 |
| June ... | ... | 106,400 | 18,700 | February | ... | 121,771 | 253,521 |
| July... | ... | 112,200 | 12,600 | March | ... | 148,091 | 26,412 |
| August | ... | 93,000 | 35,000 | April | ... | 161,207 | 23,529 |

Continued

**Table 3.** Cont'd

| | | | | | | |
|---|---|---|---|---|---|---|
| September | 100,800 | 0 | May | 163,626 | 34,870 |
| October | 89,000 | 5,900 | June | 162,796 | 45,573 |
| November | 107,000 | 0 | July | 177,165 | 52,487 |
| December | 101,700 | 0 | August | 168,997 | 83,568 |
| **1941—** | | | September | 186,751 | 47,741 |
| January | 103,700 | 0 | October | 192,360 | 60,915 |
| February | 105,700 | 10 | November | 182,919 | 41,258 |
| March | 101,800 | 0 | December | 190,809 | 48,860 |
| April | 80,390 | 497 | **1944—** | | |
| May | 87,985 | 32 | January | 179,081 | 73,869 |
| June | 102,280 | 6,156 | February | 176,687 | 110,038 |
| July | 74,360 | 21,440 | March | 179,851 | 80,734 |
| August | 70,150 | 21,800 | April | 154,465 | 66,390 |
| September | 68,294 | 8,982 | May | 181,148 | 142,582 |
| October | 53,126 | 5,921 | June | 196,882 | 38,513 |
| November | 51,864 | 15,083 | July | 249,080 | 228,631 |
| December | 52,865 | 7,500 | August | 203,385 | 128,507 |
| **1942—** | | | September | 169,023 | 342,066 |
| January | 114,383 | 5,700 | October | 173,350 | 213,476 |
| February | 103,669 | 13,780 | November | 213,342 | 95,186 |
| March | 87,406 | 5,628 | December | No subsequent figures. | |
| April | 97,696 | 5,784 | | | |

**Table 4.** Acceptance of Machine Guns by the Army Ordnance Directorate in the OKH and Wastage Returns submitted by Q.M.G. and A.H.A. in the Field and at Home, September 1939–May 1945.

| | | | | | | |
|---|---|---|---|---|---|---|
| **1939—** | | | April | 5,960 | 2,187 |
| September | 3,500 | 1,500 | May | 6,610 | 3,033 |
| October | 2,900 | 70 | June | 6,405 | 2,177 |
| November | 3,300 | 0 | July | 5,757 | 2,780 |
| December | 3,000 | 0 | August | 6,578 | 6,192 |
| **1940—** | | | September | 7,476 | 3,349 |
| January | 3,700 | 0 | October | 8,934 | 3,917 |
| February | 3,500 | 0 | November | 8,544 | 4,320 |
| March | 3,750 | 4,500 | December | 10,716 | 6,533 |
| April | 3,800 | 500 | **1943—** | | |
| May | 5,200 | 1,700 | January | 11,387 | 4,846 |
| June | 4,400 | 4,800 | February | 10,495 | 15,441 |
| July | 5,000 | 9,800 | March | 11,495 | 5,312 |
| August | 4,900 | 4,500 | April | 11,451 | 3,903 |
| September. | 4,900 | 3,700 | May | 11,731 | 2,557 |
| October | 5,700 | 300 | June | 12,883 | 2,519 |

| | | | | | |
|---|---|---|---|---|---|
| November | 6,000 | 1,000 | December | 10,716 | 6,533 |
| December | 6,200 | 800 | 1943— | | |
| 1941— | | | January | 11,387 | 4,846 |
| January | 7,580 | 450 | February | 10,495 | 15,441 |
| February | 9,070 | 0 | March | 11,495 | 5,312 |
| March | 6,760 | 128 | April | 11,451 | 3,903 |
| April | 10,170 | 1,169 | May | 12,883 | 2,557 |
| May ... | 7,370 | 1,176 | June | 14,186 | 2,519 |
| June ... | 7,770 | 2,037 | July ... | 14,186 | 10,944 |
| July ... | 6,620 | 6,481 | August ... | 16,713 | 13,863 |
| August | 6,370 | 16,590 | September ... | 16,265 | 7,215 |
| September | 6,300 | 4,140 | October | 16,558 | 10,404 |
| October | 5,853 | 3,000 | November | 16,658 | 6,981 |
| November | 3,930 | 2,138 | December | 15,704 | 5,681 |
| December | 3,424 | 3,500 | 1944— | | |
| 1942— | | | January | 16,250 | 9,734 |
| January | 3,859 | 3,200 | February | 16,562 | 16,744 |
| February | 4,878 | 4,513 | March | 18,093 | 11,613 |
| March | 5,484 | 3,452 | April | 18,631 | 7,415 |
| April | 5,960 | 2,187 | May | 19,600 | 11,826 |
| May | 6,610 | 3,033 | June | 20,122 | 4,678 |
| June | 6,405 | 2,177 | July | 24,141 | 26,369 |
| July | 5,757 | 2,780 | August | 24,788 | 9,136 |
| August | 6,578 | 6,192 | September | 26,629 | 27,341 |
| September | 7,476 | 3,349 | October | 26,252 | 24,818 |
| October | 8,934 | 3,917 | November | 25,741 | 14,412 |
| November | 8,544 | 4,320 | December | No subsequent figures. | |

**Table 5.** Acceptance of 2-cm. Guns by the Army Ordnance Directorate in the OKH and Wastage Returns submitted by Q.M.G. and A.H.A. in the Field and at Home, September 1939–May 1945.

| 1939— | | | | 1942— | | |
|---|---|---|---|---|---|---|
| September | ... | 59 | 2 | May | ... | 203 | 35 |
| October | ... | 101 | 0 | June | ... | 239 | 40 |
| November | ... | 175 | 0 | July | ... | 254 | 38 |
| December | ... | 36 | 0 | August | ... | 222 | 43 |
| 1940— | | | | September | ... | 207 | 34 |
| January | ... | 240 | 0 | October | ... | 229 | 21 |
| February | ... | 125 | 0 | November | ... | 214 | 50 |
| March | ... | 134 | 0 | December | ... | 199 | 77 |
| April | ... | 5 | 0 | 1943— | | | |
| May | ... | 59 | 15 | January | | 43 | 40 |
| June | ... | 1 | 26 | February | ... | 33 | 316 |
| July | ... | 24 | 0 | March | ... | 314 | 54 |

Continued

**Table 5.** Cont'd

| Month | | | | Month | | | |
|---|---|---|---|---|---|---|---|
| August | ... | 40 | 0 | April | ... | 276 | 36 |
| September | ... | 30 | 2 | May | ... | 379 | 24 |
| October | ... | 25 | 0 | June | ... | 369 | 13 |
| November | ... | 80 | 0 | July | ... | 377 | 135 |
| December | ... | 30 | 0 | August | ... | 384 | 147 |
| 1941— | | | | September | ... | 373 | 92 |
| January | ... | 90 | 0 | October | ... | 323 | 190 |
| February | ... | 36 | 0 | November | ... | 385 | 119 |
| March | ... | 58 | 0 | December | ... | 476 | 116 |
| April | ... | 53 | 0 | 1944— | | | |
| May | ... | 59 | 5 | January | ... | 485 | 187 |
| June | ... | 28 | 5 | February | ... | 362 | 485 |
| July | ... | 82 | 44 | March | ... | 454 | 210 |
| August | ... | 101 | 31 | April | ... | 353 | 90 |
| September | ... | 74 | 24 | May | ... | 279 | 247 |
| October | ... | 94 | 11 | June | ... | 285 | 92 |
| November | ... | 122 | 8 | July | ... | 344 | 379 |
| December | ... | 76 | 75 | August | ... | 518 | 457 |
| 1942— | | | | September | ... | 568 | 635 |
| January | ... | 126 | 19 | October | ... | 454 | 543 |
| February | ... | 218 | 59 | November | ... | 414 | 256 |
| March | ... | 196 | 30 | December | ... | No subsequent figures. | |
| April | ... | 193 | 17 | | | | |

**Table 6.** Acceptance of 5-cm. Anti-Tank Guns by the Army Ordnance Directorate in the OKH and Wastage Returns submitted by Q.M.G. and A.H.A. in the Field and at Home, September 1939–May 1945.

| 1939— | | | | 1942— | | | |
|---|---|---|---|---|---|---|---|
| September | ... | 0 | 0 | April | ... | 391 | 150 |
| October | ... | 0 | 0 | May | ... | 244 | 59 |
| November | ... | 0 | 0 | June | ... | 331 | 86 |
| December | ... | 0 | 0 | July | ... | 317 | 100 |
| 1940— | | | | August | ... | ... | 213 |
| January | ... | 0 | 0 | September | ... | 480 | 265 |
| February | ... | 0 | 0 | October | ... | 345 | 101 |
| March | ... | 4 | 0 | November | ... | 529 | 283 |
| April | ... | 16 | 0 | December | ... | 500 | 384 |
| May | ... | 3 | 0 | 1943— | | | |
| June | ... | 12 | 0 | January | ... | 448 | 209 |
| July | ... | 17 | 0 | February | ... | 342 | 335 |
| August | ... | 32 | 0 | March | ... | 357 | 187 |
| September | ... | 56 | 3 | April | ... | 264 | 232 |
| October | ... | 104 | 0 | May | ... | 223 | 100 |

| | | | | | | | | |
|---|---|---|---|---|---|---|---|---|
| November | . . . | 84 | 8 | June | . . . | 323 | 16 |
| December | . . . | 106 | 0 | July | . . . | 208 | 349 |
| 1941— | | | | August | | . . . | 349 |
| January | . . . | 142 | 1 | September | . . . | 142 | 202 |
| February | . . . | 117 | 0 | October | . . . | 101 | 203 |
| March | . . . | 113 | 11 | November | . . . | 29 | 138 |
| April | . . . | 154 | 2 | December | . . . | 15 | 162 |
| May | . . . | 177 | 1 | 1944— | | | |
| June | . . . | 163 | 21 | January | . . . | 0 | 268 |
| July | . . . | 173 | 111 | February | . . . | 0 | 320 |
| August | . . . | 250 | 76 | March | . . . | 0 | 73 |
| September | . . . | 152 | 32 | April | . . . | 0 | 36 |
| October | . . . | 241 | 52 | May | . . . | 0 | 92 |
| November | . . . | 212 | 33 | June | . . . | 0 | 30 |
| December | . . . | 178 | 149 | July | . . . | 0 | 136 |
| 1942— | | | | August | . . . | 0 | 295 |
| January | | 315 | 58 | September | . . . | 0 | 220 |
| February | . . . | 307 | 113 | October | . . . | Weapon obsolete. No further figures published. | |
| March | . . . | 324 | 99 | | | | |

**Table 7.** Acceptance of 7.5-cm. Anti-Tank Guns (Pak 40) by the Army Ordnance Directorate in the OKH and Wastage Returns submitted by Q.M.G. and A.H.A. in the Field and at Home, September 1939–May 1945.

| 1942— | | | 1943— | | |
|---|---|---|---|---|---|
| January | 0 | 0 | July. . . | 800 | 405 |
| February | 15 | 0 | August | 850 | 441 |
| March | 15 | 0 | September | 800 | 418 |
| April | 156 | 0 | October | 950 | 356 |
| May. . . | 261 | 0 | November | 645 | 259 |
| June. . . | 93 | 16 | December | 932 | 302 |
| July. . . | 176 | 41 | 1944— | | |
| August | 175 | 77 | January | 1,007 | 490 |
| September | 185 | 74 | February | 877 | 748 |
| October | 307 | 15 | March | 976 | 553 |
| November | 290 | 6 | April | 986 | 397 |
| December | 468 | 199 | May. . . | 1,014 | 692 |
| 1943— | | | June. . . | 1,016 | 309 |
| January | 500 | 108 | July. . . | 1,000 | 1,317 |
| February | 551 | 225 | August | 840 | 1,392 |
| March | 610 | 117 | September | 928 | 725 |
| April | 651 | 160 | October | 1,054 | 1,079 |
| May. . . | 700 | 161 | November | 1,025 | 546 |
| June. . . | 751 | 33 | December | No subsequent figures. | |

**Table 8.** Acceptance of 5-cm. Mortars by the Army Ordnance Directorate in the OKH and Wastage Returns submitted by Q.M.G. and A.H.A. in the Field and at Home, September 1939–May 1945.

| 1939— | | | | 1942— | | |
|---|---|---|---|---|---|---|
| September | . . . | 340 | 174 | April | . . . | 780 |
| October | . . . | 400 | 0 | May. . . | . . . | 1,100 |
| November | . . . | 479 | 0 | June. . . | . . . | 760 |
| December | . . . | 461 | 1 | July. . . | . . . | 765 |
| 1940— | | | | August | . . . | 750 |
| January | . . . | 547 | 0 | September | . . . | 750 |
| February | . . . | 440 | 0 | October | . . . | 750 |
| March | . . . | 570 | 87 | November | . . . | 750 |
| April | . . . | 740 | 0 | December | . . . | 700 |
| May. . . | . . . | 455 | 198 | 1943— | | |
| June. . . | . . . | 775 | 365 | January | . . . | 150 |
| July. . . | . . . | 630 | 46 | February | . . . | 410 |
| August | . . . | 555 | 6 | March | . . . | 550 |
| September | . . . | 520 | 5 | April | . . . | 500 |
| October | . . . | 500 | 56 | May. . . | . . . | 600 |
| November | . . . | 390 | 0 | June. . . | . . . | 600 |
| December | . . . | 420 | 0 | | | Acceptance ceased. |
| 1941— | | | | July. . . | . . . | 0 |
| January | . . . | 700 | 0 | August | . . . | 0 |
| February | . . . | 680 | 0 | September | . . . | 0 |
| March | . . . | 700 | 6 | October | . . . | 0 |
| April | . . . | 680 | 18 | November | . . . | 0 |
| May. . . | . . . | 670 | 16 | December | . . . | 0 |
| June. . . | . . . | 569 | 54 | 1944— | | |
| July. . . | . . . | 701 | 696 | January | . . . | 0 |
| August | . . . | 485 | 1,037 | February | . . . | 0 |
| September | . . . | 220 | 514 | March | . . . | 0 |
| October | . . . | 210 | 338 | April | . . . | 0 |
| November | . . . | 100 | 266 | May. . . | . . . | 0 |
| December | . . . | 100 | 558 | June. . . | . . . | 0 |
| | | | | July. . . | . . . | 0 |
| 1942— | | | | August | . . . | 0 |
| January | . . . | 200 | 413 | September | . . . | 0 |
| February | . . . | 380 | 550 | October | . . . | 0 |
| March | . . . | 1,090 | 579 | November | . . . | 0 |
| | | | | December | . . . | Weapon obsolete. No further figures published |

**Table 9.** Acceptance of 8-cm. Mortars by the Army Ordnance Directorate in the OKH and Wastage Returns submitted by Q.M.G. and A.H.A. in the Field and at Home, September 1939–May 1945.

| 1939— | | | | 1942— | | | |
|---|---|---|---|---|---|---|---|
| September | . . . | 379 | 53 | May. . . | . . . | 725 | 245 |
| October | . . . | 435 | 0 | June. . . | . . . | 625 | 203 |
| November | . . . | 335 | 0 | July. . . | . . . | 920 | 301 |
| December | . . . | 374 | 1 | August | . . . | 835 | 448 |
| 1940— | | | | September | . . . | 1,030 | 608 |
| January | . . . | 468 | 0 | October | . . . | 1,120 | 47 |
| February | . . . | 372 | 0 | November | . . . | 1,470 | 489 |
| March | . . . | 345 | 116 | December | . . . | 1,660 | 764 |
| April | . . . | 265 | 0 | 1943— | | | |
| May. . . | . . . | 440 | 137 | January | . . . | 1,505 | 615 |
| June. . . | . . . | 390 | 220 | February | . . . | 1,779 | 955 |
| July. . . | . . . | 305 | 62 | March | . . . | 1,823 | 512 |
| August | . . . | 319 | 4 | April | . . . | 1,852 | 578 |
| September | . . . | 368 | 1 | May. . . | . . . | 1,510 | 135 |
| October | . . . | 387 | 28 | June. . . | . . . | 1,522 | 426 |
| November | . . . | 398 | 0 | July. . . | . . . | 1,486 | 1,000 |
| December | . . . | 408 | 0 | August | . . . | 1,550 | 1,323 |
| 1941— | | | | September | . . . | 1,495 | 798 |
| January | . . . | 411 | 0 | October | . . . | 1,290 | 923 |
| February | . . . | 533 | 0 | November | . . . | 1,295 | 581 |
| March | . . . | 640 | 6 | December | . . . | 1,290 | 877 |
| April | . . . | 541 | 9 | 1944— | | | |
| May. . . | . . . | 535 | 15 | January | . . . | 1,320 | 977 |
| June. . . | . . . | 504 | 53 | February | . . . | 1,420 | 2,092 |
| July. . . | . . . | 435 | 349 | March | . . . | 1,420 | 1,530 |
| August | . . . | 482 | 620 | April | . . . | 1,650 | 1,083 |
| September | . . . | 293 | 299 | May. . . | . . . | 1,916 | 823 |
| October | . . . | 50 | 202 | June. . . | . . . | 1,980 | 885 |
| November | . . . | 105 | 202 | July. . . | . . . | 2,225 | 2,590 |
| December | . . . | 107 | 499 | August | . . . | 2,340 | 2,617 |
| 1942— | | | | September | . . . | 2,250 | 2,090 |
| January | . . . | 100 | 452 | October | . . . | 2,190 | 2,870 |
| February | . . . | 349 | 400 | November | . . . | 2,320 | 1,478 |
| March | . . . | 446 | 540 | December | . . . | No subsequent figures. | |
| April | . . . | 496 | 236 | | | | |

**Table 10.** Acceptance of 7.5-cm. Light Infantry Guns by the Army Ordnance Directorate in the OKH and Wastage Returns submitted by Q.M.G. and A.H.A. in the Field and at Home, September 1939–May 1945.

| | Accepted by Army Ordnance Directorate from Production. | Wastage. | | Accepted by Army Ordnance Directorate from Production. | Wastage |
|---|---|---|---|---|---|
| 1939— | | | 1942— | | |
| September ... | 74 | 21 | May... ... | 82 | 146 |
| October ... | 78 | 5 | June... ... | 79 | 62 |
| November ... | 69 | 0 | July... ... | 65 | 72 |
| December ... | 69 | 0 | August ... | 83 | 155 |
| 1940— | | | September ... | 93 | 61 |
| January ... | 70 | 2 | October ... | 80 | 54 |
| February ... | 52 | 4 | November ... | 78 | 88 |
| March ... | 38 | 18 | December ... | 130 | 67 |
| April ... | 51 | 3 | 1943— | | |
| May... ... | 85 | 60 | January ... | 130 | 83 |
| June... ... | 80 | 101 | February ... | 132 | 349 |
| July... ... | 97 | 0 | March ... | 143 | 102 |
| August ... | 91 | 3 | April ... | 154 | 49 |
| September ... | 70 | 0 | May... ... | 165 | 39 |
| October ... | 84 | 18 | June... ... | 170 | 15 |
| November ... | 74 | 0 | July... ... | 170 | 184 |
| December ... | 64 | 0 | August ... | 170 | 255 |
| 1941— | | | September ... | 170 | 107 |
| January ... | 59 | 0 | October ... | 170 | 135 |
| February ... | 103 | 15 | November ... | 170 | 84 |
| March ... | 116 | 5 | December ... | 196 | 98 |
| April ... | 111 | 19 | 1944— | | |
| May... ... | 110 | 4 | January ... | 207 | 142 |
| June... ... | 117 | 12 | February ... | 195 | 347 |
| July... ... | 150 | 156 | March ... | 195 | 226 |
| August ... | 100 | 256 | April ... | 195 | 79 |
| September ... | 65 | 135 | May... ... | 195 | 137 |
| October ... | 83 | 97 | June... ... | 195 | 55 |
| November ... | 40 | 75 | July... ... | 190 | 473 |
| December ... | 58 | 198 | August ... | 200 | 374 |
| 1942— | | | September ... | 200 | 230 |
| January ... | 40 | 148 | October ... | 157 | 302 |
| February ... | 103 | 164 | November ... | 186 | 80 |
| March ... | 216 | 142 | December ... | No subsequent | |
| April ... | 142 | 94 | | figures. | |

**Table 11.** Acceptance of 15-cm. Heavy Infantry Guns by the Army Ordnance Directorate in the OKH and Wastage Returns submitted by Q.M.G. and A.H.A. in the Field and at Home, September 1939–May 1945.

| 1939— | | | | 1942— | | | |
|---|---|---|---|---|---|---|---|
| September | . . . | 6 | 6 | May. . . | . . . | 20 | 50 |
| October | . . . | 11 | 1 | June. . . | . . . | 55 | 16 |
| November | . . . | 12 | 0 | July. . . | . . . | 35 | 15 |
| December | . . . | 19 | 0 | August | . . . | 58 | 36 |
| 1940— | | | | September | | 40 | 14 |
| January | . . . | 22 | 0 | October | . . . | 81 | 19 |
| February | . . . | 26 | 0 | November | . . . | 44 | 24 |
| March | . . . | 28 | 29 | December | . . . | 70 | 39 |
| April | . . . | 24 | 0 | 1943— | | | |
| May. . . | . . . | 14 | 11 | January | . . . | 60 | 32 |
| June. . . | . . . | 22 | 15 | February | . . . | 65 | 130 |
| July. . . | . . . | 21 | 0 | March | . . . | 75 | 29 |
| August | . . . | 30 | 1 | April | . . . | 76 | 10 |
| September | . . . | 34 | 0 | May. . . | . . . | 77 | 5 |
| October | . . . | 30 | 1 | June. . . | . . . | 66 | 3 |
| November | . . . | 13 | 5 | July. . . | . . . | 77 | 39 |
| December | . . . | 35 | 4 | August | . . . | 41 | 61 |
| 1941— | | | | September | . . . | 75 | 50 |
| January | . . . | 44 | 5 | October | . . . | 80 | 72 |
| February | . . . | 60 | 2 | November | . . . | 80 | 31 |
| March | . . . | 39 | 6 | December | . . . | 96 | 37 |
| April | . . . | 48 | 24 | 1944— | | | |
| May. . . | . . . | 60 | 1 | January | . . . | 84 | 55 |
| June. . . | . . . | 46 | 4 | February | . . . | 83 | 127 |
| July. . . | . . . | 48 | 44 | March | . . . | 86 | 113 |
| August | . . . | 48 | 51 | April | . . . | 92 | 35 |
| September | . . . | 24 | 45 | May. . . | . . . | 103 | 42 |
| October | . . . | 19 | 53 | June. . . | . . . | 130 | 30 |
| November | . . . | 45 | 34 | July. . . | . . . | 145 | 202 |
| December | . . . | 14 | 74 | August | . . . | 160 | 102 |
| 1942— | | | | September | . . . | 156 | 53 |
| January | . . . | 37 | 51 | October | . . . | 173 | 116 |
| February | . . . | 17 | 42 | November | . . . | 201 | 41 |
| March | . . . | 21 | 39 | December | . . . | No subsequent | |
| April | . . . | 18 | 20 | | | figures. | |

**Table 12.** Acceptance of 10.5-cm. Gun-Howitzers by the Army Ordnance Directorate in the OKH and Wastage Returns submitted by Q.M.G. and A.H.A. in the Field and at Home, September 1939–May 1945.

| 1939— | | | | 1942— | | | |
|---|---|---|---|---|---|---|---|
| September | . . . | 83 | 12 | May. . . | . . . | 68 | 185 |
| October | . . . | 137 | 3 | June. . . | . . . | 52 | 75 |
| November | . . . | 130 | 2 | July. . . | . . . | 81 | 83 |
| December | . . . | 133 | 1 | August | . . . | 126 | 233 |
| 1940— | | | | September | . . . | 100 | 122 |
| January | . . . | 120 | 6 | October | . . . | 108 | 86 |
| February | . . . | 92 | 4 | November | . . . | 157 | 136 |
| March | . . . | 117 | 1 | December | . . . | 242 | 156 |
| April | . . . | 135 | 0 | 1943— | | | |
| May. . . | . . . | 132 | 57 | January | . . . | 237 | 167 |
| June. . . | . . . | 139 | 84 | February | . . . | 176 | 663 |
| July. . . | . . . | 113 | 0 | March | . . . | 298 | 112 |
| August | . . . | 109 | 0 | April | . . . | 273 | 63 |
| September | . . . | 92 | 1 | May. . . | . . . | 377 | 149 |
| October | . . . | 96 | 0 | June. . . | . . . | 257 | 28 |
| November | . . . | 99 | 8 | July. . . | . . . | 288 | 195 |
| December | . . . | 108 | 3 | August | . . . | 313 | 360 |
| 1941— | | | | September | . . . | 367 | 260 |
| January | . . . | 147 | 0 | October | . . . | 459 | 213 |
| February | . . . | 102 | 0 | November | . . . | 449 | 225 |
| March | . . . | 127 | 0 | December | . . . | 606 | 270 |
| April | . . . | 140 | 6 | 1944— | | | |
| May. . . | . . . | 132 | 2 | January | . . . | 613 | 301 |
| June. . . | . . . | 89 | 53 | February | . . . | 585 | 611 |
| July. . . | . . . | 101 | 140 | March | . . . | 784 | 508 |
| August | . . . | 130 | 211 | April | . . . | 702 | 250 |
| September | . . . | 73 | 133 | May. . . | . . . | 774 | 251 |
| October | . . . | 45 | 127 | June. . . | . . . | 778 | 175 |
| November | . . . | 45 | 129 | July. . . | . . . | 881 | 980 |
| December | . . . | 21 | 468 | August | . . . | 704 | 1,218 |
| 1942— | | | | September | . . . | 638 | 364 |
| January | . . . | 43 | 198 | October | . . . | 785 | 702 |
| February | . . . | 104 | 145 | November | . . . | 509 | 310 |
| March | . . . | 129 | 326 | December | . . . | No subsequent | |
| April | . . . | 59 | 85 | | | figures. | |

**Table 13.** Acceptance of 10-cm. Guns by the Army Ordnance Directorate in the OKH and Wastage Returns submitted by Q.M.G. and A.H.A. in the Field and at Home, September 1939–May 1945.

| 1939— | | | | 1942— | | | |
|---|---|---|---|---|---|---|---|
| September | . . . | 0 (Stocks 621) | 2 | May. . . | . . . | 0 | 12 |
| October | . . . | 0 | 0 | June. . . | . . . | 0 | 14 |
| November | . . . | 0 | 0 | July. . . | . . . | 35 | 5 |
| December | . . . | 0 | 0 | August | . . . | 6 | 29 |
| 1940— | | | | September | . . . | 29 | 14 |
| January | . . . | 0 | 0 | October | . . . | 16 | 4 |
| February | . . . | 0 | 0 | November | . . . | 28 | 21 |
| March | . . . | 0 | 0 | December | . . . | 21 | 6 |
| April | . . . | 0 | 0 | 1943— | | | |
| May. . . | . . . | 8 | 14 | January | . . . | 20 | 12 |
| June. . . | . . . | 5 | 18 | February | . . . | 35 | 90 |
| July. . . | . . . | 6 | 0 | March | . . . | 35 | 9 |
| August | . . . | 14 | 0 | April | . . . | 35 | 10 |
| September | . . . | 5 | 0 | May. . . | . . . | 35 | 2 |
| October | . . . | 1 | 0 | June. . . | . . . | 45 | 3 |
| November | . . . | 1 | 0 | July. . . | . . . | 35 | 7 |
| December | . . . | 3 | 0 | August | . . . | 43 | 10 |
| 1941— | | Acceptance by Army Ordnance Directorate from Production. | Wastage. | September | . . . | 27 | 14 |
| January | . . . | 5 | 0 | October | . . . | 47 | 1 |
| February | . . . | 17 | 0 | November | . . . | 45 | 12 |
| March | . . . | 23 | 0 | December | . . . | 52 | 14 |
| April | . . . | 10 | 0 | 1944— | | | |
| May. . . | . . . | 10 | 1 | January | . . . | 52 | 24 |
| June. . . | . . . | 5 | 12 | February | . . . | 45 | 65 |
| July. . . | . . . | 15 | 19 | March | . . . | 50 | 40 |
| August | . . . | 9 | 6 | April | . . . | 43 | 15 |
| September | . . . | 5 | 12 | May. . . | . . . | 56 | 31 |
| October | . . . | 0 | 19 | June. . . | . . . | 60 | 8 |
| November | . . . | 9 | 10 | July. . . | . . . | 65 | 79 |
| December | . . . | 0 | 39 | August | . . . | 60 | 43 |
| 1942— | | | | September | . . . | 45 | 11 |
| January | . . . | 0 | 24 | October | . . . | 75 | 31 |
| February | . . . | 0 | 5 | November | . . . | 75 | 10 |
| March | . . . | 0 | 7 | December | . . . | No subsequent figures. | |
| April | . . . | 0 | 8 | | | | |

**Table 14.** Acceptance of 15-cm. Howitzers by the Army Ordnance Directorate in the OKH and Wastage Returns submitted by Q.M.G. and A.H.A. in the Field and at Home, September 1939–May 1945.

| 1939— | | | | 1942— | | | |
|---|---|---|---|---|---|---|---|
| September | ... | 51 | 13 | May... | ... | 47 | 51 |
| October | ... | 64 | 2 | June... | ... | 44 | 60 |
| November | ... | 35 | 0 | July... | ... | 56 | 155 |
| December | ... | 40 | 0 | August | ... | 58 | 129 |
| 1940— | | | | September | ... | 36 | 92 |
| January | ... | 33 | 0 | October | ... | 44 | 90 |
| February | ... | 28 | 0 | November | ... | 42 | 114 |
| March | ... | 50 | 2 | December | ... | 60 | 84 |
| April | ... | 65 | 1 | 1943— | | | |
| May... | ... | 49 | 31 | January | ... | 70 | 41 |
| June... | ... | 48 | 67 | February | ... | 45 | 240 |
| July... | ... | 39 | 0 | March | ... | 59 | 47 |
| August | ... | 40 | 0 | April | ... | 63 | 14 |
| September | ... | 36 | 48 | May... | ... | 72 | 80 |
| October | ... | 65 | 0 | June... | ... | 68 | 25 |
| November | ... | 57 | 0 | July... | ... | 131 | 65 |
| December | ... | 58 | 0 | August | ... | 115 | 109 |
| 1941— | | | | September | ... | 124 | 88 |
| January | ... | 63 | 12 | October | ... | 142 | 76 |
| February | ... | 57 | 8 | November | ... | 150 | 72 |
| March | ... | 64 | 20 | December | ... | 182 | 60 |
| April | ... | 48 | 2 | 1944— | | | |
| May... | ... | 49 | 0 | January | ... | 192 | 98 |
| June... | ... | 48 | 23 | February | ... | 180 | 165 |
| July... | ... | 41 | 90 | March | ... | 198 | 167 |
| August | ... | 43 | 113 | April | ... | 227 | 109 |
| September | ... | 32 | 42 | May... | ... | 256 | 87 |
| October | ... | 39 | 58 | June... | ... | 265 | 43 |
| November | ... | 10 | 44 | July... | ... | 273 | 402 |
| December | ... | 10 | 208 | August | ... | 240 | 256 |
| 1942— | | | | September | ... | 308 | 117 |
| January | ... | 38 | 88 | October | ... | 264 | 224 |
| February | ... | 53 | 65 | November | ... | 315 | 84 |
| March | ... | 57 | 66 | December | ... | No subsequent figures. | |
| April | ... | 98 | 45 | | | | |

**Table 15.** Acceptance of Pz. Kpfwg. IIIs. By Jn. 6 or Insp. of Pz. Tps., and Wastage Returns from the field and at Home, September 1939–May 1945.

| | Acceptance by Jn. 6 or Insp. of Pz. Tps. from Production. | Wastage. | | Acceptance by Jn. 6 or Insp. of Pz. Tps. from Production. | Wastage. |
|---|---|---|---|---|---|
| 1939— | | | 1942— | | |
| September ... | 40 | 26 | May... ... | 246 | 19 |
| October ... | 40 | 0 | June... ... | 228 | 115 |
| November ... | 35 | 0 | July... ... | 231 | 245 |
| December ... | 42 | 0 | August ... | 231 | 135 |
| 1940— | | | September ... | 217 | 184 |
| January ... | 42 | 0 | October ... | 188 | 88 |
| February ... | 49 | 0 | November ... | 178 | 266 |
| March ... | 51 | 0 | December ... | 221 | 89 |
| April ... | 51 | 6 | 1943— | | |
| May... ... | 65 | 110 | January ... | 46 | 271 |
| June... ... | 58 | 25 | February ... | 34 | 1,053 |
| July... ... | 84 | 0 | March ... | 35 | 274 |
| August ... | 87 | 0 | April ... | 46 | 249 |
| September ... | 86 | 0 | May... ... | 43 | 132 |
| October ... | 95 | 0 | June... ... | 11 | 2 |
| November ... | 82 | 0 | July... ... | 0 | 189 |
| December ... | 86 | 0 | August ... | 20 | 178 |
| 1941— | | | | Acceptance ceased | |
| January ... | 88 | 0 | September ... | 0 | 84 |
| February ... | 108 | 0 | October ... | 0 | 81 |
| March ... | 92 | 0 | November ... | 0 | 119 |
| April ... | 124 | 0 | December ... | 0 | 50 |
| May... ... | 143 | 4 | 1944— | | |
| June... ... | 133 | 27 | January ... | 0 | 43 |
| July... ... | 127 | 164 | February ... | 0 | 77 |
| August ... | 179 | 78 | March ... | 0 | 1 |
| September ... | 178 | 104 | April ... | 0 | 52 |
| October ... | 164 | 38 | May... ... | 0 | 1 |
| November ... | 206 | 116 | June... ... | 0 | 41 |
| December ... | 171 | 208 | July... ... | 0 | 9 |
| 1942— | | | August ... | 0 | 2 |
| January ... | 159 | 181 | September ... | 0 | 21 |
| February ... | 216 | 157 | October ... | 0 | 11 |
| March ... | 244 | 32 | November ... | 0 | 0 |
| April ... | 246 | 62 | December ... | No further figures published. | |

**Table 16.** Acceptance of Pz. Kplwg. IVs by Jn. 6 or Insp. of Pz. Tps. and Wastage Returns from the Field and at Home, September 1939–May 1945.

| September | ... | 0 (Stocks 211) | 19 | July... | ... | 88 | 61 |
|---|---|---|---|---|---|---|---|
| October | ... | 20 | 0 | August | ... | 84 | 37 |
| November | ... | 11 | 0 | September | ... | 93 | 69 |
| December | ... | 14 | 0 | October | ... | 99 | 54 |
| 1940— | | | | November | ... | 113 | 57 |
| January | ... | 20 | 0 | December | ... | 155 | 45 |
| February | ... | 20 | 0 | 1943— | ... | | |
| March | ... | 24 | 0 | January | ... | 163 | 98 |
| April | ... | 10 | 1 | February | ... | 171 | 348 |
| May... | ... | 20 | 77 | March | ... | 205 | 139 |
| June... | ... | 23 | 20 | April | ... | 213 | 142 |
| July... | ... | 26 | 0 | May... | ... | 272 | 16 |
| August | ... | 30 | 0 | June... | ... | 253 | 172 |
| September | ... | 17 | 0 | July... | ... | 244 | 20 |
| October | ... | 30 | 0 | August | ... | 283 | 325 |
| November | ... | 30 | 0 | September | ... | 289 | 309 |
| December | ... | 30 | 0 | October | ... | 338 | 207 |
| 1941— | | | | November | ... | 238 | 266 |
| January | ... | 31 | 0 | December | | 354 | 358 |
| February | ... | 26 | 0 | 1944 — | ... | | |
| March | ... | 28 | 55 | January | ... | 300 | 293 |
| April | ... | 36 | 0 | February | ... | 252 | 154 |
| May... | ... | 29 | 7 | March | ... | 310 | 136 |
| June... | ... | 38 | 16 | April | ... | 299 | 292 |
| July... | ... | 38 | 111 | May | ... | 302 | 98 |
| August | ... | 44 | 70 | June | ... | 300 | 285 |
| September | ... | 46 | 23 | October | ... | 187 | 179 |
| October | ... | 51 | 55 | July | ... | 300 | 441 |
| November | ... | 52 | 38 | August | ... | 300 | 418 |
| December | ... | 61 | 65 | September | ... | 180 | 771 |
| 1942— | | | | November | ... | 200 | Wastage |
| January | ... | 59 | 48 | December | ... | 132 | increasing but |
| February | ... | 58 | 49 | 1945— | | | not recorded. |
| March | ... | 8 | 10 | January | ... | 120 | |
| April | ... | 80 | 22 | February | ... | 117 | |
| May... | ... | 85 | 30 | March | ... | 53 | |
| June... | ... | 72 | 41 | April | ... | 16 | |

**Table 17.** Acceptance of 7.5-cm. Assault Guns by Jn. 6 or Insp. of Pz. Tps. and Wastage Returns from the Field and at Home, September 1939–May 1945.

| September | ... | 0 | 0 | September | ... | 70 | 32 |
|---|---|---|---|---|---|---|---|
| October | ... | 0 | 0 | October | ... | 80 | 34 |
| November | ... | 0 | 0 | November | ... | 100 | 30 |
| December | ... | 0 | 0 | December | ... | 120 | 40 |
| 1940— | | | | 1943— | | | |
| January | ... | 0 | 0 | January | ... | 130 | 30 |
| February | ... | 0 | 0 | February | ... | 140 | 251 |
| March | ... | 0 | 0 | March | ... | 197 | 139 |
| April | ... | 1 | 0 | April | ... | 228 | 48 |
| May. . . | ... | 8 | 0 | May | ... | 260 | 14 |
| June. . . | ... | 12 | 0 | June | ... | 275 | 46 |
| July. . . | ... | 14 | 0 | July | ... | 281 | 150 |
| August | ... | 16 | 0 | August | ... | 291 | 153 |
| September | ... | 30 | 0 | September | ... | 345 | 151 |
| October | ... | 36 | 0 | October | ... | 395 | 201 |
| November | ... | 30 | 0 | November | ... | 163 | 223 |
| December | ... | 44 | 0 | December | ... | 336 | 176 |
| 1941— | | | | 1944— | | | |
| January | ... | 52 | 0 | January | ... | 305 | 292 |
| February | ... | 30 | 0 | February | ... | 332 | 265 |
| March | ... | 30 | 0 | March | ... | 351 | 253 |
| April | ... | 47 | 0 | April | ... | 385 | 348 |
| May. . . | ... | 48 | 1 | May | ... | 430 | 151 |
| June. . . | ... | 56 | 3 | June | ... | 431 | 193 |
| July. . . | ... | 34 | 11 | July | ... | 467 | 979 |
| August | ... | 50 | 26 | August | ... | 372 | 434 |
| September | ... | 38 | 12 | September | ... | 421 | 627 |
| October | ... | 71 | 23 | October | ... | 409 | 337 |
| November | ... | 46 | 10 | November | ... | 441 | Wastage |
| December | ... | 46 | 19 | December | ... | 421 | increasing |
| 1942— | | | | 1945— | | | but not |
| January | ... | 45 | 53 | January | ... | 432 | recorded. |
| February | ... | 45 | 10 | February | ... | 210 | |
| March | ... | 3 | 25 | March | ... | 88 | |
| April | ... | 36 | 10 | April | ... | 0 | |
| May. . . | ... | 79 | 28 | | | | |
| June. . . | ... | 70 | 13 | | | | |
| July. . . | ... | 60 | 20 | | | | |
| August | ... | 80 | 37 | | | | |

**Table 18.** Acceptance of Pz. Kpfwg. Vs. (Panthers) by Jn. 6 or Insp. of Pz. Tps. and Wastage Returns from the Field and at Home, September 1939–May 1945. (Acceptance began in 1943.)

| January | 0 | 0 | October | 257 | 107 |
|---|---|---|---|---|---|
| February | 0 | 0 | November | 209 | 79 |
| March | 0 | 0 | December | 299 | 92 |
| April | 0 | 0 | 1944— | | |
| May | 0 | 0 | January | 279 | 129 |
| June | 0 | 0 | February | 256 | 116 |
| July | 0 | 0 | March | 277 | 19 |
| August | 0 | 0 | April | 311 | 242 |
| September | 0 | 0 | May | 345 | 114 |
| October | 0 | 0 | June | 370 | 133 |
| November | 0 | 0 | July | 380 | 358 |
| December | 4 | 0 | August | 350 | 278 |
| 1943— | | | September | 335 | 705 |
| January | 20 | 0 | October | 218 | 315 |
| February | 18 | 0 | | | Wastage |
| March | 59 | 0 | November | 318 | increasing but |
| April | 0 | 0 | December | 210 | not recorded. |
| May | 324 | 0 | 1945— | | |
| June | 160 | 0 | January | 208 | |
| July | 202 | 83 | February | 110 | |
| August | 120 | 41 | March | 42 | |
| September | 197 | 81 | April | 0 | |

**Table 19.** Acceptance of Pz. Kpfwg. Vis. (Tigers) by Jn. 6 or Insp. of Pz. Tps. and Wastage Returns from the Field and at Home, September 1939–May 1945. (Acceptance began in 1942.)

| January | 0 | 0 | October | 50 | 32 |
|---|---|---|---|---|---|
| February | 0 | 0 | November | 57 | 28 |
| March | 0 | 0 | December | 67 | 58 |
| April | 0 | 0 | 1944— | | |
| May | 0 | 0 | January | 93 | 59 |
| June | 1 | 0 | February | 95 | 13 |
| July | 0 | 0 | March | 86 | 28 |
| August | 8 | 0 | April | 104 | 96 |
| September | 3 | 0 | May | 100 | 21 |
| October | 10 | 3 | June | 107 | 89 |
| November | 17 | 0 | July | 109 | 191 |
| December | 38 | 6 | August | 100 | 91 |
| 1943— | | | September | 60 | 138 |
| January | 35 | 11 | October | 26 | 49 |
| February | 32 | 3 | | | Wastage |
| March | 37 | 16 | November | 26 | increasing but |
| April | 46 | 4 | December | 23 | not recorded. |
| May | 50 | 17 | 1945— | | |
| June | 60 | 0 | January | 22 | |
| July | 65 | 33 | February | 34 | |
| August | 60 | 40 | March | 21 | |
| September | 85 | 33 | April | 13 | |

**Table 20.** AMMUNITION. *Stocks, held by the Army, of the Principal Ammunition Types (in Rounds).*

| Type | September 1, 1939. | January 1, 1940. | January 1, 1941. | January 1, 1942. | January 1, 1943. | January 1, 1944. | November 1, 1944. |
|---|---|---|---|---|---|---|---|
| Infantry Ammunition | 6,789,000,000 | 7,168,000,000 | 9,423,000,000 | 7,180,000,000 | 4,754,500,000 | 2,096,300,000 | 1,139,300,000 |
| 2 cm. | 18,419,000 | 20,538,000 | 32,340,000 | 22,416,000 | 17,177,700 | 22,715,000 | 21,831,200 |
| 3.7 cm. | 562,900 | 1,013,000 | 2,401,100 | 2,546,000 | 2,669,400 | 926,800 | 691,600 |
| 5-cm. Mortar | 3,672,000 | 11,019,000 | 30,767,000 | 26,978,000 | 19,928,800 | 4,462,600 | 2,416,800 |
| 8-cm. Mortar | 1,865,000 | 3,776,000 | 11,793,000 | 8,660,700 | 5,111,800 | 6,257,900 | 13,214,700 |
| 7.5-cm. Light Infantry Gun | 3,506,000 | 5,618,000 | 7,796,000 | 5,382,000 | 2,897,000 | 3,582,600 | 3,161,700 |
| 15 cm. Heavy Infantry Gun | 212,500 | 504,500 | 1,153,200 | 859,300 | 245,300 | 677,600 | 823,600 |
| 10.5-cm Gun Howitzer | 16,063,000 | 17,996,000 | 23,958,000 | 11,015,000 | 10,966,100 | 9,390,400 | 7,532,200 |
| 10-cm. Gun | 821,000 | 1,301,000 | 2,357,800 | 1,824,000 | 1,547,500 | 571,500 | 1,022,600 |
| 15-cm. Howitzer | 2,882,000 | 3,438,000 | 4,961,000 | 2,478,000 | 2,633,000 | 2,517,200 | 843,300 |

Note.— The stocks are complete figures, i.e., they include all ammunition in the Army's possession, whether in depots, dumps, ammunition trains, field dumps or carried by the field army. It can be said generally of most types of ammunition that after 1st January, 1942, stocks were not sufficient adequately to equip the formations in the field, even with reduced issues, and wastage exceeded production by roughly 3 : 2, and in times of heavy expenditure as much as 9 : 2.

# APPENDIX VIII.

# POLAND 1939.

## Preliminary Planning.

In the political direction which Hitler occasionally gave service chiefs, one thing is clear and proved correct in the event: that a bloodless solution of the Polish question was impossible. This was a logical conclusion from Hitler's determination that the Polish State must be annihilated to provide "Lebensraum" for Germans. In the light of this reasoning, the Danzig question was a mere sideshow. For a time, possibly only up till the Anglo-French guarantee to Poland (31st March, 1939), Hitler seems to have believed that the Danzig question in itself was capable of political solution.

2. Hitler is less certain of his ground on the question of intervention by the Western Powers, but appears finally to have deluded himself that there was little danger in accepting the risk. In this he proved correct from the short-term point of view of the Polish campaign. From the long-term point of view he was, of course, disastrously wrong.

3. The first evidence we have of planning for the Polish campaign is a report of an interview which von Brauchitsch (Commander-in-Chief of the German Army) had with Hitler on the 25th March, 1939. At this time Hitler had not envisaged an immediate solution of the Polish problem, but it was to receive active consideration, presumably from the point of view of military planning. When the time came, Poland was to be struck so hard that it would cease to count as a political factor for generations. On the immediate question of Danzig, Hitler makes the interesting confession that he does not propose to seek a warlike solution of this problem, since to do so would be to drive Poland into the arms of Great Britain.

4. At what must have been the first staff conference on this subject, held, according to Halder, in late April or early May, Hitler seems to have taken the view that the war

against Poland could be fought as a self-contained battle without Western intervention. With an unflattering reference to the 1914 German statesman, Hitler is alleged
to have stated that he would be an idiot if he got involved in a world war "because
of this lousy corridor business". The OKH plan for this war-on-one-front gamble,
which came off, was completed shortly after. In consequence, whatever confidence
the German General Staff felt must have been tempered with some misgivings when,
in an address to his Chiefs of Staff on the 23ʳᵈ May, 1939, Hitler stated that if the
Western Powers came in, they were to be treated as the primary enemy, and Poland
was to be settled with incidentally. Even the German railway system could scarcely
cope with such a rapid change of mood on the part of the Supreme Commander.

In the same address, the question of Russia's attitude was rather cockily dismissed
with the remark that it was quite possible that Russia would not trouble herself about
the dismemberment of Poland. After the 21ˢᵗ August, 1939, however, the German
General Staff can have had few immediate qualms about Russia.

5. Eight hours before operations against Poland were due to begin, Hitler postponed D-Day for about a week, allegedly because Mussolini had produced a scheme
for mediation. Considering the German Army's state of readiness at the time, and
the political indoctrination on the fate of Poland which Hitler had given his senior
Generals, this postponement must have seemed to the General Staff a pointless and
distasteful concession to the morals of diplomacy or to Mussolini's pride.

## *The German Plan.*

6. The invasion plan involved throwing in fifty-seven divisions - in fact, the bulk
of Germany's fully-mobilised divisions – against Poland. Halder complains that the
Army which took the field in September 1939 could not bear comparison in point of
readiness with the Kaiser's Army of 1914, and that many of its ancillary units were
improvised. The campaign bears little trace of improvisation, and, considering the
condition of the Polish armies, it is difficult to see what the Germans would have
gained by waiting till 1940. Halder's contention may be his innocent contribution to
the legend that the German Generals were bundled into the war against their will and
better judgement.

7. In planning the attack on Poland, the Germans took full advantage of the opportunity, which possession of East Prussia gave them, to strike deep into the heart of

their enemy's country. The force which struck Southwards from East Prussia was the Third Army, which disposed of eight Infantry divisions. Further West, the Fourth Army deployed in Pomerania with eight Infantry and four mobile divisions. This Army, which, together with the Third Army, formed the Northern Army Group under von Bock, invaded the Polish corridor, thrust to the coast in the Danzig area, and then drove South-east towards Warsaw. Army Group South, under von Rundstedt, consisted of the Eighth Army, deploying seven divisions, from the Breslau area; the Tenth Army, with ten Infantry and seven mobile divisions, concentrated around Oppeln; and the Fourteenth Army, with twelve divisions, of which two were Panzer, in the area opposite Cracow. These forces were supported by some 1,800 first line aircraft, comprising 50 per cent. of the total strength of the Luftwaffe.

## *The Campaign.*

8. While von Bock's armies converged on the Warsaw area from the North-west and North-east, von Rundstedt's forces provided the Southern arm of a vast pincer movement, with one army directed on Warsaw from the South-west, another (the strongest) on the Vistula above Warsaw, and his third army striking due East through Cracow, Przemysl and Lvov. At the beginning of the second week of the campaign, a decision was taken that Guderian's Panzer Corps, which, after the capture of Graudenz, it was planned to switch Eastwards to spearhead the drive on Warsaw from East Prussia, should be switched still further East. It was launched in a drive Southwards to Brest Litovsk, thus cutting Polish communications from the rear. By the day hostilities ceased it had almost joined hands with von Rundstedt's Southernmost army, thus just failing to complete yet another, and still wider, ring of encirclement.

## *Polish Counter-measures.*

9. The success which attended German planning in the Polish campaign can have been aided in no small measure by an almost fundamental misappreciation on the part of the Poles. According to German intelligence maps, the Poles deployed eight Infantry divisions in the large salient formed by the province of Posen. Halder claims that he based his plans on the assumption that the Poles would take this course as Posen was German before the Great War. These forces were lost almost without striking an effective blow for the Polish cause. The Germans by-passed Posen to the

North and South, reckoning presumably that the consequent shorter distances to Warsaw compensated for the loss of the comparatively good Posen railway network. Similarly, against the German Southern Army Group, the Poles placed the main weight of their forces around Cracow; thirteen divisions were in this area, according to the Germans, as against only seven further North in the Tschenstochau area, where Rundstedt struck his heaviest blow.

10. Such arrangements as had been made with the Russians in Moscow in August appear to have remained the secret of OKW and were not passed on to OKH. However, the scant regard which OKW showed for the dispositions of troops on the ground and for movements in progress when issuing orders for withdrawals in Eastern Poland, suggests that in fact nothing but the sketchiest co-ordination can have been worked out with the Russians beforehand.

# APPENDIX IX.

# NORWAY.

(*Note*: - This section includes Finland from September 1944 onwards. Prior to this date, Finland is dealt with in the sections on the Eastern Front.)

## Invasion.

Falkenhorst, who eventually became the German C.-in-C., Norway, states that towards the end of February 1940 he was given the task of preparing for the occupation of Denmark and Norway. There were, according to him, fears that the British were going to occupy these countries, thus constituting a serious threat to Germany, her navy and her imports from Norway and Sweden. Warlimont of OKW adds that in January and February rumours of intended British landings in Norway, and especially in the Stavanger area, caused considerable alarm in German High Command quarters. It was reasonable that rumours of this sort should attract some attention so long as Finland was still at war with Russia, and there was talk of Anglo-French intervention. (The Russo-Finnish armistice was not signed till March).

2. It may be that rumours of impending Allied operations in these areas focussed Hitler's attention on the vulnerability of Germany's Northern approaches, particularly in view of Germany's unfavourable naval position. The occupation of these two countries had undoubted advantages for Germany. Apart from the factor mentioned by Falkenhorst –the security it afforded to German sea communications from Norway and Sweden and therefore to her imports of iron ore – it gave the Germans additional bases from which to attack Allied shipping. Furthermore, the occupation of Denmark ensured Germany against the Allies opening up a new front additional to the French front.

3. Plans for the operation were ready in some shape by the 6th March, and D-Day was fixed for as soon as weather would permit and there would be sufficient daylight. The campaign began, in fact, on the 9th April. It is understandable that, from the point of view of timing, the operation was unwelcome to OKH, since the German offensive in the West was due to begin only a month later. The Army commitment in Norway and Denmark was not, of itself, large, namely, some ten divisions, but it is easy to see the operation might easily have become, if it had gone badly, an embarrassment from an air and naval point of view, as it contained so many hazardous aspects. But German appreciation of British capabilities and intentions may well have been such that the risk of waiting till the conclusion of the Western campaign was considered unjustifiable.

4. The plan depended essentially on surprise. In no place did the forces to be landed at zero hour exceed 2,000 men, although, in most cases, a follow-up was planned for the same day. The ships carrying the Narvik force had to put to sea almost a week before D-Day. The margin of shipping was small – the amount of merchant tonnage earmarked for the operation was nearly a quarter of a million tons, of which only 8,000 tons were officially classified as reserve. For security reasons transports could not be armed against air or submarine attack until after D-Day. The Germans must have reckoned that deficiencies of this sort and terrain difficulties would be counter-balanced by the unpreparedness of the Norwegians and the strength of the G.A.F. some 800 operational aircraft and 250-300 transport aircraft being employed. It is interesting in this connection that in the Narvik area, where the G.A.F. could bring little weight to bear, the Germans found themselves in an extremely difficult situation after the destruction of their destroyers. Indeed, according to Falkenhorst and Warlimont they were actually considering withdrawal when the Allies evacuated.

5. Seven divisions were used for the occupation of Norway. Ports of embarkation were principally in the Hamburg-Bremen area, but Stettin and Danzig were also used for the follow-up divisions. The initial phase involved the seizure of ports all round the Norwegian coast, warships being used to land the assault troops, whose heavier equipment was carried on merchant vessels. In some cases these merchant vessels, under the guise of ordinary cargo ships, were berthed before zero hour. Air transport was also used at Oslo, Stavanger and Bergen and particularly Trondheim, which were all of great strategic importance from the air point of view. In the assault phase, three divisions were employed, one for the Oslo-Kristiansand South area, another for the Stavanger-Bergen area, and the third, a mountain division for the

Trondheim and Narvik area. Two follow-up divisions came through Oslo and two through Trondheim. The Germans appreciated that Norwegian forces consisted of six divisional districts, based principally on the main ports: two in the Oslo area, and one each in the areas of Kristiansand South, Bergen, Trondheim and Narvik.

6. Apart from the difficult situation which arose in the Narvik area, the campaign, which could scarcely have succeeded without complete surprise, went well for the Germans, the rapid establishment of complete air supremacy being an important contributory factor. A link-up took place before the end of April between the forces advancing Southwards from the Trondheim area and those pushing Northwards from the Oslo area. The Norwegian final capitulation took place on the 9th June.

## *Subsequent Strategy.*

7. Having occupied Norway, the German problem was to ensure its defence with the greatest economy of forces compatible with security. The subsequent course of German strategy in Norway is mainly a history of German efforts to solve this problem in the face of increasing man-power shortage. During the rest of 1940 the German garrison in Norway remained essentially unchanged. None of the divisions which occupied the country was removed, and only one new division came in. From this point to the end of the war defence tended to be centred principally on the main ports and strategic airfields, notably Stavanger, Trondheim, and later in the far north.

8. During the first half of 1941 there was a more noticeable increase in the number of German divisions in Norway. Several factors were at work. In the first place, a British raid in the Narvik area caused considerable alarm, and towards the end of March Hitler issued a directive alerting the German forces in Norway, referring to the possibility not merely of raids against the coast, but also of major landings. He ordered a vast reinforcement of coastal artillery. The most important factor influencing the despatch of reinforcements to Norway in 1941 must surely have been the impending attack on Russia, in which the German army of Norway was destined to play a rôle. It contributed initially three divisions to the Finnish front, and its commander became responsible for German operations in Finland and remained so until the end of the year. The reinforcement of Norway, which took place prior to the 22nd June, 1941, (attack on Russia), must have been at least partly intended to take the place of the divisions earmarked for Finland. The opening of a German front in

Finland against Russia also provided further reasons for a strong defence of Norway. Sea communications via Norway were vital for the supply and reinforcement of the Murmansk front. So long as the Germans were interested in keeping Finland in the war against Russia, they were bound to hold Norway and, in particular, to ensure that the Allies did not get a foothold in North Norway. This is the zone in which, in his directive at the end of March, Hitler ordered the main defensive effort to be made. Again, a month later, an OKW directive on the forces to be sent from Norway to Finland pointed out that in no circumstances was the defence of the Norwegian coast from Narvik Northwards to fall below eighteen battalions.

9. Reinforcements in the Spring of 1941 were the 702 and 710 Divisions, both low-category defensive formations. Their arrival and the departure of three divisions to Finland made the total of German divisions in Norway seven, at which figure it remained for the rest of the year. Their arrival also marked the beginning of a process of dilution in the German garrison of Norway. At first this process was mostly limited to taking drafts from good divisions.

10. During 1942 there was little change in the outward appearance of the German forces. There were, however, considerable changes in organisation. Following on the Vaagsö raid in December 1941, Field-Marshal List was sent to report on the defences of Norway. Apparently as a consequence of his recommendations, the coastal troops, which hitherto had been under the control of the field division responsible for the sector, were now grouped under separate static commands. In time, three coastal divisional headquarters made their appearance, two in the North and one in the South-west. The field divisions, of which during 1942 there were five in Norway, were intended to have a more mobile rôle. It was no doubt a reflection of this policy that a start was made with the formation of a Panzer division in Norway. That the Germans were increasingly preoccupied with the possibility of attacks on Norway during this period is also borne out by the fact that Commander-in-Chief, Norway, was relieved of his responsibilities in Finland at the end of 1941.

11. From 1943 onwards Norway was slowly but steadily robbed of its good divisions and G.A.F. anti-shipping by the more urgent needs of other fronts. Three left in 1943; in return four others were either transferred to Norway or formed there, but none was of the same quality as those that left. At the beginning of 1944 and in the summer respectively, two more divisions left, both for the East, and one new division was formed in South Norway.

12. In September 1944 Norway was defended by ten divisions, nearly all of low category. The number of independent units was, however, enormous. Some idea of this can be gained from a figure quoted by Jodl for the end of 1943. At that time there were over 300,000 German troops in Norway – nearly as many, although not of such quality, as in Italy, where nearly twenty Allied divisions were committed. It is, however, unlikely that the defence of Norway could have been conducted more economically. The generally indifferent and, in the North, deplorable communications imposed drastic limits on the extent to which the defence of Norway could be centralised. The coastal perimeter was over 1,000 miles long, and each zone had to be largely self-contained for defence purposes. Up till the Summer of 1944, the retention of Norway was strategically justifiable. Finland was still in the war against Russia, and therefore communications through Norway were still required, while Narvik was important as a loading point for iron ore from Sweden. The Germans could furthermore hardly court the risk of giving the Allies direct land contact with Sweden with the consequent possibility that the latter would to some extent have uncovered Denmark. Not least important were the naval bases in Norway, particularly those for submarines which constituted practically the only sphere in which Germany was still on the offensive.

13. After September 1944, circumstances arose which ultimately absolved the German High Command from passing judgment on the question of abandoning Norway. The capitulation of Finland, which took place in that month, eventually produced a large surplus of first-class troops in Norway. Although the need for these troops on other fronts was urgent, the shipping bottleneck, aggravated by the competing demands of the East Baltic transport services, prevented this surplus being completely evacuated from Norway before the general armistice occurred.

14. The Germans were in some measure prepared for Finnish defection as early as September 1943. This factor can have done little to make the event less unwelcome. The possibilities of withdrawal through Finnish ports were very limited, and in fact the Germans appear to have attempted to send only a few odds and ends out through the Gulf of Bothnia. It seems that at best they can have got little more than one division out by this route. For the eight German divisions in Finland, there was no way out except through North Norway. Four of these divisions were on the Salla Front, over 300 miles from the frontier of North Norway. They had only two roads, one of them poor. Winter conditions were only two months away. Not satisfied with these

difficulties, the Germans allowed their resentment to get the better of them, and by scorching the earth as they withdrew converted the Finns from obligatory but not very vigorous hostility into active belligerency.

15. By the end of September, OKW had decided that the retention of the Petsamo nickel mines was no longer the decisive factor in determining the extent of a German withdrawal in Finland. Germany's nickel stocks at this time were sufficient until 1946; subsequently the supply was 50 per cent. assured. It appears, however, that it was only with some reluctance that Hitler adopted a bold policy in Finland and North Norway. As late as the 1st October he envisaged holding a line (apparently covering the Finnish arm and the Petsamo nickel mines) which would have required all the German forces then in Finland, and the establishment of new bases on the lines of communication (L. of C.). On the 4th October, it appears that on the recommendation of the local commander, Rendulic, Hitler decided that the German Army of Finland should withdraw direct to the Lyngen Fjord position. This was the shortest line possible in North Norway, and in addition to the overall economy in forces which it afforded, provided effective cover for German naval bases in North Norway and for the Narvik iron ore traffic. Having made this decision, Hitler was far from allowing full local initiative at Rendulic, who was anxious to clear the Arctic Highway between Lyngen and Kirkenes as part of it became impassable by mid-November. Hitler, influenced probably by the large quantities of German stores in the North and the desire ruthlessly to remove anything which would assist the Russia pursuit, decided that Kirkenes was to be held till mid-November. With superb disregard for local conditions, he also suggested to Rendulic that he leave outposts East of the Lyngen position – a task which, on account of the vast distances, could not be carried out economically and at the same time effectively.

16. Withdrawal to the Lyngen position was, however, carried out successfully and, once the Germans were on Norwegian soil, without pursuit. Long before it had been reached, in fact on the 9th October, troops from Finland were started on their journey to Southern Norway to transfer to other fronts. Their arrival in the South was anticipated by the despatch from Norway of divisions already in the South. The removal of divisions was fairly continuous, but was gravely hampered by shortage of transport shipping.

17. Towards the end of 1944, the Germans appear to have had some fears that Sweden might be enticed into the war on the side of the Allies. In consequence, a

division was ordered from Finland into the Narvik area in October, and in January an enterprising suggestion was made that the Swedes might be deterred if a few V-Weapon sites were set up on Danish soil and ostentatiously pointed at Sweden.

18. Despite the risk of Swedish intervention, it is probable that some ten German divisions could have provided reasonable peace of mind in Norway, certainly if the Germans had withdrawn from the Lyngen position to the Narvik area, which would have been without serious strategical disadvantages. In the event, when the war ended the Germans had for transport reasons been unable to reduce the garrison below eleven divisions compared with a peak of 19 divisions in October 1944. The personnel total was over 300,000.

# APPENDIX X.

# THE WEST
# (Up to December 1942).

Phase I. – January 1933-May 1940.For the early years of the period the West was, from Hitler's point of view, merely a dangerous rear, which had to be kept neutral or inactive while he settled with Austria, Czechoslovakia and Poland. Only two Western adventures were undertaken. The first, the remilitarisation of the Rhineland in March 1936, was an essential step towards security in the West. It was a successful political gamble, since German war potential at that time was quite inadequate for a trial of strength with France, and military counter-action must have resulted in a withdrawal. The second adventure, intervention in the Spanish Civil War, was deliberately kept on a minor scale. According to General Warlimont, who was on a special mission to Franco from July to December 1936, it was decided on his return to Germany, on both military and political grounds, not to send major units of the Germany army to Spain.

2. While Hitler, confident in democratic disunity and dislike of war, always believed that he could keep the West quiet until he was ready, the leading members of the General Staff of the army took a very different view. This appears to have been due in part to a genuine apprehension of the French army, and in part to a dislike of going to war, under the leadership of a man they distrusted, at a time when the German army had by no means reached the pitch of perfection to which they hoped to raise it. In June 1938 the Chief of Staff of the army, Beck, delivered a lecture to General officers and General Staff officers in which he considered the probable results of a German attack on Czechoslovakia. He concluded that Czechoslovakia could be crushed, but that in the meantime the French Army would be able to penetrate into South-Western Germany, and that the final result would be a complete defeat of

Germany by France. The only result was that Beck was dismissed and Hitler's distrust of the Generals augmented. Certain members of the General Staff now claim that they were prepared to resist Hitler on this issue, and had mounted a plot to overthrow him, but that this was brought to nothing by the Munich agreement and Hitler's complete political triumph.

3. The only major military precaution taken in the West in these early days of German expansion was the building of the West Wall. This was begun immediately after the reoccupation of the Rhineland and was given highest constructional priority from summer 1938 until the Polish campaign. No fortifications were built North of Muenchen-Gladbach until September 1939 (when some pill-boxes and field works were constructed), a fact attributable to two main causes:-

(1) Germany's Northern frontier was considered to be too close to the Ruhr to be the basis for a sound defence line should the Allies enter the Low Countries. It would be essential for the German defence line to be advanced in order to protect the Ruhr from long-range artillery fire and close-based air bombing.

(2) It was always intended to settle the West by an attack in the North. Strong static defences in South Germany were, therefore, an essential part of this plan, to ward off any possible counter-offensive.

4. The first of these reasons affected Hitler to such an extent that, as late as May 1939, he was still considering countering Allied intervention in the coming Polish war by a lightning occupation of Holland. His confidence in Allied respect for treaties prevailed, however, and in September he left the Dutch and Belgian frontiers with a bare token garrison (three divisions only between Aachen and Emmerich). His less flattering trust in French inertia also enabled him to leave his South-West frontier very thinly manned, much to the anxiety of his General Staff. In all there were only 33 divisions in the west, none of them armoured, on the day Poland was attacked.

5. Hitler and his General Staff were at one in considering that France, if attacked in the North, by a strike through Belgium, and preferably Holland also, towards the Channel ports. This was considered the best course of action for a variety of reasons: -

(1) It would immediately move the battle front away from the vital Ruhr area (which the Allies could menace by invading, or coming to terms with Belgium and Holland).

(2) It would avoid the Maginot Line.

(3) It would secure forthwith bases for naval and air warfare against England.

(4) It enabled best use to be made of Germany's communications network.

Reason (1) was the one most frequently on Hitler's lips, as he professed always to believe that the Allies could at any time bring sufficient pressure to bear on the Low Countries to compel them to abandon their neutrality. The extent of his real belief in this, however, can be measured by the risk taken during the Polish campaign (see above).

Reason (3) was that which was probably nearest his heart, as he believed that (with suitable bases) he could bring England to her knees by air and submarine warfare alone, without risking an invasion.

6. The details of the plan of attack were subject to frequent modification, but one of these was so drastic that it is reasonable to call the gradually-evolving plan before it Plan I, and what came after Plan II.

Plan I was similar to the old Schlieffen plan, being based on a strong right wing sweeping across Belgium and Holland to the Channel ports, and then making a sharp left wheel to the Seine and Paris. The main thrust lay in the sectors of 6 and 4 Armies of Army Group B. Army Group B was allotted the bulk of the available armour and would have received the bulk of the theatre reserves. Army Group A was to push through Luxembourg and Southern Belgium and build up the defensive front on the left flank of Army Group B. Army Group C was to hold the West Wall against possible French counter thrusts.

One or other version of this plan was in force throughout the latter half of 1939, and, had Hitler succeeded in goading the Army High Command into action that year, it would have been carried out. Hitler for once failed to get his way, however. First the General Staff said that they were not ready, and then that it was too late in the year. Towards the end of December Hitler gave up the struggle and the operation was postponed to the Spring. In after years Hitler gave this as a classical instance of General Staff obstruction and claimed that, had he prevailed, he would have been able to attack Russia in 1940.

7. During the winter of 1939-40 the Allied position clarified. It became evident to the German General Staff that the French and British would not march into Belgium until the Germans did. The initial frontier battles, therefore, would be against the

Dutch and Belgians only. This point had been in doubt before and had made Plan I rather tentative and complicated, since two entirely different sets of circumstances had had to be allowed for. It now became possible to plan more definitely, and therefore with greater boldness. Moreover, by a blunder which lost Goering much favour, a German plane carrying a copy of the entire plan came down in Belgium. Plan I was therefore, mistakenly, considered as blown, as the Allies regarded this accident as an attempt at deception.

8. For these reasons Plan II was adopted in late February. It will be seen that in its early stages this was practically the Schlieffen plan in reverse. The main thrust lay with Army Group A, which was, if all went well, to cut to the coast at Abbeville, form a defensive front on the Somme, and then turn North against the rear of the Allied armies. Army Group B was to advance more slowly across central Belgium and the move of the Allies into Belgium was to be turned to their own destruction. The advance of two Army Groups was closely co-ordinated and Army Group A was not to advance West of a North-South line through Brussels until it was clear that Army Group B had the situation in central Belgium well in hand. The bulk of the armour and of the theatre reserve was to go to Army Group A, since its long salient would be susceptible at one period to attacks on both flanks. Army Group C, after an initial holding demonstration against the Maginot Line, was also to yield troops to Army Group A. This daring plan, which was the one finally employed, involved a very great risk of a shattering counter-attack from the South. Moreover large armoured forces were to advance through country so bad that a well-executed plan of demolitions would seriously have delayed their progress.

9. Hitler must receive some credit for the planning of these operations in that he always insisted that attack in the West was feasible and essential. In matters of detail he was, as usual, a great nuisance, but on the whole he did not alter the General Staff's plans. He worked off his superfluous energy by planning personally in minutest detail the attack on Fort Eben-Emael, which, since it involved the Luftwaffe, was treated as an OKW operation.

## Phase II. – May 1940–October 1940.

10. The Western offensive was an outstanding success, exceeding even Hitler's expectations. Army Group A grouped the mass of its mobile formations in a single

striking force (Group von Kleist), and led with armour all the way from Luxembourg to the sea. The foremost armoured corps, under Guderian, which crossed the frontier on the 10th May, reached Abbeville on the 20th. The infantry had little to do but follow behind and build up a Southern defensive front as quickly as possible. No French counter-attack came in from the South, and under heavy frontal pressure from Army Group B the encircled Allied armies in the North were unable to fact about in sufficient strength to break out Southwards.

11. Army Group B, despite its lack of armour, had pressed forward with great dash (attributed by Halder, Chief of the General Staff at the time to the personal ambitions of its Commander, von Bock), and by the 20th May had reached the general line Ghent-Tournai. These forces were supported by the full weight of the Luftwaffe some 3,300 aircraft out of a total strength of about 11,200 being committed to the support of the Army. Group von Kleist reached Gravelines and St Omer on the 26th May. On that day when the Allied evacuation, which was to continue until the 4th June, began, German armour was within 12 miles of Dunkirk. Then Hitler intervened decisively, forbidding the further advance of the armoured divisions. It is said that Keitel had shaken his nerve by telling him stories of Flanders mud in the last war, and that he was afraid that losses in tanks would be so heavy as to prejudice the next stage in the campaign. Undoubtedly, however, he had an exaggerated faith in the capabilities of the Luftwaffe, to which the destruction of the pocketed Allied forces was now entrusted. The army protested vigorously, but Hitler was adamant.

12. The remainder of the campaign was marked by little other than speed and competence. Regrouping was quickly carried out and Army Group B advanced across the Somme on the 5th June. The Seine was reached on the 10th June and Paris entered on the 14th. On the same day Army Group C started to break through the Maginot Line into South-Western France. Hostilities ceased on the 25th.

13. Such an overwhelmingly swift and decisive victory had not been foreseen either by Hitler or by his staffs. Hitler expected and hoped to be able to come to an arrangement with Britain without further fighting. The Luftwaffe immediately underwent a brief period of re-equipment and Hitler's energies were for a time devoted to preparations for an immense victory parade in Paris.

14. Only when it became evident that England would fight on were plans made for an invasion. Suitable landing craft were lacking and the improvisations available were safe only in fair weather. The German navy could not guarantee a secure passage of

the Channel and the Luftwaffe could not even ensure absolute air superiority. In these circumstances planning was uncertain and half-hearted and the attempt was eventually abandoned. The first extant order for the preparation of the invasion, issued by Keitel, is dated the 2$^{nd}$ July, 1940. It stated that the Fuehrer had decided that invasion was possible, and called on Commanders-in-Chief to start preparations immediately.

15. On the 1$^{st}$ August, however, Keitel issued another order stating that since Commander-in-Chief Navy had reported that the ground work could not be completed before the 15$^{th}$ September, the Fuehrer had decided that preparations should be continued up to that date, but that in the period 8-14 days after the beginning of the great air offensive (which began about the 5$^{th}$ August) he would finally decide whether or not the invasion should take place in 1940. It was not until the 12$^{th}$ October, when it was finally realised that the battle of Britain had been lost, that the invasion was finally declared postponed until 1941. In so far as it went, the general plan of operation "Sealion" was for landings by two armies, with twenty-five divisions in all, between Folkestone and Worthing. Ten divisions were to be landed in the first four days to form the initial bridgehead. After about eight days, an advance could be made to the first objective, a line Thames estuary-hills south of London-Portsmouth. The course of the battle would then depend largely on circumstances, but efforts were to be made to cut London off from the West as quickly as possible. Parachute troops were to be used only for the capture of Dover.

16. A third army might possibly have been employed for a landing in Lyme Regis Bay if necessary. Deception to simulate an imminent invasion was carried on up to the invasion of Russia, and a new genuine outline plan was prepared between April and August 1941 for use after Victory in the East.

## Phase III. — October 1940-December 1941.

17. Apart from the air blitz on England, the West was a dead theatre throughout this period. The Atlantic Wall was begun and its construction went ahead steadily. The intention was to build a strong crust of relatively small depth, the defences being concentrated: -

(1) Near important ports.

(2) In proportion to the facilities offered by the coast line for landing.

(3) In inverse proportion to the distance from ports and airfields in the United Kingdom.

A project to attack Gibraltar through Spain had to be abandoned owing to the failure to agree over Franco's price. In December 1941 there were thirty-five divisions in the West, none of which were armoured or motorised.

## Phase IV. — December 1941-December 1942.

18. Construction of the Atlantic Wall continued throughout this period, being stimulated, particularly as regards the building of anti-tank obstacles, by the Dieppe raid in August 1942.

The Allied landing in North Africa in November 1942 induced a German entry into the unoccupied zone of France, a precautionary measure to prevent landings on the Mediterranean coast.

During this period, France and the Low Countries began to be used as a refitting area for divisions from the Eastern Front. From December 1941 right up to D-day there were generally four or five divisions refitting or reforming at any one time. In December 1942, there were thirty-six divisions in the West, of which four were armoured.

# APPENDIX XI.

# THE BALKANS
# (Up to the Winter of 1941.)

NOTE. – This section includes Hungary, Roumania and Bulgaria, but from an occupational point of view only. German operations in these countries, when they became part of the Eastern Front, are dealt with in the sections on the Eastern Front.)

1. It is clear that, until Mussolini's attack on Greece (28th October, 1940), the German General Staff and Hitler wished to leave Bulgaria, Greece and Yugoslavia well alone. The realisation that, in the long run, intervention in the Balkans would have become necessary to shield the Roumanian oil fields against British attack appears to have offered some consolation, after the event, for having been forced to fight the Duce's battles and for the consequent deleterious effects on German redeployment to the Eastern Front.

2. Roumania itself was occupied during the winter of 1940-41 (under the pretext of providing schools and training formations for the Roumanian Army) as an advance preparation for the attack on Russia; but the main reason for this move was to place the Roumanian oil fields under German control.

3. As early as the 12th November, 1940, Hitler issued a directive to OKH to prepare for a possible invasion of Greek Thrace from Bulgaria with a force of some ten divisions. An early fancy of Hitler's, to send a mountain division to Albania to reinforce the Italians and thus eventually enable them to attack the Salonika defile from the rear, in conjunction with the attack from Bulgaria, did not survive the administrative objections of Mussolini and the military objections of the German General Staff.

By mid-February 1941, German plans for the occupation of Bulgaria and for pushing on into Greek Thrace were complete. (Operation "Marita"), and the number of divisions had risen to seventeen, including finally five Panzer, divisions. Furthermore, the Balkan campaign entailed a major diversion of air strength, amounting to 1,000 operational aircraft, away from the Western Front.

4. The first division crossed the Danube on the 2$^{nd}$ March (the day after Bulgaria joined the Axis), and the last was scheduled to cross on the 31$^{st}$ March. Thus, at a time when concentration against Russia was proceeding actively, the Germans planned to tie up nearly one quarter of their total Panzer force on the wrong side of one of the worst communications bottlenecks in Europe. Halder explains the large number of forces sent into Bulgaria by the need to protect the Turkish and Yugoslav flanks, about which Bulgaria was particularly anxious.

5. Of the eight divisions envisaged for the invasion of Greece, nearly all were to arrive in their concentration areas by the 6$^{th}$ March. It is difficult to see why the actual invasion should have had to wait until the 6$^{th}$ April, unless German administrative preparations were in arrears by reason of Bulgaria's recent "neutrality", or Hitler was unwilling to start until Bulgaria was well packed.

6. Before the invasion of Greece could begin, a new factor emerged in the shape of the Simović coup d'État in Belgrade. It is abundantly clear that up till this time the Germans had intended to respect Yugoslavia's sovereignty during the invasion of Greece, hoping, no doubt, to gain their ends in the former country later, at a more convenient time and in less costly manner. OKH were given eight days in which to improvise an invasion of Yugoslavia, originally without using routes through Hungary, although in the event, this condition was not strictly observed. The plan put into operation provided for, firstly, a thrust by four divisions from Bulgaria (12$^{th}$ Army) towards Skoplje with the aim of relieving the Italian East flank in Albania, secondly, a thrust by five divisions from Bulgaria (also 12$^{th}$ Army) via Nish towards Belgrade, and thirdly, the deployment of seven divisions through Styria and Hungary to complete the destruction of the Yugoslav army.

7. On the eve of the attack from Styria and Hungary, only four divisions out of seven had reached their concentration area. However, the course of the campaign in Yugoslavia justified the German General Staff's unflattering appreciation of the Yugoslav Army, but the campaign place another two German Panzer divisions at the mercy of the indifferent Balkans communications network. Furthermore, the Germans did not have to wait till Tito became a national figure before they realised that in Yugoslavia they had caught a Tartar.

8. OKH limited the initial objective in the operations against Greece to Northern Greece; only when that objective was reached could a decision be made to wheel South-west. In fact, the main German drive was Southwards. On the 20th April Greek resistance was finished. Once the Greek campaign was over, the Germans largely turned the defence and administration over to the Italians as quickly and in as large a measure as possible, confining their own commitment to some ports and airfields.

9. On the 25th April Hitler gave orders for "Mercury", an airborne operation against Crete. Warlimont, Jodl's deputy, gives as the strategical justification for this operation, which began on the 20th May, the desire to prevent British naval and air penetration into the Ægean and to secure a spring-board for operations against North Africa. The latter factor acquired added plausibility when it was realised that the Germans had by then landed forces in Tripolitania. The Germans were also working on the Vichy French in Syria and Rashid Ali in Iraq, flying in officers to organise revolt in the latter country. If Rashid Ali's coup d'État, which occurred shortly after the Crete landings, had been successful the Germans intended to exploit it by sending reinforcements. They had at the back of their mind the idea of striking south from Syria and Iraq and attacking Egypt from the East while Rommel attacked from the West. Crete would have been an extremely useful base for such a project. They apparently hoped that Rashid Ali would be more successful than turned out to be the case.

10. There can be no doubt that the necessity to intervene in Greece and Yugoslavia was a grave embarrassment to the German High Command. One of their documents speaks of the 15th May as a provisional planning date for the attack on Russia (as against the actual D-Day, the 22nd June), which suggests that the delay was at least a month. It is probable, however, that the floods in Poland that summer might have caused an equivalent delay in any case.

11. On the conclusion of the Balkan campaign, Field-Marshal List, General Officer Commanding 12th Army (which invaded Greece and Yugoslavia from Bulgaria), was appointed Commander-in-Chief, South-East – a command which included all of Serbia, part of Croatia, and the trunk communications of Greece. List, if draconic in his measures, appears at least to have been efficient and clear-minded. He was, however, hampered almost from the outset by lack of German troops, by the indifferent military ardour of the Italians, who controlled the entire coastal area of Yugoslavia, but the almost oriental inefficiency of the puppet Croat Government, and by the airy misconceptions of the Balkan situation cherished by Hitler and the OKW.

12. The bulk of the invasion armies and strong elements of the G.A.F. left the Balkans in April and May, and by June List disposed of only four "occupational" divisions in Yugoslavia, including one in Croatia and, in addition, an "occupational" division in Salonika. It was at once clear to List, when partisan trouble began in Serbia in June 1941, and became intensified in August, that the situation could not be adequately dealt with by police measures, for which alone his occupational divisions were qualified. The arrival of a field division from France in September 1941, gave him his first chance to mount a full-scale operation against the partisans in North-West Serbia, without, however any decisive success. A further two field divisions were promised for November, but only one arrived. An OKW directive issued in November 1941, defining Commander-in-Chief, South-East's main task as the protection of the metal deposits, coal-mines and munition works of Serbia, showed the first clear divergence of opinion between List and the High Command. List contended that protection of Serbia's economic resources would tie up all his forces and make it impossible for him to pacify the country by striking hard at partisan centres. This he regarded as ultimately the only sure way to the economic exploitation of the country.

# APPENDIX XII.

# THE EAST (Up to the fall of Stalingrad).

Genesis of the Russian Campaign. According to Jodl, Chief of the Operational Planning Staff in the OKW, even while the campaign in the west was still in progress, Hitler declared his intention of coming to grips with Russia as soon as the German military position permitted. This declaration may at the time have been a mere whim of Hitler's fertile imagination; or there is marked inconsistency in the decision he took after victory in the west to demobilise thirty-eight divisions as a gesture to the home front. OKH was apparently not so optimistic, and circumvented the orders.

2. Warlimont, Jodl's deputy, whose accuracy is, however, in some matters, not above suspicion, states that in July 1940 Hitler wanted to begin operations against Russia in the following autumn, but Jodl and Keitel raised objections. It is possibly worth recording another statement of Warlimont's that, after Molotov's visit to Berlin in 1940, secret hopes were cherished that Hitler would abandon his plans for a defensive war with Russia. This may be taken as one of the many indications of the misgivings with which the German General Staff approached the new war in the east. There is, however, no record of any serious concerted attempt having been made to dissuade Hitler, although the OKH referred to the completely inadequate amount of intelligence on Russia, and was answered with silence. OKH began to lay its plans as soon as it received, in August, the first definite hint of Hitler's intentions.

3. Throughout the campaign OKH remained responsible for the co-ordination of operations on the eastern front, whereas all other theatres became eventually OKW responsibilities. It was logical that OKH should be paramount in the east where initiative and decision lay throughout almost exclusively with land armies. As early as September 1940 considerable preparations must have been made, for at that time Jodl found it necessary to issue an instruction on security measures in Poland, stating that

Russia was on no account to get the impression that she was threatened. It is clear that the German-Soviet Pact was characteristic bluff on the part of Hitler. In August 1940, he intimated that he wanted punctual delivery to Russia to continue until the spring of 1941. On the 12th November, 1940, he issued an order explaining to the General Staff that "political discussions had been initiated with the aim of satisfying Russia's attitude for the time being. Irrespective of the results of these discussions all preparations for the east which have been verbally ordered will be continued".

## Intensive Planning Begins.

4. According to Halder, intensive planning began in October 1940, and by January 1941 the plan of operations was ready. The preparation of maps and communications was also in full swing, and during the winter Roumania was transformed into a German base under cover of schools and training formations.

## Hitler's First Directive.

5. On the 28th December, 1940, Hitler issued a directive to his three chiefs of services on Operation "Barbarossa", the code name for operations against Russia, stating that forces must be prepared to overthrow Russia in a quick campaign, but adding, under the heading of security, that the execution of the operations had not yet been definitely decided. If the operation became necessary, final concentration would be ordered eight weeks before the intended D-Day. For planning purposes, however, the 15th May was to be taken as a provisional D-Day for preparations which required longer than eight weeks.

6. As regards Allies, Hitler apparently already felt himself in a position to say that Finland and Roumania could be counted on to hold the Russians on the extreme flanks, although negotiations with Finland only took place in May 1941. He proved less correct in his predictions about Sweden, which he asserted would make her railways and roads available for the concentration of a German group in Finland. In the event, Sweden public opinion could stomach the passage of only one German division from Norway to Finland.

7. The key-note of Hitler's plan was the destruction of the bulk of the Russian Army, which was in Western Russia, in bold operations with deep armoured thrusts. Hitler also laid down, presumably on good advice, the broad grouping of forces,

namely, two Army Groups North of the Pripet Marshes and one South, which was eventually followed.

8. OKH contended, according to Halder, that the plan of operations could only take first objectives into account, and these it fixed for the three Army Groups at such a distance that, on the one hand, the complete destruction of the Russian forces employed at the beginning of the war could be ensured, and, on the other hand, the danger of air attack against the Reich eliminated. This latter factor applied only in the case of the Northern and Central Army Groups, for which the initial objectives were given respectively as (thus far it was in agreement with Hitler) the Leningrad area and the heights East of Smolensk; for the Southern Army Group, where prospects were less certain, the Lower Dnieper was fixed, but the need was envisaged to remove the threat of the Crimean air bases to Roumanian oil. OKH maintained that a firm decision on the future course of operations could only be taken after these first objectives have been reached, but that Moscow would have a decisive rôle. To this Hitler replied that thinking of Moscow was out of date, and thus revealed a fundamental difference between the approach of OKH to the problem and his own. He apparently refused to believe that a decision on the continuation of operations must await the outcome of the frontier battles and the immediately following phase. He had already decided that the reduction of Leningrad should inevitably have priority over an assault on Moscow.

9. This was a foretaste of Hitler's fatal intuition that the best prospect of success in the East lay with his two out Groups of Armies, Army Group North and Army Group South. It is said that in 1942 two cities at either extremity of his long front, Stalingrad and Leningrad, exercised an almost mystical influence on Hitler's military inspirations; but as early as 1941 his neglect of the Centre was destined to lead to a frightful holocaust in front of Moscow.

10. In this connection, it is interesting to discover that, from the Russian point of view, the most critical time in Moscow was in mid-October, when German troops actually entered the suburbs and the diplomatic corps was evacuated. There was real panic in the city and for several days the police did not function; even the N.K.V.D. disappeared and public transport broke down. The Government, however, kept its head, and Stalin remained in the Kremlin and broadcast to the people. The Germans were, however, turned back from the suburbs, and an early frost helped save the city. On the 7th November, six days before the issue of Hitler's orders to take Moscow that

year, the Annual Red Army Parade was held in Red Square, both as a gesture of defiance and because, by then, the situation had been more or less restored. It is difficult to understand German inaction to take Moscow in October, unless one assumes that they had an unexpected success in front of Moscow which the German generals must have wished to exploit, but which Hitler himself stopped.

11. On the final objective of the operations against Russia, Hitler's directive of the 28th December becomes nebulous. This was described as the formation of a defensive screen against Asiatic Russia on the general line Archangel-Volga. In this way, if it proved necessary, the G.A.F. could knock out the Urals, the last industrial area left to Russia. The maintenance of a defensive screen on such a 2,000 mile front with any degree of security and for any length of time – details below the Hitler planning level – staggers the imagination. It is thus clear that from the very beginning there was a grave clash of opinion between Hitler and the Army. Henceforward, there are two main conceptions of strategy nearly always completely divergent; the Army General Staff strategy, backed by expert knowledge, at least until the autumn of 1942, and Hitler's school of thought, which had executive power.

## *Effect on Balkan Campaign (see also Annex V).*

12. The Balkan campaign intervened on the 6th April, and by tying up twenty-seven field divisions, of which no less than seven were Panzer, delayed the opening of the Russian campaign by what appears to have been well over a month. Halder claims, as a further consequence of the Balkan campaign, that it reduced the strength of forces which could be concentrated in Roumania and thus condemned Army Group South to a purely frontal attack. This contention is by no means proven.

## *Hitler's Hopes of Early Decision in East.*

13. When the Russian campaign opened on the 22nd June, 1941, Hitler had, in Halder's opinion, the preconceived idea that Russia would, despite the advanced season, be forced to make peace in 1941, thus making further prosecution of the war hopeless for the Western Allies. Immediately before D-Day he promised the Gauleiters of Germany that he would be in Leningrad in eight weeks. On the 21st June, 1941, Warlimont, in a directive on North Africa doubtless expressing Hitler's views, described the rosy strategical possibilities which might arise in the Mediterranean by

the end of 1941, after the successful conclusion of the Eastern campaign. According to Halder, these views were not shared, much less encouraged, by the Army General Staff. Hitler, spoiled by the quick successes of his early campaigns, refused to take account of road conditions and terrain, and the progress never proved fast enough for his liking.

14. The forces deployed for the initial assault on Russia numbered 123 divisions, of which 17 were Panzer and 13 motorised; these were supported by the main striking power of the G.A.F., comprising approximately 2,500 aircraft. A further 24 divisions, including 2 Panzer divisions, were in OKH reserve, but only half were available before the 4$^{th}$ July, 1941. In the South, the Germans were supported by some 15 Roumanian divisions. Halder regarded this number of divisions as sufficient for the frontier battles, but inadequate to cover the much greater needs which would arise as the battle progressed, particularly as Hitler had the illusion of the need for a continuous front, and did not understand the principle of concentration of force. He had, however, refused a more complete use of the Reich's man-power on account of the effect on home morale of the war in the East. He stressed that numerical inferiority must be offset by knocking large chunks out of the Russian front and destroying the opposing forces completely – a proposition in itself acceptable to the General Staff, but not when combined with Hitler's continuous demand for speed.

## *The Finnish Campaign.*

15. Operations in Finland were run as an almost separate theatre, being directly under OKW and no concern of OKH, although Finnish operations on the Ladoga front were expected to conform to some extent with the German forces directed on Leningrad. The initial German commitment in Finland was only three divisions – two in the Far North and one on the Kandalakscha front, all drawn from Norway, and with the very limited air support. This force was so small in relation to the rest of the Eastern Front and the main lines of strategy so simple that it is convenient at this point to treat the Finnish theatre as a whole.

16. Presumably some material investment in Finland in the shape of German divisions was a precondition for fully capitalising Finnish hatred of the Russians. It promised to be a cheap investment, since by obtaining the Finns as Allies the Germans secured their Baltic flank against Russian amphibious threats and set the stage for

operations designed to cut Russia's Northern communications with her Western Allies. Furthermore, the Finns were able to deploy an army of 12 good divisions in the Lake Ladoga area, and thus provide some support for the main German operations in the Leningrad area. In addition, Finnish co-operation secured for Germany the valuable nickel deposits in the Petsamo area.

17. But the Germans overreached themselves and were unable to achieve all these advantages. The Finns were unable to strike a decisive blow in the battle for Leningrad, and the German operations fell a long way short of cutting the Murmansk railway. OKH opinion of this OKW theatre was that OKW had no idea of the difficulties of campaigning in the far North and set tasks which far exceeded the capabilities of the troops. That this is not mere OKH prejudice is proved by the frequent postponements and changes in plan which OKW had to make for the German forces in Finland.

18. The two main operations in which German forces were to be employed after the securing of the Petsamo area, were an attack on Murmansk and on the Murmansk railway in the Kandalakscha area. This was laid down in April 1941. In July operations against Kandalakscha were in progress, but were stopped, and the Finns were given the task of cutting the railway with German help at a point slightly further South. In September Kandalakscha again came on the German programme for October, but in October was postponed till the following year. The attack on Murmansk was stopped in September 1941, after considerable German losses was envisaged for 1942, and remained a fond hope at least until the end of the year.

19. German reinforcement of Finland continued in the latter part of 1941, and by the spring of 1942 there were 6 German divisions in Finland, but throughout the campaign German air strength remained extremely weak on this front. When the Russia-Finnish armistice was signed there were 8. Although the Finnish theatre was mismanaged by OKW and produced no spectacular operational successes, there can be no doubt that the basic conception of a Finnish front against Russia was sound. Besides the advantages quoted above, it tied up Russian divisions at relatively small cost to the Germans. In summer 1942 the number of Russian divisions on the Finnish front was estimated to be four times as many as the number of German divisions, as against less than twice as many on the rest of the Eastern front. In the summer of 1944 the proportions were six times and three times respectively. For this reason alone it was worth while for the Germans to keep the Finns in the war as long as

possible. For the contingency of Finnish defection they were, however, prepared at least as early as September 1943, and made strenuous and successful efforts to avert in March 1944. The respite was temporary, and the Finns came out of the war against Russia in September the same year.

# DEPLOYMENT ON THE MAIN FRONT.

## *Army Group North.*

20. On the main front Army Group under Field-Marshal von Leeb attacked on a front stretching from the Grodno area to the Baltic. The Army Group had in all 28 divisions. These included a Panzer Group of 6 mobile divisions in the centre. They were supported by some 500 aircraft. The Germans estimated that they were opposed on this front by 31 Russian divisions, of which 23 were rifle divisions. Not all of these, however, were immediately opposite East Prussia, some being on the Baltic coast.

## *Army Group Centre.*

21. Army Group Centre under Field-Marshal von Bock deployed on a front extending from the Pripet Marshes to the Grodno area. This Army Group had 50 divisions which included the biggest force of German armour, 15 mobile divisions forming 2 Panzer groups, 1 on either flank. For this reason the main G.A.F. alone support forces, amounting to about 1,000 aircraft, were deployed on this front. The Germans estimated a total of 35 Russian divisions, of which 25 were rifle formations, to be on this front.

## *Army Group South.*

22. South of the Pripet Marshes lay Field-Marshal von Rundstedt's Army Group South which had 45 German divisions including a Panzer group of 9 mobile divisions on the Northern flank, together with some 800 aircraft in support. There were, in addition, 17 Roumanian divisions and a few Hungarian brigades. Russian forces opposed to this Army Group totalled, according to the German appreciation, 53 divisions, of which 38 were rifle divisions.

## Comparison of Forces.

23. The 123 German divisions were thus, in the German estimate, opposed by 119 Russian divisions, and at least 5,000 aircraft. The Germans estimated, however, that, apart from these and 17 Russian divisions on the Finnish front, there were 6 divisions in the Moscow area, 11 in the Caucasus and no less than 33 unlocated – a very considerable unknown. The Germans thus reckoned with a total of 186 Russian divisions. That they grossly under-estimated is tacitly implied in a speech Jodl made to the Gauleiters at the end of 1943 when he said that it was only by the discovery of such vast personnel and armaments resources at the disposal of her enemy that Germany herself was goaded to achieving peak production! Halder comments on this subject that intelligence on the Russian forces in the frontier area was reasonably accurate but was unable to grapple with the problem of Russia's strategic resources.

# FIRST PHASE OBJECTIVES.

24. The first phase objectives fixed for the invasion of Russia involved along almost the whole front drives to a depth of nearly 300 miles into Russian territory and on the front of the Army Group Centre to a depth of 450 miles. It is clear from maps available that OKH won the day in the question of first phase objectives or at least managed to keep Hitler's feet on the ground.

## Army Group North (First Phase).

25. On the Army Group North's front, the Infantry army on the left flank was to cut off and mop up the Baltic States by a wide sweep through Schaulen, Tartu and Tallin. The Panzer Group was to drive through Dvinsk to an area just short of Lake Ilmen supported by the Infantry army crossing the frontier on its right flank. Hitler's plan for this Army Group was to take Leningrad in the first phase, with a subsidiary thrust into Estonia. As a gamble this might have succeeded, but a firm plan to drive direct on Leningrad in this fashion might well have made it impossible to detach sufficient forces to mop up the Baltic States. Hitler's plan would have involved maintaining out of a total of 29 divisions not merely an attack group strong enough to take one of the

key centres of Soviet Russia but also some degree of protection for a flank of nearly 450 miles.

## Army Group Centre (First Phase).

26. In the Army Group Centre the plan involved thrusts by a Panzer group and an Infantry army from each of the extreme flanks. The Northernmost of these two thrusts starting from the area North of Grodno was directed via Molodeczno on the Vitebsk and Polotsk areas. The Southern thrust was launched from the Brest-Litovsk area via Baranovicze and Minsk and directed on the Smolensk and Mogilev areas. Hitler's plan for the first phase operations on Army Group Centre's front advocated a remarkable dispersion of effort, to begin even before the main forces reached the Smolensk area. As soon as the River Beresina was crossed Infantry forces were to be detached Northwards and Southwards and once the armour had reached Orscha it was to swing off to the flanks – one Panzer Group to Lake Ilmen and the other Southwards in support of Army Group South. Hitler was apparently satisfied that this should leave only Infantry forces to pursue in the second phase, the attack on Moscow, distant 250 miles from Smolensk! These views, although at this stage successfully outvoted by OKH, completely hamstrung the planning for the second phase of the campaign.

## Army Group South (First Phase).

27. In the Army Group South's area the OKH plan took the form of a vast turning movement with the main weight of attack launched between Przemysl and Luck and swinging South-eastwards between the Rivers Bug and Dnieper. Kiev was captured in the first phase. From the Carpathians southwards along the Pruth – manned chiefly by Roumanians and a few Hungarians – there were to be holding actions only except for a drive by the German Eleventh Army across the Northern Bukovina to Mogilev Podolsk on the Dniester. Hitler found himself in substantial agreement with these plans apart from being more ambitious in objectives between the Bug and the Dniester and the wish to launch the eight Infantry divisions of the Eleventh Army in a 200-mile drive across two major rivers to Odessa. Warlimont claims that the German achieved strategic surprise and that considerable portions of the Red Army even on the frontier areas were not even alerted.

*Completion of First Phase.*

28. By the third week in July the first phase of the campaign was over and the objectives set by OKH substantially reached. In the Leningrad area they had even been exceeded, but Leningrad was far from encircled and there were Russians still to mop up in Estonia. In the South, Rundstedt's main thrust between the Bug and the Dnieper had made slower progress in frontal assaults than had been envisaged. Kiev was still in Russian hands. According to Halder, however, the Russians facing Rundstedt were becoming increasingly demoralised and there were indications that they had begun to abandon the area up to the River Donetz.

# CONFLICT BETWEEN OKH AND HITLER.

29. At this stage in the campaign there arose between Halder and OKH a fundamental clash of opinion which, according to Halder, had a decisive influence on the course of the war in the East. OKH took the view that Timoshenko's Army Group, which lay in front of Moscow and whose will to fight was unbroken, constituted the main Russian strength and must, therefore, in accordance with traditional German principles of strategy, be defeated first before decisive results could be achieved in Russia. Furthermore, Moscow itself constituted a military, political and industrial nerve centre, whose capture would have incalculable effects.

Hitler poured sarcasm and ridicule on OKH's plans for a drive on Moscow and favoured the capture of the Crimea and the Eastern Ukraime industrial area and the cutting of Russia's Caucasian oil supplies. This time and, it appears, on every subsequent major issue Hitler's views prevailed.

*Hitler decides to make main effort in South.*

30. Hitler's first proposal for weakening Army Group Centre was made on the 19th July, 1941. Army Group South was to continue to mop up the Russian armies West of the Dnieper and Army Group Centre was to detach forces Southwards to prevent the escape of Russian forces across the Dnieper to the East. Army Group Centre was also to detach armour to Army Group North to strike through the Valdai Hills and cut the Moscow-Leningrad railway as a preliminary to the renewal of the attack on Leningrad. The depleted Army Group Centre was to attack towards Moscow with infantry forces only.

31. The full enormity of the revolution which Hitler had wrought in German principles of strategy was revealed in the more detailed instructions issued by Keitel four days later.

After the destruction of the Russians West of the Dnieper and as soon as the strategic and administrative situation allowed, the Southernmost Panzer Group of Army Group Centre, then in the Briansk area, was to drive Southwards and join hands in the Kharkov area with Rundstedt's Panzer group driving Eastwards. The two groups (which would include about 16 mobile divisions) were then to push on across the Don to Caucasia. This set Rundstedt's Panzer Group, which as yet had not even a bridgehead across the Dnieper, a drive of some 600 miles, based on an increasingly lengthening and more difficult line of communication.

32. On the 30th July Hitler was forced to order a postponement of the regrouping for these operations largely owing to the need to give ten days' rest to the two Panzer Groups of Army Group Centre. Army Group Centre was ordered on to the defensive and Army Groups South and North were directed to continue operations with their own forces, the latter resuming operations against Leningrad with increased air support drawn from the Central Front. A directive issued on the 12th August indicates a renewed rise in Hitler's confidence and Army Group Centre was again ordered to allot a few divisions to Army Group North. It was made clear that the attack on Moscow must not take place until the Leningrad operations were complete.

## OKH Advocate Moscow.

33. On the 18th August OKH made a last determined attempt to substitute their own strategy for Hitler's. By this time Army Group Center had already set Panzer Group Guderian attacking towards Army Group South, in the area West of the River Desna. OKH were in agreement that the attack on Leningrad should be continued, but wished the scope of operations in the Southern sector of the front to be drastically reduced. They proposed that on the Moscow front two attack groups should be formed, each of just under 20 divisions and with a total of about 10 mobile divisions. The Northern one was to strike from the Veliki Luki area through the Valdai Hills towards Moscow, while the other converged on the Russian capital from the Roslavl area. The tasks of Army Group South were mainly to tie down Russian forces by covering the flank of the attack on Moscow from the Roslavl area and to gain bridgeheads across the Dnieper between Kiev and Dnyepropetrovsk. OKH envisaged that later

this Army Group should with its own forces push on to Kharkov, the middle Donetz and the Crimea.

Halder describes the effect of these proposals on Hitler as explosive and the reaction as charged with insults. Hitler's written reply reasserting his views on strategical priorities in Russia crystallises this decisive cleavage of opinion between O.K.H. and the Supreme Commander.

## Operations in South: August to September 1941.

34. Meanwhile Guderian's attack Southwards, whatever its strategic merits and demerits may have been, prospered, and by the first week in September a vast pocket of Russian forces was in process of formation in the triangle Konotop-Kremenchug-Kiev. At this time Hitler had already begun to turn his attention back to the Central Sector where he still thought a decisive attack could be launched before the winter. He envisaged the end of September as a probable timing. Timoshenko's armies, the main strength of which was packed between Smolensk and Moscow, were to be encircled by two thrusts converging from the Bjelj area Eastwards and from the Roslavl area North-eastwards. The encirclement of Leningrad, of whose actual capture even Hitler now seems to have despaired for 1941, was to be so complete by the end of September that Army Group North could detach mobile forces and return Richthofen's close support Air Corps to Army Group Centre in good time. After the encirclement of Timoshenko's army, von Bock was to continue the attack on Moscow with his left flank on the Volga and his right on the Oka.

## September 1941: Hitler turns attention back to Centre.

35. But the battle of Kiev, as the operations against the pocket East and South-east of Kiev were called, although skilfully conducted, was not complete until the 24th September. In consequence forces switched back from the Ukraine for Army Group Centre's offensive, which began on the 2nd October, were exhausted, and M.T. was in a bad state of repair. A further consequence of this small margin of time seems to be that there was no alternative to launching Guderian's Panzer Group in a drive well South of the main centre of attack. This thrust made, it is true, spectacular progress,

taking Orel and encircling Briansk. Some of the armour which it consumed might well, however, have produced a more decisive concentration of effort further North where, despite reinforcements from Army Group North, the left arm of the main pincer movement was comparatively weak in armour, having only five mobile divisions. Despite these factors, however, and the onset of autumn road conditions, less than a week after the offensive opened, the attack made good progress, and by mid-October the Moscow-Leningrad road was cut North-west of Moscow. Hitler, who thought that the Battle of Kiev had represented the decisive turning point in the resistance of the Red Army, was optimistic. By the end of October the Germans stood less than 40 miles West of Moscow. At the same time, according to Guderian, there had been a marked stiffening in Russian resistance.

## *13th November, 1941 - Hitler orders attack on Moscow.*

36. On the 13th November Hitler's orders for an "autumn campaign" designed to take Moscow before the end of 1941 were issued. The plan was opposed by Bock, Commander-in-Chief, Army Group Centre, and by Guderian, probably the most experienced German Panzer Army commander on the Eastern front. Suggestions from the field that the army should dig in for the winter received no consideration. The left flank of the attack rested on the Volga and the right flank was secured by Guderian's Panzer Army starting from the Tula area and driving Eastwards South of the Oka. This latter movement was to prelude a strong attack on Moscow by 4th Army North of the Oka. Until the end of November, steady but unspectacular, and certainly not decisive, progress was made. The infantry corps in Guderian's Army had inadequate winter clothing. Temperatures were as cold as 20° below zero, which, together with supply difficulties and bad airfields, seriously reduced the support which could be given by the G.A.F.

37. Fourth Army's attack was launched on the 4th December, already a few days late, but completely misfired on account of the extreme cold on the eve of the attack. In these temperatures automatic weapons and tank motors failed to function. At the same time as 4th Army's abortive attack, Guderian's army failed to take Tula and retreat became inevitable North and South of the Oka. North-west of Moscow also, the German third Panzer Group had come to a stand-still and was forced to begin a retreat.

# WINTER 1941–42.

38. Baulked in the attack on Moscow, Hitler turned his attention to the flanks. Army Group North had reached Lake Ladoga in September, thus cutting off Leningrad. Against the advice and bitter opposition of OKH, Hitler had pressed on with the attack in this area across the River Volkhov to Tikhvin hoping that in this way he would force the Russians to retire from the Eastern shore of Lake Ladoga, thus enabling him to join hands with the Finns. On the 8th December Army Group North was ordered to hold its ground on the Tikhvin-Volkhov road and railway and to seize the opportunity to clear up the remaining Russians in the Lake Ladoga area.

This stubbornness led to losses which Army Group North could ill afford. At the same time Army Group South, which had reached Rostov and Kharkov and had occupied most of the Crimea, was ordered to make preparations to capture Sevastopol and for an attack during the winter to reach the line of the Lower Don and the Donetz as a precondition for operations against the Caucasus. For Army Group Center Hitler's directive of 8th December gave some promise of rest, when it stated that the bulk of the Army was to go as soon as possible on to the defensive on an economical front. Such hopes were completely dashed by another order he issued only a week later that Army Group Centre was to make no major withdrawal but was to fight for every inch of ground until reserves came from the West. Only then could it withdraw to the planned rearward position. A few days later on von Brauchitsch (Commander-in-Chief of the Army) asked for, and was eagerly granted, his retirement.

## *Discussion of Hitler's and OKH's Strategy in 1941.*

39. At this point consideration must be given to the question of whether the greater strategical merit lay in Hitler's plan in August 1941 to push on in the South before going for Moscow or in the OKH's plan which was diametrically the opposite. Halder describes Hitler's decision to go for the industrial area of the Eastern Ukraine and to advance towards the Caucasian oil as a second-rate objective which could at best lead only to the quick collapse of an already weakened front at the cost of an irreplaceable loss of time and strength. While it is true that Halder may have overestimated the decisiveness which the fall of Moscow would have had on the Russian war effort, it

was on the other hand proven by events that the loss of the Eastern Ukraine did *not* cripple the Russian armament industry as Hitler hoped. In Hitler's favour it could be said that by pushing on in the South he was exploiting success, but it is doubtful whether it could ever be decisive success. The gravest charge which can be laid against Hitler's strategy, is that he could not, Halder says, recognise the limits between the possible and the impossible. He may have hoped that by cutting off Russia's supplies of oil from the Caucasus he could achieve decisive results. He should have recognised, from the point of view of timing alone, that this objective was beyond his grasp, especially as he was still determined to strike also at Moscow before the winter.40. For OKH it must be said that their plans were within the capacity of the troops, that they aimed at annihilating the strongest and most threatening Russian force then in the field and would have produced a definite, even if not decisive, success. Under Hitler's influence the battles of 1941 culminated in withdrawals along almost the whole front with the troops strained nearly beyond the limits of human endurance, the myth of German invincibility broken, and the G.A.F. seriously weakened and exhausted by ruthless sustained operations.

# OPERATIONS DURING 1942.

41. After the retirement of Brauchitsch, Hitler assumed direct command of the Army on the Eastern front. The one salutary result of the change in command was the fact that the G.A.F. was forced to disgorge a vast number of superfluous personnel for the armies in the East. On the other hand Hitler's refusal to make strategic withdrawals resulted, when the front was finally stabilised in mid-January 1942, in a series of uneconomical and dangerous salients.

## *Preliminaries for 1942 Offensive.*

42. According to Halder, Hitler at once began to think about a Spring offensive. Halder claims that in the view of the Army General Staff an offensive continuation of the war was no longer possible in view of Russian strength, as available German forces were only just sufficient for a strong defence with strategic reserves. Hitler, confident that the Russians had reached the limits of their strength, believed that a renewal of

the offensive, if only in the South, would lead to complete Russian collapse. He had even begun to dream of the Persian Gulf. According to a directive issued on the 5th April, 1942, Hitler's plan for the whole front was to hold in the centre, reach the Caucasus and then switch forces northwards to capture Leningrad.

43. As a preliminary to this vast programme there were to be local operations to make the troops conscious of their superiority and to clear the Kerch peninsula and seize Sevastopol. These operations began in late May, first in the Kharkov area where a deep Russian salient was eliminated following an abortive Russian spoiling attack. The attack on Sevastopol followed in early June. The main operations began at the end of the same month. At one time OKW appears to have intended that they should begin in mid-May and reach Stalingrad by the end of June.

44. When the offensive began, the flow of replacements had for three months kept ahead of casualties, but the margin must have seemed deplorably thin for the great battles which lay ahead. According to Halder the wastage of the winter battles, both in men and material, had been largely made good in the divisions first engaged in the new offensive. These received first priority, those further South were not so fortunate. The administrative situation was good for the moment but the future must have seemed precarious.

## *The Plan for the South.*

45. The plan involved over 100 divisions, of which 70 were German, including 18 Panzer and motorised divisions, supported by 1,500 aircraft. In the outline the scheme provided in the first place for a series of encirclements produced by three successive thrusts Eastward and South-eastward which were intended to bring the German front to the Don in preparation for the final drive to the Caucasus.

The first thrust was from the area North-east of Kursk with seven mobile divisions and was directed on Voronezh, supported by a subsidiary drive from the Kharkov-Bjelgorod area with a force including two mobile divisions. These forces were then to continue down the Don, and link up with a second thrust from the Isyum area, which brought another five mobile divisions into the battle. Finally these forces were to be joined by a third thrust from the Taganrog-Stalino area. During this preliminary phase opportunity was to be taken to seize any cheap bridgeheads across the Lower Don.

In the second and what it was hoped would be the decisive phase of the summer offensive, some thirty German divisions, half motorised or Panzer, were to drive down to the Caucasus occupying the Maikop oil centre and the passes on the Ossetian and Grusinian military highways. The security of this operation depended on the Germans and their Allies being able to hold a 799-mile flank from Orel Southeastwards, thence along the Volga to Astrakhan. For this task, out of the original total of just over 100 divisions, it was calculated to use no less than seventy divisions. Half these were satellite including some ten Italian formations.

To the General Staff, despite these impressive totals of forces, it must have seemed that there was little enough in hand if unforeseen difficulties should arise on this long and vital flank. They were strenuously opposed to the plan.

## Course of 1942 Offensive.

46. By the 23$^{rd}$ July the German front was closing the Don along almost the whole sector of attack. Hitler felt confident, and believed only relatively weak Russian forces had escaped encirclement; a view not shared by the General Staff, who were convinced that the Russian forces West of the Don had made a strategic withdrawal. Von Bock was dismissed for his failure to produce more prisoners in support of Hitler's views. Even Hitler, however, recognised that a new Russian Group was in process of concentration in the Stalingrad area. Despite this he now took two steps which had catastrophic effects on his already perilously small margin of force. Manstein, whose Eleventh Army had been reducing Sevastopol, was ordered to send five of his divisions with medium and heavy artillery to the Leningrad front, although OKH had been specifically ordered to include these divisions in their planning for the Caucasus operations. Manstein's divisions were duly railed to the Leningrad area, but before they could be used for the assault on the city (projected for early August) they had to be committed in defence and were bled white in Russian attacks. Only very shortly afterwards, Hitler became convinced that political pressure would force the British to invade in the West in 1942 and he insisted that France should be reinforced with some valuable divisions from Army Group South. About a dozen were sent, including some newly refitted mobile divisions.

47. When on the 23$^{rd}$ July Hitler issued his directive for the continuation of operations, the Southern front had been split into two Army Groups, Army Group B in

the Northern Sector and Army Group A in the Southern. Army Group B was made responsible for capturing Stalingrad and pushing down the Volga to Astrakhan. This meant that in the main scheme Army Group B had the rôle of giving flank protection to the drive to the Caucasus. This was the task of Army Group A, which was to push Southwards and at the same time secure the Caspian and Black Sea Coasts. It was to receive support from the crossing of the Kerch Straits to be carried out by the remainder of the 11th Army, but the resources of the G.A.F. were inadequate to support Army Group A, since the main air effort had to be continued at Stalingrad.

## *Situation late September 1942.*

48. By late September Hitler's map should have shown him the precarious situation of his Southern Armies. Army Group A had, it is true, reached the foothills of the Central Caucasus, but had not secured even the Grozni oil. The main oil resources at Baku were still 300 miles from its grasp. As against the thirty German divisions it was planned to send into the Caucasus there were only some dozen now deployed, and most of these were facing Westwards towards the Black Sea flank. Army Group B's task had proved more formidable than had been envisaged. In its gigantic flank protection task it had been planned to use thirty-seven German and a similar number of satellite divisions. These totals had been exceeded and the figure of German divisions deployed between the Astrakhan and Orel areas stood at well over forty. 6th Army's position in the Stalingrad area was already dangerous. Its sixteen divisions were flanked in the North by Italians and Roumanians, and in the South by a thin screen of Roumanians.

49. According to Halder OKH reserves no longer existed, and grave warnings of the weakness of the Eastern front as a whole were provided by Russian attacks against Army Group North in the Leningrad area and against Army Group Centre, where there had been noticeable crises at Vyazma and Rzhev. On Hitler's personal orders, the inadequate reserves of the Army Group, which should have been husbanded for defence, were used in an abortive attack much further South at Sukhinichi.

## *Halder dismissed.*

50. It was in the late September of 1942 that Halder's relations with Hitler reached their climax. Halder's appreciations of the steadily stiffening Russian resistance

around Stalingrad and in the Caucasus and of the improved fighting qualities of the Russian army were met with fits of rage. Another bone of contention was that Hitler had already developed his passion for forming new divisions so that old and experienced cadres were starved of replacements. For the last five months of 1942 the flow of replacements to the front as a whole was less than half the casualty rate, and to the Southern Sector, it only met one-third of the number of casualties. It was in this situation that Hitler decided to draft half a million men from the over-established ranks of the G.A.F.; but instead of using these to fill the ranks of impoverished divisions he formed new G.A.F. field divisions, whose rawness and incompetence became a byword in the East.

Hitler rid himself of the embarrassment of Halder's professional ability in September. Henceforward, Hitler said, it was no longer expert knowledge that counted, but the fervour of National Socialist beliefs. These remarks, which saluted the departure of Halder and the arrival of Zeitzler, were an ominous watchword of an army stretched from Leningrad to the Caucasus, with well over a third of its forces committed in a vast salient.

## October 1942: Germans Lose Initiative in South.

51. In October, the German Southern Army Groups began to lose the initiative. On the 10th October it was unofficially announced that the reduction of Stalingrad would be left to the G.A.F. and siege artillery. Soon after, the advent of winter conditions put an end to German attempts to cross the Western Caucasus range and, while further East progress continued, it was at an ever-diminishing rate and stopped in mid-November.

On the 9th November the Russians began their counter-offensive in the Stalingrad area and opened what proved for the Germans a winter of almost unmitigated disaster.

## Stalingrad.

52. The Russians attacked North-west and South of Stalingrad and tore great gaps in the Roumanina line at both points. Within a few days, 6th Army was surrounded in Stalingrad and requests from Paulus (G.O.C. 6th Army) that it should be allowed to break out were refused. An attempt to regain contact by a counter-attack from the South-west, made principally with three Panzer divisions, was repulsed just before

Christmas. The garrison finally surrendered in February after an appalling siege which cost Germany twenty field divisions and nearly 200,000 men.

In the Caucasus, Hitler again delayed withdrawal dangerously long, waiting till the counter-attack to relieve Stalingrad had failed. The retreat was hampered by attacks from three sides; the Russian progress towards Rostov forced the bulk of the German Caucasus army to withdraw into the Taman peninsula.

# APPENDIX XIII.

# THE BALKANS
# (From the Winter 1941-42 to 1945).

Towards the end of 1941, List appears to have been able to serve both his own and the OKW's conceptions of strategy by launching a sharp two-division attack against a strong force of partisans installed in the ore region of Western Serbia. This success, coupled with the onset of winter and possibly to some extent Mihailovic's increasing willingness to fight the Communists, produced a substantial measure of pacification in Serbia which lasted through the summer of 1942. A less welcome immediate consequence was the loss of two divisions to the East (January 1942), where the winter crisis of 1941-42 was at its height. To some extent, their departure was offset by the entry of three Bulgarian divisions into Southern Serbia.

2. In Croatia, partisan trouble was centred principally in Bosnia, and the Germans were unable to achieve any decisive success, as the partisans crossed the weakly-held demarcation line into Italian-occupied Croatia. A proposal by List to limit German responsibilities at the end of 1941 by placing the whole of Croatia under Italian command was vetoed by Hitler on account of the probable political repercussions on the Croats. Later, List proposed that there should be a unified command (obviously German) in all anti-partisan operations. Only, however, as a result of a conference at Keitel's level (March 1942) and the promise of nominal command in the Balkan operations to the Italians, could the latter be induced to take any serious action against the partisans.

3. In the midst of these troubles, List appreciated that the loss of his two field divisions, his inferiority at sea, and in the air, and the difficulties of supply meant that

since Autumn 1941 the situation in the South-east had changed in favour of the Allies, and his forces could no longer guarantee its defence. Looked at from the Allied point of view, List's appreciation must be classified as unjustifiably pessimistic.

4. The British victory at Alamein (November 1942) resulted in a sharp rise in German interest in the defence of Greece, which had hitherto been mainly an Italian concern. A directive issued in the last days of 1942 by Hitler, emphasising Commander-in-Chief South-east's responsibility for the defence of South-east Europe and the outlying islands, mentioned the contingency of satellite (*i.e.*, Italian and Bulgarian) troops coming under German command in the event of an Allied landing. Special attention was to be directed to coastal defence in the Dodecanese, on Crete and in the Peloponnese. But it was only very gradually, in the spring and summer of 1943, that German anxiety began to express itself in terms of troop movements, since Yugoslavia continued to absorb nearly all the forces the Germans could spare. Here the German order of battle was undergoing a nominal, but in reality not very imposing, increase in numbers by the formation of new divisions from local recruitment and racial Germans. In addition, the Belgrade area was selected for the resurrection of two German divisions destroyed at Stalingrad, and another field division was brought in from the Caucasus for refit. Thus, by May 1943, the Germans had a paper showing of eleven divisions in Yugoslavia.

## *Operations against the Partisans.*

5. In the winter and early spring of 1942-43 Loehr, formerly commanding the G.A.F. in South Russia, who had succeeded List, was able to stage a fairly large-scale attack on the partisans in Bosnia (operation "Weiss"), four divisions being involved. It seems clear that he hoped that the fruits of this attack might, if accompanied by wise political measures, produce a substantial measure of pacification in Croatia. On the 27th February, 1943, he wrote that operation "Weiss" could only lead to permanent results if followed by political, economic and administrative reforms. The Croats were not in a position to govern themselves, and the discontent which was fostered in the Croat forces and all State enterprises by lack of regular pay and by poor living conditions constituted a sharp stimulus to Communism. Loehr proposed a German-directed Government, which would inspire new confidence and carry out the necessary administrative reforms. Failure to do so, or delay, would have to be paid for dearly in

German blood. Loehr's keen political insight (possibly a little dimmed by his touching faith in the virtues of German political methods) was not rewarded by the appropriate reforms in Croatia. In May and June 1943 a further large-scale operation against the partisans was carried out in an endeavour to separate Herzegovina and Montenegro and to encircle Tito's forces in Western Montenegro.

## German fears of Allied Invasion.

6. By the time this operation (called Schwarz) was nearing completion, a very considerable regrouping of the German forces in the Balkans was taking place, directed principally to reinforcing the defences of Greece. This redeployment (called Constantine) began in May, and involved the move of three divisions from Yugoslavia to Greece, and a Panzer division from Brittany to the Peloponnese. The latter move appears to have been a whim of Hitler's, which prevailed against the expert advice that the terrain in the Peloponnese was unsuitable for tanks. At the same time, the nucleus of what became Assault Division Rhodes was being shipped from Salonika to its destination. As a result of these changes, the Germans had, in the Summer of 1943, five divisions on the Greek mainland, two of which were in the Peloponnese. At the same time, the OKW allotted additional independent battalions for coastal defence in Greece, and authorised increased Bulgarian help in Southern Serbia and Northern Greece. The date at which Constantine was planned is not clear, but the immediate incentive which caused it to be put into effect may well have been the conclusion of the Tunisian campaign. The Allied invasion of Sicily seems to have increased rather than abated German anxiety, since it is clear from a Hitler directive of the 26th July (the day Mussolini fell) that an Allied attack on the Ægean "blocking front" (Rhodes-Crete-Peloponnese) was considered a course within Allied capabilities, as were landings on the Greek West coast and on the Ionian Islands. It was also reckoned that an Allied landing in Southern Italy would bring the Yugoslav coast under threat.

7. Hitler's directive is naturally much more assertive as concerning the Italians. German command is effectively established in the whole of Greece, with nominal concessions to Italian pride. It appears, however, that a declared German intention to put four German divisions at key points on the Adriatic coast of Yugoslavia before the end of July was successfully frustrated by the Italians. The background to this bid by

the Germans is plain, for as early as the 19<sup>th</sup> May a draft directive (never issued in final form) prepared at Hitler's headquarters laid down the measures to be taken "if the defence of the Balkans became the task of German and Bulgarian troops alone".

8. In contrast to the skilful and economical use which Commander-in-Chief, South-east, had consistently made his limited resources, are the reinforcement plans worked out by OKW during this period. At best they can be described as pious hopes, but to Commander-in-Chief, South-east, they must have seemed more like fraudulent promises. Warlimont states that Hitler, at one stage during his mounting anxieties over the Balkans (presumably Spring and Summer of 1943), ordered the transport tables to be prepared for the move of twelve divisions to the Balkans, mostly from the East. In July, when the unusually bad start of the Kursk offensive should already have aroused in a wiser commander misgivings about Russian strength, Hitler gave Commander-in-Chief, South-east, airy promises about a strategic reserve army of six divisions from the East (including two mobile), which it was proposed to form along the Belgrade-Larissa railway.

9. In the weeks before the Italian armistice there was some reorganisation of the chain of command in the Balkans. The functions of Commander-in-Chief, South-east, which had been exercised by the Commander-in-Chief of Army Group E at Salonika (Colonel-General Loehr), were transferred to Army Group F, newly established at Belgrade under Field-Marshal Weichs. Army Group E remained at Salonika, but was subordinate to Army Group F. A further measure, designed to tighten the chain of command in Yugoslavia, was the introduction of Headquarters Panzer Army 2 from the Eastern Front to command all operations in Yugoslavia. Operations had previously been the responsibility of the various territorial commands.

## *Effect of Italian Armistice.*

10. The Italian armistice (8<sup>th</sup> September, 1943) can, as shown above, have constituted no strategic surprise for the Germans, the possibility having been envisaged for at least four months. Even this, however, and any more precise forewarning they may have had nearer the day, can have been small compensation for the enormity of the tasks with which the Italian defection faced them. In Yugoslavia and Albania there were nineteen Italian divisions, and only eight German divisions. In Greece the forces were more evenly balanced, the Italians having eight divisions and the Germans seven. The day

of the armistice found the Germans with a fairly large-scale anti-partisan operation on their hands in Western Croatia. The main feature of immediate German counter-measures in Yugoslavia and Albania was the drive to the coast, which had been exclusively in Italian occupation, and the disarming of the Italian forces. The former task the Germans accomplished with considerable expedition, seizing the main ports with forces earmarked in July or earlier, although the partisans had gained control of some stretches of the coast. For nearly two months, however, the partisans maintained a grip on the islands, which hampered coastal shipping. Disarming the Italians seems to have been an administrative rather than a tactical problem. The Germans encountered little resistance from their demoralised ex-Allies, who seemed glad enough to be rid of the necessity of keeping up a pretence of being hostile to the partisans.

The Germans were similarly successful in putting the Italians out of harm's way in Greece, where, since Mussolini's fall, they seem to have been able to carry out a much greater degree of infiltration among Italian units in vulnerable areas than had been possible in Yugoslavia.

In Crete and the Ægean Islands, the tale was similar. In Crete the Germans had rather more than one division, which proved adequate to overpower the single Italian division. The Germans already garrisoned certain islands in the Northern Ægean, and had a strong force on Rhodes. Only on Samos and a few islands in the Dodecanese was it possible to establish British garrisons. With one exception these were speedily liquidated by an improvised German amphibious force supported by dive-bombers.

## *Measures to Fill the Gap.*

11. The crisis thus surmounted, the Germans set about finding reinforcements for the Balkans. These came, not in the shape of the promised legions from the Eastern Front, but as single divisions culled from all quarters of the German globe. By these and similar diverse means, including local recruitment, the Germans were able at the end of 1943 to count over twenty divisions in Yugoslavia, Albania, Greece and the islands. There were, besides, a large garrison of non-divisional units, so that, according to Jodl, the total number of German service personnel garrisoning the Balkans at the end of 1943 was over 600,000. This was nearly twice the total for Italy (although there was a vast difference in quality), and nearly half the total for the West.

12. The tying up of this prodigious number of troops in an intrinsically singularly unproductive theatre of war, coupled with Italian defection, must, or at least should, have caused the Germans to consider some reduction in their commitments in the Eastern Mediterranean and the Balkans. The problem of making such a decision can, of course, only be viewed against the background of Hitler's refusal to give ground at any but the ultimate price coupled with the undue prominence he gave to political factors in questions of strategy. A fair case could be made in late 1943 for holding Italy on political grounds and by reason of the number of good Allied divisions this contained. Holding Italy at this time implied in its turn denying the Allies cheap access to Yugoslavia. This in itself should not, however, have precluded consideration being given to yielding some ground in Greece and the outlaying islands.

13. There is evidence to suggest that the Germans tended to regard the defence of the Balkans as indivisible, and the Ægean Islands and Crete as the forward defence line in this system. But their experience of our operations in the Eastern Mediterranean in September 1943 should have led them to appreciate that the British Middle East Command was scarcely in a position to exploit German withdrawal. Owing to their lack of intelligence, which led them to exaggerate the strength of the Allied forces in the area, they continued to think that they needed strong forces there to dispel Allied landings, which would threaten the Roumanian oil and the southern part of the Eastern Front line of communications. They continued to be sensitive about Turkish neutrality and feared that any British success in the Eastern Mediterranean might encourage them to throw their hand in with the Allies.

14. In the autumn of 1943 the Germans launched a strong offensive against the partisans in Slovenia, designed to clear the main L. of C. from Austria. In the winter of 1943-44 they carried out another large-scale operation in Bosnia lasting nearly two months (January-February). This offensive, besides being an answer to the formation of the Partisans' Free Yugoslav Government in November, was an attempt by the Germans to secure vital lines of communication to the coast as a precaution against Allied invasion, and to seize the Dalamatian Islands. In most of these aims, the offensive did not achieve decisive results. In particular, it failed to destroy large numbers of partisans, but by clearing the partisans from the islands it denied them access to sea-borne supplies. In May and June 1944, the Germans made another offensive in Bosnia, this time with the additional object of capturing Tito, presumably in the hope

that the partisan movement would fade out with Tito. Again there was no decisive success, although the Germans effected a temporary clearance of routes leading to the coast.

## Plans to counter Allied landings.

15. There is adequate evidence in the form of OKW maps of the extent to which the Germans were preoccupied with the danger of Allied landings in the Balkans in early 1944. These maps show planned counter-measures in the event of a landing against the North or South Adriatic coast or against the Salonika area, or in the event of a combination of two or all of these contingencies. There is some justification for assuming that Commander-in-Chief, South-East, regarded the South Dalmatian coast as the most threatened point, and this is emphasised by the strenuous efforts made to keep open his L. of C. through Bosnia. Apart from the regrouping within the Balkans planned for these emergencies, the defence of the Yugoslav coast was to be reinforced by two divisions from Italy, two divisions from the West, and seven regiments from Germany. While this is further proof that Hitler still did not regard investment in the Balkans as throwing good money after bad, the details of the reinforcement plan suggest that in respect of the Yugoslav communications system the OKW was out of touch with the elementary principles of time and space. As an instance, it appears that it was planned to rail two S.S. Panzer divisions from the West to Eastern Serbia in just over two weeks. In actual fact, a month might have been a more realistic timing.

16. To German fears of Allied invasion of the Balkans was added anxiety over two satellite countries, Roumania and Hungary, and probably also (though specific evidence is lacking) Bulgaria. A plan for dealing with Roumania was in existence as early as January 1944 (Margarethe II), and involved an attack from four sides. The plan for dealing with Hungary was called Margarethe I, which suggests that Hungary fell into disrepute as an ally before Roumania. In mid-March it was intended to use seven to eight divisions against Hungary, including four to five from Yugoslavia, and two from the West. In the event, Hungary succumbed to only five.

17. The number of contingencies in South-East Europe for which the German General Staff had to plan at this time should in itself have drawn attention to the insolvency of the German position in the Balkans. If all the chances against which it was considered necessary to plan had materialised, it is difficult to see how the

Germans could have mastered the situation. It was of course, strategically correct at this time, when the Eastern Front still lay east of the Dniester, to make sure of Roumania and therefore also of Hungary. The paramount importance of this task should, however, have dictated some concentration of the German defence forces in the Balkans, instead of leaving them sprawled inside a perimeter which measured 2,000 miles from the River Isonzo to the river Maritza.

## *The withdrawal begins.*

18. Not until the last days of August, when the Russians had broken through the Galatz Gap, did the withdrawal begin. It is difficult to believe that Hitler, in so long delaying a decision which had long been recommended by the Commander-in-Chief in Greece, can have had any conception of the road conditions and the other difficulties which beset troop movement in the south-east. In early September the Bulgarians went over to the Russians, thus exposing the German escape route through Macedonia, and by early October the Russians themselves had blocked the main L. of C. further north.

19. German policy was to give priority to saving the best troops. The field divisions on Crete and Rhodes were brought to the mainland mainly by air transport. The forces which remained in the islands were concentrated in the western half of Crete, and in a few islands in the Cyclades and Dodecanese. Some 20,000 Germans were thus left to work off their patriotic fervour on short commons in the remotest outposts of the Reich until the general armistice.

On the Greek mainland, the last German soldier crossed the frontier into Yugoslavia or Albania in the first few days of November. Further withdrawal through Yugoslavia encountered many problems: the necessity to detach forces northwards to make a front against the Russians in the Belgrade area, the need to build up a strong eastern flank against the Bulgarians who were now attacking into Macedonia, the onset of winter and the need to clear the partisans from every road required for the withdrawal of the main body.

By Christmas 1944, the worst phase of the withdrawal, the passage of nearly a quarter of a million troops over indifferent roads through partisan country south-west of Belgrade, was complete, and there was only a small German enclave east of the River Drina. This withdrawal may rank as one of the great military feats of history.

20. At this stage the Germans should have taken stock of their priorities in Yugoslavia in order to see what further economy of forces they could effect. They held too long to different salients in the Sarajevo and Bihac areas, in addition to their Syrmian front between the Rivers Sava and Drava. Some divisions had already been transferred to Hungary, but in January there were still fifteen German divisions in Yugoslavia. Political factors appear to have been dominant in the decision to make no further withdrawal; and the Germans could have hoped for little further co-operation from the tottering Croat State if by their withdrawal they allowed Tito uninterrupted sway over Southern Croatia. The Croat State was not, however, worth preserving for its own sake, and the probable loss of its support should not have precluded the Germans from making a withdrawal provided the latter was on a large enough scale, for instance, to a line covering Zagreb.

21. When in mid-March the evacuation of Sarajevo was at last authorised, the salient had already been thinned out to a dangerous extent, in consequence of the need to find forces for an operation across the River Drava into Southern Hungary. Withdrawal from the salient was not complete until mid-April. By this time the rapidly deteriorating situation in Hungary and Italy had undermined the whole German position in Yugoslavia. General withdrawal westwards between the Rivers Sava and Drava became necessary, and continued at a quickening pace towards Austria until the armistice.

# APPENDIX XIV.

# THE WEST (1943-1945).

*Phase V. — December 1942-September 1944.*

1. The Allied invasion was long foreseen, and great efforts were made to prepare for it adequately. The building of the Atlantic Wall continued, being greatly stimulated by Rommel's inspection, and blistering comments, in December 1943. A new development then introduced was the under-water obstacle, placed along important beaches from the Dutch-Belgian frontier to Normandy. A considerable amount of flooding was also undertaken.

2. Although the weaknesses of the wall were well realised (Rundstedt now calls it "just a bit of cheap bluff"), in particular its lack of depth and its effect of tying down large forces to the coast, nevertheless the Germans do seem to have over-estimated its value as an initial obstacle.

3. The Army was also built up, and on D-Day there were sixty divisions in the West, of which nine were Panzer and one Panzer Grenadier. Allowing for Hitler's obstinacy in refusing to give ground in minor theatres of war in order to free troops, this was not an unreasonable allocation. Efforts, by no means unsuccessful, had also been made to build up equipment, and some of the Panzer Divisions were outstandingly well equipped for the German Army at that time.

Replacement arrangements, on the other hand, both for men and equipment, were pitifully inadequate, unless the invasion could be swiftly repelled. Though in April 1944 petrol stocks were at their peak since 1941, from then onward these declined so rapidly that overall shortages became acute.

4. Hitler's passion for clinging to ground applied in the West as elsewhere. Rundstedt was ordered to hold fast everywhere. Any invasion, wherever it takes place, must be defeated on the coast. A glance at the map of dispositions on D-Day shows the degree of dispersal that this involved, since there was hardly any point in

the West (even including Spain, for which various counter-invasions were planned) which was not at one time or another appreciated as a possible landing area. Southern France was a particular cause for anxiety, it being thought that a preliminary diversionary attack might be made there.

In particular, the following points stand out: -

(1) There were as many as 14 Inf. Divs., 3 Pz Divs. And 1 Pz. Gren. Div. in France South of the Loire.

(2) There was no central infantry reserve, all infantry divisions (other than those engaged on security duties) being on or immediately behind the coast. (As a result, in the Normandy battle, there was a chronic infantry shortage).

Rundstedt now states that had he been given a free hand, he would have written off the South of France, garrisoned it with skeleton forces only, and built up his strength North of the Loire.

5. Other influences on initial dispositions were differences of opinion among the local commanders as to whether the armoured reserve in the North should be forward on the coast or held back in the Paris area (in the end a compromise was reached), and the gradually hardening belief that the main danger areas were the Contentin Peninsula and the Pas de Calais.

The fact that the Allies would have air superiority was realised by the Germans, though its extent was not foreseen. The scale on which troops could be landed on open beaches was not appreciated. It is doubtful, however, if full realisation of either of these factors would have led to any fundamental changes in dispositions.

6. Once the Allied landing had begun, Commander-in-Chief, West, would have stood a better chance had he immediately appreciated it as our main effort and been allowed a completely free hand by OKW. Neither of these conditions was fulfilled. Owing partly to gross over-estimates of the total Allied forces available and partly to a belief that the only correct way for the Allies to invade was to land in the Pas de Calais, build a defensive front on the Somme and march for the Ruhr (Rundstedt to this day considers our actual strategy most unmilitary), 15th Army was left almost intact throughout the most critical week of the Normandy fighting. Admittedly Allied air power hampered all troop movements, but the main reason why Normandy was not quickly reinforced was that the Germans delayed moving. Moreover, Commander-in-

Chief, West, was stringently forbidden to yield ground, so that he was forced to fight in a narrow area where he was a sitting target for air attack and even naval bombardment. The latter factor was one to which Rundstedt and several of his senior commanders appear to have attached a quite exaggerated importance, possibly as being one of the few features in this novel battle which they could thoroughly comprehend. German armour was forced into the line to hold ground and for want of sufficient infantry support was never able to free itself to deliver a large-scale counter-attack. Rundstedt now considers that had he been allowed freedom of manoeuvre, he could have done better. In view of his petrol and ammunition shortage, however, mainly attributable to the success of Allied air attack on his communications, and of the vastly superior mechanisation of the Allies, this is doubtful.

7. By the end of July the Normandy situation was hopeless. The Germans might then have attempted to cut their losses by withdrawing to the Seine and Yonne and evacuating South and South-West France. Such a withdrawal, although hazardous, might possibly have led to an immense saving in men and equipment and eventually to an orderly retreat to the West Wall. It was, however, steadfastly refused by Hitler. As a result, there was a complete rout in the West (over 400,000 prisoners of war were taken in August and September) and the situation was only saved by the not unnatural failure of the Allied supply line under the stress of such rapid advances.

## Plan VI. – September 1944-May 1945.

8. During this period Germany made her last fling in the West, the Ardennes offensive, launched on the 16th December. It would be misleading to consider this as though it were in any way calculated or professional in its conception. Hitler had indeed a basic plan to deal a shattering blow in the West while the Eastern Front was quiet, and then to shift his main effort to the East to meet the coming offensive there. No sane German with knowledge of the real situation imagined this plan to be feasible, however, and the Ardennes offensive is best regarded as an expression of Hitler's desperate desire to attack and escape from the misery of constant and unsuccessful defence.

9. If Hitler could no longer command confidence, he could at least enforce action, and every effort was made to build up strength in the West for the offensive. From October to December, the West was, as compared with the East, given the highest

supply priority it had yet enjoyed. That only 25 divisions were finally available for the attack and that fuel supplies were inadequate even for these, is but a measure of Germany's overall poverty.

The plan for the offensive was as follows: -

(1) The main thrust was to be made by the 6th S.S. Pz. Army via Liege towards Antwerp.

(2) 5th Pz. Army was to thrust from the Eifel via Namur towards Brussels, covering the West flank of 6th S.S. Pz. Army.

(3) 7th Army was to take over the protection of the Southern flank of 5th Pz. Army.

(4) Three or four days after the beginning of the offensive (by which time it was calculated that 21st Army Gp. would have begun to withdraw forces to the South) a reinforced Corps Group from 15th Army was to thrust south-west towards Maastricht.

This 15th Army attack was subsequently dropped in order to spare more troops for the main effort.

10. The weakness of the plan is obvious. A long salient was to be driven through very difficult country, and through the midst of a mobile and well-equipped enemy, with forces so small that an adequate flank guard would be impossible. It is clear that had the Germans succeeded in crossing the Meuse they would only have increased the scale of their defeat.

Commanders in the field, in particular Model of Army Group B, which was responsible for carrying out the whole operation, in vain tried to persuade Hitler to accept a more modest plan, under which the Pz. Armies were to turn North after reaching the Meuse, and, in conjunction with 15th Army, attempt to destroy the Allies East of the Meuse.

11. The operation failed from the start as 6th S.S. Pz. Army was repulsed in its initial assault, nor, owing to adverse weather could the attack on Allied airfields be carried out until 1st January. Surprise, the only major weapon available to the Germans in the absence of adequate forces and supplies, was thereby to a large degree wasted. 5th Pz. Army was more successful, and had the whole operation been called off after the first week, it might have been considered a successful spoiling attack. It

was allowed to drag on, however, with heavy casualties and equipment losses, until Allied pressure and the imperious demands of the Eastern front compelled retreat.

12. By now the Russian offensive had opened, and Germany's overall position was hopeless. Troops were transferred to the East, and the West lost its high supply priority. Hitler's usual refusal to yield ground led to the bouncing of the Rhine at Remagen (Commanders were forbidden to cross to the East of the river in time), and to encirclement in the Palatinate, but cannot really be claimed to have done more than hasten an inevitable end. Thus ended a campaign in which the initiative was with the Allies almost continuously from D-Day.

# APPENDIX XV.

# THE EAST (1943-1945).

*Russian Winter Offensive, 1942-43.*

The encirclement of Stalingrad was followed by further Russian attacks until by the end of January the whole Southern Front as far North as Voronezh had been assaulted. As at Stalingrad, the Russian break-throughs were made easier by the disintegration of the satellite formations, this time Hungarians and Italians. In February the Germans began to counter-attack in the Upper Donetz area, regaining ground, and further North recapturing Karkov, which had fallen to the Russians. By the end of March 1943, however, when the spring thaws brought some stability to the front, the German line in the South was practically back to the starting points of the previous spring, and in the Centre had been pushed back beyond Kursk.

2. The Russians had not confined their attacks to the South, and the bankruptcy of Hitler's strategy was revealed at many points along the whole front. Attacks against the German salient West of Moscow began in mid-November. This expensive monstrosity, only 150 miles across the neck, but about two and a half times as long around the perimeter, tied up at this time nearly 50 German divisions. Its retention, it is true, denied the Russians a valuable railway network, but the Germans were forced to withdraw in early March.

3. In mid-January the Russians substantially raised the siege of Leningrad by the recapture of Schluesselburg, a starved front where, according to the German maps, there was only one infantry division in reserve. Despite these disasters the Germans were able, during the spring and early summer of 1943, at least partly to make good the appalling losses of the winter. From March to June replacements to the Eastern front exceeded casualties by 300,000. Nevertheless, the crisis which had been reached in the German war effort is shown by the fact that in no subsequent

month up to the end of the war did the Germans find sufficient drafts to make good their losses in the East.

## Kursk Offensive, July 1943.

4. Even Hitler, it appears, had no intention of making a large-scale offensive in 1943, but according to Warlimont, he could not bring himself to withdraw to the line dictated by Russian successes and thus regain the initiative. The Kursk offensive was fathered by Zeitzler. Keitel is alleged to have thought it was necessary on political grounds, the Army Group Commanders in the sector were in favour and Hitler gave his grudging approval. Guderian, at this time Inspector of Panzer Formations, was opposed to it on account of the Russian defences, but Geschmack, the German Chief of Air Staff, did not hesitate to commit the strongest possible air support to this attack, employing at least 1,000 first-line aircraft amounting to half the total G.A.F. strength on the Eastern Front.

5. The attack on the Kursk salient was launched with thirteen Panzer divisions striking from the North and the South against the neck of the salient. There were a further two Panzer divisions in OKH reserve. This concentration, from which no more than a tactical success was expected, left the rest of the long front sorely depleted of mobile and even infantry reserves.

## Russian Counter-Offensive, 1943.

6. Despite very intensive air support, the attack did not succeed in breaking the main Russian defences, and once the German armoured force was solidly committed in this unprofitable struggle, the Russians launched their counter-offensive, striking in the first instance in the Orel sector. By the end of the year, there was scarcely a sector from the Smolensk area to the Black Sea which had not felt the weight of Russian attacks.

7. Documentary evidence from this point until the end of 1944 is very scanty, and the strategical decisions and capabilities of the Germans during this period can only be deduced from the course of operations and the German situation maps.

8. The Russian attacks exploited every weakness in the enemy's line and gave him no respite in which to rest and refit his slender reserves of armour, while the G.A.F. were fighting a heavy battle, the control of air strategy having also passed to the

Russians. The attack against Orel was followed by a blow against Byelgorod South of the original Kursk salient. The next blow was in the direction of Smolensk from the South-east. In the last few days of August the Russians launched a drive on Kiev from the North-east, and in the extreme South attacked across the River Mius.

9. In no case were the Russian advances so spectacular as the Germans had achieved in their summer offensive. In a sober appreciation of the situation, however, the German General Staff must inescapably have come to the conclusion that the strategical and, to a large extent, the tactical initiative both on the ground and in the air had passed to the Russians. The supreme direction of the Russian showed superb timing and planning. Their tactical handling was also good, and it must have been disconcerting to the Germans to realise that now for the first time the Russians were able to make headway against them under summer conditions. It is true that their progress was comparatively slow, and where it came up against German Panzer divisions it almost invariably stopped. But the German Panzer divisions, switched with great skill from sector to sector, were wearing thin, and it must have become increasingly clear to the German that in a battle of attrition the odds were not all in his favour. This apparently unlimited capacity of the Russian to increase the scope of his attacks must have shaken even Hitler in his belief that "The Russian was dead" (apparently his favourite form of encouragement for Halder).

10. By the beginning of October the German line was back to the Dnieper from Zaporozhye to the Gomel area, with Russian bridgeheads North and South of Kiev. From there the line ran Northwards in front of Orscha and Vitebsk (thus denying the Russians the bridgehead of land between the upper reaches of the Rivers Dvina and Dnieper). North of the Vitebsk area the line was still unattacked and therefore unchanged. In the extreme South, South of Zaporozhye, the Germans still stood forward of the Dnieper, covering communications to the Crimea on the general line Zaporozhye-Melitopol. The Taman peninsula, which had been garrisoned in the main by forces withdrawn from the Caucasus, was in process of evacuation to provide troops for the Crimea and for the Southern Ukraine. In its heyday the Taman peninsula had nearly 20 divisions committed in its defence, more than half of them German. Examination of the tactical situation in the South suggests that this commitment was militarily justifiable, and not merely a whim of Hitler's. So long as the Southern extremity of the main front lay forward of the Perekop isthmus, the most economical defence of the Crimea consisted in holding Taman, and thus denying the

Russians bases for exercising their indifferent amphibious talents on the Crimea. In fact, so long as the German retained a foothold Eastward of the Kerch Straits, the Crimea was defended only by a thin screen of Rumanians. The defence of the Crimea was, at least at this stage, vital to the Germans, since its loss would have given the Russians bases for air attacks on the Rumanian oilfields and left the deep German Southern flank perilously exposed to seaborne attack. A further advantage of holding the Taman peninsula while the Germans stood as far forward as the Taganrog area was that it effectively closed the Sea of Azov, and thus afforded increased flank protection.

11. During October the Russians continued to make progress principally on the Southern front, although in the North they took advantage of the lack of German reserves to seize Nevel, a railway junction of great importance to the Germans. In the Ukraine they increased and improved their bridgeheads North and South of Kiev, in particular driving well across the Lower Dnieper up to the Krivoi Rog area. By early November, a thrust Westward from the Melitopol area had reached the Dnieper and cut off the Crimea. For four months, however, the Germans retained a bridgehead across the Dnieper at Nikopol, covering the manganese resources.

12. On the 3$^{rd}$ November the Russians launched out from their bridgeheads North and South of Kiev. The Germans evacuated the city, and further to the South-West lost the railway junction, controlling the main railway, to the Dnieper Bend forces. In mid-November the Germans counter-attacked with Panzer divisions newly arrived from Italy and the West, and drove the Russians back some distance towards Kiev. North-East of the Pripet Marshes, however, the Russians continued to push on. Further German counter-attacks West of Kiev during December again failed to achieve decisive results, and towards the end of the year and in January 1944 the Russians crossed the old Polish frontier West of Kiev and almost reached the Russian Bug further South.

## Russian Offensive Continues, 1944.

13. The New Year brought no respite for the Germans in the South, and produced new difficulties in the North Centre and North, where the front was almost stripped of armour and without any substantial reserve of any quality. In mid-December, the

Russians began to widen their Nevel salient, and in mid-January they struck at the German forces round Leningrad and rapidly dislodged them from their positions. In the North the German front was not stabilised until mid-March on the general longitude of Lakes Peipus and Pskov. In the South there were few pauses in the Russian drive. During January they continued to thrust Westwards into Poland, and in early March were in a position to turn Southwards along the old Polish frontier. The ceaseless strain of operations extending the whole length of the front also brought out increasingly the growing exhaustion of the Luftwaffe deprived of any breathing space for recuperation.

14. In later January and early February they inflicted heavy losses on the Germans further to the South-East by pocketing a salient at Smela. In early March, beginning in the Krivoi Rog area, the Russians attacked on almost the whole front South of the Pripet Marshes. By mid-April, when the front began to stabilise, the Russians had crossed in quick succession the Bug, the Middle Dniester and the Upper Pruth, and had reached the Carpathians. In the South, Odessa had fallen, but the Germans still held the Lower Dniester. In the extreme South-East corner of old Poland the Germans escaped the worst consequences of a dangerous encirclement by means of strenuous counter-attacks carried out by two S.S. Divisions brought straight from France.

## Crimea Liberated, April 1944.

15. In April, also, the Russians began the liberation of the Crimea, and in the third week of that month, after only a few days' fighting, the German and Roumanian forces were hemmed in around Sevastopol. The original garrison of the Crimea when first cut off was 3 German and 9 Roumanian divisions, but two more German divisions were flown in before the end – one as late as March. The bulk of the Roumanian divisions and some German forces were evacuated in good time, but Hitler effectively prevented an orderly withdrawal of the main German garrison. When on the 8th May he authorised complete evacuation, Sevastopol had already fallen and German losses were considerable.

# SUMMARY OF THE STRATEGIC SITUATION ON THE EASTERN FRONT, WINTER, 1943-44.

16. During the period July 1943 to April 1944 an examination of German strategy on the Eastern front can only take into consideration the manner in which the Germans organised and conducted their defence. Russian superiority in resources of men and material, which enabled them to be strong almost everywhere along a 1,300 mile front, precluded for the Germans any choice between offensive and defensive.

17. The tactical handling of the German formations was of high quality, and their retreat under heavy pressure skilfully conducted, even when at times dangerously delayed. Until February 1944 no large German forces were cut off. The two encirclements which occurred in March (Smela) and April (Horodanka) may well reflect a sharp increase in Hitler's interest and intervention in tactics at divisional and regimental level.

18. In assessing German strategy at this time it would be of considerable value to have a responsible and unbiased German appreciation of Germany's prospects. The controversy which preceded the abortive Kursk offensive suggests that even Hitler doubted whether the war could still be won offensively. In a speech made to Gauleiters at the end of 1943 Jodl referred to U-boat warfare as the only theatre in which Germany was on the offensive. In view of this fact, and the heavy defeats suffered during 1943 at the hands of the Russians, the German General Staff must have begun to realise that success in the East could only come by winning the battle of attrition. That there was a great deal of deception at the highest German level as to who was really winning the battle of attrition is clear from the fantastic German estimates of Russian casualties. If any member of the High Command already doubted whether the Russian were being bled white faster than the Germans they may have concluded that Germany could no longer win the war in the East, and that the European struggle could only go in her favour if the Anglo-Americans were driven into the sea with heavy losses when they landed in the West. The only reasonably safe way out of the Russian difficulty – namely, by political means – could presumably never be reached unless Hitler was removed, a proposition which responsible Germans seem either to have shunned or mismanaged.

19. In consequence, by the end of 1943 the prosecution of the German campaign in the East had become a strategical impossibility. The Germans could not hold the positions they had reached. On the other hand, they could only afford to carry out a large-scale strategical withdrawal if in the process sufficient time were gained to win the battle of attrition in the East and to defeat the expected Anglo-American invasion of the West.

## Advantages of Strategic Withdrawal.

20. The advantages to be gained by carrying out a strategical withdrawal were obvious. In the first place, the front would have become shorter and the defence, in consequence, more solid. This economy would not, however, have been enormous, and in the first instance would have applied only North of the Pripet Marshes. By bending the line back to the Dvina, the overall saving in frontage, as compared with the situation at the end of 1943, would have been only 20 per cent. Withdrawal to the general line Dniester, Polish Bug or Vistula, Niemen would have produced practically no further economy. The German administrative position would, of course, have been considerably improved, and the anti-partisan commitment on the L. of C. reduced. By scorching the earth during withdrawal, the Germans could have laid very considerable administrative difficulties on the Russians. Further offensive activity on the part of the Russians would have been delayed by the need for redeployment. It should, however, be remembered that to some extent the Russians could bridge administrative deficiencies with his abundant man-power. Another advantage of strategic withdrawal would have been the opportunity afforded for resting and refitting the German forces. This factor would, however, have been partly offset by the reduced casualties on the Russian side.

## Disadvantages of Strategic Withdrawal.

21. The disadvantages were also great. Reference must again be made to Halder's strategical conception of the Russian campaign. After the initial battles, which aimed at the destruction of the Russian frontier armies, he foresaw as next phase for the sector North of the Pripet Marshes, pushing the line sufficiently far forward to secure the Reich against Russian air attack. To achieve this, he foresaw the Smolensk

and Leningrad areas as objectives. By 1943, the Germans can have had little fear of Russian long-range bomber attack, but they could reasonably expect Russia's Western Allies being offered almost unlimited use of air bases on Russian soil. Similar conditions obtained in the South, where the vulnerable points were not, however, on Reich soil, but in the Roumanian oilfields.

22. The political consequences of a strategic withdrawal would have been far-reaching. Psychologically, the German people themselves were probably ill-prepared for such a measure; the effect on Germany's allies could have been disastrous. It would have become painfully obvious to them that their territory was important to Germany only so long as it directly assisted the German war effort. If the Baltic States were voluntarily given up, the Finns might well have come out of the war many months before they did in fact leave the alliance. In the South, the Roumanians, who had imperial ambitions in Transnistria, would have reacted unfavourably if the Germans had begun a voluntary withdrawal in the Ukraine. In view of the Ploesti oil resources, Roumanian co-operation was as vital to the Germans as it was doubtful (the latter shown by German plans for occupying Roumania in early 1944).

23. Perhaps the most important disadvantage of strategic withdrawal was that it would have brought the Russians prematurely to within striking distance of German soil in the North, and of the Roumanian oil in the South. In the Eastern war, space only really became an ally of defence when it was measured in scores of miles. For propaganda to the German people, Goebbels had made much of the fact that the war was kept a long way from Germany's frontiers. Against an enemy who could accept a vastly greater casualty rate than any Western nation, no defence line in itself could be considered inviolate. It was desirable, therefore, that Germany's defences against the Russians should stand as far East as possible for as long as lay within the capabilities of her armies. Once the Russian armies were in a position to strike at German soil or the Roumanian oil, the collapse of Germany would, if the Western Allies were still unbeaten, become merely a question of time.

24. For these reasons, it is difficult to make out a decisive case for strategic withdrawal in the East after the disasters of 1943. Whatever the strategical policy, however, there is sufficient evidence that Hitler's interference in the tactical conduct of the war robbed commanders of their local initiative, and must have cost heavier casualties than were justifiable. A major shortcoming of German policy during the period 1943-summer 1944, was the failure to build strong

rearward positions. Up till August 1944, no defences were built in the East. That this was Hitler's responsibility is proved by his statement to Guderian that if he built defence lines in rear of the front, his generals would at once want to withdraw to them.

25. In the second week of June (a few days after D-Day in the West), the Russians attacked the Finns on the Ladoga front, but although the Mannerheim Line was broken, the Germans kept the Finns in the war by a *tour de force*, mainly political.

## Russian Summer Offensive, 1944.

26. On the 22$^{nd}$ June, the Russian summer offensive began with an attack on a broad front North of the Pripet Marshes. This front was unaccountably weak in reserves of any kind, and had practically no armour. Practically all the German Panzer divisions were grouped South of the Pripet Marshes. Doubtless it was appreciated that the Russian drives through Southern Poland or the Galatz Gap constituted the greatest threat to the German war potential; but the Northern half of the front seems to have been left unwarrantably exposed.

27. In Southern Poland the Germans had eight Panzer and Panzer Grenadier divisions in reserve, and eight in Roumania. As the Russian offensive gathered way, these reserves were gradually drawn on. When the Russians in mid-July struck South of the Pripet Marshes, three Panzer divisions had left Southern Poland for sectors further North, and by the end of August, when Southern Roumania was attacked, German reserves in the extreme South had sunk to three mobile divisions.

28. It was mid-August before the Russian offensive between the Baltic and Carpathians showed signs of halting. It had swept forward to the Baltic coast West of Riga (the Germans shortly after regained contact with the large pocket thus formed in Estonia and Northern Latvia), it had almost reached the East Prussian frontier, it had come within an ace of capturing Warsaw, and South of Warsaw had reached the Vistula. East of Cracow, there was a Russian bridgehead across the Vistula. In Southern Poland, the front lay along the foothills of the Carpathians.

## Attack on Roumania.

29. The Russian offensive against the Galatz Gap in Southern Roumania began on the 20$^{th}$ August. Three days later Roumania, whose forces held a large portion of

the sector attacked, changed sides and the German southernmost Army Group was involved in catastrophe. Some twelve German divisions were surrounded and destroyed and the Ploetsi oilfields – Germany's main source of mineral oil – were lost. The German forces which escaped annihilation withdrew skilfully through Transylvania towards Hungary, and at the same time a Russian drive from Poland into Slovakia, aimed at cutting the German line of retreat, was thwarted.

The effect of the debacle in Roumania on the German situation in the Balkans has been dealt with in Annex VII.

## German Strategy in Hungary.

30. Until the end of the war Hungary, Germany's last remaining effective ally and one of her principal remaining sources of mineral oil, was a magnet for German armour and her defence seemed to receive priority over all other sectors of the Eastern Front. It is difficult to believe that Hungary's economic contribution alone can have justified the German resources in men and armour which were squandered on the Hungarian front. Important factors may well have been Hitler's unwillingness to give ground at any price and a certain evil loyalty to an ally he had brought to the verge of destruction. He could also, with some logic, regard a stubborn defence of Hungary as a contribution to the security of Austria and the Southern redoubt area generally.

By the end of 1944 the German armies which had retreated into Hungary from Roumania only some ten divisions strong had grown to over thirty divisions, of which eight were Panzer. These reinforcements had been collected from many quarters, including Italy and the Balkans, but the armoured reinforcement had been carried out principally at the expense of the Central Sector of the Eastern Front.

By the end of October the Russians had reached the Danube on a broad front South of Budapest, but the Germans had survived the uncertainties which accompanied the Szalasy *coup d'État*. By the end of the year 1944 the Russians had reached Lake Balaton and locked a German garrison of three divisions in Budapest which had been under siege conditions for nearly two months.

## Operations on remainder of Eastern Front.

31. On the remainder of the Eastern Front Russian operations during the autumn and early winter of 1944 were mainly on the extreme of Northern flank. Following

on the capitulation of Finland in early September, the Russians launched an attack against the German forces in Eastern Latvia and Estonia aimed at completing their control of the Gulf of Finland. This was followed in October by a drive to the coast North of Memel, which cut off the German forces in the Baltic States from contact with East Prussia. Had Hitler wished to withdraw his Baltic State armies into East Prussia, it should have been possible to break through in the first few days of encirclement. He seemed, however, determined to retain a foothold in the Baltic States. The main justification produced for this policy was that it contained large numbers of Russian forces – an argument of doubtful validity unless the ratio of Russian forces thus contained was considerably greater than on other sectors of the front. A second argument in favour of the retention of the Baltic States was that it maintained substantial freedom of passage for German shipping in the East Baltic – a position which the Russian navy seems to have been unwilling and unable to challenge.

When the Baltic States were first cut off there were thirty-seven divisions in the Army Group North which controlled the area. At the end of 1944, when the German holding was reduced to Western Latvia and the islands of Dago and Oesel had passed to the Russians, the garrison was still over thirty divisions.

32. On the Central Sector of the front the Russians attacked East Prussia in October and made a small penetration, but were thrown back in a manner which must have provided some fillip for German morale. Further South, the Germans were unable to prevent the establishment of Russian bridgeheads across the Narev North of Warsaw; these became jumping off points for the Russian winter offensive.

33. German situation maps of late 1944 are literally criss-crossed with green lines denoting positions "under construction" stretching as far back as the Oder. They began to appear as early as August, but by the end of the year none was shown as completed. They must have been less impressive on the ground than on the map.

## Situation January 1945.

34. There is adequate day-to-day evidence to show that in the last four months of the war on the Eastern Front Hitler exercised a complete strategical and tactical stranglehold on operations. At the height of the retreat through Poland even mile-to-mile withdrawals required Hitler's approval, and during a crisis in Hungary in March his sanction had to be sought for regrouping on a divisional level. Even more than

in the past he showed that he had no conception of the limits between the possible and impossible. It is to the credit of the German field commanders that to the end there was no serious break in discipline in sectors such as East Prussia and Latvia, where the task set the Army Groups was to all intents and purposes a rank and costly impossibility.

35. It is, however, also clear that Hitler did not want for good advice from the Army General Staff and from his field commanders; but his strategy followed a divergent course independent of advice. In particular, his disregard for Intelligence must have been phenomenal. On the 5th January, 1945, an appreciation by Foreign Armies East predicted with very considerable accuracy the broad lines taken by the Russian offensive, which began a week later. The appreciation emphasised the success the Russians had achieved in drawing off strong German reserves from the fronts of Army Groups A and Centre (Carpathians to Baltic) and the consequent need to create fresh reserves. Yet when the Russian offensive began German dispositions, especially of armour, were such as to suggest that, compared with Hungary, all other sectors were of only secondary importance. There were eight German panzer and panzer grenadier divisions in Hungary, including two fresh from the Warsaw area and another fresh formation recently arrived from East Prussia in exchange for a battered division. On the whole of the rest of the front there were only thirteen panzer and panzer grenadier divisions. It is true that nearly all of these were in reserve, but they could provide only slender reinsurance for the many sectors of the front where the Russians had deployed enormous strength. Even more incomprehensible is the fact that no attempt had been made to "false-front" the Russians. Early in January the Commanders-in-Chief of Army Groups A and Centre had asked and been refused Hitler's permission to withdraw respectively from the salient between the two Vistula bridgeheads and from the Narev bridgeheads to the East Prussia frontier. In the case of the Vistula salient alone, this refusal involved eight divisions being put out of action in the first few days of the Russian offensive.

36. Some conception of the stretch in German defence can be gauged from the situation in the Baranov bridgehead area. The Germans estimated that there were five Russian armies in the bridgehead proper. Strung round the perimeter were seven German infantry divisions, which could not fail to take heavy casualties in the initial artillery preparation. In close reserve were five regiments; army group reserves for

the area were three panzer and panzer grenadier divisions. As Guderian says, there were no strategic reserves for the whole front.

## Course of Russian Offensive, January 1945.

37. The course of the Russian offensive in its initial phase was briefly as follows: Attacking first from the Baranov bridgehead on the 12th January they swept across Southern Poland and reached Oppeln on the 24th January. Two days after the first attack, they struck again North and South of Warsaw, pinching out the Polish capital and driving Westwards into Posen and North-westwards towards Elbing. Land communications between East and West Prussia were cut on the 26th January. The attack against the Eastern frontier of East Prussia began on the 20th January and by the end of January had almost reached Königsberg.

38. After the *coup* of the 20th July, 1944, Guderian had succeeded Zeitzler as Chief of Staff of the Army. Now in the first days of the offensive Guderian requested Hitler almost daily to move troops from the West and to make reinforcements available from Hungary by cancelling the attack intended against Budapest. His appeals were strongly reinforced on the 20th January by Foreign Armies East was appreciated that the Russians aimed at reaching the line Breslau-Posen-Bromberg as a preliminary for the final assault on Berlin; the front could only be cleaned up if the Russians were stopped and thrown back to the line Cracow-Chestochowa-Thorn-Danzig. The appreciation therefore recommended drastic measures. The Armies in Latvia, which had fulfilled their rôle and now tied up only half as many Russian divisions as before, should attack Southwards and link up with the German forces in East Prussia. Subsequently East Prussia itself should be abandoned. Its loss mattered less than losing Berlin. To such requests Hitler's response seems to have been too timid and piecemeal. On the 16th January Army Group A (Central and Southern Poland) which had been allocated six divisions, mostly panzer and panzer grenadier, from Hungary, the West and East Prussia, was informed it could have no more reinforcements for two weeks and was ordered to stand finally on a line which had already been crossed at one point. Hitler paid even less heed to the suggestion by Foreign Armies East that Latvia and East Prussia should be given up. Powerful German armies were left in these areas till the end of the war with the primary rôle of tying down Russian divisions. To some extent the defence of the two zones was linked. So long as Latvia was

held it was important also to hold a port in East Prussia as a link in sea communications with Latvia. Subsequently the desire to hold East Prussia necessitated in time the sacrifice of strong forces in defence of the Danzig-Gdynia area.

## *Course of Events in East Prussia and Latvia.*

39. All these forces suffered heavy casualties, and the thirty odd divisions shut up in East Prussia were bled white. Although until early February at least the forces in East Prussia were under orders to restore land communications with West Prussia, the subsequent course of the war in East Prussia and Latvia had little direct connection with operations on the remainder of the Eastern front and can conveniently be disposed of at this point.

Little freedom of action was allowed the commanders. Towards the end of February Commander-in-Chief, East Prussia, whose forces were divided into three separate pockets was refused permission to form one consolidated front on the grounds that on one front he would tie up fewer Russian divisions.

Hitler refused a similar request a month later when one of the East German armies containing the remnants of 12 divisions had been compressed into a strip of coast less than 6 miles deep.

40. In the case of Latvia, Hitler ordered the evacuation of three divisions to the Reich on the 16th January and periodically ordered further withdrawals. The number reached about ten by early March and in total probably corresponded fairly closely to German shipping capabilities. Subsequently, however, no further evacuations were ordered, apparently because Hitler was unable to regard Latvia purely as a source of reinforcements and was adamant that his troops should not yield a yard of ground despite Russian attacks. On the 17th March he definitely refused to countenance general evacuation. Only on the 3rd May, when the German situation had long become hopeless and Hitler was dead, was permission given to abandon Latvia and Prussia.

41. Superficially Hitler's contention that holding East Prussia and Latvia contained Russian divisions was true. Undoubtedly, also, Russian deployment on the Oder front must have been delayed by German resistance on the West and East Prussian flank. In mid-March there were fifteen Russian armies on the Latvian and East Prussian fronts against only ten on the Berlin-Stettin front. But the ration of Russian to German

forces was approximately the same on both sectors. What Hitler seems above all to have failed to appreciate was that with the initiative on the side of the Russians, he was less in a position to disperse his forces than they were, and that no strategy was sound which did not concentrate the maximum of forces to defend the heart of the Reich. Thus sixty German divisions fought their last battles in pockets in West Prussia, East Prussia and Latvia without contributing vitally to the ultimate defence of the Reich. By contrast the Berlin-Stettin sector of the Oder front was manned, when the Russians made their final assault, by less than thirty divisions, many of them nondescript.

## German Counter-measures on Berlin Front, February 1945.

42. German counter-measures to meet the main Russian threat to Berlin began to take shape towards the end of January. By this time the Russians had reached and in places crossed the Upper Oder, and were within fifty miles of the Oder opposite Berlin. There was still adequate deployment room for the Germans in Pomerania and West Prussia, where, with the help of fresh divisions from Latvia, Russian progress was being slowed down. In the first instance the German counter-measures seem to have been concerned primarily with the Northern half of the Russian drive towards Berlin. Plans for counter-attacking the Silesian flank of the Russian drive came later, in February.

43. On the 21st January Hitler's orders were issued for the setting up of Army Group Vistula under Himmler with the task of preventing East Prussia being cut off and to supervise the concentration of newly allocated forces. This Army Group also became responsible for the defence of the Berlin sector.

## The Transfer of 6th S.S. Army to Hungary.

44. Following a preliminary instruction on the 20th January, orders were issued on the 22nd January for 6th S.S. Pz. Army and its four Panzer divisions, together with a further two Panzer and Panzer Grenadier divisions and two mobile brigades (all then in the West) to be placed at Hitler's disposal for eventual counter-attack after the Russian drive had been checked. There is good evidence that all these forces were to move to the area of Army Group Vistula. Only two days later, Hitler ordered two of the divisions of 6th Pz. Army into the Vienna area, and by the 28th January had decided that the other two should also go South for a counter-attack in Hungary. Thus

unaccountably Hitler squandered such limited chances he had of achieving any major tactical success against the Russians facing Berlin. There are indications that as late as mid-March Hitler deluded himself that this reinforcement of Army Group South was only temporary, but the decision to give Hungary priority over Brandenberg can only be described as pathological. The immediate result was that for the counter-attack Southwards from the Arnswalde area into the Northern flank of the Russian armies facing Berlin, only some ten divisions could be made available and of these only two were Panzer. At least three divisions had had to be prematurely committed before the attack began. The inexperience of the Army and Army Group responsible constituted a further obstacle to success, and by the 18th February this attack, which it was hoped would remove the threat to Berlin, was branded a failure. A similar plan to attack the Russian flank further East came to nothing, and at the beginning of March the Russians reached the Baltic on a broad front East of the Oder, forming a large German pocket in East Pomerania and West Prussia. This pocket was condemned to protect the area Danzig-Vistula estuary until the War's end.

45. Meanwhile, at the beginning of February, 6th SS. Pz. Army H.Q., located in the Frankfurt area and separated from its divisions, was ordered to plan an attack Northwards across the Southern arm of the Oder bend opposite Berlin, using five Panzer and Panzer Grenadier divisions from the West. It was intended to meet an attack Eastwards from the Kuestrin area and destroy the Russians in the Oder bend. Unless these schemes were part of a cover-plan of which G.O.C., 6th Pz. Army, Dietrich was one of the victims (he produced a plan on the 9th February), they can only be described as wishful thinking, in view of the way Hitler had sidetracked his reserves of armour. With this doubtful exception, therefore, the Germans were prevented by lack of forces from planning a simultaneous attack against both the Northern and Southern flanks of the Russian salient directed against Berlin.

46. When, in mid-February, the Arnswalde attack against the Russian Northern flank had come to a standstill, the German situation further South had become dangerous. The Russians had reached the Oder opposite Berlin and had established bridgeheads; South of the Oder bend they were well across the river and closing the River Neisse. Breslau was surrounded, and the Moravska Ostrava industrial area threatened. Hitler was persuaded to call off the Arnswalde attack in order to provide mobile reinforcements for the Berlin and Neisse fronts. Typical of this lack of insight into the difficult tactical situation was an order he then made for

preparing an ambitious counter-attack Northwards through Liegnitz deep into the Russian Southern flank, a proposal which the Army Group Commander (Schoerner) seems to have been successful in shelving. An attempt to make Army Group South (Hungary) responsible for the provision of reserves in the Moravska Ostrava area, a reasonable division of labour in view of the overall strategic situation, did not meet with Hitler's approval.

Meanwhile, the Germans were manning the Berlin front with a heterogeneous collection of troops. At the end of February in this sector unorthodox formations composed of depot and training units and N.C.O. and officer schools outnumbered regular divisions by nearly two to one. The front held in much the same shape until mid-April, largely, no doubt, because the Russians were not yet ready to launch their final blow. Similarly along the Neisse and Silesian fronts there was little change of position during March and the first fortnight of April.

47. It was, however, some time before Hitler lost the offensive spirit on the Berlin front. On the 11th March he insisted on using some of his precious reserves from the Neisse and Berlin fronts in an attack Southwards from the Stettin bridgehead. The reason for this attack was alleged to be the critical condition on the right flank of the Second Army, already pocketed 150 miles to the East. It is difficult to see what headway Hitler can have hoped to make against Russian strength in the Stettin area. The next day he was considering stopping this bridgehead along the East bank of the Oder. He appears finally to have resigned himself to the defensive on the Oder front only on the 20th March.

## Operations in Hungary.

48. At this point some consideration must be given to operations in Hungary. Undaunted by Army Group South's failure to relieve Budapest in the first half of January, an even more ambitious scheme was prepared, presumably inspired by Hitler. Originally the new plan was to come into effect at short notice before the end of January, and involved converging attacks Eastwards from the area South of Lake Balaton and Northwards from Yugoslavia across the Drava. The object was to destroy Russian and Russian-satellite forces West of the Danube. The scope of the plan was then widened to include an attack Southwards from the area North of Lake Balaton, with the object of regaining the Danube line. Army Group South pointed out that preconditions for the plan were the despatch of two to three more infantry divisions

and some replacements for his Panzer divisions, whose overall deficiencies exceeded 600 S.P. guns and tanks! It was presumably to support this unpromising undertaking that Hitler was inspired to send to Hungary the four S.S. Panzer divisions from the West and another mobile division from Italy. What he hoped to gain from this venture is made clear in a directive he issued on the 5th February. The tasks of Army Group South were to protect the industrial areas North and South of Lake Balaton (Szekesfehervar and Komarno on the one hand, and Nagykanisza on the other) and to prevent Russian entry into the Vienna basin. It seems at least questionable whether Hungary's economic resources (principally oil), even at this period of dwindling German sources of supply, can have been worth such high stakes.

49. Preparations for the operation dragged on through February. In the meantime, Budapest fell and the presence of 6th S.S. Pz. Army in Hungary was prematurely advertised by the use of two of its divisions in a limited attack North of the Danube. The attack began on the 5th March simultaneously from the area North of Lake Balaton South-eastwards and Eastwards, from the area South of Lake Balaton Eastwards and from Yugoslavia Northwards across the Drava just west of its confluence with the Danube. The latter attack, made with four divisions, established bridgeheads but was unable to exploit and obtain bridgeheads across the Danube some 40 miles further North as planned. The attack from the area South of Lake Balaton also made little progress. The main attack from North of Lake Balaton, in which eight Panzer divisions were used, was up against major difficulties from the outset. No preliminary operation had been possible to neutralise strong Russian forces on the high ground West of Budapest, and they remained a menace to the flank of the German attack. A week before the attack, Army Group South reported that none of the important ammunition natures was up to 100 per cent. of a first issue (that is, they were sufficient for less than ten days' fighting), but the Army Group could "manage" for petrol and oil if the weather did not break. This was a precarious administrative basis for an attack involving such a large proportion of Germany's armoured forces.

50. By the 16th March the attack had come to a standstill within ten miles of the Danube. Hitler's approval for a renewal of the attack was overtaken by a Russian counter-attack from the high ground West of Budapest. This developed into a general offensive which spread North of the Danube in the last week of March. Hitler's standfast orders could not do duty for prepared positions, and none of the defence lines planned were complete.

In early April, the Bratislava Gap was pierced, and in mid-April Vienna fell. Subsequently the Germans were able to offer stiffer resistance South of the Danube, once again at the expense of the Berlin front, which, although hourly expecting the main Russian offensive, was milked to provide further armoured reinforcements for Army Group South. This desperate move must be assumed to mark the last attempt on Hitler's part to secure the Southern redoubt area against further Russian progress.

## THE RUSSIAN OFFENSIVE, APRIL 1945.

51. German dispositions on the 16th April, when the last Russian offensive began between the Sudeten Mountains and the Baltic, gave few grounds for optimism. The Berlin-Stettin sector of the Oder front was held by only twenty-three German divisions, seven of which were classified, very nominally, as reserves. Some of these divisions were mobile, but there was no regular Panzer division among them. Further South, the Neisse front had no reserves. Judging by artillery ammunition expenditure in the first few days, the Berlin front must, however, have had a fairly generous allocation of artillery and of ammunition.

In a week the Russians reached the outskirts of Berlin and broke the Neisse front. In the second week a German army was surrounded South-East of Berlin, Berlin was besieged, and the Lower Oder crossed on a wide front. On the 25th April the Russians and Americans linked up. The Russians were also pushing into Czechoslovakia from the North-East and South-East.

52. At this stage there was small room left for strategical principles, but the tradition of issuing orders died hard. As late as the 27th April, Army Group Centre was still under orders to hold the Moravska Ostrava industrial area. The main theme, however, was the relief of Berlin, which Hitler seems to have considered as a rallying point for his armies in the last hours of National Socialism. Only on the 30th April was hope abandoned of re-establishing contact with Hitler in Berlin, but not before Hitler's Chief of Staff had made a signal to the luckless Ninth Army encircled South-East of Berlin and assigned a rôle in the relief operations – "The Fuehrer expects the Ninth Army to do its duty". Hitler's death on the 30th April removed the last real objection to official recognition that the war was lost. On the 2nd May Jodl stated that Doenitz was determined to continue the fight against the Russians, but against the

Western Allies only in so far as they interfered with this object. At this stage these orders could affect only the Army Groups South of the link-up - notably Schoerner's Army Group Centre, which was still relatively intact and covered the Northern and Eastern approaches to Czechoslovakia. Only indirectly was this policy an anti-Bolshevik crusade, the main objects being to gain time for political ends and to save as many civilians and valuable personnel as possible from the Russians.

# CONCLUSION.

53. From the information available on the course of operations in the East emerges the inescapable conclusion that at least from late 1941 onwards Hitler had an almost exclusive prerogative of ultimate strategic decision. As the war continued his interference in the tactical sphere also became more and more marked. It follows that without his malevolent influence the disasters which the Germans suffered in Russia would have been less calamitous. It seems, however, none the less true that even had the German Army been spared the handicap of Hitler's amateur leadership, it would still not have escaped final disaster. That the Germans succeeded in overcoming and holding for two years such a vast area of Russia is a tribute to the efficiency of their war machine and to the skill of its professional direction. By the tacit admission of some of their leading generals, however, these were still inadequate to overcome a country of such vast strategic resources as Russia. Halder implies that the German forces were sufficient for the frontier battles and not for all that lay beyond. Even had his strategy been accepted in 1941 and resulted in the fall of Moscow, that blow may well not have been decisive and he has so far offered no suggestions how the campaign could then have been continued to a decisive conclusion in Germany's favour. Rundstedt explains that he was "not enthusiastic" when he was called to take command of Army Group South in 1941. Warlimont expressed the hopes felt by high German officers in late 1940 that a way out could be found without recourse to war. It is clear that there was a strong realisation in the German High Command that in launching an assault on Russia they were undertaking something beyond the capabilities of their armies.

# APPENDIX XVI.

# THE MEDITERRANEAN.

Note. – This section does not deal with Crete, which is included in the Annexes on German Strategy in the Balkans.

## I.– EGYPT AND NORTH AFRICA.

Operations to the end of 1941.

The Germans appear to have been interested in North Africa as early as September 1940, when General Thoma visited the Italian armies in Libya and Western Egypt as an observer. According to his own account, he reported to Hitler that the Germans would have only small successes in North Africa and that the final result would be disaster. On the 12$^{th}$ November, 1940, Hitler issued a directive stating that the question of using German ground forces in North Africa would only arise when the Italians reached Matruh. However, he envisaged the possibility that G.A.F. support might be given earlier, and also issued a warning order for a Panzer division to be made ready. As this was a month before the British counter-offensive, the original motive for intervention in North Africa appears to have been a desire to capitalise Italian success rather than to assist Italian defence.

In spite of representations from Raeder, and suggestions by Jodl and possibly Goering, it is clear that the OKW in limiting their desire to capitalise on Italian success, did not appreciate the vital importance of the Mediterranean theatre to the Allies. Further, they did not fully take into account the necessity of securing their sea communications in the area, nor the extent to which command of the Mediterranean could be exploited in the implementation of their war at sea. Thus at a time when the wholehearted support of the Italians might have gained decisive success the Germans hung back. It was only when threatened with an Italian collapse in North Africa early in 1941 that Germany was spurred into reinforcing her Allies.

2. By New Year, 1941, however, the situation had completely changed. The Italians had been pushed back beyond the frontier between Egypt and Cyrenaica, and their incapacity to defend Libya with their own resources had become obvious. On the 11$^{th}$ January, 1941, Hitler stated that the situation in the Mediterranean demanded German intervention on strategical, political and psychological grounds: Tripolitania must be held. A "blocking" formation, equivalent in strength to a Panzer division, was to be sent to North Africa in February.

3. By the time the first German troops were ready to begin the crossing to North Africa, doubt already existed in German and Italian circles whether Tripolitania could be held long enough to justify German intervention. In mid-February, however, the British advance came to a standstill, and a few days later Hitler issued orders for a regular Panzer division (15$^{th}$) to be sent to Tripolitania as soon as the original expeditionary force had crossed. (The nucleus of the original expeditionary force was a Light Division (African Model), which eventually became the 21$^{st}$ Panzer Division and some 200 close support aircraft).

4. In the spring and summer of 1941, OKH was responsible for the German troops in North Africa, although tactically these were under the Italian High Command in Libya. It is useful to outline the views of Halder, Chief of Staff of OKH, on the strategical prospects of German intervention in North Africa. He claims that at the outset he regarded these as strictly limited, and held the view that while operations in Libya and beyond should be conducted offensively whenever opportunity offered, the campaign could, in the ultimate, do no more than gain time. Eventually, the Axis must reckon with the loss of North Africa, but German investment in this theatre was essential and strategically justified in order to keep Italy in the war as long as possible. In spite of the numerical superiority of Italian Naval Forces, Halder at this stage realised that the scope of operations in North Africa would be limited by the extent to which he could secure his maritime supply lines. The transfer of strong G.A.F. units to Greece and Sicily did prove an effective counter, and was costly to the British naval forces operating in this area, and they also made Malta virtually untenable as a base for anything but aircraft. In fact, the effective control of the Mediterranean was at one time almost within Axis grasp. This fact does not seem to have been fully appreciated, or if it was, it was not exploited effectively.

5. Rommel, who commanded all German forces in Africa from the start, was an opportunist *par excellence*, with a natural aptitude for desert warfare. He must have found the cautious directives which he received from OKH and OKW repugnant in the extreme. He was fully alive to the glittering prospects which North Africa offered to the side which seized the initiative and used it boldly; he seems to have been less conscious of the difficulties of getting supplies and reinforcements across the Mediterranean. There is, however, no evidence that, at least in the first year of the campaign, Rommel's powers of local decision and initiative were restricted by the directives which he received from Germany.

6. Rommel's initial task was to build up a mobile German and Italian attack force behind the Italian blocking front at Agheila. On the 21st March OKH ordered Rommel to prepare for the recapture of Cyrenaica. The initial phase was to get Agedabia. Whether operations directed on Tobruk could continue immediately or must await arrival of 15th Panzer Division (mid-May) depended on how many British forces were destroyed in the Agedabia operations. It is typical of OKH's caution that Rommel was not required to submit his detailed plan until the 20th April. Before this date, Rommel reached Sollum. He had seized the chance offered him by the transfer of strong British forces from Cyrenaica to Greece.

7. Agedabia was taken on the 3rd April, and on the same day Rommel received orders from Hitler calling for the utmost circumspection. Further attacks were to be very limited in objective until the arrival of the 15th Panzer Division. In particular, Rommel was not to expose his flank by turning Northwards towards Benghazi. Even after the new Panzer division had arrived, Hitler's directive continued, no large-scale offensive, such as an attack on Tobruk, was to be envisaged. Rommel presumably found the loophole he required in these orders in a statement that new conditions might prevail if the bulk of the British forces were withdrawn from Cyrenaica.

8. In forty days Rommel's forces covered over 500 miles. On the last day of April and the first day of May an attempt was made, using nearly all the German forces, to take Tobruk. Some penetration was made, but the German Africa Corps suffered unwelcome losses. In warning against a repetition of such an attempt before the troops were rested and refitted, OKH made it clear that "possession of Cyrenaica with or without Tobruk, Sollum and Bardia was the primary task of the Africa Corps". To ensure this task during the hot summer months, a permanent position was to be prepared in the Gazala area, which could, if the situation demanded, be more easily

defended than the frontier. At the same time Rommel was ordered to prepare a supply base for the continuation of the offensive after the hot summer months were over.

9. As this directive clearly implies that OKH regarded the continuation of the offensive into Egypt as secondary in importance to the secure defence of Cyrenaica, it is well to examine at this point what ideas the German High Command had in 1941 on strategy in the Mediterranean as a whole. About the time when the attack on Russia was launched, Warlimont signed an OKW directive detailing the strategic tasks which might arise from a successful conclusion of the campaign on the Eastern Front. One of these was an attack on the British position in the Mediterranean and the Near East by concentric attack from Libya through Egypt, from Bulgaria through Turkey, and possibly also from Transcaucasia through Iran. In North Africa, Tobruk was to be secured as a base for a German-Italian attack against the Suez Canal. Preparations were to be completed by November. Existing German formations in North Africa were to be brought up to strength, but no new ones shipped across. The German attack on Russia in the summer of 1941, necessitated the withdrawal of part of the G.A.F. from the Mediterranean. In spite of the defensive policy of the Italian Navy, the lack of a common strategy between the Axis, and failure of the Axis to secure effectively their lines of communication to Africa, it would still have been possible to mount an expedition against Malta. It was not until Hitler's glittering dreams of a swift victory over Russia had been shattered that, too late in the day, the Germans realised the vital importance of the Mediterranean theatre and the North African campaign though this had been frequently stressed by OKM.

10. A detailed survey of the prospects and requirements of operations designed to overthrow the British position in the Middle East was made during July 1941 by OKH in a study called "Orient". OKH reached the conclusion that there could be no improvement in the supply situation in North Africa unless there were an operation against Malta, or unless Malta could be held down or alternatively weakened by an attack against Gibraltar. The main effort against the British position in the Mediterranean and the Near East must, therefore, be made through Anatolia and the Caucasus. If Turkey were not disposed to allow the Germans transit facilities, no operations would be carried out from the North until 1942. In that case, by means of troop concentrations in Roumania and Bulgaria, Turkey should be blackmailed to the greatest extent possible without weakening the Eastern Front. Even in the event of Turkish acquiescence, sufficient forces for an attack to the Persian Gulf from Turkey

could only be concentrated in Southern Anatolia by early 1942. The same timing would apply for concentration in Transcaucasia for attacking through Iran.

11. If the evidence here presented is correct the conclusion in the "Orient" study is remarkable and seems to be an astonishing example of thinking in terms of land warfare with a complete disregard of maritime factors.

12. In spite of the attack on Russia, Germany still had the means by energetic measures and a determined policy at least to establish control of the sea communications in the Central Mediterranean but seems to have been completely blind to the fact. True in anticipation of rapid victory over Russia, plans were made for the neutralisation of Malta and the capture of Gibraltar with the ultimate object of occupying Egypt, but even then the possibility of securing the supply lines to North Africa seems to have been disregarded as the objective was to be achieved by uneconomical mass operations via Syria and the Persian Gulf. If this was so there can be few examples in history of a "greater maritime inferiority complex".

13. In accordance with these views, OKH suggested a tentative programme of operations for the future, assuming that the Eastern campaign had been successfully concluded. In the autumn of 1941 Malta should be neutralised, Gibraltar should be attacked, and Tobruk captured. For the latter operation OKH envisaged mid-September as a provisional timing. During the winter 1941-42, if Turkish approval were forthcoming, an invasion of Syria, based on Southern Anatolia and directed on Palestine, should be carried out. In accordance with the success of these operations, the German Africa Corps should invade Egypt. If the operations during the winter were successful, they would be followed in early 1942 by a concentric attack on the Persian Gulf, made by a Panzer corps each from Anatolia and from Transcaucasia. If the operations envisaged for the winter of 1941-42 had not been possible owing to Turkish opposition, the suggested programme for 1942 was an attack from Bulgaria through Turkish Thrace into Anatolia, coupled with an attack from Transcaucasia into North-East Turkey and North Iran.

14. The forces envisaged for these operations were considerable even without those deploying from Transcaucasia. If Turkey was acquiescent, it was estimated that some ten divisions would be required, half Panzer and motorised. If Turkey opposed German penetration, twenty divisions would be required for the drive to Anatolia, nearly half of them mobile.

15. From this OKH study emerge several conclusions of great importance for understanding German strategy in the Mediterranean. In the first place, OKH was committed to the view that, in a grand Mediterranean strategy, the main effort could not be made in North Africa, but rather through the Levant and Iran. In the second place, the forces required for an attack through the Levant and Iran were so great that there could be no grand Mediterranean strategy until Russia was beaten. In the "Orient" study the end of September 1941 seems to have been taken as the planning date for the release of forces from the Eastern Front. In view, however, of the doubts expressed by Halder and other German generals of similar status (admittedly after the event) whether the Russian campaign could have been conducted in 1941, OKH planners must have been very sceptical whether the "Orient" study would serve any useful purpose for a considerable time to come. This scepticism in itself must have tended to make the OKH reinforcement policy for North Africa niggardly, even within the limits of the shipping situation.

16. On the 27th July Rommel submitted his views on the question of continuing the offensive against Egypt. Assumptions were that Tobruk was in German hands and that the Allies were prevented from attacking Cyrenaica by German threats from Turkey and the Caucasus. Otherwise, there could be no German offensive. The plan had four phases following in quick succession. The first objective was in the Alamein area, the second was the Nile. The third phase involved seizing crossings over the Nile and the final objective was the Suez Canal. The scheme was clearly ambitious, but the success which Rommel had in his 1942 offensive suggests there was a little unfairness in the ribald comments which OKH wrote in the margin of his 1941 plan.

The plan involved no nominal increase in the number of German divisions (a third was then in process of formation from miscellaneous units) but a considerable number of drafts and miscellaneous units – nearly 40,000 men in all, as against an actual strength at that time of only some 60,000. Rommel also asked for additional tank battalions for his Panzer divisions, and the Italian reinforcements required would have involved shipping three more divisions.

17. In Rommel's view, administrative reasons would make it impossible to begin the offensive until February; OKH thought April a more likely date. One of the main administrative difficulties was the provision of adequate supply columns. Rommel's nearest good port was over 300 miles from the front, and this could not handle all the required sea intake. OKH estimated that supply units in adequate numbers could

only be sent to North Africa in good time if the Russian campaign was to all intents and purposes finished by October 1941. OKH were less justified when they quibbled over the miscellaneous combatant units requested by Rommel. These they estimated were equivalent to more than one whole Panzer division, and could only be sent at the expense of the Eastern Front. The proportionate loss to the Eastern Front, where there were then over fifteen Panzer divisions, seems small in comparison with the decisive effect on the Allied strategic position which might have been achieved had the OKW not been blind to the fact!

18. By the end of August, OKW had decided in agreement with the Italians that operations for the remainder of 1941 should be limited to an attack on Tobruk in mid-September. Prospects of staging an attack with limited objectives, much less of driving to the Suez Canal, within the foreseeable future did not exist, even if Tobruk was taken in the autumn. For the moment, the Sollum front was to be held, but withdrawal to the Gazala position might be considered if Tobruk were not taken. Renewed attempts were to be made to improve the administrative situation by using Bizerta as an intake port. Warlimont states, however, that the French successfully evaded concessions given to the Germans and Italians for the use of this port for military supplies.

19. By the end of 1941 the importance of sea communications in the Mediterranean had been forced upon OKW. U-boats and some light craft had been sent to the Mediterranean theatre. In addition the G.A.F. were reinforced in Sicily. This strengthening of the naval position evoked some offensive spirit in the Italians, and their midget craft succeeded in immobilising in one operation the only two battle-ships then in the Mediterranean. In addition, the operations of U-boats, small craft and G.A.F. had altered the position in the Mediterranean to one where the Axis virtually controlled the central area although they did not hold Malta. It was now pos-sible, with the newly won mastery of the sea and air, for the Axis to regain supremacy in North Africa, although their forces had recently been driven out of Cyrenaica with heavy losses to men and material.

## Operations during 1942.

20. There is no evidence whether there had been any material modification in these decisions by the 18$^{th}$ November, when Eighth Army launched its offensive

into Cyrenaica. Rommel was making ready to attack Tobruk in the near future, but it is not known whether this stroke was to be followed by a bold drive into Egypt. The Germans decided to stay and meet Eighth Army's attack. They failed to wrest the initiative from the Allies and suffered heavy tank losses. A heavy toll was, however, also taken of Allied tanks, and the initial impetus taken out of the offensive. Subsequently, Rommel took the only course open in desert fighting after a costly tank battle to the side which did not have the initiative. He refused further serious engagement, and shortly after the New Year was back to the Aghelia position. By this means, he shortened his own lines of communication and facilitated the rest and refit of his troops, his administrative build-up, and thus the winning of local superiority. In turn, the Allied communications were unduly stretched, and build-up of supplies could continue only by drastic reduction in the forces in contact with Rommel. Allied administrative difficulties were further aggravated by German command of the Sollum defile, where a small garrison held out for two months.

21. Rommel was quick to capitalise this situation, and before the end of January launched a bold counter-stroke, which in two weeks took him forward to the Gazala position. At this time, there was an improvement in the Axis sea transport situation, brought about by the transfer of strong air forces from the Eastern Front to the Mediterranean where Malta came under heavy and sustained air attack. It is probable also that Rommel's recent successful come-back from Agheila had increased his willingness to take risks and to make do with a much less lavish administrative situation than he had envisaged in 1941 for his offensive into Egypt. Especially, his hand was strengthened by the proven superiority of his tank and anti-tank weapons, although his air support did not exceed 150-200 aircraft. He was thus able in the early summer of 1942 to anticipate Allied preparations for attack by going over to the offensive himself. His successes must have surpassed even his own expectations. Notable among these successes were the destruction of the bulk of the Allied armour in Cyrenaica, the capture of Tobruk and the division which garrisoned it, and the capture of large numbers of Allied vehicles and stores. These victories opened the way to Egypt. The decision to push on was German and contrary to Italian intentions. The Italian viewpoint can be appreciated. The majority of the Italian divisions had only a very low degree of motorisation, and they would suffer most from the continually lengthening L. of C. Benghazi was over 300 miles from the frontier, and even when Tobruk port

was in full operation the L. of C. to the Lower Nile would still be over 350 miles. In the case of a reverse, the Italians would be the first to suffer.

22. In the early days of 1942 Rommel felt the added freedom which resulted from his improved supply position. Convoys to Africa passed as near as 100 miles to Malta. The German U-boat successes and the presence of the German Air Force encouraged the Italian Fleet to contest the command of the sea in the Eastern Basin. This situation was not exploited to the full. The turning-point was the failure of the Italian Fleet to destroy the convoy from Alexandria to Malta on the 22nd March. This failure continued in the minds of the German High Command because of the complete lack of offensive qualities in the Senior Naval Italian Commanders.

23. And yet the immediate results gave the impression, correct or incorrect, that Rommel's bold strategy was sound. He had advanced 200 miles into Egypt before the Allies were able to stabilise the front at Alamein in the latter half of July. This month brought a revolution in the German reinforcement policy. An infantry division from Crete was flown in, closely followed by a first-class parachute brigade group. Both these formations arrived, however, too late to sustain Rommel's offensive, but the infantry division was hustled into the line suffering from dysentery to support the defence. Had these reinforcements been on hand, acclimatised and provided with their heavy equipment, when Rommel crossed into Egypt, the course of the North African campaign might well have been different. It is true that their despatch in late 1941 or early 1942 would not have been easy, and could only have been carried out at the expense of administrative build-up. Their presence might, however, have been more telling than the weight of supplies they would have displaced. In contrast to Rommel, the German High Command seems to have been slow in learning to take risks in North Africa. They seem to have carried the principle of main effort so far that they failed to see that one German division in North Africa could produce much greater results than one German division on the Eastern Front. The high stakes were worth some risk of administrative break-down and even of eventual disaster for the comparatively small forces involved.

24. Rommel's last offensive in Egypt was staged in the last days of August and the first few days of September 1942, and completely misfired. The attack seems to have been backed by completely inadequate petrol resources and it neglected growing British air strength, which together with naval forces had begun to take an increasing toll of Axis shipping. It is a matter for question, therefore, whether Rommel himself still seriously believed that this attempt to turn the Alamein

position from the south would really bring him to the Lower Nile. His defeat was especially significant in that the operation marked the first occasion in the desert when a fully-fledged tank attack had been repulsed without the opposing side moving its armour. It is worth that throughout the campaign the Axis army was never supported by naval forces.

## *The case for strategic withdrawal.*

25. The Germans should at this stage have given serious thought to the question of making a strategic withdrawal to the frontier. Their sea L. of C. was becoming increasingly difficult thanks to continuing air and naval success against shipping and the land L. of C. was equally strained. The nearest port (Tobruk) was nearly 300 miles from the front, but the main port was still Benghazi, 500 miles away. The Allies had shown that they had much improved anti-tank tactics and weapons even if the Germans had no intelligence of the Sherman tank.

26. The obstacles to strategic withdrawal were also considerable. It would have been a hard blow to public opinion both in Italy and Germany. It is furthermore probable that neither Hitler nor Mussolini could abandon the idea that the Delta was within their grasp. This is proven of Hitler at least by his orders to Rommel to hold the Alamein position when the Allies had already broken through. Withdrawal of the four Italian infantry divisions would also have been a difficult problem, and this factor must have provided some incentive to stand at Alamein and try to hold the Allies. For the same reason an attempt to "false-front" would have been scarcely possible. Thus, too late in the day, Hitler and Mussolini realised the vital necessity of occupying the Delta if the Allies were to be beaten. Had they in 1940, '41 or early '42 devoted the energy to its capture with which they now persisted in the attempt, they might have succeeded.

27. According to Warlimont, when Rommel saw things were going badly at Alamein he decided to pull out against orders. He delayed, however, sufficiently long to suffer heavy casualties in men, tanks and guns. Rommel carried out a skilful withdrawal but the Italian infantry were abandoned to their fate. There was no major German stand till administrative difficulties halted the Allies at Aghelia towards the end of November.

## Operations ending in the surrender in Tunisia.

28. Thus the Allies had succeeded with naval and air forces vastly inferior to those of the enemy in so harrying the short-supply route to North Africa that the enemy's army was brought to a standstill. Meanwhile, despite the enemy's U-boats and air reconnaissance, the Allies had succeeded in sailing a convoy of some 500 ships to land a force in North-West Africa. It is too early to assess the reasons why the German Intelligence gave no warning and sea and air patrols failed to detect this armada and bring it to battle, but it sealed the fate of the German armies in North Africa.

29. According to Warlimont the Allied landings in French North Africa came as a complete surprise to the Germans, although in 1941 Warlimont himself had been engaged in negotiations with the French designed to improve their defences in Tunisia.

30. There was no German division available in Italy for despatch to Tunisia, but the Germans acted with commendable resource and rapidity. Replacement and similar units intended for Rommel were sent across to Tunisia by air and destroyer. By the end of November there were some 20,000 Axis troops in the country, about a battalion of tanks, and 100 close-support aircraft, together with some 250 L.R. Bombers based in Italy and Sardinia. With these forces and the handicap which bad weather and a lengthening L. of C. imposed on the Allies, Tunis was narrowly held.

31. There were two objects to be gained in Tunisia. Firstly, to protect the rear of Rommel's forces withdrawing through Tripolitania; secondly, to delay as long as possible Allied preparations for a landing in Italy. North Africa could be defended at smaller cost in German men and equipment than Italy. Warlimont claims that Hitler as late as the winter 1942-43 had visions of an attack by an *élite* army as far as Morocco, but German policy is probably more correctly expressed by Jodl, who in late 1943, speaking of Tunisia, said that "this battle on the periphery had created a capital of space which Germany was still living".

32. The Germans attempted nothing beyond the scope of delaying actions. In Tripolitania the Germans paused on each bound long enough to enable the Italians to clear out and to force the Allies to deploy. By late February they had withdrawn from Tripolitania and were subsequently back on the Mareth Line. By this time two German field divisions had arrived in Northern Tunisia and in the latter half of the

month, with the aid of a division from Rommel's forces, it was possible to launch a well-stage attack against the southern sector of the West Tunisian front.

33. For administrative reasons the attack could not go far, but it was a successful spoiling attack and relieved the pressure in the north. An attempt to achieve a similar success against Eighth Army in the Mareth area by using the bulk of the German armour in Tunisia was a complete and costly failure. By the end of March the Eighth Army had turned the Mareth position and the Germans were forced to begin withdrawing northwards. In Mid-April they were back on the bridgehead covering Tunis and Bizerta which they held when the Allies launched their final assault. By the end of March the Germans should have realised that the situation was hopeless and that their delaying action was in its closing phase. They continued, however, to reinforce and the bulk of two divisions was sent over in the last two months. Drafts were sent in almost up to the last day. The shipping and aircraft required for these reinforcements would have been more usefully employed in bringing ammunition and petrol. The same sea and air communications which had failed to sustain the North African armies were equally inadequate to ensure the safe return to Europe when they no longer had the supplies to fight, and so when the fighting ended on the 12th May nine German army divisions and two flak divisions laid down their arms – a total, with G.A.F., of nearly 150,000 Germans.

# II.- ITALY, SICILY, SARDINIA AND CORSICA.

34. The loss of the Axis foothold in North Africa left Italy dangerously exposed. The hope that the Italians would fight better in defence of their homeland than they had fought in defence of their African empire can have given little comfort to the Germans. There was no complete German division in Italy, and according to Warlimont, the Italians were not keen that there should be. In Sicily, however, there were several thousand drafts and miscellaneous troops who had been awaiting passage to Tunisia, and these became the nucleus of a Panzer Grenadier division.

35. There were two phases in the German reinforcement of Italy. The first phase includes those measures taken to provide a German stiffening of the Italians on the assumption that the latter would do something in their own defence. The second phase includes the more considerable reinforcements whose despatch seems to have been planned from the outset mainly for the contingency that the Germans might

have to shoulder the main burden of defence in Italy. For the sake of convenience these two phases are dealt with separately although preparations for the second phase (called "Alarich") began on the 24$^{th}$ May and were therefore concurrent with the execution of the first phase.

36. The German problem of reinforcement in Italy was complicated initially by great uncertainty as to where the Allies would strike. They feared an Allied landing in the Eastern as well as the Western Mediterranean, although wisely they gave the latter preference almost from the beginning. In the first instance they seem to have regarded Sicily and Sardinia as almost equally threatened. They thought amongst other things that Sardinia might be used as a stepping-stone to Southern France. An OKH appreciation of mid-May recommended that in each island, Sicily and Sardinia, there should be two German mobile formations. The appreciation stated that if Sardinia were lost, Upper Italy would be acutely threatened with grave consequences for the defence of the whole of Italy, Southern France and the Balkans. Southern Germany would also be brought under the threat of air attack.

37. At first the despatch of troops to Sicily and Sardinia appears to have proceeded at practically equal rates. The decision in mid-June to send the Goering Panzer Division, reformed after partial destruction in Tunisia, to Sicily may indicate that at that stage the Germans began to appreciate that Sicily was more immediately threatened. At the end of the month, however, Kesselring was still unable to appreciate categorically that Sardinia stood less chance of being invaded than Sicily. Corsica began to receive German troops, eventually of brigade strength, in mid-June; from the outset its defence appears to have been placed in a lower category than that of Sicily and Sardinia.

38. Meanwhile reinforcements were arriving in Italy proper from France, beginning at the end of May and rising by the end of June to four divisions (all Panzer or Panzer Grenadier). As the number of forces in Italy and the principal islands remained substantially unchanged up till the Allied landings in Sicily, operations in this island will be dealt with briefly at this point.

39. When the Allies landed in Sicily on the 10$^{th}$ July there were two German divisions on the island, one division in an advanced state of formation on Sardinia and a brigade concentrating on Corsica. Of the four divisions in the mainland two were in Central Italy and two in Southern Italy. The two divisions on Sicily had a counter-attack rôle and were in close reserve behind the Italian coastal defences – one in

the general area Western Sicily and one in Eastern Sicily. Kesselring appreciated, wrongly, that there would be a strong Allied landing on the west coast of the island.

From the outset Kesselring realised that Sicily could only be held if the Italians were willing to fight. On the fourth day of the action Hitler, referring to the collapse of Italian resistance, appreciated that the Allies could no longer be thrown into the sea and directed that the German troops should withdraw, imposing the maximum delay, to a line round the base of Mount Etna covering the north-east corner of the island. A parachute division was to be flown in from France and a Panzer Grenadier division in Southern Italy made ready for shipment across the Straits of Messina. In front of and on this line in north-east Sicily the Germans offered tenacious resistance. Evacuation to the Toe of Italy began, however, in early August and in about a fortnight the four German divisions of the Sicily garrison were ferried across the narrow Straits with comparatively light losses. The weight of the Allied bombing offensive which preceded the landing not only pinned down a considerable portion of the defensive fighter force and severely restricted bomber operations, but also materially reduced German air strength both in Sicily and Sardinia.

40. At this point the narrative must revert to the second phase of German reinforcement in Italy – the preparations which were covered by the code name "Alarich". These preparations were entrusted to Field-Marshal Rommel who eventually received for this task an Army Group Staff (Army Group B) in the Munich area. The original directive issued to him in late May instructed him to prepare for the concentration of some half dozen Panzer and Panzer Grenadier divisions from the Eastern front, in three groups respectively in the Villach area, the Innsbruck area and South-East France, where they were to be available for the rapid reinforcement of Italy. At the same time he was to prepare a supply base in these areas which could if necessary support more than twice that number of divisions in Italy. It was doubtless the abortive Kursk offensive which prevented the Germans from fulfilling these lavish promises to Rommel. Only one Panzer division came from the East and the majority of Rommel's forces were "Stalingrad" infantry divisions resurrected in France.

41. Up till the end of June the Germans appreciated that there was unlikely to be any immediate political crisis in Italy, although they could see that the country was war weary and they realised that the Italian armed forces were in no shape to do battle on their own. On the 25th July however Mussolini was deposed and the Germans

must have appreciated that the defection of Italy had become a probability unless they showed a strong hand. It is nevertheless worth noting that for at least a fortnight Kesselring cherished fond hopes describing himself as an "inveterate friend of Italy".

42. On the 28th July instructions were issued by OKW on the measures to be taken in the contingency of Italian defection ("Achse"). Sicily and Sardinia were to be evacuated, the forces in Sardinia crossing to Corsica. As soon as the evacuation of Sicily was complete, the German forces in Southern Italy were to move Northwards. Rommel's Army Group was to take over command in the whole of Italy and seize the coastal areas Genoa-Leghorn and Venice-Trieste, and the Apennine crossings between Leghorn and Ancona. Rommel was never in fact appointed German Commander-in-Chief for the whole of Italy. Such an appointment would have made for intolerable relations with Kesselring who was nearly two years his senior in rank. Accordingly Rommel's command was confined to Northern Italy and Kesselring remained German Commander-in-Chief in Central and Southern Italy. This dualism lasted till November, 1943, when Kesselring became Commander-in-Chief of the whole of Italy.

43. On the 1st August OKW reported that "Achse" was to be expected soon. It was difficult to take overt action. If the suspicions of the Italians were aroused the position of the German forces in Sicily and Southern Italy might be jeopardised. On the 30th July however the Germans ordered the "Alarich" movements to begin and two days later managed to persuade the Italian High Command that the dispatch of further German divisions to Italy was essential to prevent those in the South from being cut off by new Allied landings. Fear on the Italian's side that they might arouse German suspicions must have made it difficult for them to refuse. The German movements into Northern Italy continued and by the time the evacuation of Sicily was complete there were in all seventeen German divisions complete or concentrating in the Italian area. North of the general line Pisa-Rimini was Rommel's command with four divisions in the Genoa-Spezia area, two in the Po plain and two on the L. of C. in North and North-East Italy. There were eight divisions under Kesselring's command in Central and Southern Italy and another under his command in Sardinia. The Germans still hesitated however to take precipitate action against the Italians although they had a scheme to overthrow the Badolio regime and rescue Mussolini. According to Jodl, Hitler had prepared a political and military ultimatum to the Italians when the Allied landing fleet appeared off Salerno.

44. German views on strategy in Italy from the close of the Tunisian campaign up to the date of Italian defection (8th September, 1943) are closely influenced by the dwindling value of the Italians as Allies.

45. Initially Kesselring decided that Sardinia, Sicily and Southern Italy should be defended, and this view was shared by a representative of OKH who visited the Italian theatre late in June. The rapid collapse of the Italian forces in Sicily and the prospect of Italian defection produced a marked change in the situation. The chances of an Allied landing on the Italian mainland achieving rapid success were increased and German forces defending Southern Italy would therefore run the risk of being cut off. It appears that for this reason Jodl in early August considered the Germans delayed too long in Sicily although the time gained must have been useful for concentration in Northern Italy. In the third week of August Hitler directed that the German forces in Southern Italy should be prepared to march Northwards and that three mobile divisions were to be concentrated in the Naples-Salerno area which he regarded as the most threatened piece of coast. At no time in August do the Germans appear to have envisaged abandoning Central Italy as well as Southern Italy. By that time Jodl appreciated that the likelihood of Allied landings on the Ligurian coast had diminished.

46. When the Allies landed in the Toe of Italy on the 3rd September, the German forces in this area were already thinning out and committed to delaying actions only. Two mobile divisions were thus moving Northwards to reinforce the Panzer division in the Salerno area when the Allies landed there on the 9th September. Italian defection was quickly dealt with. Rome was seized and in the North Rommel's strong forces stamped out the isolated centres of Italian resistance.

47. After the initial attempts to throw the Allies into the sea at Salerno had failed the Germans began to pull back pivoting on the area North of Salerno. The transfer of the Sardinia garrison to Corsica began almost immediately since the Genoa area was no longer considered to be threatened and the defection of the Italians had removed the possibility of a serious defence of the Island. The evacuation of Corsica to the mainland followed.

48. German strategy at this time is made clear in a directive issued by Hitler on the 4th October. It was, he said, to be expected that the Allies would launch a major operation from Italy against the Yugoslav coast, but it was not yet clear whether this would be based on Southern Italy or whether the Allies would first push further North, and then strike at the North Yugoslav coast and Istria. The German front

was to be stabilised on the general line Gaeta-Cassino-Ortona. A German counter-offensive against Apulia was to be prepared in case the Allies should not pursue their attack Northwards, but instead stage a landing in the Balkans. Other evidence shows that an ambitious project to envelop the Allied right flank was duly worked out by Kesselring's staff.

49. The German front stabilised on the general line laid down by Hitler, and there was much fighting but little movement until the front was broken in the Allied summer offensive of May 1944. But the number of German divisions required for its defence continued to grow. Hitler has envisaged seven including two in reserve. During the winter the total was nearer ten. The total number of German divisions in Italy had also grown, and before the end of 1943 had reached twenty despite transfers to the Eastern front. The total remained at over twenty till the end of the Italian campaign. In December it was decided that Italy should provide two mobile divisions for the West in the New Year, but wholesale withdrawals were never considered and even the two divisions earmarked did not go.

50. When the Allies landed at Anzio on the 22$^{nd}$ January, 1944, behind the main German front, the Germans were alive to the risk of Allied amphibious operations against the Italian coastline, but were ill-prepared for a landing at the precise point chosen. They diverted, however, reserves moving down from Northern Italy and a division from Southern France, and by bold transfer of armoured and other units from the main front were able to contain the Allied bridgehead.

51. The Germans showed themselves determined to hold Rome at all costs despite their difficult L. of C., and the costly commitment of two separate fronts which arose after the Anzio landings. During February Kesselring appears even to have been directed to plan an elaborate spoiling attack on the Cassino front, but notes written in the plan suggest that his staff was sceptical of success, and he was apparently successful in getting the plan shelved.

52. When the Allies launched their Summer offensive on the 12$^{th}$ May, 1944, the Germans had twenty-three divisions in Italy and of these sixteen were South of Rome. A continuous line intended to cover Rome was in course of preparation, but had hardly passed the stage of survey. When Rome fell on the 4$^{th}$ June all but three of the German divisions in Italy had been drawn into the battle, and German losses in men and material had been substantial. The most economical method of defence

would have been to refuse further engagement and withdraw to the Apennines. This was forbidden by Hitler. The Gothic Line which ran from Spezia to Pesaro, was, he said, in only an elementary state of preparation and needed months of work. It was the last line of defence in Italy and the political and military consequences would be enormous if the Allies broke the line and poured into the Po Plain. Kesselring was to gain the maximum of time, and to stand at the latest on the general latitude of Lake Trasimeno. Kesselring was given five fresh divisions and by skilful defensive action gained two months.

## *The last phase in Italy.*

53. Soon after the Allies penetrated the first defence of the Gothic Line in early September, the enemy must have begun to make tentative preparations for strategic withdrawal. There are indications that administrative preparations for the evacuation of North-west Italy were to be complete by the end of October. But such preparations for withdrawal were apparently never more than planning measures for the eventuality of a crushing defeat, involving hasty evacuation across the Po. A voluntary withdrawal to the Alps would have resulted in considerable economy of force, and would have released welcome reinforcements for the Western Front or for Hungary, but it does not appear to have been considered seriously by Hitler. Apart from being totally out of keeping with his strategic conception of defence to the utmost on the line held, it would have meant the loss of the industrial and agricultural areas of Northern Italy – a serious economic consideration – and would also have given the Allies medium bomber bases from which to intensify the air assault on Southern Germany. In the Autumn the success of Kesselring's defensive battles on the Northern slopes of the Apennines, and along the rivers on the Eastern flank must have encouraged the belief that the Allies could be kept out of the Po Plain. Italy continued to receive its reinforcements.

54. When the Russians launched their winter offensive on the 12th January, 1945, the time for strategic withdrawal in Italy was past. The railways out of Italy were in such poor condition that the surplus produced by a large-scale withdrawal would have taken months to move. Nevertheless the Germans managed laboriously to move four divisions out of Italy to reinforce the Eastern Front between the beginning of the year and the start of the Allied Spring offensive.

55. Thus when the Allies launched their last offensive in Italy on the 9th April, 1945, there were still twenty-one German divisions under Kesselring's command, and these included some of the best and strongest formations in the German army. German defence was nevertheless handicapped by lack of petrol and ammunition, and by Hitler's refusal to countenance even tactical withdrawals. The Germans were unable to reorganise on the Po, and before the Lower Alps position could be manned German resistance in Italy had completely disintegrated.

# APPENDIX XVII.

# GERMAN NAVAL STRATEGY AND CONDUCT OF THE WAR AT SEA.

SUMMARY.

Preparatory Phase.

(1) Evasions of the Versailles Treaty, under cover of seemingly non-military measures.

(2) Plans as result of London Naval Agreement: war with England not expected till 1944-45; fleet adequate only for Germany; continental designs; 35 per cent. allowed in surface ships not built.


*Phase I September, 1939, to August, 1940.*

Raeder's Policy:

(1) Bold use of big ships as raiders; expansion of U-boat production and reliance on U-boats as the chief means of attacking British sea communications; mine warfare.

(2) Invasion of France and Norway provides well placed additional U-Boat bases.

(3) Failure of non-combat torpedo pistol undermines the confidence of the U-Boat arm in its weapon, and robs the Germans of many successes.

(4) Complete blockade of England declared August, 1940.

(5) Bad co-operation between the Navy and the Air Force; this handicaps the Navy throughout the whole war.

## Phase II. — *From fall of France to War with Russia.*

(1) Plans for invasion of England abandoned in Autumn, 1940, to the great relief of the German Naval Staff.

(2) The German Naval Staff begins to stress the importance of the Mediterranean theatre of war.

(3) The German Navy is surprised by the rapid British counter-measures to the new magnetic mine.

(4) The German Naval Staff is informed of the projected attack on Russia only when the plans were already well advanced in October 1940. Raeder is strongly opposed to the project.

(5) Divergence of views between Hitler and Raeder over necessity of enlisting the co-operation of the French Navy.

## Phase III. — *From attack on Russia to retirement of Raeder, January, 1943.*

(1) Sees the peak period of success of the German war at sea.

(2) Raeder presses for intensification of U-Boat warfare. The German Air Force engaged in Russia is unable to help the Navy.

(3) System of blockade running for essential supplies from the Far East is introduced.

(4) Naval representations on the necessity of capturing Malta and holding Tunis ignored: Hitler wishes to concentrate on Eastern offensive.

(5) Disagreement between Hitler and Raeder over big ship policy. After the loss of the *Bismarck* in raider operations the Naval Staff considered that the main rôle of the heavy ships was to tie down considerable British forces in Home Waters and that this justified their maintenance. Hitler disagreed. *Scharnhorst*, *Gneisenau* and *Prince Eugen* withdrawn from Brest. Later Hitler, incensed by

*Lutlow's* lack of success against a Murmansk convoy, orders that all big ships be put out of commission.

(6) January 1943, Raeder resigns. Doenitz succeeds him 30$^{th}$ January, 1943.

## Phase IV, January 1943 to Invasion, June 1944.

(1) The turning-point in the war at sea.

(2) Doenitz obtains absolute priority for building U-Boats. Big ships to be paid off except *Tirpitz* and *Scharnhorst*, which are to operate from Norwegian bases.

(3) Germany's serious U-Boat losses; shortage of escort vessels and local defence craft. The Allies superior in intelligence, air cover and Radar development.

(4) Weakness of the Italian Navy; it would be unable to prevent an Allied landing in Sicily or Sardinia.

(5) New types of U-Boats being tried, with long submerged endurance and high submerged speed. Preliminary trials of Walther U-Boats with high under-water speed.

(6) Encouragement of technical developments and research. End of 1943, setting up of Department of Scientific Research for the Navy. Allied counter measures have gained the lead, however, and the development of the new type U-Boat and its technical improvement came too late to regain the ascendancy.

(7) Increased production of E-Boats. Plans for new air-mine offensive.

## Last Phase. - Invasion and after.

(1) Counter measures to invasion:

(a) Creation of Small Battle Units Command. Probably attributable to Doenitz alone, and influenced by experience gained in Mediterranean.

(b) Anti-invasion ground mine.

(2) After Invasion: rapid deterioration of situation. Walther Boats not in time. Success of "Schnorchel". Troops evacuated by sea from East Prussia. Delaying action in the Scheldt.

(3) Final Defeat.

# INTRODUCTION.

Contemporary records indicate the main features of German Naval Strategy as planned or desired by the Naval Staff. The following is an outline of these features and of the general conduct of the war at sea. A detailed account of the U-Boat campaign is contained in Appendix XVIII.

## *Preparatory Phase.*

1. In the years following the 1914-18 War, Germany took measures to avoid the Versailles Treaty. Prototypes of U-Boats were built in foreign countries – orders were evaded to destroy coastal defences – youth movements and sport clubs built up to provide naval training. As the Army and Air Force had priority, Naval formations allowed by Treaty were used as "cover" for military and air rearmament.

2. After the London Naval Agreement of 1935, Germany was confident that war with England in the near future would be avoided, and in consequence, so far as surface ships were concerned, she did not build up to her allowance of 35 per cent. of British strength. The following tables show the actual strength of the fleet in 1939, and the strength allowed under the Anglo-German Agreement of 1935:-

|                  | Actual strength. | Allowed strength. |
|------------------|:----------------:|:-----------------:|
| Capital ships    | 2                | 5                 |
| Aircraft carriers| . . .            | 2                 |
| Cruisers         | 11               | 21                |
| Destroyers       | 21               | 64                |
| Submarines       | 57               | 57                |

(The 11 cruisers include 3 pocket battleships.)

3. Although it was clearly impossible for Germany to reach the agreed strength in the four years between 1935 and the outbreak of the war, she could probably have approached it more closely, at any rate, in cruisers and destroyers, had she given the matter priority. Moreover, she could have prepared the way for a rapid expansion in submarines – in case of war – than she actually achieved in 1939 and 1940.

4. On the outbreak of war Raeder recorded how he had been given to understand by Hitler that war against England would not be likely until 1944-45, by which time the German Fleet would have possessed ships of all types in sufficient numbers to make England hesitate. This statement reveals a gap between higher policy and the means for enforcing it, which perhaps more than any other feature dominates the naval events of the war years.

## Phase I, from outbreak of war to the fall of France — September 1939 to June 1940.

5. When war broke out, the naval resources, both in U-Boats and surface ships, were considered inadequate for decisive results, and it was therefore Raeder's policy to expand the U-Boat production as rapidly as possible for the waging of decisive war against shipping, and to employ the big ships boldly against Allied shipping. Later they were augmented by Armed Merchant Cruisers which operated with considerable success. Big ships were ordered to avoid action with enemy warships except when the enemy force was inferior in strength. Raeder also required that as soon as possible an intensive mine warfare should be launched against the principal British harbours and approaches and that the G.A.F. should be used in sufficient numbers for this purpose.

6. In October 1939 Raeder first advised Hitler that the capture of Norway would provide valuable bases from which U-Boats could operate against Atlantic convoys. Hitler at this time was more interested in the invasion of the Low Countries. Perhaps the main motive for the German invasion of Norway was the fear of a British occupation, which would have threatened the vital ore supplies from Sweden and closed the approaches to the Baltic.

7. In this phase the German naval strategy conformed to the general plan as revealed by Hitler's directives. The U-Boats could operate only in small numbers and were ordered to conform to the usages of Prize Law and to avoid incidents with neutral, and particularly American, ships. These restrictions were gradually removed until in August, 1940, a complete blockade of England was declared, and only Irish ships were exempted from attack. The background for this period was provided by Hitler's belief that when France was defeated, England would be induced to come to terms.

8. Important divergences of opinion had already revealed themselves between Raeder and Goering, concerning the employment of aircraft for naval purposes.

At the outbreak of war Raeder had only five partially trained squadrons of reconnaissance machines and fighters at his disposal. In brief, Raeder wanted a sufficient number of suitable types of aircraft to be allocated to the Navy permanently for mine-laying operations and also for naval reconnaissance. The crews were to be trained and operations to be controlled by the Navy. Goering was unwilling to surrender so much to the Navy, and considered that the German Air Force should operate under his centralised control, whether its tasks be over the land or over the sea. It is noteworthy that this important question, the solution of which would largely govern the success or failure of the mine and U-Boat offensive against shipping, was never thrashed out round a table between Goering, Raeder and Hitler. The procedure, on the contrary, was that Raeder pointed out the deficiencies to Hitler, who usually promised to discuss the matter with Goering. It is known that at that time the Reichsmarshall went his own way in many matters affecting co-operation with the Navy. In the result the Navy suffered a serious handicap throughout the war, recognised but not removed by either Raeder or his successor. It is true that Doenitz in June 1943 claimed to have obtained all that was required from the G.A.F., and he may have done so for a short time, but by then the G.A.F. was heavily committed to other vital tasks and the results were never satisfactory.

9. The German invasion of Norway in April 1940 and the fall of France provided Raeder with bases enabling U-Boats to operate further afield in the Atlantic, and to remain longer in the operational areas. A serious weakness in the design of the magnetic pistols of U-Boat torpedoes became evident at this stage and it lost the Germans many opportunities of sinking Allied ships off Norway. This also seriously undermined confidence in the U-Boat and its weapons.

10. In June 1940 Raeder was not satisfied with the speed of production of U-Boats. He was told by Hitler that after the fall of France the German Army would be reduced and that all efforts would be concentrated on building up the Navy and Air Force for the defeat of England. When Raeder realised, as will appear later, that no such policy was being pursued, he began to have misgivings as to the strategic conduct of the war.

## Phase II. From the fall of France to the attack on Russia — June 1940 to June 1941.

11. The naval share of the hasty preparations for the invasion of England was completed by the 15th September, 1940, which was the original planned date for the

attack. Raeder's attitude at the time was that invasion should be undertaken only as a last resort, as such an operation under the prevailing circumstances could only be regarded as a gamble. There was general relief among the leading naval authorities when reasons were found for postponement and finally cancellation of the invasion. A later review of this phase by the German Naval Staff ended with this statement: "Finally, just as in Napoleon's invasion plans in 1805, the fundamental condition for success, namely, command of the sea, was lacking".

12. At this time Raeder began to stress the importance of N.W. Africa (Dakar) and Spain to the successful prosecution of the war against England. At the end of September 1940 the Naval Staff considered that the main effort of Germany should be concentrated on the Mediterranean, with emphasis on Gibraltar and Suez: Raeder's view was that a major operation should be launched against the British in the Mediterranean, so as to succeed before the United States could come into the war. Against England herself the war should take the form of intensified U-Boat operations and air-mining. There were great expectations from the results of mines with new acoustic and magnetic firing mechanisms, which were to be laid in the approaches to the principal British ports. Raeder and his naval staff were prone to over-estimate the surprise value of this weapon; in other words they under-estimated the speed and efficiency of British counter-measures.

13. Unknown to Raeder, the Chief of Staff of OKW was, in September 1940, making preparations for the attack on Russia. Hitler had already decided after the "Battle of Britain" that the last continental opponent must be eliminated before the major attack on England could be taken up in earnest. His decision was then given to Keitel and Jodl only. The intention against Russia first became known to the Navy by official top secret documents on the 30th October, 1940. Naval circles, and particularly Raeder and his advisers, were intensely against this plan. Early in December a memorandum was produced by the Naval Staff (and marked to Hitler) which demanded the strongest concentration of all weapons for the destruction of British shipping and supplies, and warned against other undertakings that would weaken this main effort and prolong the war. It is not known whether Hitler weighed these arguments in relation to his other problems, but it is certain that on the 27th December, 1940, Raeder, in a personal interview with the Fuehrer, recorded in the strongest terms his disapproval of attacking Russia before England had been defeated. This warning evoked the curt reply from Hitler that Russia must first be eliminated.

14. In reviewing these events in 1944, Raeder stated "I accommodated myself, as was my only possible course, to the force of circumstances."

15. The German Admiralty was vitally interested in securing the active collaboration of France. Towards the end of 1940 Raeder repeatedly asked the Fuehrer to make generous concessions to France of a kind which would not only encourage her to fight for the defence of her North African territories against Allied attacks, but bring her actively into the Axis partnership. Raeder attached particular importance to Dakar and Tunis, which he regarded as vital strong points for ensuring the protection of the "southern flank" of Europe. It was essential, because of Germany's limited naval power, to enlist the active help of France and to make use of her bases to secure mastery of the Mediterranean while Britain was still weak in that area. This might have led to the capture of Suez and would then probably have brought Spain with her valuable naval bases into the war.

16. Hitler, however, felt that France could not be trusted, and that the claims of Italy (who was jealous of any concessions to France) must be considered. He therefore approved the support of France only to the extent that would allow her to defend her African possessions. He did not wish her to take an active part in the war.

17. These two factors, the decision to attack Russia and Germany's failure to secure the use of the French Naval bases, was vitally to affect the future of German Naval operations.

18. To sum up, Hitler's interest at the end of 1940 was focused primarily on the East and secondarily on the South, while Raeder wanted Germany's total effort to be concentrated mainly towards the West and the South. That Raeder failed to influence the Fuehrer reflects no discredit on the Naval Commander-in-Chief as a strategist, but serves to illustrate Hitler's habit of making major strategic decisions without the concurrence of his chief professional advisers.

## Phase III. From commencement of Russian war to the retirement of Raeder (June 1941 to January 1943).

19. This phase saw the peak period of success of the German war at sea. U-Boat production had been stepped up and technical improvements made. The occupation of Norway and France had afforded well-placed operational bases for the U-Boat war in the Atlantic. U-Boat morale was at its highest. U-Boat sinkings were reasonable in

proportion to Allied sinkings and if these rates could be maintained, although unprepared for war with England at the outset, Germany had a reasonable hope of establishing an effective blockade. Despite losses the bold use of surface forces had pinned down the British Navy and was paying a satisfactory dividend. Commerce raiders had been equipped and were operating with success. Co-ordination of air strategy and air co-operation was still lacking. The Air Force remained "continentally minded" and this factor may have been decisive in Germany's battle with England which, now that invasion and bombing had failed, must be decided at sea.

20. During this phase the Naval High Command saw victory within reach and constantly urged not only increased air support, but the whole readjustment of German strategy to make the results of the war at sea decisive: control of the Mediterranean by the occupation of Gibraltar, Malta and Suez and the establishment of U-Boat bases in North Africa and Spain, but Germany's continental commitments precluded her taking these measures which might have cut England's sea communications and brought the war against England to a decisive conclusion. Even had it been possible for Germany to adjust her continental plans to support her maritime strategy the naval High Command spoke with so little authority and the OKW was so constituted that it is unlikely that the step would have been taken.

21. After the commencement of the war on Russia, Raeder's policy was to press for still greater U-Boat production and to dispose his surface and U-Boat forces with the object of inflicting the heaviest losses on British shipping. He also had to contend with the growing losses in Axis shipping to North Africa. Wherever possible the weakness of the German Navy must be compensated by enlisting the resources of the over-run countries. Plans were made to co-ordinate the building of small standard cargo ships in Italy and Greece, but results proved disappointing. The German Navy could no longer count on support from the German Air Force for mining and reconnaissance operations against British shipping on any scale sufficient to produce decisive results against England. The G.A.F. was heavily committed on the Eastern Front, and was beginning to face growing air resistance from the West.

22. England's unchallenged command of the sea had cut off all German overseas trade, and a system of blockade running for essential supplies from the Far East had been introduced. Later on, owing to the ever-increasing danger of these operations, surface blockade runners were forced to give place to U-Boat blockade runners.

23. The American occupation of Iceland was disturbing, and the increasing help from America, with supplies to England, did not justify any optimism over the results of U-Boat operations. U-Boats had also to be sent to North Norway for attacks on the Russian convoys and to the Mediterranean and South Atlantic. A certain lack of cohesion in planning objectives for U-Boats is evident towards the end of 1941. Raeder wanted concentration of effort against Atlantic shipping, but gave way to Hitler's demands for activity in other theatres.

24. Raeder had been assured by Hitler in July, 1941, that the Russian campaign would be completely successful for Germany by October at the latest. It may well be that this confident assurance persuaded him to face a situation which by then was already quite out of harmony with his own conception of the best strategic conduct of the war. When the United States joined the Allies, Raeder thought that the transfer of American shipping to the East would cause considerable shortages of supplies to Britain. Otherwise he did not appear unduly concerned, since he considered that this policy of using his big ships to tie down the British Home Fleet in northern waters would greatly embarrass England in the defence of her eastern possessions.

25. In December 1941 Raeder was pressed by Hitler to send the big ships (*Scharnhorst*, *Gneisenau*, *Prinz Eugen*) then based on Brest to Norway, where they would, he considered, be of greater use for repelling possible British landings and for attacking Russian convoys. After careful preparation the ships left Brest in February 1942, for German ports. Two of them were damaged by mines while approaching the Heligoland Bight. Raeder, in commenting on the reasons for the move, states that Goering failed to provide adequate A.A. protection for the ships while at Brest. The Naval Staff considered this port tenable with adequate A.A. and smoke defences, and as a base more suitable than Norwegian ports.

26. On the 15th June, 1942, after several previous endeavours by the Naval Staff to persuade Hitler to capture Malta and thereby make possible the drive on Suez, and a link-up with the Japanese in the Indian Ocean, Hitler told Raeder that this operation was not possible while his Eastern offensive was in progress. The Naval Staff commented that the capture of Malta would be difficult, but that it was a strategic necessity, and that the opportunity would not recur. A principal motive was to eliminate the island as a base for British attacks on the Axis convoys to Libya. These attacks were causing serious losses and imperilling supplies to the advancing Axis armies.

27. The Allied landings in North Africa in November 1942 had caused a concentration of a number of U-Boats in the Western Mediterranean and to the West of Gibraltar. According to Doenitz, then Flag Officer, U-Boats, the results achieved by these boats were not sufficient to justify their withdrawal from Atlantic operations. The naval staff were disappointed that the German Air Force did not put up a better performance in attacking the Allied invasion fleet, and criticised the lack of training of G.A.F. crews in attacking ships.

28. On the 19th November, 1942, Raeder made what was to be his last effort to stem the course of events which he had predicted two years earlier. He made an earnest appeal to Hitler to hold Tunis at all costs so as to save the "southern flank of Europe", from the major Allied offensive which would follow.

## German surface ships – Raeder resigns.

29. The hazards of raider operations by German battleships, pocket battleships and heavy cruisers had in the course of three years of war resulted in the loss of *Graf Spee* and *Bismarck*. The pocket battleship *Scheer* had achieved some success in the distant raider operations between November 1940 and March 1941. The Battle Cruisers *Scharnhorst* and *Gneisenau* and the Cruiser *Hipper* also operated successfully. The *Hipper* in September and October 1940, the *Scharnhorst* and the *Gneisenau* between January and March 1941. During the 59 days that *Scharnhorst* and *Gneisenau* were at large twenty-one ships were sunk or scuttled and one captured. But the German Naval Staff now regarded the big ships mainly as a strategic counter which tied down a considerable force of British warships and escorting craft in home waters. There was also the threat to the Allies' northern sea route supplying Russia.

30. Raeder considered that these were sufficient reasons for keeping the ships in commission, and that lack of results, particularly against the Arctic convoys, was in great part due to insufficient air support by the G.A.F.

31. Hitler was greatly upset by the loss of *Bismarck* in May 1941 and by the general lack of results with the big ships. During a discussion with Raeder in December 1941 concerning the move of the Brest ships to Norway, he had suggested an alternative that the ships should be put out of commission, their crews being trained for U-Boats and their guns used for coastal defence. This provoked a strong defence by Raeder of the rôle of big ships.

32. At the end of December 1942 *Lutzow* and *Hipper* were engaged in an operation off Northern Norway against a Murmansk bound convoy. Hitler had expected good results and was greatly incensed when the British Radio announced the failure of this attack. The German Admiralty could provide him with no information, because the German ships were still at sea and preserving W/T silence. Hitler stormed against the German Navy in general and the big ships in particular. He sent for Keitel to take down a directive ordering the disbandment of the ships and the employment of the crews in more useful tasks, such as U-Boat warfare. The guns of the ships were to be mounted at strategic points along the Norwegian coast. He ordered Raeder to state his reasons in writing why big ships were necessary to the German war effort.

33. Early in the New Year (1943) Raeder presented his memorandum and asked to be relieved of his post as Commander-in-Chief of the Navy. "I feel (he said) that after the Fuehrer's remarks about the Navy, I can no longer count on his confidence in my leadership". His resignation was accepted "on grounds of health" and when asked by Hitler to propose a successor he recommended Admiral Carls, or, failing him, Doenitz.

34. On the 30th January, 1943, Doenitz became Commander-in-Chief of the Navy. From then until the end of the war Raeder, though kept informed of events, was not consulted, and had no contact with his successor.

## Phase IV. The Navy under Doenitz — January 1943 — May 1944.

35. During this phase Germany lost the initiative and was forced on to the defensive. By improved radar and technical equipment, increased air cover and surface escorts, the Allies succeeded by a narrow margin in mastering the U-boat at sea. U-boat losses were increasing, and the sinkings of Allied merchant shipping was steadily declining. Germany's diminishing resources were pitted against the mounting effort of the Allies. At the same time the extent of our air cover and the accuracy of our Intelligence had brought home to the German High Command that the operation of surface warships so far from their bases was proving too hazardous. The life of commerce raiders was becoming ever shorter and losses of surface blockade runners to the Far East had become so high that their operation was stopped and Germany had to rely on U-boats for the exchange of essential commodities with the Far East.

36. Meanwhile, the mounting Allied Bombing Offensive was diverting more and more of Germany's much needed man-power and material to the purely defensive

task of protecting her vital installations both on Germany's long occupied coastline and inland. At the same time, the threat of amphibious operations, the increased scale of air attacks, air mining, and attacks by surface ships and submarines against her merchant shipping were likewise forcing on Germany a further dispersal of effort to make good her losses and to build and repair her minesweepers and escort vessels which alone could decrease these growing losses.

37. The Naval High Command realised that her standard U-boats were fighting a fast losing battle and had no hope of achieving their object – the effective blockade of the United Kingdom. The U-boat, however, still afforded the only hope of defeating England, or at least hindering the build-up of those forces destined for the invasion and occupation of the Continent. The construction of standard U-boats was therefore stopped, and the highest priority accorded by Doenitz to scientific research in the hope of outstripping the Allied technical devices which had sealed the fate of the standard U-boat.

38. At the same time, Speer, Minister of Armament Production, was charged with the mass production in the shortest possible time of two types of U-boat which it was hoped would be able to operate successfully despite Allied counter-measures.

39. These two types (the Type XXI and XXIII) had increased battery capacity which gave them a considerably improved submerged performance and were intended to fill the gap until the more effective Ingolin propelled (Walther) U-boat had overcome its teething troubles and could be put into service in effective numbers.

40. These measures, which might have been effective if put in train earlier, came too late. Germany's position was deteriorating in every way. Her resources of manpower and material were inadequate to provide for her mounting needs, the protection of the wide areas she had occupied (and refused to quit) against the Allies mounting offensive and at the same time to wage an offensive war in the East and in the West. Not only was the introduction of the new type U-boat started too late but shortage of man-power and materials, disruption of her communications, damage to her factories by bombing and the loss of her eastern Baltic building yards (to which one-third of her new U-boat production was allocated) progressively delayed their production.

41. In naval matters the one hope in a situation which everywhere showed signs of deterioration was the pursuit of intensified warfare against Allied shipping. The Naval Staff realised that without ships, the Allies could not bring the war to a successful

conclusion. Both Hitler and Doenitz also required that no special steps be taken to rescue crews of sunken ships, since they considered that provision of crews for new ships was a principal problem of the enemy.

42. In his first conference with Hitler in February, 1943, Doenitz asked for and obtained absolute priority for building of U-boats. He also produced details for paying off the big ships as desired by Hitler, but within a few weeks revised this plan so as to keep *Tirpitz* and *Scharnhorst* in operation in Norwegian waters.

43. In March 1943 Doenitz became anxious over the serious losses in operational U-boats. He attributed these to treachery ("since the enemy apparently knows accurately the dispositions of the boats"); and to enemy air and radar superiority. There was also a serious shortage in escort vessels and local defence craft. The remedy, he said, lay in more U-boats and ships of those types.

NOTE: - The first indications that U-boat buildings were slowing down were at first attributed by the Allies to the effect of the bombing, shortage of material and similar causes, but it was not long before the true reason became apparent.

44. Early in May Doenitz went to Italy to discuss matters of defence with Italian and German authorities. On his return he reported to Hitler that Italian naval forces would be too weak to attack the Allied ports of embarkation or the invasion fleet, and could not prevent landings in Sicily or Sardinia. Neither island had been properly supplied with defences. The Italian High Command showed a reluctance to make shipping available for this purpose, and Germany could not help.

45. At the end of May a review of the U-boat war by Doenitz revealed his increasing alarm over heavy Atlantic losses, caused by enemy carrier-borne aircraft and by lack of up-to-date radar in U-boats. He wanted specially trained air crews and suitable aircraft to work with the U-boats. Naval overall requirements in personnel revealed serious shortages. Preliminary trials of the new Walther U-boats with high underwater speed were promising.

46. Doenitz encouraged all technical developments in U-boats, acoustic torpedoes and radar. Although he was constantly in touch with Hitler particularly on the Italian situation after the invasion of Sicily, there is no evidence that Doenitz possessed or expounded views on the general strategic problems of the war. He confined himself almost entirely to the problems of U-boat operations, over which he retained the direct control which he had exercised in his previous post.

47. In August 1943 Doenitz discussed with the Chief of Staff of the G.A.F. plans for a new air mine offensive against the South-East coast of England, using a new firing mechanism for the mines. The extent of the operations must be limited because of insufficient air power. Doenitz also encouraged increased production of E-boats and increased operational use on the East and South-East coasts of England.

48. In September 1943 Hitler, encouraged by a recent slight revival of successes by U-boats in the North Atlantic, referred emphatically to U-boat warfare against shipping as being the only way of easing German difficulties in the prevailing general war situations.

49. At the end of 1943 Doenitz set up a Department of Scientific Research for the Navy; "to wrest from the enemy his lead in the field of physical science (particularly radar) is a matter of decisive importance". By this date the lead of the Allies in radar was so great that Doenitz's purpose remained unaccomplished.

## Phase V. Measures against Invasion — 1944.

50. In the last phase of war, Germany, deprived of the initiative, was forced on to the defensive on all fronts, and no longer had the resources of men or material necessary for defences let alone offence. She strove to make good her lack of these resources by the development of novel weapons in a desperate attempt to achieve technical supremacy despite her dwindling assets. To this phase belong the V-1 and V-2 and in the naval sphere the whole agglomeration of clock-work toys including the Biber and Molch midget U-boats, the one-man torpedo, explosive motor boats, swimming saboteurs and the rest of the paraphernalia entrusted to Vice-Admiral Heye to develop under the K.D.K.

51. Early in 1944 Doenitz gave his thoughts to measures for repelling Allied invasion in the West. German cruisers in the Baltic could not be transferred to the West, as their crews consisted of trainees for U-boats. As a result of experience in the invasion of Italy, Doenitz ordered the rapid construction of fifty midge U-boats, and expansion in the production of simple "oyster" mines for coastal defence. Various types and large numbers of midget U-boats were later given priority equal to that of normal U-boats, and by June 1944 over 17,000 naval officers and ratings had been earmarked for this new branch of the Navy. A detailed analysis of results obtained by this weapon up to the end of the war is not available. But the German records indicate

that its extensive development at a time of many other pressing claims on personnel and industry was attributable to Doenitz himself, and was not a result of the deliberations of the Naval Staff. When the invasion took place, the level of production of this weapon, and the state of training of the crews were not sufficient to have any serious influence on the course of operations.

52. Production was also behind with the anti-invasion ground-mine (a cheaply-built concrete sinker containing explosive) and the oyster mine was not yet available. It is stated by the Germans that at the time of the invasion only 30 per cent. of the planned defensive minefields had been laid. Delays were caused by shortage of mine-laying vessels and by growing difficulties in sea and land transport of the mines from the factories.

## After the Invasion.

53. Doenitz defined the principal task of the Navy as attacks on the Allies' supply lines and transports using all available means. The intensive air attacks to which German ships of all kinds were exposed hampered the execution of this task. There were not enough mine-sweepers to ensure freedom from mines for ships on passage between German and Dutch ports, at the very time when the Allies increased their air mining activity.

54. The story from now on shows rapid deterioration in the naval and general situation, and the scope of naval strategy recedes as the local tactical disasters multiply in every theatre of war. The Navy had to adapt its limited resources to the urgent problems of supply to isolated garrisons, protection of essential shipping, and co-operation with the retreating Armies in the East and West.

55. In one respect there was still hope for the Navy. The recent fitting of Schnorchel to some U-boats had proved an undoubted success, and had enabled the boats to operate close to the coastal shipping routes remaining submerged for very long periods and thus avoiding detection from the air. A programme for fitting this apparatus to all U-boats was put in hand. Moreover the new Walther boats promised to revolutionise U-boat warfare. It was claimed for these boats that they could proceed at 27 knots submerged and could reach Japan without ever needing to surface. In February, 1945, Doenitz told Hitler that the first boats would be in operation within two months. He reckoned without the Allied air offensive on the assembly yards in the West, and the Russian capture of the building yards in the East.

56. The U-boat as a weapon of offence certainly showed a revival in the closing months of the war, and its potential danger remained great until the end.

## The final stage.

57. The withdrawal of troops from East Prussia, the loss of Gdynia, and the threat to the Baltic training ground for U-boats imposed a severe strain on naval resources. A large proportion of the Navy's total personnel had remained locked up in the West when the German Armies were driven back to the Rhine. The Navy played a part in the delaying action in the Scheldt. The loss of U-boat bases in France, the uncertainty of the supplies to Norway, and the growing menace in the air, made the problem of U-boat bases and repair facilities ever more difficult. In the records of the almost daily meetings between Hitler and Doenitz in February and March, 1945, there is evidence that hopes of salvation, such as might come from the wonder U-boats, were as a straw to a drowning man. Perhaps the only satisfaction that Doenitz derived from the situation was the appreciation by Hitler of the work of the well-disciplined special brigades of naval ratings who had been sent to carry out demolitions at danger points on the crumbling Eastern front, and of the efficient arrangements for evacuating troops by sea from isolated East Prussia to the Western Baltic ports.

58. From the time of his appointment as C.-in-C. until the last moment Doenitz appeared to have the full confidence of the Fuehrer. He was made Chief Administrator for Northern Germany when the country was threatened with bisection, and in the last days he was appointed successor to the Chancellor.

# CONCLUSION.

59. The above brief survey of German naval strategy between 1939 and 1945 covers the more vital aspects of a wide subject. While Raeder was in office, there were many opportunities for influencing the course of strategy. The turn of the tide reduced these opportunities for his successor, who in any case showed no outstanding capacity for strategic problems.

60. In spite of heavy losses the German Navy could justify the large effort that was put into the U-boat arm by pointing to the destruction of shipping, which at its peak

came near to achieving decisive results and to the huge resources that the Allies were forced to devote to the building of ships and the protection of supply routes throughout the greater part of the war. That the German naval effort was not decisive must be attributed largely to Raeder, who held the highest office from 1928 to 1943. He failed to impress on either Hitler or the OKW that the success of a strategy involving world-wide operations depended at least as much on sea-power as on other factors. The naval aspect of strategy, both in the planning and the conduct of the war, was excessively subordinated to the continental aspect. But viewing this defect on the wider basis of the supreme direction of Germany's was, we find in the comprehensive contemporary archives an almost complete absence of references to joint strategic planning. This void is eloquent of a most serious weakness. It can be inferred that just as Hitler in matters of aggression strove to deal with one victim at a time, so in matters of military policy he often dealt with each of his advisers separately, and reserved to himself the right of absolute decision.

61. It is therefore idle to reflect that Germany's destiny after the outbreak of war might have assumed a different shape if, in the days of her ascendancy, she had utilised the sound strategic judgment of Raeder.

# APPENDIX XVIII.

# GERMAN U-BOAT STRATEGY IN THE WAR.

## INTRODUCTION.

*Appreciation by the U-Boat Command.*

That the German Navy was not prepared for war with England has already been remarked upon in the previous Appendix on German Naval Strategy. In March, 1939, Raeder explained to Senior Naval Officers and their Chiefs of Staff that the Fuehrer did not want war with England and therefore there was no need to prepare for it, and in July, 1939, a little more than a month before the outbreak of war Admiral Raeder reiterated this statement in a speech to U-Boat Officers at Swinemunde.

2. Nevertheless many German Naval Officers believed that German policy must eventually lead to conflict with England, and certain staff appreciations and plans were accordingly drawn up.

## The Basic Principles of U-Boat Warfare.

3. The German Staff appreciation was on the following lines: -

(i) England is dependent for her very existence on sea communications, these are vulnerable and must be attacked.

(ii) England's lead in the construction of surface warships, particularly of the heavy types, is such that even if Germany makes its maximum constructional effort British superiority cannot be overtaken in time to affect the outcome of the war.

(iii) Britain's sea communications must, therefore, be attacked by Cruiser Warfare, Raiders and U-Boats.

(iv) Of the above, the U-Boat is Germany's most effective weapon.

(v) The U-Boat brought Britain near to defeat in the War 1914-18, but was itself defeated by the introduction of the convoy system. "Concentrations of ships in convoy" must, therefore, be countered by "Concentrations of U-Boats".

(vi) Basically the U-Boat has undergone little change during the past 25 years, but great technical improvements have been made. The modern U-Boat is armed with better torpedoes having non-contact pistols and bubbleless ejection; it is capable of greater diving depths and has increased resistance to attack due to welded pressure hulls. It can also transmit and receive signals when submerged, and has been modified so that all U-Boats are now capable of laying mines.

(vii) A/S defence, on the other hand, has made no decisive progress since 1918.

(viii) The U-Boat, therefore, is not an obsolete but an efficient modern weapon. Produced in sufficient numbers it can make a decisive contribution to the war against Britain if its bases and departure routes can be sufficiently protected. Once at sea it can operate freely in spite of enemy Naval superiority in surface craft, but sufficient numbers of U-Boats are necessary if a decisive result is to be achieved.

## Conclusions of the U-Boat Command.

4. For the U-Boat to achieve success it was necessary for its personnel to have a firm faith in their U-Boats, to be well trained in individual and concentrated attack tactics in reconnaissance and in co-operation with aircraft which supplement the U-Boats' limited capabilities of reconnaissance.

5. Every effort must be concentrated on the technical development of the U-Boat and its equipment and on its production in sufficient numbers.

## The U-Boat Situation at the Outbreak of War.

6. The U-Boat Command entered the war with good morale and well-trained personnel. Training and technical standards were equal to the requirements of the duties

which had to be performed, but the number of U-Boats were quite inadequate for the task in hand. It was not until September, 1939, that the extension of the U-Boat Building Programme was energetically undertaken. It was later realised that with greater energy and bolder conception an even greater effort could have been made. British Merchant Shipping production was estimated by the German High Command at 100,000 tons per month.

## Under-Estimation of Allied Anti-Submarine (A/S) Effort.

7. Whereas the probability of Anti-Submarine (A/S) and Radar detection of U-Boats by surface ships was reasonably appreciated, the potential threat of radar detection by patrolling aircraft as it was eventually developed was not foreseen.

8. The foregoing shows the general lines of appreciation by the German Naval Staff, it is not clear, however, whether at any time before or during the early part of the war the decisive importance of the U-Boat offensive was properly recognised by the other branches of the German High Command.

# SEPTEMBER, 1939 TO APRIL, 1940.

9. When war with England became an actuality the programme for building a homogenous Fleet was dropped and only ships which were nearly ready were completed. A considerable increase in the U-Boat construction programme was ordered. Whereas previously the monthly output was only about 2 to 4 U-Boats, the new programme ordered in September, 1939, was intended to reach, in stages, 20 to 25 U-Boats a month.

10. The principal types of U-Boat with which Germany entered the war were the type VII of 517 tons carrying 12-14 torpedoes; the type IX of 740 tons and the small U-Boat of 250 tons which could only be used for training and coastal operations. In the opinion of the U-Boat Command the first possessed all the qualities necessary for successful U-Boat warfare: easy to handle, difficult to see at night, and yet having the necessary offensive strength and radius of action. The second type, though less handy to manoeuvre and more complicated to handle, had greater endurance and carried more torpedoes. Both types had proved their effectiveness in peace-time exercises.

11. A building time of some 21 months was envisaged for the U-Boats ordered in September, 1939. These boats, therefore, could not be counted on for operations for two years. As a result it seemed probable that the provision of a strong U-Boat Arm would be very late, if not too late, for the decisive prosecution of the U-Boat war. Despite the greater successes achieved in 1942 with the growing numbers of U-Boats, the average tonnage sunk by each U-Boat each day of 1942 was only about one tenth of that achieved in 1940.

## Early U-Boat Strategy.

12. At the outbreak of the war the 250-ton U-Boats, by reason of their small radius of action, operated only in the North Sea and the vicinity of the Orkneys. The 517-ton U-Boat operated off the West Coast of England. Improvements in the design of this type enabled it to operate as far from home as the North Coast of Spain, and the 740-ton U-Boat could operate off Gibraltar. Passage to and from the attacking areas was made round the Shetlands. Attempts to shorten the distance to the U-Boat-attacking areas by sending them through the Channel proved too costly, and after one or two attempts this route was abandoned.

## The Development of the Sink-at-Sight Policy.

13. In the early days when, despite the declaration of war by England and France, it was hoped to confine the war to Poland, considerable restrictions were placed on the operation of U-Boats. Later a Blockade Area round England was declared, in which all Merchant Ships could be attacked, and with the introduction of the Convoy System, U-Boats were given freedom of attack on all Merchant Ships under Warship escort.

## Early U-Boat Operations.

14. In the winter of 1939 the number of U-Boats at sea in operational areas never exceeded 10 and at times was no more than 2. To this period belong such operations as the penetrations of Scapa Flow, Moray Firth, the Firth of Forth, Shetland Passages, Loch Ewe and the Bristol Channel. These operations resulted in the sinking of the Battleship *Royal Oak*, damage to the Cruiser *Belfast* and to the Battleship *Nelson*. That they did not achieve greater success was attributed by the German Naval Staff to torpedo failures.

*Initial Successes of the Magnetic Mine*
*and Failure of the Magnetic Torpedo Pistol.*

15. These operations were carried out with a mixed outfit of mines and torpedoes. Whereas the Magnetic Mine proved itself effective in the first months of the war the reverse was true of the Magnetic Pistol. Torpedoes exploded before reaching the target or did not detonate at all. As Magnetic firing had been relied on, accurate depth keeping and contact firing had been neglected. These failures had a marked influence on the successes of the U-Boat Arm in the first months of the war, and robbed the U-Boats of successes which they would otherwise have gained during the Norwegian Campaign. The crews lost confidence in the weapon and the personal influence of the C.-in-C. U-Boats was necessary to restore their morale. It was not until long after that the technical faults of the torpedoes were ascertained and rectified.

*U-Boat Losses.*

16. Losses of U-Boats up to April 1940 were high in proportion to the number of U-Boats operating although British defence was still weak. This was due to the lack of war experience of the crews and to technical defects in the boats, such as faulty exhaust valves and the like which only became apparent under war conditions.

# APRIL 1940 – OCTOBER, 1940.

17. The occupation of the Biscay ports eliminated the long journeys of the U-Boats to and from their operational areas and made it necessary at this time for Germany to operate her U-Boats from Norwegian bases. The advantage of eliminating long journeys to and from their bases was seen immediately in the doubling of the number of U-Boats available in the actual operational areas. The war against shipping was increasingly successful until October 1940. Most of the British destroyers and Escort Vessels were either lost or under repair as a result of the Norwegian Campaign, and the evacuation from Dunkirk or tied to the South Coast of England by the threat of invasion. The U-Boats proceeding from the Biscay ports were quickly in contact with their targets, since they were able to operate close to the English approach Channels. The U-Boat losses were exceptionally small, technical defects were overcome and

torpedoes fitted only with impact pistols were used. U-Boats still operated singly as up to then there was no difficulty in finding suitable targets in the vital areas close to the English Coast.

# OCTOBER 1940 – DECEMBER 1941.

## *Introduction of U-Boat "Pack Tactics".*

18. From October 1940 the picture West of England began to change for the U-Boat Arm. For England the danger of invasion was over and escort vessels were once more available for A/S defence. The Royal Air Force was being used increasingly for the protection of the shipping routes and the Convoy System was becoming generally used. As a result it was becoming more difficult for U-Boats to operate close inshore and convoys were located less frequently. U-Boats were at sea for lengthy periods without sighting any shipping and the great successes of the summer came to an end. The U-Boat Commands decided, therefore, from October 1940 on the controlled operation of U-Boats at sea against convoys located by systematic search. This was called "pack tactics" which were developed in the knowledge that location would be the main problem in the U-Boat War as concentration of ships in convoys would make them more difficult to find. The organisation and control of the U-Boats was carried out by the U-Boat Command originally in Paris, but later transferred in November 1940 to Lorient. The first convoy attacks at the end of October 1940 succeeded with very good results, but the attacking U-Boats quickly exhausted their torpedoes so that after these short but successful operations they had to be withdrawn. As there were no replacements to relieve them, operations were not renewed till the beginning of December when further successful convoy attacks were made. These actions showed the German High Command that U-boat tactics were being developed on the right lines and that it was necessary to keep strict control of the boats until contact was made with the convoy and that thereafter the U-Boats must have complete freedom of action.

## *Successes of Night Attacks.*

19. It was further proved that attacks at night by surfaced U-Boats were the most successful. The U-Boat could get within firing range and deliver its attack more quickly

and certainly than if it attacked submerged by day. The U-Boat "Aces" of that time who developed this system of concentrated night attack were loud in the praises of the 517-ton U-Boat and did not wish to exchange them for the larger type.

## U-Boats Forced Further Afield. The Difficulty of Finding their Targets and the Need for Better Reconnaissance.

20. The winter of 1940 to 1941 revealed the further concentration of English shipping into convoy, and the continual extension of the English surface and air A/S defences which forced the U-boat dispositions further and further out into the Atlantic. Time was necessary, therefore, for concentrating the U-boats from their reconnaissance positions, if a successful attack on a convoy was to be launched. It was no longer any use locating a convoy about 24 hours before it ran under the English Coast as there was then not sufficient time to direct the other U-boats onto the target and carry out the attack. The U-boat itself with its limited range of vision was the worst possible medium of reconnaissance. The aircraft was therefore the vital and necessary comple-ment to the U-boat. That this was lacking was the fault of the High Command who in peace time had created a Naval Air Arm which in war time was incorporated in the Luftwaffe. The type of aircraft developed by the Luftwaffe was suitable for land war-fare but did not meet the needs of the Navy. Pressure exerted by the U-boat Command and representations to the Fuehrer in September 1940 resulted in a Squadron of long-range F.W. 200 being attached to the U-boat Arm based at Bordeaux. The result of this air co-operation was entirely unsatisfactory, as the personnel were inexperienced in navigation, ship recognition and naval co-operation generally. Owing to the limited range of the aircraft they could only operate on the English-Gibraltar convoy routes. On the main shipping routes in the North Atlantic U-boats still had to rely on their own reconnaissance. As a result of this lack of adequate air reconnaissance and as the new building programme had not yet materially increased the number of boats in oper-ation, in the year 1941 showed only very limited successes in Merchant Ship sinkings.

## Effect of Policy of United States.

21. For political reasons U-boats had been ordered to avoid under any circumstances attacks on American Merchant or Warships and U-boats were forbidden to operate west of Newfoundland. They were, therefore, unable to locate English bound convoys

close to their port of departure, e.g., near Halifax. Furthermore, the United States had declared the Western Hemisphere to be their Zone of protection, and although neutral had announced that they would attack any German warships in this area. The occupation of Iceland by the Americans early in 1941 and its use as a base for air reconnaissance increased the difficulties of passage through the Icelandic waters for the U-boats and foreshadowed more active participation by the United States.

22. The U-boat Arm was convinced, however, that its limited successes were only due to failure to find the enemy and that this would improve as soon as greater numbers of U-boats were available. They regarded the future with confidence.

## The Entry of Italy into the War.

23. After the conquest of France and the entry of Italy into the war in June 1940 and the opening of the North African Campaign a small number of U-boats were continually employed in the Mediterranean. Here conditions for U-boat operations were comparatively unfavourable and the U-boats achieved only limited successes although they did succeed in sinking the *Barham*.

## The Declaration of War on Russia.

24. The declaration of war on Russia had little immediate effect on the conduct of U-boat operations, except that it demanded a further dispersal of the U-boat effort, so as to attack the Arctic Convoys to Russia.

25. In the Black Sea the Russians possessed an overwhelming Naval superiority over the few Units of the Roumanian Navy. The latter was strengthened by six 250-ton German U-boats which were transported from Germany over land and by river and canal and by a number of landing craft and auxiliary vessels which were fitted out there. The Russian Black Sea Fleet remained, however, inactive.

## United States Enters the War.

26. The American declaration of war as a result of the Japanese attack on Pearl Harbour on the 7th December, 1941, came as a surprise to the German Naval Command although it had probably been clear that the eventual entry of the United States into the war was inevitable. The change brought about thereby at first simplified the

problem for the U-boat Command. The ban on operations in North-American waters was immediately lifted and in December, the only six U-boats then available for the purpose were equipped to operate in American waters. The total of U-boats available for service was still small and no large increase in the monthly rate of production could be expected until the spring of 1942.

## Early U-Boat Successes off the American Coast.

27. Though the number of U-boats operating off the American Coast were small, their successes were outstanding. The U-boat Commanders were experienced and the American defences were inadequate, undeveloped, and the personnel inexperienced. All available boats were therefore sent to this area in order to exploit to the full a favourable situation which was not expected to last for more than a few months. It did last, however, until the end of September 1942, and U-boat operations so far afield were fully justified by results, despite the long passages to and from their bases.

Even when conditions off the East Coast of America became relatively hazardous, an extension of operations into the less dangerous Caribbean area was again justified by the striking results which were achieved.

## Withdrawal from American Coast Waters.

28. Towards the latter part of 1942, when convoys had been effectively instituted in the Caribbean and on the East Coast of America, and when A/S measures in these areas had been increased and perfected, the U-boats once more moved on to the ocean trade routes, where their successes continued.

## Anglo-American Landings in North Africa — Concentration off Gibraltar and Decrease in the U-Boat Sinkings.

29. Although an Allied landing in North Africa had been to some extent foreseen by the German High Command, the Admiral commanding U-boats, though constantly pressed to do so, had refused to divert U-boats from their main task — the blockade of England — in order to intercept an attempted landing in North Africa until it was known that such an operation was in fact taking place. The landing, when it did take

place, came as a surprise. Every U-boat that could reach the scene of action within ten days was ordered there immediately. This resulted in a considerable reduction in the tonnage sunk which was not compensated by the sinkings off Gibraltar. Allied A/S measures, particularly from the air, in these waters were very effective and U-boat losses correspondingly high. The diversion of U-boats to the Mediterranean resulted in a shortage of boats in the Atlantic and a consequent reduction in the number of convoys sighted and attacked.

## Review of U-Boat War in 1942.

30. Although due to Allied counter-measures individual U-boats were only sinking one-tenth of that accounted for by individual U-boats in 1940, 1942 was the most critical year of the U-boat war so far as the Allies were concerned. It is clear, therefore, that had Germany had sufficient number of U-boats to profit by Allied unpreparedness in 1940 they might have won the Battle of the Atlantic.

31. By November 1942 Allied shipping losses by U-boat action had reached almost 80 per cent. of their final total, whereas U-boat losses were by then not 19 per cent. of the total lost throughout the war. At this time new Allied shipping was hardly sufficient to make good current losses, whereas the number of U-boats was increasing rapidly.

32. The aircraft threat to surfaced U-boats was developing, but aircraft radar had not yet been perfected. Evasive routeing had become increasingly successful, but, speaking generally, U-boat attack in 1942 was superior to the defences. The increased number of boats operating facilitated the location of convoys, and U-boats operating on the surface were not detected in sufficient time to enable convoys to avoid them.

33. Meanwhile, however, Allied counter-measures were gradually being perfected, and as will be seen they eventually gained the upper hand in the struggle, but only in the nick of time.

## U-Boat Operations in early 1943.

34. Although in January/February 1943 there had been a marked falling off in the number of convoys located, the prospect that surfaced tactics against convoys might come to an end did not appear immediate. The number of U-boats produced was

steadily rising and the number operating in the Atlantic progressively increased despite diversion to the Mediterranean, and to the Arctic for attack on Russian-bound convoys. In March 1943 a satisfactory number of convoys were sighted and some of the most successful convoy attacks of the war were fought. The system of controlling the U-boats from Headquarters situated on shore had been perfected. By this means unrestricted W.T. communication was possible without necessitating the U-boat breaking wireless silence except for the briefest signals. It was at this time that the U-boat successes reached their peak. The number of U-boats operating was continually increasing and losses were slight. The range of action of all types of U-boat had been considerably extended by the use of supply U-boats from which about 10 operational U-boats could draw supplies of fuel and provisions and thus extend their period of patrol in the attack area without returning to their bases. Surface tankers were also used for maintaining U-boats in the more distant areas.

35. The protection of the U-boat shelters in the Biscay ports had rendered them immune from bombing attacks so that the repair and maintenance of U-boats returned from patrol could be satisfactorily carried out.

36. Great strides had also been made in the development of U-boat torpedoes. The circling and zig-zag torpedoes had improved the percentages of hits on ships in convoy and the acoustic torpedo was coming into production whereby escort vessels about to attack a submerged submarine could themselves be attacked without the U-boat surfacing. Although anxiety was felt about the development of enemy air support over the Atlantic, the advantages mentioned above gave reason for expectation of the satisfactory continuance of U-boat operations.

## Co-operation with Japan.

37. Owing to the great distance separating the European and Far Eastern theatres of war, co-operation between the German Naval Staff and the Japanese Admiralty was at first limited mainly to the exchange of information and war experience through small Naval liaison staffs. The rapid advance of the Japanese to the edge of the Indian Ocean made a measure of direct co-operation possible. In order to avoid mutual interference the meridian of 70° East was fixed as the dividing line of the respective operational areas. It was incumbent upon each partner to obtain the other's approval before crossing the line.

38. The establishment of Penang as a German U-boat base enabled the Japanese demands for increased co-operation to be met to a considerable extent.

## *Operations Against Arctic Convoys.*

39. The Anglo-American convoys to Murmansk and Archangel, which had now been instituted, presented an objective of strategic importance against which U-boats from Norwegian bases were operated in conjunction with surface forces and aircraft. Furthermore, U-boats were employed on mining the Channels connecting the Barents Sea with the Kara Sea and the approaches to the Kola Inlet.

## *Allied Mining Offensive.*

40. The Allied air-borne offensive was at this time becoming more and more intensive in the coastal waters of the Bay of Biscay, the Channel and the North Sea, and particularly in the shallow waters of the Western Baltic and the Baltic approaches. It was only for short periods when new types of mines were employed that the German Naval Command was unable, generally speaking, to counter this threat, but only at the cost of diverting an ever increasing amount of man-power and material to the defensive task of mine clearance. It was not until the winter of 1944-45 that the cumulative effect of the mining offensive began to be felt, and really serious difficulties were encountered, particularly delays in the trials and working up of the new U-boat types which ultimately found themselves so congested in the Baltic that they had considerably to curtail their normal programmes.

41. Although in March, April and even September 1943, successful convoy attacks were still being carried out, by May it was clear that the Allied air strength in the Atlantic, not only of long-distance aircraft, but also of carrier-borne aircraft, had increased enormously. Of even greater consequence, however, was the fact that U-boats could be located at a great distance by Allied radar, without previous warning on the search receivers with which U-boats had now been fitted. Their location was followed by a heavy attack from surface ships and aircraft before the U-boat had sighted the convoy. If, in spite of this, a convoy was sighted, the fire power of the convoy and its escorting aircraft forced the U-boat to submerge before it could attack. U-boat losses, which had previously been some 13 per cent. of all the boats at sea, rose rapidly up to 50 per cent. In May 1943 alone, 43 U-boats were lost. These losses were

not only suffered in convoy attacks but everywhere at sea. There was no part of the Atlantic where boats were safe from being located by day and by night by aircraft. The U-boat approaches to the Bay of Biscay were continually patrolled and U-boat losses in these areas were particularly high.

## German Counter-Measures.

42. Under these circumstances the previous method of surfaced attack on the convoy could no longer be contained. U-boat successes in the Western Atlantic had also considerably diminished. Counter-measures against the increased air threat were started with all speed: -

(1) To produce as quickly as possible a new U-boat which could operate and attack successfully without ever surfacing;

(2) Until these new boats are ready for operations, to make every possible alteration to the existing U-boats so that they could operate despite the enormous radar superiority and air power of the Allies.

## Appointment of Doentiz to the Supreme Command of the Navy.

43. On the 30th January, 1943, Commander-in-Chief, U-Boats, had been appointed Supreme Commander of the Navy. He was, therefore, in a position to deal personally and energetically with these important problems of naval warfare. By this time, too, the whole of German industry had been placed under the direction of the Armament Minister, Speer. He was given the order to produce with all speed the new type 21 and type 23 U-boats. By means of increased battery capacity and improved streamline, there boats were designed to give a submerged speed nearly twice that of the normal types. Their introduction was in the nature of a stop-gap until the new Hydrogen-Peroxide (Ingolin) propelled "Walther" U-boats could be produced.

44. At the same time the defensive armament of the old type U-boats was improved against aerial attack by the increase in their A.A. armament. This measure succeeded by September 1943 in reducing the number of losses as compared with the month of May 1943.

45. It was finally clear, despite the attack in September 1943, that surfaced warfare for U-boats had come to an end. It was now a matter of filling in time till the new types could be ready for action. The Schnorchel, whereby U-boats were enabled to remain continually submerged without having to surface to charge their batteries, was introduced at this time. In the months after September 1943, when U-boat warfare was achieving little success and sustaining high losses, the U-boats continued to operate with the object of forcing the Allies to maintain constant reconnaissance in the air and on the sea, and thereby divert effort which would otherwise have been available in other theatres of operation. During the summer of 1944 the Schnorchel experiments were finished and a start was made in installing the gear. The boats so fitted did not need to surface at all, and the U-boat losses dropped suddenly by more than half. Virtually no boats on passage to or from their operational area were lost. By its use, U-boats could operate again the focal areas close to the coast which had been barred to the U-boats even in 1939 and 1940, when the defences were at their weakest. The first U-boats fitted with Schnorchel were ready at the beginning of the Invasion and were used between the Isle of Wight and the Mouth of the Seine where they operated successfully considering the difficult conditions produced by strong currents, shallow water, powerful fighter and radar defences.

## *Withdrawal in Russia and loss of Balkans and Rumania.*

46. The loss of the Rumanian oil reduced the already small fuel supply of the German forces and led, in the Navy, to a strict reduction in consumption. The fuel necessary for the U-boat war, however, remained unreduced.

In the Baltic, the retreat of the northern army group from Leningrad to the Narva position in January 1944, made the blockade of the inner gulf of Finland very difficult, but it was continued without reduction until the Autumn of 1944. The Anglo-American aerial offensive in the Baltic became increasingly heavy during 1944, but by energetic counter-measures the essential areas were kept free from mines.

## *Invasion of France.*

47. The loss of France was a set-back of the utmost gravity for the conduct of the U-boat war, all the strategic advantages arising from the possession of the Biscay ports were lost in one blow. The U-boats had to fall back on the Norwegian and home bases.

The long passage swallowed up a large part of the boats' operating time, and as previously mentioned it had to be made submerged.

Besides the set-backs in other theatres already dealt with the increased Allied air offensive became more and more effective. The destruction of industrial installations caused frequent interruptions in the production of armaments. Damaged communications caused widespread traffic hold ups which seriously hampered the transport of material and supplies. By concentrating on the vital necessities, however, it was still possible to keep production and transport going and to meet essential commitments.

## Construction of Prefabricated U-Boats.

48. In the meantime, during 1944 the construction of U-boat types 21 and 23 was being pressed on with all vigour. As soon as the constructional plans were completed the boats were put into production. The construction of engines was turned over to industries widely spread throughout Germany. The hulls of the boats themselves were manufactured in sections inland and then transported to the building yards for assembly. In this manner in spite of the heavy air attacks on German industry the production figures planned were on the whole maintained up to the end of 1944. In spite of intensified bombing, at the beginning of 1945 there were already a considerable number of both new types of boat in commission.

## First Operations by Prefabricated U-Boats.

49. In March 1945, several type 23 boats were for the first time sent to operate off the English East coast. Operations confirmed to the full the hopes that had been entertained. By virtue of their high submerged speed, attack and subsequent withdrawal could be carried out effectively and without damage. Out of seven trips, of which five proved successful, no boats were lost in spite of the strongest opposition. The U-boat personnel had great confidence in the new types and a progressively increasing number of boats were to be operated in the coming months. It was now expected that the U-boat war would develop into a new phase. Considerable successes had already been achieved by old type boats fitted with Schnorchel on operations of long duration without a single surfacing being necessary. The strain on crews who remained up to 70 days submerged proved surprisingly small, but the most important

result was the removal of the continual nervous tension in U-boat crews caused by attacks by aircraft.

Type 21, with its great range of some 22,000 miles, was capable of operating in all the important hunting areas without ever surfacing.

This development of the German U-boat war was, however, cut short by the German capitulation.

## *Summary of Results.*

50. Germany commenced the war with 60 U-boats. By the end of the war she had completed a further 1,110 U-boats. They sank over 14 million tons of Allied shipping, and a large number of Allied warships. The most critical year for the Allies was 1942, after that they gradually gained the ascendancy in the struggle, and by the end of the war they had destroyed 782 U-boats and 30,000 men out of the 38,000 in the U-boat arm had lost their lives.

# APPENDIX XIX.

# GERMAN AIR STRATEGY.

## The German Conception of Air Power.

At the outbreak of war in September 1939 the German Air Force mustered some 3,650 first-line aircraft of which approximately one-third were long-range bombers. During the formative years of the Luftwaffe, *i.e.*, from the appointment of General Leutnant Wever as Chief of Air Staff in 1934, the development of the idea of strategic air warfare was certainly uppermost in the minds of the German General Staff and the Supreme Command; Goering and Wever undoubtedly favoured the development of the G.A.F. on strategic lines and as a direct result of this belief the G.A.F. was organised as an independent arm with emphasis on the formation of long-range bombers for strategic employment.

2. Reliance was placed on their high speed enabling them to outdistance the types of fighters then available to oppose them and thus to be able to dispense with strong fighter cover. The experiences of the Spanish Civil War, coupled with the development of the conception of the "Blitzkrieg", resulted, however, in increasing attention being given to the employment of the Air Force as a close support arm for the Army, the vulnerability of the German bombers being marked even with the inferior types of fighters which they then encountered; it must be remembered that, apart from Goering, the senior officers of the G.A.F. carried little weight in High Command circles dominated as they were by powerful personalities strong in the Army tradition. Thus it came about that in the campaigns against Poland and Norway the whole of the air forces employed were used in tactical close support, and the Battle of France, to which virtually all available elements of the G.A.F. were committed, did nothing

to cast doubt on High Command policy; the isolated attacks on factories in Warsaw, Paris and Marseilles may be regarded perhaps as strategic operations, but there is no question of the employment of the G.A.F. bomber arm in these campaigns on anything approaching the Allied conception of strategic bombing.

3. So long as the Germans were fighting against weak nations or enjoying overwhelming superiority it may be said that their air strategy as adopted justified itself by results. Their great failure lay in the incredible optimism and over-confidence in high places, particularly on the part of Hitler himself and his political entourage, which could envisage nothing but easily-won success and was incapable of foreseeing the strength and resources of the Powers to which they became progressively opposed, in what they refused to regard as a long-term struggle. So far as the G.A.F. is concerned, it cannot be said, however, that responsible officers on the Air Staff were unaware of the consequences of war with the Western Powers and Field-Marshal Milch, Inspector-General of the G.A.F., claims to have said in 1939: "We should be crazy to enter into a war at all now". He realised fully that Germany was in no way ready for such a war either as regards technical equipment or training, but the strained relations between Milch and Goering had made it impossible for his views to find support, quite apart from the fact that Hitler himself was totally unreceptive to such opinions although holding Milch in considerable esteem.

## The Battle of Britain and its Consequences.

4. With the fall of France, German air strategy found itself confronted with the problem of defeating the R.A.F. in order to establish the necessary air supremacy as a prelude to the invasion of Britain. The problem differed in every respect from those which had hitherto been met so successfully and the German Air Staff had to face the fact that, owing to their lack of foresight, they had failed to envisage the strategic use of air power in such circumstances, nor had their bombers and fighter crews the necessary training and experience to operate efficiently under such conditions. With the failure to bring the R.A.F. to battle in large-scale fighter sweeps and of the subsequent attempt to destroy the R.A.F. on the ground, mass daylight bombing raids on Southern England and London brought out the resulting weaknesses in the G.A.F., first by demonstrating the numerical inadequacy of the fighter force to provide escort, now realised as essential, on the scale required, due also partly to their

lack of range, and secondly, by the tactical mis-employment of the fighters, as close escort at the insistent demand of Goering and the bomber units. This rendered the effective carrying out of their duties almost impossible. Add to this the absence of any adequate system of fighter control and the poor planning of operations as a whole, and a major failure of German air strategy becomes apparent.

5. With the failure to achieve victory in the Battle of Britain, the German High Command had to find an alternative means of eliminating Britain and adopted a pol icy of strategic night bombing and blockade, for neither of which the High Command was prepared. The strength of the long-range bomber force (now mounting to some 1,300 aircraft) was such, however, that a formidable scale of attack could be mounted and sustained, and, with increasing experience and the adoption of navigational aids, much heavy damage was inflicted during the eight months' long attack maintained between September 1940 and May 1941.

## Naval Air Strategy.

6. Most of the G.A.F. operational activity from the end of the Polish campaign to the attack on Norway consisted of anti-shipping operations (including reconnaissance) over the North Sea and off the East Coast of Britain; this activity comprised minelaying and isolated attacks on the Firth of Forth, Scapa Flow, &c., by long-range bomber units specially trained for such operations. With the fall of France, these forces were further strengthened by the employment of the long-range F.W. 200's operating from the West Coast of France and Norway against shipping in the Atlantic, supplemented by land-based long-range bomber types in conjunction with long-range bomber units engaged on minelaying and torpedo operations. The combined effect of these forces was such as to cause grave difficulties to shipping at almost all points round the British coast during the winter of 1940-41, but remained effective only so long as German air supremacy was maintained in British home waters.

7. From 1941 onwards the German anti-shipping forces consisted for the most part of long-range reconnaissance aircraft based in Western France, in Norway primarily for U-boat co-operation, and for general purposes in the Mediterranean, together with a land-based torpedo bomber force of some 100 long-range bomber type aircraft. During 1941 and 1942 the latter force was strategically based partly in North Norway, where it constituted a major threat to the convoy route to North Russia, in

the Central Mediterranean and in the Black Sea. The effects of this relatively small force on Allied naval strategy and commitments were greatly disproportionate to its size, and the failure to develop this arm more vigorously can only be ascribed to the general subordination of the Luftwaffe as a whole to military requirements in the field, and to the fact that the bomber force could be, and frequently was, used to supplement the specialist units against shipping, *e.g.*, in the Mediterranean.

8. While it is true that in anticipation of the Allied landing in the West, a belated attempt was made in 1943 to expand the specialist anti-shipping forces by the development of very long-range reconnaissance aircraft, the conversion of further bomber units to torpedo operations and the introduction of other units operating with guided missiles, the decline of the G.A.F. had already set in and the anti-shipping force, hampered by lack of training and fuel shortages, became increasingly ineffective against growing Allied air supremacy. When the time came, its efforts against the landing forces off the Normandy beachhead resulted in utter fiasco and the anti-shipping force passed into oblivion. As in other matters, the recognition of the inestimable value of strong and effective naval co-operation came too late for the waning ability of Germany to meet her mounting commitments and steadily deteriorating strategic situation.

## Consequences of the Development in the War Situation on the Southern and Eastern Fronts.

9. So far, though they had been unable to win the vital Battle of Britain, German air supremacy in other respects was undisputed with its forces concentrated in a single main theatre of war. From the Spring of 1941 onwards, the whole situation radically changed with the extension of the war first to the Balkans and Mediterranean, culminating in the brilliant, though expensive, capture of Crete by air-borne forces, and subsequently against Russia. In both these theatres the overwhelming employment of air power again brought dazzling results with the Luftwaffe again committed to the close support of the army; once again the rapid success so nearly achieved against Russia blinded Hitler and his staff to the consequences of such a vast extension of the war for which the resources of the G.A.F. no longer remained adequate. Inevitably a division of German air strength became necessary, with no less than 50 per cent. of it employed on the Eastern front. Moreover, as the year went on, the increasing effect of R.A.F. bombing began to call for the build-up of a night-fighter force to supplement the anti-aircraft defences.

10. Apart from the division of forces to meet excessive commitments, German air strategy in the first six months of the campaign against Russia did more than anything else to bring about the ruin of the Luftwaffe. The bomber force, after eight months' strategic bombing operations by night against Britain and at the peak of its efficiency, was sacrificed to the tactical support of the army, and experienced crews and vast numbers of aircraft were frittered away in low-level daylight close support operations against strong ground defences. Similarly, the close support forces proper, consisting of dive bombers and fighters, were ruthlessly employed on the most intensive scale with little or no respite up to the end of the year, leaving them in a state of virtual exhaustion.

11. The turn of the year 1941-42 saw a further increase in German air commitments with the development of operations in the Mediterranean; this led to the doubling of G.A.F. strength in that theatre and entailed a withdrawal of Luftflotte 2 from the Eastern Front. Yet at this time G.A.F. strength had declined, reflecting the heavy wastage in the East, and most significantly aircraft production had failed to show any increase and, in fact, remained at the end of 1941 substantially at the same level as in 1940; nor, apart from the introduction of the F.W.190 confined to the Western Front, was there any sign of new and improved types of aircraft coming forward to maintain the quality of technical equipment.

## Strategic Advantages of Mobility.

12. Overburdened as the G.A.F. was with its mounting commitments, further increased by the entry of the United States into the war, to an appreciable extent it was still possible at this stage to offset its numerical inadequacy for its tasks by virtue of the great degree of mobility which existed in all categories. While this outstanding feature of the G.A.F. was of particular importance tactically in the spaces of the Eastern Front, strategically also with the aid of numerous first-class airfields in Central and Western Europe, it was possible to re-deploy all categories, and notably the long-range bombers, at extremely short notice from one theatre to another as the situation required. Thus, until the advent of overwhelming Allied air superiority from the end of 1942 onwards, formidable German striking power in relation to the opposing forces could always be shifted with great rapidity to reinforce any one particular theatre, although adequate air strength in all could not be maintained simultaneously.

## *1942.*

13. The dominant features during 1942 were the increasing G.A.F. commitment on the Western Front with the arrival in due course of the United States Bomber Force, coupled with the need for reinforcing the night-fighter defence of Germany, the maintenance of air strength in the Mediterranean at 700-800 aircraft in an effort to knock out Malta and so close the sea-route, and concentration of all other available forces to support the campaign in Russia, where the bulk was committed to the Southern Front. Once again, notwithstanding the experiences of 1941, German strategy was to commit the G.A.F. wholesale to the assault on Stalingrad and the Caucasus. The ruthless employment of the G.A.F. in the Stalingrad operations, and more particularly its deliberate sacrifice to Hitler's determination to relieve the surrounded 6th Army, had the most adverse and far-reaching effects on the long-range bomber arm from which it was never to recover. This is accounted for by the fact that the advance training establishments were stripped of aircraft and crews for supply duties in which crippling losses were incurred and which German resources were never able subsequently to make good; later in 1943, fuel shortages, already becoming felt in 1942 were to restrict training and the need for increased fighter production, together with the growing allocation of long-range bomber types to the night-fighter force, spelt the doom of the long-range bombers as a strategic force, and substantially reduced their effectiveness for other types of operations.

## *The Turn of the Tide.*

14. The Stalingrad *débâcle* and the German defeat of El Alamein, followed by the Allied landing in North Africa, marked the turning-point of the war and threw German strategy as a whole on the defensive; it also brought the German Air Staff face to face with a fundamental change in the air situation, one of attrition which they had no resources to meet, and which the mobility of the G.A.F. could no longer counter. Moreover, German overall air strength at the turn of the year 1942-43 had fallen to the low level of less than 4,000 aircraft.

15. Not only did the Mediterranean theatre, with the palpable threat of an Allied lodgement in Southern Europe, demand still greater German air strength to be committed to that area; the development of the Allied heavy bomber offensive against Germany from British bases both by day and by night, so long threatened and

foreseen, also began to materialise and, steadily growing in weight, could only be met by the withdrawal of fighter forces from the operational theatres and a further heavy expansion of the night-fighter arm. This situation, which was to be increasingly a dilemma for the German Air Staff, called for a rapid expansion in fighter output and a striking recovery in total air strength was made to some 6,000 aircraft by June 1943, which, however, could not be maintained due primarily to heavy losses in the Mediterranean.

16. Henceforth German air strategy was to be governed exclusively by the vital need for defence of the Reich behind which lay the threat of the Allied invasion in the West; with more space to lose in the East, the G.A.F. commitments against Russia had in the circumstances inevitably to be reduced and from the end of 1942, on Hitler's express orders, only obsolete or obsolescent aircraft were in the main employed on that front. In the Mediterranean, following the collapse of Italy and the severe wastage suffered by the Luftwaffe in the process, German air strategy had to be content with no more than a small token force to support the Italian campaign, a situation which continued up to the conclusion of hostilities. The defence of Southern Germany, Austria and Hungary and the Balkans against bombing from Italian bases effectively pinned down such fighter forces as might have been available for the support of the front and thus added to the already formidable problem of defence of the contracting German perimeter.

17. Perhaps the last success which the Germans can claim in the strategic employment of the G.A.F. occurred in the autumn of 1943, when with limited forces transferred from the Russian Front local air supremacy was made possible to support the recapture of Cos and Leros in the Eastern Mediterranean. The air operations supporting this were in the true model of 1940 and 1941 and demonstrated once again the decisive value of air supremacy in attaining strategic objectives.

## The Mounting Problem of Defence.

18. The year 1944 was to be one of growing frustration for the G.A.F. with defence as the inevitable key-note of its strategy. During the first six months of the year no less than 75 per cent. of the fighter forces were tied down in defence of the Reich against the "round the clock" Allied bomber offensive accompanied by long-range fighter escort by day. Fighter production in consequence became of paramount importance

and in a desperate and hopelessly belated effort to meet this situation all available resources were devoted to this end; this led, on the one hand, to the setting up of the Jaegerstab and the conversion of all available aircraft production resources, under Speer's direction, to the output of fighters and, on the other, to the complete elimination of the bomber arm. The latter, after a brief and ineffective return to strategic bombing against London in February 1944, followed by an intensive period of sea-mining operations productive of no result comparable to the effort expended for some two months following the Allied landings in France, finally disappeared from the scene of active air operations.

## *The Final Stages.*

19. From then onwards until the capitulation, German air strategy, in so far as it can be said to have existed at all, lay exclusively with fighter defence. Notwithstanding the crippled condition of the fighter force, following the retreat to the Rhine, a surprising recovery in strength took place during the autumn of 1944, directly reflecting the remarkable success attained in the reorganisation and concentration on fighter production, which reached a new peak of nearly 2,000 aircraft by the end of the year. But numbers were no longer sufficient, and other factors, notably the acute shortage of fuel caused by Allied strategic bombing and the loss of Roumanian oil, imposed serious handicaps both on training and operational activity, thus limiting the effective employment of the substantial force available. A final all-out attack by the fighter force against Allied airfields in the West on the 1st January, 1945, caused crushing losses both of aircraft and particularly of irreplaceable experienced pilots.

20. From the autumn of 1944 onwards the night fighter arm remained the only element of the G.A.F. still retaining anything of its former efficiency; extremely well equipped and with abundance of crews of long-standing experience, this force alone appeared capable of effective employment against Allied bombers. But with the loss of forward radar and reporting systems in the West, the relentless improvement in British bombing technique and equipment, and hampered by lack of fuel, the night fighter force also could no longer play its part against the overwhelming strength pitted against it, and the final bankruptcy of the G.A.F. became inevitable.

## The Failure of Jet Aircraft.

21. The jet-propelled aircraft afforded the Germans the only hope that they might at the eleventh hour yet revolutionise air strategy. The primary jet-propelled aircraft were the Me. 262, Ar. 234 and to a much lesser extent the Me. 163. These came into front-line use in the late summer and autumn of 1944 (the Volksjaeger He. 162 and other similar types never came into effective operational employment). Here again the deliberate interference of Hitler in German air-staff plans led to these aircraft, with their valuable characteristics as fighters, being mainly employed initially as bomber-aircraft, for which they were in no way suited; although this decision was reversed in January 1945, the effect of bombing of production centres and communications rendered impossible the development of the jet force to any appreciable size (some 250 aircraft being available in the concluding stages of the war) in spite of the most determined efforts to concentrate on their production to the exclusion even of normal fighter types.

## Conclusion.

22. It is undoubtedly a fact that during the last six months of the war the relations between Hitler and the air staff increasingly deteriorated and, with the already long-standing eclipse of Goering, the air staff became more and more unable either to exert their influence in the necessary quarters or to pursue policies based on their own judgment in the light of operational experience. Even if the German air staff had been right in their opinions at all material stages of the war (and there is reason to believe that they were frequently aware of the errors committed in the employment of the G.A.F.), the failure of German air strategy was part and parcel of the failure of German military strategy as a whole, the result of the blind optimism and confidence of Hitler and his entourage in final victory, and their wilful refusal to foresee and prepare against the consequences of military commitments undertaken far beyond their resources. The days of their own air supremacy had shown how vital a factor it was under the existing conditions of war, and the failure to build up German air power on a scale commensurate with their military commitments, even at the expense of other arms, played a leading part in the down-fall of Hitler's Reich.

# *Notes*

## Introduction

1　See Donald McLachlan, *Room 39: Naval Intelligence in Action, 1939–45* (London: Weidenfeld & Nicolson, 1968), p. 248, and Percy Cradock, *Know Your Enemy: How the Joint Intelligence Committee Saw the World* (London: John Murray, 2002), p. 302.

2　TNA CAB 146/497, J.I.C. (46) 33 (Final), 'Some Weaknesses in German Strategy and Organisation, 1933–1945', 20 October 1946.

3　Gill Bennett, *Churchill's Man of Mystery: Desmond Morton and the World of Intelligence* (Abingdon, Oxon: Routledge, 2007), p. 160.

4　See F. H. Hinsley et al., *British Intelligence in the Second World War: Its Influence on Strategy and Operations*, volume I (London: HMSO, 1979), p. 160 and Percy Cradock, *Know Your Enemy: How the Joint Intelligence Committee Saw the World* (London: John Murray, 2002), pp. 7–11.

5　TNA CAB 146/498, 'MI14 Draft Papers and Lists Prepared for the Chiefs of Staff Committee Report (JIC (46) 33)', July 1945.

6　TNA WO 208/5568, 'War Diary: Directorate of Military Intelligence', 'M.I.3.', Appendix 3.

7　Noel Annan, *Changing Enemies: The Defeat and Regeneration of Germany* (London: Harper Collins, 1995), p. 2.

8　The obituary of Lord Annan, *The Daily Telegraph*, 24 February 2000.

9　TNA CAB 146/497, J.I.C. (46) 33 (Final), 'Some Weaknesses in German Strategy and Organisation, 1933–1945', 20 October 1946, pp. ii–iii.

10　Richard Overy, *Why the Allies Won* (London: Jonathan Cape, 1995).

11　See Patrick Howarth's *Intelligence Chief Extraordinary: The Life of the Ninth Duke of Portland* (London: The Bodley Head, 1986), p. 201.

12　*Codebreakers: The Inside Story of Bletchley Park*, edited by F. H. Hinsley and Alan Stripp (Oxford: Oxford University Press, 1993), pp. 11–13.

13　Richard Overy, *Why the Allies Won* (London: Jonathan Cape, 1995), pp. xi–xii.

14　Sir Michael Howard, *Captain Professor: A Life in War and Peace* (London: Continuum, 2006), p. 188.

15 TNA CAB 146/497, J.I.C. (46) 33 (Final), 'Some Weaknesses in German Strategy and Organisation, 1933–1945', 20 October 1946, p. iii.

16 Ibid.

17 Michael Howard, *British Intelligence in the Second World War: Strategic Deception*, volume V (London: HMSO, 1990), p. 46.

18 To date, Dick White is the only figure to have been both Director-General of the Security Service, MI5, and Chief of SIS. See Keith Jeffery, *MI6: The History of the Secret Intelligence Service, 1909–1949* (London: Bloomsbury, 2010), p. 749.

19 H. R. Trevor-Roper, *The Last Days of Hitler* (London: Macmillan & Co, 1947).

20 Noel Annan, *Our Age: A Portrait of a Generation* (London: Weidenfeld & Nicolson, 1990), p. 201.

21 TNA FO 1110/220, 'Proposed Visit to UK by Dr Andrews of Logistics Division – Psychological Warfare', 18 March 1949, p. 3.

22 *Hitler's War Directives, 1939–1945*, edited by H. R. Trevor-Roper (Edinburgh: Birlinn Ltd, 2004), p. 13.

23 Wilhelm Diest et al., *Germany and the Second World War: The Build-up of German Aggression*, volume I (Oxford: Clarendon Press, 1990), p. 8.

24 Horst Boog et al., *Germany and the Second World War: The Global War: Widening of the Conflict into a World War and the Shift of the Initiative, 1941–1943*, volume VI (Oxford: Clarendon Press, 2001), p. 5.

25 TNA CAB 146/497, J.I.C. (46) 33 (Final), 'Some Weaknesses in German Strategy and Organisation, 1933–1945', 20 October 1946, pp. 23–7.

26 See in particular Fritz Redlich, *Hitler: Diagnosis of a Destructive Prophet* (Oxford: Oxford University Press, 1999); David Owen, *In Sickness and in Power: Illness in Heads of Government during the Last 100 Years* (London: Methuen, 2008); and *The Hitler Book: The Secret Dossier Prepared for Stalin from the Interrogations of Hitler's Closest Personal Aides*, edited by Henrik Eberle and Matthias Uhl (London: John Murray, 2005).

27 TNA CAB 146/497, J.I.C. (46) 33 (Final), 'Some Weaknesses in German Strategy and Organisation, 1933–1945', 20 October 1946, p. 23.

28 Ibid., p. 24.

29 See TNA CAB 81/95 – CAB 81/129, 'War Cabinet and Cabinet: Committees and Sub-Committees of the Chiefs of Staff Committee: Minutes and Papers'.

30 TNA CAB 146/497, J.I.C. (46) 33 (Final), 'Some Weaknesses in German Strategy and Organisation, 1933–1945', 20 October 1946, p. 42.

31 Ibid.

32 Ibid., p. 23.

33 Henry A. Murray, 'Analysis of the Personality of Adolph Hitler With Predictions of His Future Behaviour and Suggestions for Dealing with Him Now and After Germany's Surrender', OSS Confidential, No. 3 of 30, October 1943, Cornell University Law Library, Donovan Nuremberg Trials Collection.

34 Walter C. Langer, 'A Psychological Analysis of Adolph Hitler: His Life and Legend', October 1943, RG 263, the Records of the Central Intelligence Agency,

US National Archives and Records Administration, Washington DC. See also Walter C. Langer, *The Mind of Adolf Hitler: The Secret Wartime Report* (New York: Basic Books Inc, 1972).

35 David Jablonsky, *Churchill and Hitler: Essays on the Political-Military Direction of Total War* (London: Frank Cass, 1993), p. 237.

36 Fritz Redlich, *Hitler: Diagnosis of a Destructive Prophet* (Oxford: Oxford University Press, 1999).

37 Ibid., p. xi.

38 Lord Moran, *Churchill: The Struggle for Survival* (London: Constable, 1966).

39 Hugh Trevor-Roper, *The Last Days of Hitler* (London: Macmillan & Co Ltd, 1947), pp. 65–6.

40 *The Wicked Wit of Winston Churchill*, edited by Dominique Enright (London: Michael O'Mara Books Ltd, 2001), p. 111.

41 Ian Kershaw, *Hitler, 1936–1945: Nemesis* (London: Allen Lane, 2000), p. 411.

42 Ibid., p. 612.

43 Ibid.

44 David Owen, *In Sickness and in Power: Illness in Heads of Government during the Last 100 Years* (London: Methuen, 2008), p. 34.

45 Fritz Redlich, *Hitler: Diagnosis of a Destructive Prophet* (Oxford: Oxford University Press, 1999), p. 243.

46 Ibid., p. 239.

47 Ibid., p. 243.

48 Ibid.

49 David Owen, *In Sickness and in Power: Illness in Heads of Government during the Last 100 Years* (London: Methuen, 2008), p. 27.

50 Ibid., p. 35.

51 Fritz Redlich, *Hitler: Diagnosis of a Destructive Prophet* (Oxford: Oxford University Press, 1999), p. 333.

52 John Lukacs, *The Hitler of History: Hitler's Biographers on Trial* (London: Weidenfeld & Nicolson, 2000), p. 45.

53 Ibid.

54 Ian Kershaw, *Hitler, 1936–1945: Nemesis* (London: Allen Lane, 2000), p. 728.

55 Fritz Redlich, *Hitler: Diagnosis of a Destructive Prophet* (Oxford: Oxford University Press, 1999), p. 275.

56 David Owen, *In Sickness and in Power: Illness in Heads of Government during the Last 100 Years* (London: Methuen, 2008), p. 35.

57 *The Hitler Book: The Secret Dossier Prepared for Stalin from the Interrogations of Hitler's Closest Personal Aides*, edited by Henrik Eberle and Matthias Uhl (London: John Murray, 2005), p. 294.

58 Ibid.

59 Ibid., p. 164.

60 Ibid., p. 295.

61 Bernd Freytag von Loringhoven with François d'Alançon, *In the Bunker with Hitler: The Last Witness Speaks* (London: Weidenfeld & Nicolson, 2006), p. 15.

62 TNA CAB 146/497, J.I.C. (46) 33 (Final), 'Some Weaknesses in German Strategy and Organisation, 1933–1945', 20 October 1946, p. 27.

63 Ibid., p. 59

64 Michael Howard, *British Intelligence in the Second World War: Strategic Deception*, volume V (London: HMSO, 1990), p. 46.

65 Ibid.

66 Ibid., pp. 48–50.

67 See TNA CAB 154/105, 'The German Intelligence Services and the War', H. R. Trevor-Roper, 1945.

68 TNA CAB 146/497, J.I.C. (46) 33 (Final), 'Some Weaknesses in German Strategy and Organisation, 1933–1945', 20 October 1946, p. 47.

69 Ibid., p. 31.

70 Thaddeus Holt, *The Deceivers: Allied Military Deception in the Second World War* (London: Weidenfeld & Nicolson, 2004), p. 106.

71 Keith Jeffery, *MI6: The History of the Secret Intelligence Service, 1909–1949* (London: Bloomsbury, 2010), pp. 382–6.

72 Christopher Andrew, *The Defence of the Realm: The Authorised History of MI5* (London: Allen Lane, 2009), pp. 244–7.

73 Roger Moorehouse, *Killing Hitler: The Third Reich and the Plots against the Führer* (London: Jonathan Cape, 2006), p. 66.

74 A rare instance of the report's authors alluding to the role played by intelligence in their war against Hitler appears on page 174, paragraph 35. TNA CAB 146/497, J.I.C. (46) 33 (Final), 'Some Weaknesses in German Strategy and Organisation, 1933–1945', 20 October 1946.

75 See P .R. J. Winter, 'Penetrating Hitler's High Command: Anglo-Polish HUMINT, 1939–1945', *War in History*, volume 18, no. 1, January 2011, pp. 90–1.

76 TNA KV2/964, 'Carl Marcus', CX report, 'Germany. Rivalries in the RSHA etc.', German Department, 12 February 1945.

77 Richard Breitman et al., *US Intelligence and the Nazis* (Cambridge: Cambridge University Press, 2005), p. 114.

78 See Walter Schellenberg, *The Memoirs of Hitler's Spymaster*, Introduction by Alan Bullock, Foreword by Richard J. Evans (London: Andre Deutsch, 2006), p. 40 and TNA KV 2/755, Kurt Jahnke.

79 See P. R. J. Winter, 'Penetrating Hitler's High Command: Anglo-Polish HUMINT, 1939–1945', *War in History*, volume 18, no. 1, January 2011, pp. 92–108.

80 Keith Jeffery, *MI6: The History of the Secret Intelligence Service, 1909–1949* (London: Bloomsbury, 2010), pp. 380–2.

81 Klemens von Klemperer, *German Resistance against Hitler: The Search for Allies Abroad, 1938–1945* (Oxford: Oxford University Press, 1992), pp. 194–7.

82 F. W. Winterbotham, *The Ultra Secret* (London: Weidenfeld & Nicolson, 1974).

83  The official history of the Secret Intelligence Service was published in September 2010. See Keith Jeffery, *MI6: The History of the Secret Intelligence Service, 1909–1949* (London: Bloomsbury, 2010).

84  The selection of Germany as a potential target for the atom bomb had been mooted in August 1944 in response to Hitler's V-Weapon campaign against the United Kingdom, and was recorded in the wartime diaries of Captain Guy Liddell, head of the Security Service's counter-espionage section, B1. See Nigel West, *The Guy Liddell Diaries: Vol. II: 1942–1945: MI5's Director of Counter-Espionage in World War II* (Abingdon, Oxon: Routledge, 2005), p. 222.

85  John F. Williams, *Corporal Hitler and the Great War 1914–1918: The List Regiment* (London: Frank Cass, 2005), p. 196.

86  *The Oxford Companion to the Second World War*, edited by I. C. B. Dear and M. R. D. Foot (Oxford: Oxford University Press, 1995), p. 203.

87  David Jablonsky, *Churchill and Hitler: Essays on the Political-Military Direction of Total War* (London: Frank Cass, 1994), p. 165.

88  Gerhard L. Weinberg, *A World at Arms: A Global History of World War II* (Cambridge: Cambridge University Press, 1994).

89  Ibid., p. 558.

90  F. H. Hinsley et al., *British Intelligence in the Second World War: Its Influence on Strategy and Operations*, volume II (London: HMSO, 1981), p. 119n.

91  Only one brief allusion to 'chemical warfare projects' is made in the report. See TNA CAB 146/497, J.I.C. (46) 33 (Final), 'Some Weaknesses in German Strategy and Organisation, 1933–1945', 20 October 1946, p. 98.

92  F. H. Hinsley et al., *British Intelligence in the Second World War: Its Influence on Strategy and Operations*, volume II (London: HMSO, 1981), p. 116.

93  Gerhard L. Weinberg, *A World at Arms: A Global History of World War II* (Cambridge: Cambridge University Press, 1994), p. 464.

94  Ibid.

95  TNA CAB 146/497, J.I.C. (46) 33 (Final), 'Some Weaknesses in German Strategy and Organisation, 1933–1945', 20 October 1946, p. 79.

96  Ibid., p. 42.

97  TNA CAB 163/6, 'Report to the Joint Intelligence Sub-Committee, The Intelligence Machine', 10 January 1945.

98  Michael Herman, 'The Post-war Organization of Intelligence: The January 1945 Report to the Joint Intelligence Committee on "The Intelligence Machine"', chapter 1. Robert Dover and Michael S. Goodman (eds), *Learning from the Secret Past: Cases in British Intelligence History* (Washington DC: Georgetown University Press, 2011), p. 1.

99  Ibid., p. 14.

100  TNA CAB 163/7, Misc./P (47) 32, 'Review of Intelligence Organisations, 1947: Report by Air Chief Marshal Sir Douglas Evill', 6 November 1947.

101  Richard Overy, *Why the Allies Won* (London: Jonathan Cape, 1996), pp. 10–11.

102  Ian Kershaw, *Hitler, 1889–1936: Hubris* (London: Allen Lane, 1998), p. 243.

103 Wilhelm Deist et al., *Germany and the Second World War: The Build-up of German Aggression*, volume I (Oxford: Clarendon Press, 1990), p. 23.

104 Major-General Sir Kenneth Strong, *Men of Intelligence: A Study of the Roles and Decisions of Chiefs of Intelligence from World War I to the Present Day* (London: Cassell & Company Ltd, 1970), p. 41.

105 Hugh Trevor-Roper, *The Philby Affair: Espionage, Treason and Secret Service* (London: William Kimber, 1968), pp. 71–2. Trevor-Roper's claim is supported by the conspicuous absence of any reference to *Mein Kampf* in SIS's pre-war memorandum on Hitler. See TNA FO 1093/86. Incidentally, it would appear that while most of Whitehall's intelligence services remained intellectually unmoved by *Mein Kampf*, the pre-war director of the Security Service, MI5, Sir Vernon Kell, was more alive to the importance of Hitler's polemic informing the JIC that the Nazi leader's intentions were indeed to be found within the book's covers. See John Curry, *The Security Service, 1908–1945: The Official History*, Introduction by Christopher Andrew (London: Public Record Office, 1999), p. 112.

106 TNA CAB 81/97, J.I.C. (40) 144, 'Germany's Next Move: Alternative Draft by Professor Hall', 30 June 1940, p. 2.

107 TNA CAB 146/497, J.I.C. (46) 33 (Final), 'Some Weaknesses in German Strategy and Organisation, 1933–1945', 20 October 1946, p. 3.

108 Ibid.

109 The rare exceptions to this being Sir Horace Rumbold, one-time British Ambassador to Berlin, and Sir Maurice Hankey, one-time Cabinet Secretary. See respectively, Ian Kershaw, *Making Friends with Hitler: Lord Londonderry and Britain's Road to War* (London: Allen Lane, 2004), p. 40 and p. 43; and Stephen Roskill, *Hankey: Man of Secrets, 1931–1963*, volume III (London: Collins, 1974), pp. 84–5.

110 Michael Cockerell et al., *Sources Close to the Prime Minister: Inside the Hidden World of News Manipulators* (London: Macmillan, 1984), p. 89.

111 Patrick Howarth, *Intelligence Chief Extraordinary: The Life of the Ninth Duke of Portland* (London: Bodley Head, 1986), p. 201.

112 TNA CAB 146/497, J.I.C. (46) 33 (Final), 'Some Weaknesses in German Strategy and Organisation, 1933–1945', 20 October 1946, p. ii.

113 Noel Annan, *Changing Enemies: The Defeat and Regeneration of Germany* (London: Harper Collins, 1995), pp. 131–2.

114 For the best account of this strategic deception, see Ben Macintyre, *Operation Mincemeat: The True Spy Story that Changed the Course of World War II* (London: Bloomsbury, 2010).

115 Ewen Montagu, *Beyond Top Secret U* (Newton Abbot: Readers Union Ltd, 1978), p. 140.

116 Sir Arthur Wellesley, the 1st Duke of Wellington and victor of the Battle of Waterloo, often pondered what was on the 'other side of the hill' when trying to second-guess the intentions of his enemies. See Basil Liddell Hart, *The Other Side of the Hill: Germany's Generals, Their Rise and Fall, with Their Own Account of Military Events 1939–1945* (London: Macmillan, 1993), p. 7.